INSTRUCTOR'S RESOURCE MANUAL
with
SOLUTIONS MANUAL

to accompany

Krugman/Wells/Olney
Essentials of Economics

Janet Koscianski
Shippensburg University

Diane Keenan (Contributor)
Cerritos Community College

Martha L. Olney (Contributor)
University of California-Berkeley

WORTH PUBLISHERS

Instructor's Resource Manual and Solutions Manual
by Janet Koscianski
to accompany
Krugman/Wells/Olney: Essentials of Economics

Printed in the United States of America

ISBN 13: 978-0-7167-6240-9

ISBN 10: 0-7167-6240-4

First printing 2007

Worth Publishers
41 Madison Avenue
New York, NY 10010
www.worthpublishers.com

PREFACE

This Worth Publishers is pleased to offer an exciting and useful supplements and media package to accompany the Krugman/Wells/Olney textbook. The package has been crafted to help instructors teach their survey of economics course and to help students grasp concepts more readily.

The Instructor's Resource Manual is an ideal resource for instructors teaching survey of economics. The manual includes:

- Chapter-by-chapter learning objectives

- Chapter outlines

- Teaching tips and ideas

- Hints on how to create student interest

- Common misunderstandings that are typical among students

- Activities that can be conducted in or out of the classroom

- Detailed solutions to every end-of-chapter problem from the textbook

General Teaching Tips

Research on college student learning shows:

- Students will understand the material in more depth, and retain it longer, if they are actively engaged with the content.

- Students will find the material more interesting when it relates to something from their own experience.

- Students' attention spans start to wander after 25 minutes into a lecture presentation.

- Any student will not respond to discussion questions posed to the whole class, yet will respond easily and more freely to another student or as part of a team.

- Instructor emphasis on mastery of key transferable concepts rather than coverage of material will ensure that students do not just memorize material and will retain it longer.

Features of This Instructor's Resource Manual

The Hook

The Creating Student Interest section under each topic gives you a "hook" to start the presentation. We raise issues and questions that tie the economic concept with something closer to students' own experiences. These are ways to start off the presentation of the material in a way that engages student interest.

Using Pairs of Students

Pair activities are a great way to break up the pace of a lecture and ask students to actively respond to the material. Many students are reluctant to respond to instructor's questions to the whole class but will respond freely to another student. In addition, the research shows that when students verbalize the material they retain it longer.

You can pair up students before the start of the lecture (it is more effective for you to create the pairs than to let students form their own pairs, as some students may be left out and/or friends will socialize.) Let students know that at some point in the lecture you will pose a discussion question or present a case study or application for the pairs to consider. Take a minute to have the students in each pair introduce themselves.

After 20–25 minutes, stop the lecture and use one of the many pair activities suggested in this manual. When the activity has been completed, resume the lecture.

Experiments and Team Activities

Choose concepts that are very important for student mastery for the more time consuming team activities. These range from 10 minutes of class time to 45 minutes. These have been found to help students interact with and apply the material and therefore retain it longer. Explain to students that they will be working in teams to practice with the material; however, their grade depends on their own individual effort and not on team effort. You may or may not want to award points for participating in the activity.

Organize teams prior to the activity. Teams of four or five students work best. These can be informal teams of students or more formally organized teams. The more organized teams may work together over a longer time period, and so you may want to combine students with differing academic abilities. You can use data from tests to ensure academic heterogeneity of teams. Again, we strongly suggest that you form the teams and do not allow students to form their own teams. This prevents socializing among friends and makes sure that a few teams do not have all the most academically talented students.

Teams can be used in large lecture hall settings as well. It is best to organize the teams prior to class and to explain to the class why you will be using teams. Tell students to ignore the furniture set-up in the room and cluster together in their team. Also indicate that you need them to turn their attention back to you when you give a hand signal, for example. If well organized, you should be able to go from a lecture presentation to a team activity and then back to lecturing or whole-class discussion.

Don't assume that students are learning only if you are lecturing. Students learn in many ways; especially if actively engaged in an activity and asked to verbalize the material, *they are learning*.

About the Author

This manual was conceived and written by an individual with significant teaching and writing experience in economics. In approaching the task of writing this manual for fellow instructors, Dr. Janet Koscianski of Shippensburg University relied on her 15 years of experience in teaching undergraduate economics. She is also the coauthor of *Microeconomic Theory: An Integrated Approach* © Prentice Hall, 2002. We hope that you will find her level of expertise and insights into teaching have enhanced the usefulness of this manual.

Acknowledgments

Thanks are due to a number of people for the making of this manual. Janet Koscianski (Shippensburg University) crafted this book with the help of material and advice provided by Diane Keenan (Cerritos Community College) and Martha L. Olney (University of California–Berkeley). Editorial and production guidance were provided by the economics supplements team at Worth: Marie McHale, Eve Conte, Wendy Boulding, and Stacey Alexander.

Contents of Instructor's Resource Manual

Contents of Solutions Manual

chapter **1**

First Principles

Chapter Objectives

Students will learn in this chapter:
- A set of basic principles for understanding the choices individuals make in the face of scarce resources. These principles are: (1) Resources are scarce. (2) The real cost of something is what you must give up to get it. (3) "How much?" is a decision at the margin. (4) People usually exploit opportunities to make themselves better off.
- A set of principles for understanding how individual choices interact. These principles are: (1) There are gains from trade. (2) Markets move toward equilibrium. (3) Resources should be used as efficiently as possible to achieve society's goals. (4) Markets usually lead to efficiency. (5) When markets don't achieve efficiency, government intervention can improve society's welfare.

Chapter Outline

Opening Example: All economists use a set of common principles that apply to many different issues.

I. Nine Basic Principles of Economics

II. Individual Choice: The Core of Economics

  A. *Definition:* **Individual choice** is the decision by an individual of what to do, which necessarily involves a decision of what not to do.

  B. Resources are scarce.

    1. *Definition:* A **resource** is anything that can be used to produce something else.

    2. *Definition:* Resources are **scarce**—the quantity available is not large enough to satisfy all productive uses.

    3. Resources include natural resources and human resources—labor, skill, and intelligence.

    4. Limited resources means society must make choices.

  C. The real cost of something is what you must give up to get it.

    1. *Definition:* The real cost of an item is its **opportunity cost:** what you must give up in order to get it.

    2. Opportunity cost does not have to be just monetary cost.

D. "How much?" is a decision at the margin.

1. Most decisions of interest to economists involve decisions at the margin. An example is, Should I spend one more hour studying economics or should I spend it on chemistry?

2. *Definition:* You make a **trade-off** when you compare the costs with the benefits of doing something.

3. *Definition:* Decisions about whether to do a bit more or a bit less of an activity are **marginal decisions.** The study of such decisions is known as **marginal analysis.**

E. People usually exploit opportunities to make them better off.

1. People will exploit opportunities until the opportunities are fully exhausted.

2. People respond to incentives. For example, if the salaries of MBAs rise, more students will go to business school.

3. *Definition:* An **incentive** is anything that offers a reward to people who change their behavior.

4. Economists are skeptical of attempts to change people's behavior that do not change their incentives.

III. Interaction: How Economies Work

A. *Definition:* **Interaction** of choices—my choice affects your choices, and vice versa—is a feature of most economic situations. The results of this interaction are often quite different from what the individuals intend.

B. There are gains from trade.

1. *Definition:* In a market economy, individuals engage in **trade:** They provide goods and services to others and receive goods and services in return.

2. *Definition:* There are **gains from trade:** People can get more of what they want through trade than they could if they tried to be self-sufficient. This increase in output is due to **specialization:** Each person specializes in the task that he or she is good at performing.

   a. In *The Wealth of Nations,* Adam Smith wrote about the benefits of specialization.

C. Markets move toward equilibrium.

1. *Definition:* An economic situation is in **equilibrium** when no individual would be better off taking a different action.

2. The fact that markets move to equilibrium is why we can depend on markets to work in a predictable way.

D. Resources should be used as efficiently as possible to achieve society's goals.

1. *Definition:* An economy is **efficient** if it takes all opportunities to make some people better off without making others worse off.

2. When an economy is efficient, it is producing the maximum gains from trade possible, given the resources available.

3. There are trade-offs between using resources efficiently and attaining equity in the distribution of goods.

   a. *Definition:* **Equity** means that everyone gets his or her fair share. Because people can disagree about what's "fair," equity isn't as well-defined a concept as efficiency.

E. Markets usually lead to efficiency.

    1. The incentives built into a market economy ensure that resources are usually put to good use, that all opportunities to make everyone better off have been exploited.

    2. The economy as a whole benefits if each individual specializes in a task and trades with others.

F. When markets do not achieve efficiency, government intervention can improve society's welfare.

    1. Markets fail to achieve efficiency for three principal reasons.

        a. Individual actions have side effects (externalities) that are not properly taken into account.

        b. One party attempts to capture a greater share of resources for itself.

        c. Some goods by their very nature are unsuited for efficient management by markets.

Teaching Tips

Economics Is About Individual Choice

Creating Student Interest

Ask students to think about an economic choice they made recently and to think about the benefits and opportunity costs of that decision. Have some students share their choices with the class. As they share their economic choices, help clarify the trade-offs involved.

Common Student Misunderstandings

Students often think that economics is the study of "money." Asked why they want money, they will probably respond that they want to buy goods with it. Point out that these goods are produced with scarce resources.

Given the affluence of the U.S. economy, it is not as obvious to some students that resources are scarce. Emphasize that as of 2004, the United States had only so many people in the labor force—147 million people—and in 2000 only 25.6% of people over 25 held a bachelor's degree. (Sources: www.whitehouse.gov/fsbr/employment.html for labor force; Table 227 of www.census.gov/prod/2004pubs/03statab/educ.pdf for educational attainment.)

Students may not immediately understand the phrase "decisions at the margin." Give them some concrete examples such as, Should I buy one more CD? Should I work one more hour for pay? Should I take one more class?

Presenting the Material

This chapter acquaints students with the core issues of economics. Ask students: What is unique about economics? How does it differ from sociology or psychology? Help them understand that economics is fundamentally about choices made with resource constraints.

Using the Case Study in the Text

A Woman's Work (text pages 10–11)

Ask students the following questions:
  1. How has women's participation in the labor force changed? (33.9% were in the labor force in 1950, and 60.2% were in the labor force in 2000.)
     (Source: *The Economics of Women, Men and Work,* by Francine D. Blau, Marianne A. Ferber, and Anne E. Winkler. Saddle Brook, NJ: Prentice Hall, 2002.)
  2. Which of the nine principles of individual economic choice explains the change? (People exploit opportunities to make themselves better off.)

Activities

A Woman's Work (text pages 10–11; 5–10 minutes)

Pair students and ask them which of the principles of individual economic choice are illustrated in the following:

  • The improvement of home production technology (washers, dryers, microwave ovens, etc.) (The opportunity cost of working was reduced because it took less time to complete household chores.)
  • Women's wages rose over this period. (Women took advantage of the opportunity to earn more at paid work.)
  • The prices of homes rose more rapidly than wages, making it more difficult for a single earner family to purchase a home. (The opportunity cost for women to be out of the labor force rose, and so people face trade-offs.)

Book tip: Ann Crittenden's *The Price of Motherhood* (New York: Metropolitan Books, 2001) has a good description of the opportunity costs and benefits of deciding to stay home and raise a child rather than working for pay.

Making Choices (5–10 minutes)

Ask students to identify which of the first four principles of individual economic choice is illustrated in each statement below.

  • Because of the higher gasoline prices in Europe, people drive smaller cars there than in the United States. (People take advantages of opportunities to make themselves better off.)
  • You are weighing the advantage of working more hours this month. (You make decisions at the margin, because resources are scarce.)
  • Mothers of young children must weigh returning to paid work or remaining home to be with their child. (People face trade-offs.)
  • You decide that four classes are enough for this semester and decide against the fifth class. (You make a decision at the margin.)

Difficult Choices (10–20 minutes)

Form students into pairs or teams, then present one of the following **scarcity scenarios.**

  • A society that has 500 children is threatened by a disease that strikes only children. A pharmaceutical company (owned by stockholders) has manufactured a pill that reduces the chances of getting the disease from 90% to only 10%. The company is only able to produce 500 pills at the present time. If parents can get more than one pill it reduces the chance of their child dying. How do you allocate the pills? How do we as a society preserve incentives for the pharmaceutical firm to take risks and come up with more and/or a better medicine? This illustrates the issue of scarcity and the tension between equity (making sure that all children get the antidote) and efficiency (encouraging profit-oriented pharmaceutical firms to innovate).

- Many issues in medicine illustrate scarcity and economic choices. For example, a liver transplant costs $200,000. Should everyone who has liver disease get the transplant regardless of his or her ability to pay? If everyone cannot get one, should a very old patient or a young patient get the transplant? As a second example, we now have the technology to save premature babies who are below 1,000 grams in weight—despite a high probability that these children will be handicapped. Should we use society's scarce medical resources to save them? These issues illustrate tough economic choices involving health care.

- One of the most immediate economic choices for many college students is how many hours per week to work for pay and how many hours to spend studying and attending classes. Pair students and ask them what factors influence their choices. How do the ideas of opportunity cost and making decisions at the margin influence their choices?

Economic Interactions

Creating Student Interest

Ask pairs of students to interpret the famous quote from *The Wealth of Nations* by Adam Smith: "It is not from the benevolence of the butcher, the brewer, or the baker that we expect our dinner, but from their regard to their own interest. We address ourselves, not to their humanity but to their self-love, and never talk to them of our own necessities but of their advantages." (*The Wealth of Nations,* Book 1, Chapter 2; http://geolib.com/ smith.adam/woncont.html). (This quote illustrates the idea of specialization and gains from trade, and the idea that people take advantage of opportunities to better themselves.) Ask students how a market economy, which is built on self-interest, requires cooperation among millions of individuals. What are some examples of cooperation in a market economy?

Ask students: Why do people trade? Get them to see that trade is mutually beneficial. At what point in history do they think specialization began?

Common Student Misunderstandings

Students may take for granted the high degree of specialization characteristic of a modern economy such as the United States. Have them think about what their lives would be like if they had to be self-sufficient in producing all the goods they consume.

Students may find it difficult to understand the text definition of *efficiency*. It asserts that **efficiency** occurs when opportunities to make everyone better off have been fully exploited. This implies that resources cannot be rearranged in a way that makes someone better off without making someone else worse off. Cite examples of "inefficient" situations, such as long lines at the Department of Motor Vehicles.

Students may find the definition of equilibrium in the text abstract. It states that an economic situation is in **equilibrium** when no individual would be better off taking a different action. Give a concrete example, such as a vendor at a swap-meet who adjusts his price to make sure he sells off the entire inventory.

Presenting the Material

The five principles of market interaction will be explored more thoroughly in future chapters, but they can be introduced briefly at this point. The motivation for trade is that trade is mutually beneficial. Use yourself as an example: You teach economics; one of your students can fix computers. You each specialize and then trade: you teach economics to your student and the student fixes your computer. As a result, more economics is taught and more computers are fixed. The trade would not take place if both sides did not benefit.

Markets moving toward equilibrium is a rather abstract idea for students but give a concrete example: If a T-shirt vendor at a tourist attraction prices her shirts above the equilibrium, she will be left with unsold shirts. She will have to lower the price to sell off the excess inventory; hence, markets move to an equilibrium price.

The idea that resources "should" be used efficiently follows from the economic fact of scarcity. Because wants are unlimited and resources are scarce, it makes sense to use those resources efficiently. Efficiency is defined as making the most of the gains from trade given the limited resources society has. If everyone is made better off from a choice and no one is made worse off, then the trade is deemed efficient.

That markets usually lead to efficiency follows from built-in profit incentives—competitive markets pressure firms to use resources efficiently. For example, FedEx, under competitive pressure from UPS, invested $150 million to outfit drivers with handheld packaging devices. The result is they can cut 10 seconds from every delivery. This efficiency saves FedEx $20 million per year in total cost. (Source: "Behind Productivity: Service Sector Delivers" *Wall Street Journal,* November 7, 2003.)

Ask students to think of possible "market failures" and often they will mention monopoly and environmental damage. Additionally, you can add cases of asymmetric information.

Using the Case Study in the Text

Choosing Sides (text page 13)
Ask students the following questions:
1. Once the rule of driving on the right side of the road was established in the United States, why were there incentives for people to conform to that? (If they didn't, they would collide with oncoming traffic.)
2. In what way was driving on the right an "equilibrium" situation? (The rule became established as the norm and was self-enforcing.)

In the News
Use the following article from *The Wall Street Journal* as a case study.

More Students Enroll in Nursing Programs
by Kris Maher
Staff Reporter of *The Wall Street Journal*

From The Wall Street Journal Online, September 2, 2003.

The number of students entering nursing, a profession that has been facing a drastic shortage for nearly a decade, is finally on the rise. But the crisis is far from over, and recent events have only added uncertainty to the profession's recovery.

The total U.S. student-nursing population rose 3.7% in 2001 and 8% in 2002, according to the American Association of Colleges of Nursing, which represents more than 570 nursing schools. But the current figures are still 10,000 students shy of the roughly 128,000 enrolled in 1995, when enrollments began to fall. Moreover, with a large number of practicing nurses leaving the field, the enrollment level is not nearly high enough to meet the one million new and replacement nurses that will be needed by 2010, as estimated by the Bureau of Labor Statistics.

Many in medicine fear that over that span, prospective nurses will be discouraged by such rising threats as bio-terrorism and severe acute respiratory syndrome. Earlier this month, 150 anxious medical workers in Taiwan resigned, fearing unsafe working conditions, after several doctors and nurses died from the contagious new respiratory ailment.

The dearth of openings in many other professions could also make nursing more attractive to college students as well as career changers.

Right now, the profession is stuck in a vicious cycle, with many current and former nurses maintaining that the biggest reason people are leaving the field, ironically, is the problems caused by chronic understaffing. "The infectious diseases that we're exposed to are not what tip the balance," says Pat Greenberg, executive director of the Nurse Alliance of New York State/1199 Service Employees International Union, which represents 27,000 nurses in New York State. "No, I really think that it's the nursing work conditions that are driving nurses out of the profession."

Many registered nurses start out earning between $35,000 and $40,000 a year.

Indeed, the job has gotten more stressful over the past two decades. Hospital staffs grew much leaner during the 1990s. With managed-care companies monitoring admittances, hospitals are also more selective about whom they admit, which means the average patient in a hospital is sicker today than he was a decade ago. Nurses have far more to do with far less support, and many have left stressful emergency rooms, operating rooms and intensive care units.

Ask students the following questions:

- Which principles involving market interactions are illustrated in the article?
- What caused the increase in the number of nurses?
- What trade-offs do nurses face?
- Is this market moving toward equilibrium?

chapter 2

Economic Models:
Trade-Offs and Trade

Chapter Objectives

Students will learn in this chapter:
- Why models—simplified representations of reality—play a crucial role in economics.
- Three simple but important models: the production possibility frontier, comparative advantage, and the circular-flow diagram.
- The difference between positive economics, which tries to describe the economy and predict its behavior, and normative economics, which tries to prescribe economic policy.
- When economists agree, and why they sometimes disagree.

Chapter Outline

Opening Example: The Wright Brothers created a wind tunnel to test models of airplanes. Testing models is cheaper and safer than building full-scale versions. Economists use models in the same way.

I. Models in Economics: Some Important Examples

   A. *Definition:* A **model** is a simplified representation of a real situation that is used to study that real situation.

   B. Models allow economists to see the effects of only one change at a time.

   C. *Definition:* The **other things equal assumption** means that all other relevant factors remain unchanged.

   D. Economic models make use of mathematical tools, especially graphs.

II. Trade-offs: The Production Possibility Frontier

   A. *Definition:* The **production possibility frontier** illustrates the trade-offs facing an economy that produces only two goods. It shows the maximum quantity of one good that can be produced with available resources and technology for any given production of the other.

   B. The graph of the production possibilities frontier shows the possible combinations of two goods which can be produced given the scarce resources of the society.

   C. A point inside the frontier is a feasible combination of two goods that can be produced, but does not use all resources fully, and a point outside the frontier is not feasible given the current amount of resources. See text Figure 2-1, shown below.

The Production Possibility Frontier

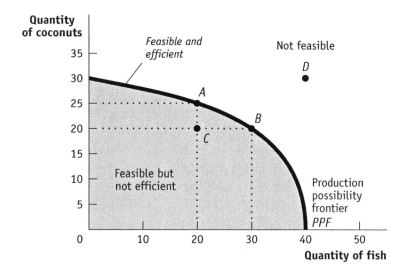

D. The production possibility model illustrates the concepts of:

1. Efficiency: Any point on the frontier represents an efficient use of resources, and any combination of goods inside the frontier represents a point of inefficiency.

2. Opportunity costs: The negative slope of the frontier means that an increase in the production of one good must require a sacrifice of some quantity of the other good.

3. The law of increasing costs: If the frontier is bowed out, the opportunity costs increase as more of one good is produced because resources are not easily transferable from the production of one good to another.

4. Economic growth: Over time as a society gains more resources, the production possibility frontier shifts outward. See text Figure 2-3, shown below.

Economic Growth

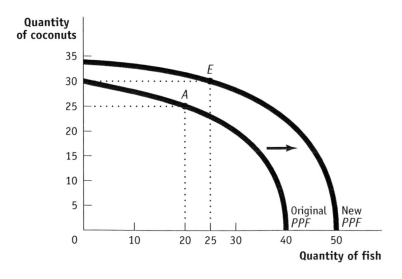

III. Comparative Advantage and the Gains from Trade

A. *Definition:* An individual has a **comparative advantage** in producing a good if the opportunity cost of producing the good is lower for that individual than for other people.

B. *Definition:* An individual has an **absolute advantage** in an activity if he or she can do it better than other people can. Having an absolute advantage is not the same thing as having a comparative advantage.

C. Comparative advantage, not absolute advantage, is the basis for the gains from trade.

D. The gains from trade are illustrated in text Figure 2-6 (shown below), with a straight line production possibility frontier for each of two countries:

Comparative Advantage and International Trade

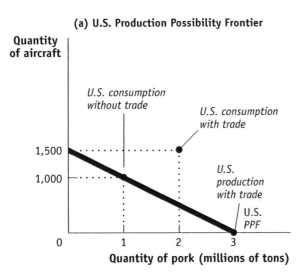

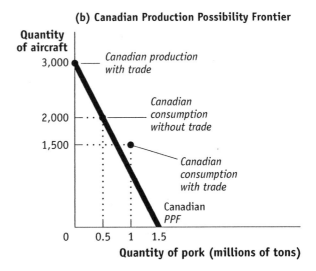

IV. Transactions: The Circular-Flow Diagram

A. *Definition:* Trade takes the form of **barter** when people directly exchange goods they have for goods they want.

B. *Definition:* The **circular-flow diagram** is a model that represents the transactions in an economy by flows around a circle.

C. *Definition:* A **household** is a person or a group of people who share their income.

D. *Definition:* A **firm** is an organization that produces goods for sale.

E. *Definition:* Firms sell goods and services that they produce to households in **markets for goods and services.**

F. *Definition:* Firms buy the resources they need to produce—**factors of production**—in **factor markets.**

G. The circular-flow diagram is a simplified picture of an economy, as demonstrated in text Figure 2-7, shown on the next page.

Circular-Flow Diagram

H. The circular-flow diagram can help us understand how the economy manages to provide jobs for a growing population.

    1. The number of jobs isn't fixed, because it depends on how much households spend; the amount households spend depends on how many people are working.

V. Positive Versus Normative Economics

A. *Definition:* **Positive economics** is the branch of economic analysis that describes the way the economy actually works.

B. *Definition:* **Normative economics** makes prescriptions about the way the economy should work.

C. *Definition:* A **forecast** is a simple prediction of the future.

D. Models are especially helpful in answering "what if" questions such as, How will revenues change with a tax cut? The answer is a predictive one, not prescriptive; it does not tell you if the policy is good or bad.

E. Economists do engage in normative economics. Economic analysis can be used to show that some policies are clearly better than others, especially if one solution is more efficient than another. For example, most economists would favor subsidies to renters over rent control laws as a more efficient solution.

VI. When and Why Economists Disagree

A. Because economists have used different models and made differing simplifying assumptions, they can arrive at different conclusions.

B. Many disagreements are eventually resolved by the accumulation of evidence.

C. Economic analysis is a method, not a set of conclusions.

Teaching Tips

Models in Economics/Production Possibility Frontier

Creating Student Interest

Ask students why economists have to rely on simplified models to explain underlying economic principles.

Ask students to describe the difference between a model airplane and the actual plane.

Common Student Misunderstandings

Students may have trouble understanding what the production possibility frontier illustrates. Explain that it is a simplification of a very complex economy, one in which only two goods are produced. The frontier shows the possible combinations of *production of two goods* that the economy is capable of producing using existing land, labor, capital goods, and technology.

Presenting the Material

Use students "producing" grades as a simple example of a production possibility frontier. Put economics on the vertical axis of a graph and accounting on the horizontal axis. Students' time and energy are fixed for the moment, and putting more time into one subject involves a lower grade in the other subject. (Assuming that the student is equally efficient in "producing" both subjects, the production possibilities graph is a straight line.) Points on the frontier show the possible combinations of grades that the student can achieve.

Use an example of a country that can produce wheat or airplanes. Here are the points on the production possibility frontier:

Maximum Annual Output Options	Wheat	Airplanes
A	1,000	0
B	800	150
C	600	250
D	400	325
E	200	375
F	0	400

Ask students: What is the opportunity cost of expanding production from 150 airplanes to 250 airplanes? (200 wheat.) Why is the production possibility graph negatively sloped? (Given scarcity, producing more of one good means producing less of the other.) Why is it bowed out from the origin? (Because of increasing opportunity cost.)

Using the Case Study in the Text

Models for Money (text page 21)

Ask students the following questions:

1. Who models for money? (There are dozens of consulting firms who use models in offering advice or forecasting future events.)

2. What is Global Insight and what does it do? (Global Insight is the world's largest economic consulting firm. It creates economic models to aid businesses and governments in their decision making.)

Activities

Increasing Your Productivity (3–5 minutes)

Pair students. After presenting the production possibility frontier for an economics and an accounting class as noted above, ask students to brainstorm what will cause the frontier to shift outward? (They might become better organized and study more efficiently, or they might purchase high speed Internet access to speed up their research time, a technological innovation that would boost productivity.) Ask a few pairs to report.

From Depression to War (3–5 minutes)

Pair students and have them place three historic points on a production possibility frontier for the U.S. economy: 1932 economic depression, 1942 full war mobilization, and 1944 consumer goods are sacrificed for the production of military goods. Have them put military goods on the vertical axis and consumer goods on the horizontal axis. (1932 is inside the PPF, 1942 is on the PPF, and 1944 is a movement upward on the PPF.)

Comparative Advantage; Modeling the Gains from Trade

Creating Student Interest

Ask students if they agree with Adam Smith's idea, implied by the Chapter 1 quote, that if it is cheaper to buy a product from another country than to make it yourself, you should buy the product.

Ask students why trade has persisted throughout history. (Obviously, trade is mutually beneficial.) You can show students pictures of the "Silk Road" in China, which is still visible from satellite pictures above earth. Or, if you have access to a U.S. History text, you can show a map of the pre-Columbian trade routes.

Provoke a discussion by asking students if the U.S. economy would be better off without importing so many clothing items from China.

Common Student Misunderstandings

Students confuse absolute advantage with comparative advantage. Explain that absolute advantage means you can produce more than someone else can. Comparative advantage means that you can produce something at less cost relative to another person.

Students often have difficulty in calculating the opportunity cost of producing a particular good in a country. See the simple example below to guide them through the calculation.

Presenting the Material

Give a simple example of two economies that can produce the following two goods, in the same time period, with a fixed amount of resources. Assume a straight line production possibility frontier.

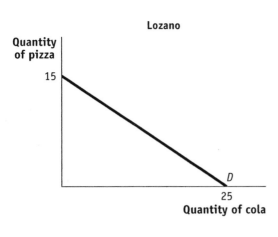

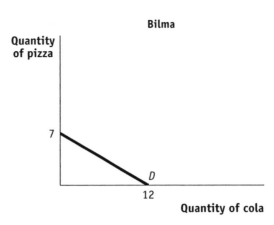

	Quantity of pizza	Quantity of cola
Lozano	15	0
	0	25
Bilma	7	0
	0	12

Indicate that Lozano has an absolute advantage in both goods. Students often need help in seeing how to calculate the opportunity costs of producing both goods in each country. The opportunity cost of pizza in Lozano is the ratio of cola to pizza, or 25/15 = 1.67, and the opportunity cost of pizza in Bilma is 12/7 = 1.7. Thus, Lozano has the comparative advantage in pizza and Bilma has the comparative advantage in producing Cola.

Using the Case Study in the Text

Rich Nation, Poor Nation (text page 33)

Ask students the following questions:

1. Why are some countries poor? (Their workers are not as productive as workers in richer economies.)

2. Why do consumers in the United States import so much cheap clothing from poor countries? (Despite their poverty, poor countries have a comparative advantage in producing clothing relative to the United States.)

Work It Out

Gains from Trade (text page 28)

This numerical exercise calls upon students to mathematically demonstrate their understanding of the following concepts:

- Absolute advantage
- Comparative advantage
- Specialization
- Gains from trade

Activities

Comparative Advantage (10–15 minutes)

Pair students and ask them to do two tasks in 30 seconds, such as drawing the same-sized Xs on a page, and turning the pages of a book. The first person does the task, while the other person records the quantity produced. Given the data for both goods for both partners, have the pairs calculate their opportunity cost of producing each good.

U.S. Comparative Advantage (2–3 minutes)

Make a list on the board or overhead with student answers to this question: What comparative advantages does the United States have? Then, point out that their answers are all the top exports of the United States.

Pros and Cons of Trade (3–5 minutes)

Pair students and ask them to brainstorm the pros and cons of the following proposition: "The United States should limit imported textiles from China" or "The United States should prohibit the import of products from abroad that are made with child labor."

The Circular-Flow Model

Creating Student Interest

Students can trace the path of a dollar spent at their local mall. Ask them to think about how their spending is tied to employment.

Common Student Misunderstandings

In trying to understand the circular-flow diagram, students need help in differentiating between the product markets and the factor markets. Define these two markets clearly before you present the model.

Students may be unclear about what the circular flow represents. Explain that it represents economic transactions, such as buying clothes at a mall, purchasing more labor, or buying raw materials.

Presenting the Material

Identify and define the two major components of the diagram first: households and firms. Then draw in the upper loop—the spending loop—of the circular-flow model. Use a concrete example of their spending money on clothes at a local store. Then add the bottom loop of the model, the factor market.

Activities

Tracing the Circular Flow (5–10 minutes)

Pair students and tell them they will trace the following events through the circular flow: (a) the introduction of a new technology which boosts productivity; (b) the decision of consumers to save more money; and (c) an increase in government spending.

Simulating the Circular Flow (15–30 minutes)

In a lecture, add banks, government, and exports and imports to the circular flow. Divide the class into the following groups: households, firms, workers, sellers of raw materials, sellers of capital goods, banks, exporters, and importers. Introduce an event into this hypothetical economy: consumers decide to spend more money and save less. Give this event card to the household group. Have this group write down how it will affect them and pass it on to the next group they feel will be most immediately affected. The next group writes down its impact on them and passes it on. Make sure the event passes to each group. Have one group use the circular-flow diagram to illustrate on the board how the event affected the economy.

Normative Versus Positive Economic Analysis

Creating Student Interest
Ask students to make a clearly biased statement concerning the economy. Then ask them to make a perfectly objective statement.

Common Student Misunderstandings
Students may not understand the term *positive economics*. Make clear that positive is not the opposite of negative. Positive economics explains the way the world works.

Presenting the Material
Lecture on specific material using a normative approach. Stop and ask students if they would label the presentation as normative or positive.

Using the Case Study in the Text

Economists in Government (text page 36)
Ask students the following questions:
1. Why are so many economists in government? (Because government makes economic policies.)
2. Do all the economists in government disagree with one another all of the time? (No, economists agree on a broad range of economic decisions.)

Activities

Positive or Normative? (3–5 minutes)
Read the following sentences to the class, and ask students to label each one as normative or positive:
- "More than 60% of women are in the labor market." (positive)
- "Rent control laws should be implemented because they help to achieve equity or fairness in housing." (normative)
- "Society should take measures to end gun violence." (normative)
- "People who smoke pass on increased medical costs to the whole society." (positive)
- "Single mothers are more than twice as likely as married mothers to be in poverty." (positive)

Change It to Normative (5–10 minutes)
Pair students. Ask one student in each pair to write a positive economic statement of fact, and the other student to rewrite the statement as a normative one. Ask a few pairs to report.

Appendix

Creating Student Interest

Have students discuss the relationship between calories consumed and weight. What is the independent variable? What is the dependent variable?

Common Student Misunderstandings

Students forget the basic set up of a graph; that each point on the graph refers to a specific quantity on the vertical axis and horizontal axis. Use a demand curve to illustrate: point A on the demand curve means that at a price of $1.00, consumers will buy 200 of the good, for example. You may want to point out which axis on the graph is referred to as the vertical axis and which is the horizontal axis.

Presenting the Material

Give an example of data and how a graph is set up, then explain how to interpret the graph.

Year	Health Expenditures as a Percent of GDP
1950	4.5%
1960	5.3%
1970	7.1%
1980	8.9%
1990	12.2%
2000	13.4%

(Source: *The Economics of Health and Health Care*, S. Folland, A. Goodman, and M. Stano. Prentice Hall, 2001.)

Ask students the following questions:

1. With health expenditures as a percent of GDP on the vertical axis of a graph and years on the horizontal axis of the graph, plot the data on the graph.
2. Is the line positive or negatively sloped? (It is positively sloped, as the years have increased, the percent share of GDP has increased.)
3. Is it a linear function? (No, the line is not a straight line.)
4. What does the graph not tell us? (It does not indicate what is causing the increase in health expenditures as a percent of GDP.)

Activity

Causal Relationships (5–10 minutes)

Ask students to think of some causal relationships between health expenditures and other variables. Identify the variables that may increase or decrease health expenditures. What is the dependent variable? (Health expenditures.) What independent variables can influence total health spending as a percent of the GDP? (Some possibilities: percentage of population over 55, government mandated health programs, percentage of population who are smokers, degree of bureaucracy in medical care structure, etc.)

chapter 3

Supply and Demand

Chapter Objectives

Students will learn in this chapter:
- That the market for a good can be described with two curves: a demand curve and a supply curve.
- That a competitive market is made up of many buyers and sellers and no seller can control the price.
- What the demand curve is and what causes it to shift.
- What the supply curve is and what causes it to shift.
- How the supply and demand curves determine a market's equilibrium.
- How the equilibrium price of a market is affected by shifts of the demand and supply curve.

Chapter Outline

Opening Example: Wayne Gretzky's retirement is used as an example of changing demand and supply and what happens in the market.

I. Supply and Demand: A Model of a Competitive Market

   A. *Definition:* A **competitive market** is one in which there are many buyers and sellers of a good.

   B. *Definition:* The **supply and demand model** is a model of how a competitive market works.

II. The Demand Curve and the Demand Schedule

   A. *Definition:* A **demand schedule** shows how much of a good consumers are willing and able to buy at different prices.

   B. *Definition:* A **demand curve** is a graphical representation of the demand schedule. It shows how much of a good or service consumers want to buy at a given price.

   C. The demand schedule and demand curve are illustrated in text Figure 3-1, shown on the next page.

   D. *Definition:* The **quantity demanded** is the actual amount consumers are willing to buy at some specific price.

   E. *Definition:* The **law of demand** says that a higher price of a good, other things equal, leads people to demand a smaller quantity of the good.

The Demand Schedule and the Demand Curve

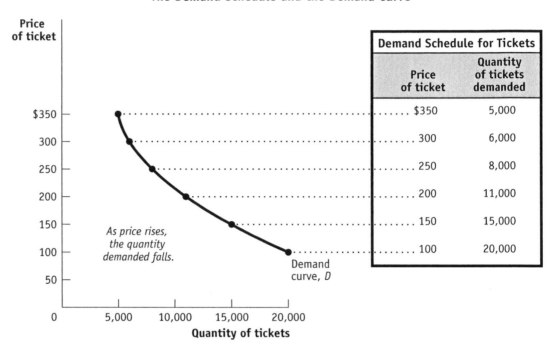

Demand Schedule for Tickets	
Price of ticket	Quantity of tickets demanded
$350	5,000
300	6,000
250	8,000
200	11,000
150	15,000
100	20,000

1. The law of demand implies that the demand curve will be downward sloping: the higher price of a good, the less consumers want of it.

F. *Definition:* A **shift of the demand curve** is a change in the quantity demanded at any given price, represented by the change of the original demand curve to a new position, denoted by a new demand curve.

   1. If consumers want more of the good at any given price, the curve shifts to the right. If consumers want to buy less of a good at any given price, the curve shifts to the left.

G. *Definition:* A **movement along the demand curve** is a change in the quantity demanded of a good that is the result of a change in that good's price.

H. The difference between a shift of the demand curve and movement along the demand curve is illustrated in text Figure 3-3, shown below.

Movement Along the Demand Curve Versus Shift of the Demand Curve

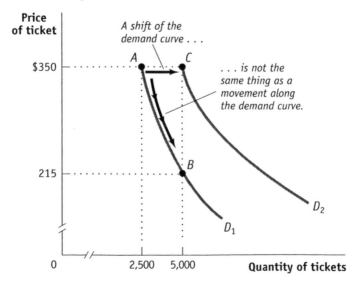

I. Factors that shift the demand curve

    1. Changes in the prices of related goods

        a. *Definition:* Two goods are **substitutes** if a fall in the price of one of the goods makes consumers less willing to buy the other good.

        b. *Definition:* Two goods are **complements** if a fall in the price of one good makes people more willing to buy the other good.

    2. Changes in income

        a. *Definition:* When a rise in income increases the demand for a good—the normal case—we say that the good is a **normal good.**

        b. *Definition:* When a rise in income decreases the demand for a good, the good is an **inferior good.**

    3. Changes in tastes

    4. Changes in expectations

III. The Supply Curve

    A. *Definition:* The **quantity supplied** is the actual amount of a good or service sellers are willing to sell at some specific price.

    B. *Definition:* The **supply schedule** shows how much of a good or a service producers are willing to sell at some specific price.

    C. The supply schedule and supply curve are illustrated in text Figure 3-5, shown below.

The Supply Schedule and the Supply Curve

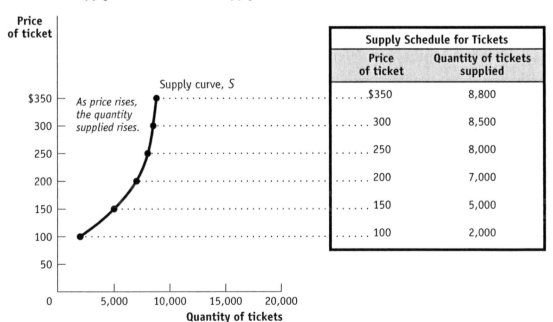

Supply Schedule for Tickets	
Price of ticket	Quantity of tickets supplied
$350	8,800
300	8,500
250	8,000
200	7,000
150	5,000
100	2,000

    D. *Definition:* A **supply curve** shows graphically how much of a good or service sellers are willing to sell at any given price.

        1. The supply curve is upward sloping because, all else equal, as the price of a good rises, people are willing to sell a greater quantity of a good.

    E. *Definition:* A **shift of the supply curve** is a change in the quantity supplied of a good at any given price. It is represented by the change of the original supply curve to a new position, denoted by a new supply curve.

        1. If supply increases, the curve shifts to the right; if the supply decreases the supply curve shifts to the left.

F. *Definition:* A **movement along the supply curve** is a change in the quantity supplied of a good that is the result of a change in that good's price.

G. The difference between a shift in the supply curve and movement along the curve is illustrated in text Figure 3-7, shown below.

Movement Along the Supply Curve Versus Shift of the Supply Curve

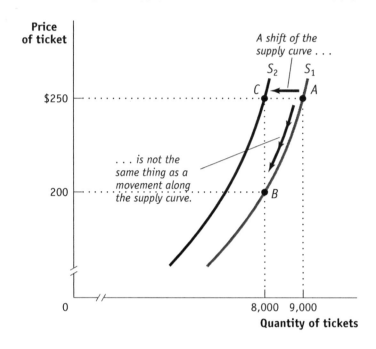

H. Factors that shift the supply curve

1. Changes in input prices
   a. *Definition:* An **input** is a good that is used to produce another good.

2. Changes in technology

3. Changes in expectations

IV. Supply, Demand, and Equilibrium

A. *Definition:* A competitive market is in equilibrium when price has moved to a level at which the quantity demanded of a good equals the quantity supplied of that good. The price at which this takes place is the **equilibrium price,** also referred to as the **market-clearing price.** The quantity of the good bought and sold at that price is the **equilibrium quantity.** Market equilibrium is illustrated in text Figure 3-9, shown on the next page.

1. Why do all sales and purchases in a market take place at the same price? In any market where buyers and sellers are around for some time they will observe which price works best for them. If a seller is trying to charge above the equilibrium price, buyers will shop elsewhere.

2. Why does the market price fall if it is above the equilibrium price? The quantity supplied in the market is greater than the quantity demanded. Excess supply causes the market price to fall.
   a. *Definition:* There is a **surplus** of a good when the quantity supplied exceeds the quantity demanded. Surpluses occur when the price is above the equilibrium level.

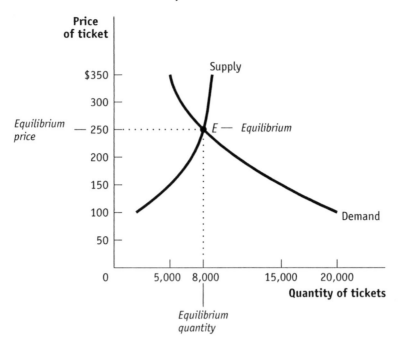

Market Equilibrium

3. Why does the market price rise if it is below the equilibrium price? The quantity supplied is less than the quantity demanded and there will be excess demand, causing the price to rise.
   a. *Definition:* There is a **shortage** of a good when the quantity demanded exceeds the quantity supplied. Shortages occur when the price is below its equilibrium level.

V. Changes in Supply and Demand

A. What happens when the demand curve shifts
   1. An increase in demand (the demand curve shifts right) leads to a rise in both the equilibrium price and the equilibrium quantity.
   2. A decrease in demand (the demand curve shifts left) leads to a fall in both the equilibrium price and equilibrium quantity.

B. What happens when the supply curve shifts
   1. An increase in supply (the supply curve shifts right) leads to a fall in the equilibrium price and a rise in the equilibrium quantity.
   2. A decrease in supply (the supply curve shifts left) leads to a rise in the equilibrium price and a fall in the equilibrium quantity.

C. Simultaneous shifts in supply and demand
   1. The results for equilibrium quantity and equilibrium price depend on the direction of the shifts in supply and demand, and by how much these curves shift.

Teaching Tips

The Demand Curve

Creating Student Interest

Pair up students and ask: What did you buy recently, and why? Then ask a few pairs to report. List on the board the various factors that influenced their decisions. These will range from "it was convenient" to "I wanted it." Often, students will say they "needed" to buy something. However, if you ask them if they had a substitute, they will understand that they preferred the item. From the list on the board, it is clear that price is just one of many factors that can influence demand. Indicate that we will focus on price first and how it influences the amount consumers want to buy.

Common Student Misunderstandings

At first, students are not clear as to exactly what a demand curve represents. They need to understand that each point on the demand curve indicates the amount people are willing to buy at that specific price. For example, say: "Let's assume we do a survey of consumers and the quantity of sodas they are willing to buy at two prices. If the price is $2.00, consumers will buy 200; however, if the price falls to $1.00, they will buy 500. (The key phrase here is "if the price changes.") We are not, at this point, indicating what the actual equilibrium price is, only indicating consumer preferences given hypothetical prices.

Presenting the Material

Do a quick survey of three students in the class and their demand for gallons of gasoline per week. Ask them how many gallons they will buy at various prices (assume a particular octane level). A hypothetical example may look like:

Price	Quantity (gallons) demanded per week	Quantity (gallons) demanded per week	Quantity (gallons) demanded per week	Total market demand Schedule
	Jim	Ricardo	Leticia	
$2.40	5	10	10	25
$2.20	8	12	10	30
$2.00	10	15	10	35
$1.80	14	18	10	42
$1.60	16	20	10	46
$1.40	18	20	10	48

Follow the survey by drawing the demand curve given the three responses.

Using the Case Study in the Text

The Great Gretzky (a running example that starts on text page 56)
Ask students:

1. Most hockey fans are not willing to pay four times the face value of a ticket to see Wayne Gretzky's last hockey game. Illustrate that on a demand curve for the

game. (This is illustrated by a movement up the demand curve. As the price rises, the quantity demanded falls.)

2. Why do consumers prefer lower prices to higher ones? (Consumers are constrained by a fixed income, and there are substitute goods available.)

Activity

Drawing a Demand Curve (30–45 minutes)

Organize students into groups of 5 or 6 students. Each team will survey the quantity demanded for a specific product. Assign each team only one product to survey. Some possibilities:

A private parking space on campus

A new Dell laptop computer

A three-ring notebook

Note-taking service per hour

Units for college courses at your campus

A flat-panel high-definition TV

1. Teams brainstorm five possible prices for their product, from high to low.
2. Teams agree on how all members will conduct the survey. For example, they can ask: "If the price is ____ , how many will you buy?" or, "If the price is _____ , will you buy it?" (A "yes" is counted as 1, and a "no" is counted as 0.)
3. Each team member interviews two students in the class regarding their demand for the team's product.
4. Students return to the team and add the quantity demanded at each price for all team member surveys.
5. Teams draw the demand curve for their product and post it on the board.

In the News

Use the following article from the St. Petersburg *Times* as a case study.

Computer Sales Brighten a Bit

St. Petersburg (FL) *Times*, December 10, 2001.

Price cutting in the personal computer market is boosting sales. PC sales following the September 11th attacks fell, however, since November 2001 a mild surge is evident in stores, on the Web and through direct sales. Computer maker Hewlett Packard reports that sales were up 20% over Thanksgiving of 2000. Dell, the leader in the price-cutting, hopes to encourage consumers to add more powerful computers and to buy more machines. Prices of complementary electronic products, such as color printers, scanners and digital cameras have also been cut to boost PC sales. The increase in computer sales has occurred in spite of the significant growth in sales of home entertainment systems and devices such as DVD player's surround-sound audio systems, and wide-screen televisions, encouraged by large price cuts and a trend toward staying at home instead of going out for entertainment. A sustained increase in computer sales is unlikely until businesses start replacing their machines. Until then, computer maker profits will be under a downward pressure.

Ask students:

1. In what way is the law of demand illustrated in the article? (The reduction in the price of computers is boosting sales.)

2. What does a drop in the price of printers do to demand in the PC market? Show both markets graphically. (PCs and printers are complementary goods. As the price of printers falls, the quantity demanded for PCs rises. Graphically, this is a movement down the demand curve for printers and a shift to the right in the demand curve for PCs.)

3. Draw a demand curve for computers. Illustrate how a fall in price causes the quantity demanded to rise. (This is shown graphically as a movement down the demand curve for PCs.)

Shifts in the Demand Curve

Creating Student Interest

Ask students to think of products that have rising sales. What factors influence that demand? Flat-panel TVs and cellular phones with picture-taking capabilities are some current (2007) examples.

Common Student Misunderstandings

Students confuse a change in quantity demanded with a shift in the demand curve. Have students recall the survey on gasoline. Emphasize that the survey held "all else equal." This means that buyers did not know the location of the gas station or if it takes credit cards, for example. If only price is changing, then this change in quantity demanded is illustrated by a movement along the demand curve.

Presenting the Material

Use a simplifying chart to make the distinction between a shift in demand and a change in quantity demanded: Put price on the left and all the other factors that can cause a shift in demand to change on the right. Indicate that if price is causing the change in the quantity demanded it is represented by a movement along the demand curve. On the right, factors that change demand, such as a change in tastes or income, cause a shift in the demand curve.

Using the Case Study in the Text

Beating the Traffic (text page 62)
Ask students:

1. How can a city reduce the demand for traffic by lowering the price of a substitute? (Cities reduce the price of subway and bus rides.)

2. How can a city reduce the demand for traffic by raising the price of a complementary good? (Cities raise the price to park in a garage.)

3. As a result, show graphically what happens to the demand for the highway. (The demand curve for traffic shifts to the left.)

Activity

Shifts and Movements Along the Demand Curve (5 minutes)
Give examples that are in the same general market to illustrate the difference between a shift and a movement along the demand curve, as shown on the next page.

Example	Movement along the demand curve	A shift in the demand curve
1. Mammoth Mountain hikes the price for ski tickets and sales plummet.	X	
2. Lack of snow keeps the skiers away.		X
3. An increase in the excise tax on cigarettes causes younger smokers to quit.	X	
4. Cutting cigarette ads from TV causes cigarette smoking among teens to fall.		X
5. Nike sales fall as Skecher shoes gain popularity.		X
6. Teens have had it with the high price of Nike Air Jordans.	X	
7. Mortgage rates are at an all time low, and new home loan applications soar.	X	
8. A booming economy spurs home sales.		X

In the News

Use the following article as a case study.

Is Skechers in a LA Gear Comeback?

www.tickertapedigest.com, July 2002.

> Skechers, the Los Angeles based shoemaker, is not just an athletic shoe company but also turns out oxfords, boots, sandals and semi-dressy shoes and even a sneaker that has wheels! Founded by Robert Greenberg, who started the sports shoe company LA Gear, the company makes shoes in China and sells them in 100 countries. Skechers can be bought in specialty shops run by the firm and in department stores. The company's sales are running at $600 million and for 2000, their profit was up 83% or $1.08 a share from 60 cents a share the year before.

Ask students:

1. Why have the sales of Skechers shoes increased? (They appeal to consumers' tastes.)
2. Would the demand curve for Skechers shoes shift right or left? (The demand curve shifts to the right.)

The Supply Curve

Creating Student Interest

Ask students if they have recently sold an item. Did they want to sell it for a low price or a high price? Why? Did they sell it too quickly, or did it take a long time to sell? Could they have sold it for a higher price? In this discussion, you are putting students in the role of a seller and showing them how price can act as an incentive to sell.

Common Student Misunderstandings

Students confuse a change in quantity supplied with a shift in the supply curve. Make clear that the law of supply assumes *ceteris paribus* conditions. Everything else constant, a higher price gives sellers an incentive to produce more. This assumes their costs of production do not change.

Presenting the Material

Ask students to write down how many hours they are willing to tutor economics students at the following hourly wage rates: $16.00, $12.00, $10.00, $8.00, $6.00. Then ask three students to report their responses. Add up the hours at each wage, and derive the upward-sloping supply curve. Note: A few students may choose to work fewer hours as the wage rises, but generally the overall response produces an upward sloping supply curve.

Using the Case Study in the Text

Down and Up on the Farm (text page 67)

Ask students:

1. Why did European farm policies increase agricultural production? (In the 1960s, European governments started guaranteeing farmers high prices, hoping the farmers would not respond by increasing production.)

2. Show the effect of the European policies on a supply curve. (This is shown as a movement up the supply curve.)

3. How did Ghana's food policies create a shortage? (The government held the price below the global equilibrium price.)

4. Show the effect of Ghana's policy on a supply curve. (This is represented as a movement down the supply curve.)

Activity

Generating a Market Supply Schedule (5–10 minutes)

Ask students about their willingness to sell their labor time at the wages listed below. Put the wages on the board, and ask students to write down how many hours they are willing to work per week at each wage. Choose three students to report.

Wage per hour	Student 1	Student 2	Student 3	Market Supply
$20.00	40	25	20	85
$15.00	30	20	15	65
$10.00	25	15	10	50
$8.00	20	10	8	38
$6.00	10	5	5	20

Add the three responses, and plot the supply curve for labor time on the board. Even if a few students choose to work less hours per week when the wage rises, most students will want to work more hours. (The substitution effect generally dominates the income effect of a higher wage.)

In the News

Oil Prices and Production

www.oilprices.com, July 2002.

The Rotary Rig Count is the average number of drilling rigs actively exploring for oil and gas. It is a measure of the oil and gas industry's confidence in future prices.

At the end of the Arab Oil Embargo in 1974, the rig count was below 1500. It rose steadily with crude oil prices to over 2000 in 1979. From 1978 to the beginning of 1981 domestic crude oil prices exploded from a combination of the rapid growth in world energy prices and deregulation of domestic prices. Forecasts of crude oil prices in excess of $100 per barrel fueled a drilling frenzy. By 1982, the number of rotary rigs running had more than doubled.

It is important to note that the peak in drilling occurred over a year after oil prices had entered a steep decline, which continued until the 1986 price collapse. For the next few years the towns in the oil patch were characterized by bankruptcy, bank failures and high unemployment.

Ask students:

1. Why does the amount of drilling increase as the price increases? (There is more profit incentive for the producer.)
2. Show a supply curve that illustrates the influence of price on the production of oil. (The supply curve will be upward sloping.)
3. Why might production increase even after prices have dropped? (There may have been investments in oil production which cannot be withdrawn immediately.)

Shifts in the Supply Curve

Creating Student Interest

Quicksilver is a producer of beach wear. Ask students under what conditions could the company produce more shirts at the existing price? Quicksilver could adapt a better technology in production, for example. Tell students we are now looking at conditions, other than a price increase, that will cause sellers to supply more goods to the market.

Common Student Misunderstandings

Students often have a hard time understanding why the supply curve shifts right or left as the result of a change in the costs of production. Illustrate with a cost of production increase for an airline company. If the price of jet fuel rises, an airline company will have to supply fewer flights at that same price. Show on the board those two points on the two supply curves, before and after the cost increase.

Presenting the Material

Give the example of Gillette when it came out with the Mach 3 razor. The company reconfigured the production line so that the production of razors doubled per hour. Changing technology represents a determinant of supply and causes the supply curve to shift to the right.

Price of razors	Quantity before the new technology	Quantity after the new technology
$5.00	100,000	200,000
$4.00	80,000	160,000
$3.00	60,000	120,000
$2.00	40,000	80,000

Activities

Movement Along the Supply Curve versus Shifts in the Supply Curve

The examples below can be passed out to students or discussed in class.

Example	Movement along the supply curve	A shift in the supply curve
1. As home prices rise, more people put out a For Sale sign.	X	
2. Personal bankruptcies rise with the recession, forcing homeowners to sell.		X
3. College grads avoid teaching jobs as starting salaries fall.	X	
4. Worsening working conditions in urban schools chase away prospective teachers.		X
5. As the price of airline tickets rise, airlines add more flights.	X	
6. The price of jet fuel drops and airlines expand the number of flights.		X

In the News

An Oil Price Forecast

www.oilprices.com, July 2002.

> In a semi-annual survey of the oil and gas industry, Standard & Poor's oil and gas equity analyst Tina Vital sees increasing risks to U.S. supplies of oil and gas going forward.
>
> Depletion of existing U.S. oil and gas wells, limited access to known low-cost reserves (in foreign lands or on U.S. federal lands), trade restrictions, environmental regulations and political and economic unrest in Latin America and the Middle East are among the causes cited.

Based on the article, in which direction will the supply of oil curve for the United States shift from the following?

- Depletion of existing wells (the supply curve shifts left)
- Trade restrictions (the supply curve shifts left)
- Environmental regulations (the supply curve shifts left)
- Political unrest in Latin America and the Middle East (the supply curve shifts left)

The Equilibrium Price

Creating Student Interest

Ask students to think about housing prices in two nearby cities. Why are the equilibrium prices different?

Common Student Misunderstandings

Students often memorize that the equilibrium price is where the two lines cross. Help them to understand that a market continuously informs buyers and sellers where the equilibrium price is so that both adjust their bid and ask prices. This price "clears" the market in that all unsold products must be reduced in price to sell. In a specific real estate market, the market may be moving toward an equilibrium price, as stubborn sellers are forced to lower their prices if they wish to sell now.

Presenting the Material

Give a specific numerical example of an equilibrium price in the razor market.

Price	Quantity demanded	Quantity supplied	
$5.00	120,000	200,000	Surplus QS > QD
$4.00	160,000	160,000	*Equilibrium QD = QS
$3.00	180,000	120,000	Shortage QD > QS
$2.00	220,000	100.000	Shortage QD > QS

Here the quantity demanded is equal to the quantity supplied at a price of $4.00. This price will clear the market. There is no shortage or surplus at that price.

Activities

Class Simulation: Buying and Selling Turquoise (30 minutes)
- Divide the class in half and assign one side to be buyers of turquoise and the other, sellers of turquoise.
- Prepare a set of playing cards as indicated below.

    Buyer cards read "Do not pay more than $250" (for example)

    The quantities are: $225 (3) $250 (3) $275 (3) $300 (3) $325 (2) $350 (2) $375 (2) $400 (2)

    Seller cards read, "Do not sell for less than $275" (for example)

    Print up an equal amount of buyer cards and seller cards.

Ask a student to help you pass out the cards to the buyers and sellers in the class. Students draw one card from the stack.
- Tell buyers to buy the turquoise as cheaply as possible, and sellers to sell as high as they can. If students do not make a trade during the session, they take the entire amount on the card as a loss.
- Students have 3–4 minutes to make a deal. Buyers try to get the cheapest price they can, and sellers try to get a high price. When two students agree on a compromise price, they shake hands and come to the board; a recorder keeps track of the trades.
- Students also keep track of their trades in each round. (If buyers make a deal below the amount on their card, they count that as a profit.)
- Run the simulation for at least three rounds, rotating buyers and sellers. At the end of the game the chart will appear as shown on the next page.

Price	Round 1	Round 2	Round 3	QD, QS
$400		x		1, 64
$375	xx			3, 63
$350	xx	x	x	7, 61
$325	xxx	xxx	xx	15, 57
$300	xxxx	xxxx	xx	25, 48
$275	xxxxxx	xxxxx	xxx	39, 38
$250	xxxxx	xxxxxx	xxxx	54, 24
$225	xxxx	xx	xxx	63, 9

From the data on the board, you derive the demand schedule from the completed trades by counting the trades from top to bottom cumulatively.

The demand schedule of the above example will be:
$400 = 1

$375 = 3 (The buyer who paid $400 would also be willing to buy at $375 if he or she had the opportunity. The trades are totaled cumulatively as you move down to lower prices.)

$350 = 7

$325 = 15

$300 = 25

$275 = 39

$250 = 54

$225 = 63

1. Given the data, what was the equilibrium price? Students can see where most trades took place. They can also plot the demand and supply curves and determine the equilibrium price more precisely.
2. Ask: Why if the game is played for more rounds do the trades start to cluster around the equilibrium price? Clearly, the market acts as a feedback mechanism, informing market participants of what trades are more likely to take place.
3. Ask what would happen to the equilibrium price if the price on the buyer cards (in effect, an increase in income) were to double? The equilibrium price will rise.

A Ticket Shortage (10–15 minutes)

Pair students and give them the following scenario: You are responsible for a concert on campus and have sold out all the tickets at $20 a piece. Unfortunately, there are 100 students outside the concert who still want to get in and are angry and frustrated.

1. Is $20 the equilibrium price? (No, we know that this price is below the equilibrium price because it causes a shortage.)
2. How do you remedy the ticket shortage? (Raise the price for future concerts, expand the capacity of the arena.)
3. Put the three graphs on the next page on the board. Ask students to label each graph and identify what kind of solution it represents for the ticket shortage.

4. Which solution would fans prefer? (Fans would like a free voucher for a future concert.) Concert organizers? (They would like a higher price for future concerts.)

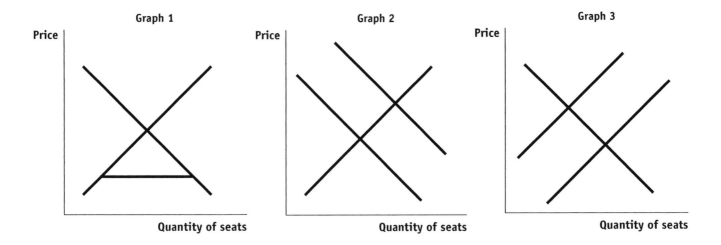

Graph 1 indicates that the cause of the shortage was a price set below the equilibrium price. To remedy this problem for future concerts, the ticket price must be equal to the equilibrium price. Graph 2 shows a shift in the demand curves for the concert. Students must speculate on possible ways in which the demand for the concert can be reduced. One solution that students often come up with is to give angry concert fans a voucher for a future concert. In graph 3, there is a shift in the supply curve for the concert. Students brainstorm how the supply of seats could be expanded, such as renting additional chairs for the concert.

In the News

Vacant Luxury Rooms With a View

LA Times, July 18, 2002.

This article refers to a drop in tourism in the United States following 9/11.

> Luxury homes with panoramic views of the Pacific Ocean are going vacant this summer, following the September 11th attacks, and the slowing economy. Wealthy foreigners and upscale Americans are passing on extended vacations at California beaches. Danielle Purcell manages many of these drop-dead gorgeous properties that hug the sands. She originally offered one for rent at $20,000 per month and found no takers and subsequently lowered the rent to $16,000 and still no interest. Purcell is up against a 2.2% drop in tourist travel this summer, as travelers spend less on travel, take shorter vacations and stay closer to home.

Ask students:

1. Are these luxury homes priced above, below, or at the equilibrium price? (Because there are so many unsold rentals, their rental price is above the equilibrium price.)

2. Is $16,000 the equilibrium price? (No, there is still a surplus at this price.)

3. Is there excess supply or excess demand of these luxury homes? (There is excess supply.)

4. What will happen to the rental price of the homes that remain vacant? (The rental price will continue to fall.)

Changes in the Equilibrium Price

Creating Student Interest

Ask students to identify some products whose prices have changed recently. Ask them to speculate on what demand factors and supply factors were responsible for the change in the equilibrium price.

Common Student Misunderstandings

Students may have difficulty interpreting a supply and demand graph that shows a change in the equilibrium price. Make sure that the graph you draw on the board is clearly labeled, showing the demand curve before a change and the demand curve after the change. Help students to locate the first and second equilibrium prices on the graph.

Presenting the Material

Help students analyze why the equilibrium price for a specific product changed. Use a simple example such as an increase in the price of new homes. Go through the steps in the analysis.

1. Did the demand for new homes shift? What caused this change in demand? (Buyers may expect higher prices in the future.) Did the demand curve shift right or left as a result?

2. Did the supply of new homes shift? What caused the change in supply? (The price of lumber may have risen.) Did the supply curve shift to the right or left?

3. Draw the demand and supply for new homes. Label the old and new demand curves D_1 and D_2, and label the old and new supply curves S_1 and S_2. Now find the old equilibrium price and label that P_1 on the vertical price axis, and label the new equilibrium price on the vertical axis P_2.

Using the Case Study in the Text

Demand, Supply, and Controlled Substances (text page 76)

Ask students:

1. Why is it so hard to eliminate the illegal drug trade? (It is profitable for sellers and there is a high demand for the drugs.)

2. What does a restriction in the supply of drugs do to the street price of drugs? (It raises the equilibrium price.)

3. Suggest policies to reduce the demand for illegal drugs. (Educational programs to reduce demand, this will shift the demand curve to the left.)

Work It Out

Supply and Demand (text pages 77–78)

This exercise demonstrates the manner in which equilibrium price and quantity are computed mathematically and represented graphically. It also covers the concepts of surpluses and shortages, as well as distinguishing between movement along a demand (supply) curve and shifts of a demand (supply) curve.

Activities

Applying Analysis to a News Article: Supply and Demand (20–30 minutes)

Ask students to bring in an article from a newspaper, magazine, or relevant online source that is about a specific market and indicates a change in price of the product. For smaller classes, you can bring in several copies of the *Wall Street Journal* and pass these around to teams of students. Ask them to:

1. Identify the relevant market.
2. Describe the nature of the change in the market: shift in demand or shift in supply.
3. Describe the direction of the shift.
4. Describe what induced the shift.
5. Indicate the effect of the shift on the equilibrium market price. Indicate when you can predict the change in the equilibrium quantity, and indicate when you cannot.

Additional Examples: Changes in the Equilibrium Price (5–10 minutes)
Pair students and give them the following examples to analyze.

Example	Demand shifts right or left?	Supply shifts right or left?	Equilibrium price up or down?	Equilibrium quantity up or down?
1. Demand for colorful prom night attire boosts sales of fuchsia cummerbunds.	Right		Up	Up
2. The expiration of drug patents increases the number of generic drugs available to consumers.		Right	Down	Up
3. Panic reigns on Wall Street as millions of stockholders sell simultaneously.		Right	Down	Up
4. GM and Ford overestimate demand and produce too many cars in the midst of a slowdown in the economy.	Left	Right	Down	Indeterminate
5. The entry of hundreds of nail salons in southern California drags down price and profits.		Right	Down	Up
6. Airline pilots negotiate a dramatic salary increase, and airlines are forced to raise ticket prices.		Left	Up	Down
7. Mexico opens a deep-water port in Ensenada and shippers shun the LA port. (The market is shipments through the LA port.)	Left		Down	Down
8. Luxury home sales fall as the stock market sputters and wealth falls.	Left		Down	Down
9. Competition in the fast-food industry increases the number of restaurants.		Right	Down	Up
10. Parking fees for the New York Yankees skyrocket and ticket sales fall. (The market is for baseball tickets.)	Left		Down	Down

chapter 4

The Market Strikes Back

Chapter Objectives

Students will learn in this chapter:
- The meaning of price controls and quantity controls, two kinds of government intervention in markets.
- How price and quantity controls create problems and make a market inefficient.
- Why economists are often deeply skeptical of attempts to intervene in markets.
- Who benefits and who loses from market interventions, and why they are used despite their well-known problems.
- What an excise tax is and why its effect is similar to a quantity control.

Chapter Outline

Opening Example: Rent control and taxi licenses are given as examples of what happens when the logic of the market is defied by government intervention.

I. Price Controls

    A. *Definition:* A **price control** is a legal restriction on how high or low a market price may go.

    B. Price controls are enacted by governments in response to political pressures from buyers and sellers.

II. Price Ceilings

    A. *Definition:* A **price ceiling** is a maximum price sellers are allowed to charge for a good.

    B. Modeling a price ceiling: A price ceiling is set below the equilibrium price. A price ceiling set above the equilibrium price has no effect. This is illustrated in text Figure 4-2, shown on the next page.

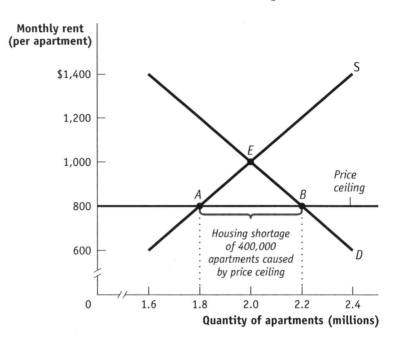

The Effects of a Price Ceiling

D. *Definition:* A market or an economy is **inefficient** if there are missed opportunities: Some people could be made better off without making other people worse off.

E. Price ceilings often lead to inefficiency in the form of

   1. Inefficient allocation to consumers: People who want the good badly and are willing to pay a high price don't get it, and those who care relatively little about the good and are only willing to pay a low price do get it.

   2. Wasted resources: People spend money and expend effort in order to deal with the shortages caused by the price ceiling.

   3. Inefficiently low quality: Sellers offer low-quality goods at a low price even though buyers would prefer a higher quality at a higher price.

F. Price ceilings also lead to black markets.

   1. *Definition:* A **black market** is a market in which goods or services are bought and sold illegally—either because it is illegal to sell them at all or because the prices charged are legally prohibited by a price ceiling.

G. Price ceilings are enacted because

   1. They do benefit some people.

   2. When they have been in effect for a long time, buyers may not have a realistic idea of what would happen without them.

   3. Government officials often do not understand supply and demand analysis.

III. Price Floors

A. *Definition:* A **price floor** is a minimum price buyers are required to pay for a good.

B. *Definition:* The **minimum wage** is a legal floor on the wage rate, which is the market price of labor.

C. Price floors lead to **excess supply;** the quantity supplied is greater than quantity demanded at the set price. Price floors are ineffective if set below the equilibrium price.

D. Modeling a price floor: Graphically, a price floor is a price set at a price that is above the equilibrium price. This is illustrated in text Figure 4-4, shown below.

The Effects of a Price Floor

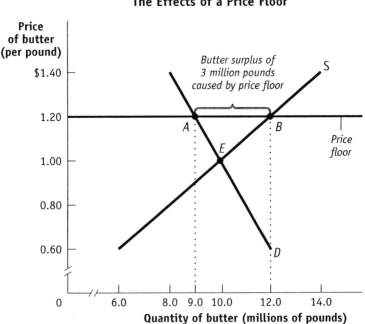

E. Price floors often lead to

1. **Inefficient allocation of sales among sellers:** Those who would be willing to sell the good at the lowest price are not always those who actually manage to sell it.

2. Wasted resources. Government price floors set about the equilibrium price cause surpluses which the government buys and destroys. Minimum wages result in fewer jobs available and so would-be workers waste time searching for a job.

3. Goods of **inefficiently high quality:** Sellers offer high-quality goods at a high price, even though buyers would prefer a lower quality at a lower price.

4. Illegal activity.

F. Government officials often disregard warnings about the consequences of price floors, either because they believe that the relevant market is poorly described by the supply and demand model or, more often, because they do not understand the model.

1. Minimum wage laws are an example of price floors. Relatively high minimum wages in Europe lead to higher levels of unemployment and black markets in labor. In contrast, the minimum wage in the United States is set closer to the equilibrium wage, and labor is relatively more productive in the United States.

IV. Controlling Quantities

   A. *Definition:* A **quantity control,** or **quota,** is an upper limit on the quantity of some good that can be bought or sold. The total amount of the good that can be legally transacted is the **quota limit.**

   B. *Definition:* A **license** gives its owner the right to supply the good.

   C. *Definition:* The **demand price** of a given quantity is the price at which consumers will demand that quantity.

   D. *Definition:* The **supply price** of a given quantity is the price at which producers will supply that quantity.

   E. Modeling a quantity control. This is shown graphically by a vertical line set at the quantity limit, as illustrated in text Figure 4-6, shown below.

Effect of a Quota on the Market for Taxi Rides

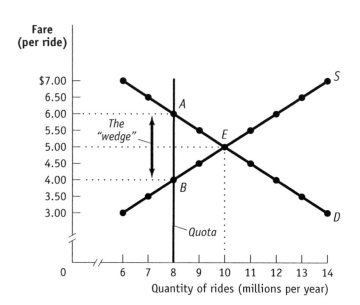

Fare (per ride)	Quantity of rides (millions per year)	
	Quantity demanded	Quantity supplied
$7.00	6	14
6.50	7	13
6.00	8	12
5.50	9	11
5.00	10	10
4.50	11	9
4.00	12	8
3.50	13	7
3.00	14	6

   F. *Definition:* A quantity control, or quota, drives a **wedge** between the demand price and the supply price of a good. The difference between the demand and supply price is the **quota rent,** the earnings that accrue to the license-holder from ownership of the right to sell the good. It is equal to the market price of the license when the licenses are traded.

   G. The opportunity costs of quantity controls are
      1. Inefficiencies, or missed opportunities, in the form of mutually beneficial transactions that don't occur.

      2. Incentives for illegal activities.

   H. Taxi medallions in New York City and clam fishing in New Jersey are given as examples of quota controls.

V. Surprise Parallel: Taxes

   A. *Definition:* An **excise tax** is a tax on sales of a good or service.

   B. An excise tax is similar in effect to a quota. A tax increases the supply price of a good corresponding to any given quantity of the good.

C. Modeling the effect of an excise tax: The tax shifts the supply curve up by the amount of the tax. This is illustrated in text Figure 4-7, shown below.

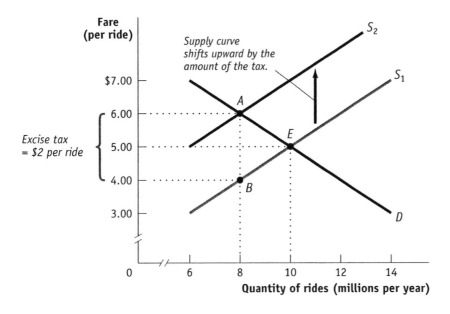

Effect of an Excise Tax Levied on Sales of Taxi Rides

D. *Definition:* The **incidence** of a tax is a measure of who actually pays it.

E. The incidence of a tax is not always split evenly between buyers and sellers and will depend on the demand and supply curves. (Elasticity is covered in Chapter 5.)

F. The amount of revenue collected by an excise tax is equal to the area of the rectangle whose height is the wedge that the tax drives between the supply and demand curves and whose width is the quantity bought and sold under the tax. This is illustrated in text Figure 4-9, shown below.

The Revenue from an Excise Tax

G. Who pays the FICA? This tax is similar to an excise tax on the sale and purchase of labor. Both employees and employers pay a percentage out of earnings. Most economists believe that workers bear the full burden of the tax in the form of a lower wage.

Teaching Tips

Price Ceilings

Creating Student Interest

Two issues that will spark debate are (1) Is a price control on apartment rental rates a good idea if the goal is to ensure a diversity of renters? What is the opportunity cost? (2) Should price controls be put on pharmaceutical medicines still under patent? What are the benefits and costs of such a proposal?

Common Student Misunderstandings

Students may think that a "ceiling" is high; therefore, it should be shown graphically as a price above equilibrium. Explain that a price ceiling holds prices down and is shown graphically below the equilibrium price. Clarify that the purpose of this price set by government is to prevent a price from rising to the equilibrium price.

Presenting the Material

Consider this concrete example to illustrate a price ceiling.

Rent	Quantity demanded (units rented per month)	Quantity supplied (units for rent monthly)
$1,400	1,000	2,000
$1,200	1,100	1,500
$1,000	1,200	1,200
$800	1,500	1,000
$600	1,800	750
$400	2,100	600

1. If a price ceiling of $800 is set on apartment rentals, how much of a shortage is created? (500 units)

2. How would this shortage manifest itself in the market? (In the short run, many renters will be unable to find an apartment. In the long run, there will be a lack of construction of new apartment buildings.)

How does a price ceiling of $800 "defy the logic of the market"? (The market is dictating an equilibrium price of $1,000, which would not result in a shortage.)

Work it Out

Showing a Price Ceiling (text page 89)

Students are asked to use the information presented for a hypothetical bottled water market to mathematically and graphically demonstrate their understanding of the concept of a price ceiling, shortages, and market efficiency.

Using the Case Study in the Text

Oil Shortages in the 1970s (text page 90)

Ask students the following questions:

1. Why did oil prices rise in most of the world but not in the United States? (The United States had a price ceiling on oil in the 1970s.)

2. What were the consequences of price ceilings in the United States in the 1970s? (Shortages of oil and long lines of cars at gasoline stations.)

Activities

Rent Control (10–15 minutes)

Pair students and ask them to brainstorm the pros and cons of rent control laws. Ask them to share their arguments with the whole class. Additional discussion questions are

> How is this issue an example of the trade-off between equity (fairness) and efficiency?
>
> How do rent control laws cause the "market to strike back"?

Price Ceilings and Essential Goods (3–5 minutes)

Pair students to discuss the following scenario:

> During the Northridge earthquake in Los Angeles County, water was in short supply in the Valley and the price of bottled water skyrocketed. The city invoked a state law which prohibits businesses from charging more than 5% extra for certain "essential goods" 30 days after a natural disaster. Ask students: should a state be able to put price ceilings on "essential" goods following a natural disaster, or should market prices prevail?

Prescription Medicines (15–30 minutes)

To stimulate discussion, hand out the following excerpts from an article in favor of a price ceiling on prescription medicines and assign it as homework. In class, group students and have them critically analyze the pros and cons of the issue.

Offering Hope: At a Price

by Katharine Greider
The Nation, July 9, 2003.

"America's Pharmaceutical Companies: New Medicines New Hope." This was the tag line of full page ads appearing in national magazines last year. But this message of hope has a dark side. Faced with a proposal to limit drug prices, industry representatives invariably respond by insisting the measure will put an end to research into terrifying diseases like Alzheimer's and cancer hitting us where we live. Certainly pharmaceutical companies take on risk by spending very large sums in their laboratories . . . yet, well over half the drugs approved in the United States between 1989 and 2000 were "product-line extensions" using old active ingredients, according to a study released in May 2002 by the National Institute for Health Care Management. . . . These standard-rated product-line extensions, contributed most to increased consumer spending on new drugs in the five years leading up to 2000. With true breakthroughs few and far between drug companies are flooding the market with new dosages, new combinations and otherwise rejiggered forms of their older medicines. . . .

According to a report by Representative Bernie Sander's office, the breast-cancer drug tarnoxifen, which costs Canadians about $34 per treatment, sets back an uninsured American more than $240 and was the product of 140 clinical trials sponsored by our government.

While the average Fortune 500 Company saw declining profits in a difficult environment in 2001, drug companies on the list actually boosted their profits by 33 percent, according to an analysis of Fortune 500 data by Public Citizen. These titan drug makers took 18.5 percent of revenues as profit, eight times the median for all other Fortune 500 companies.

Price Floors

Creating Student Interest
Ask students: Should the minimum wage be raised? Should it be eliminated? How do minimum wage laws go against "the logic of the market"?

Common Student Misunderstandings
Students may think that a price "floor" should be shown graphically below the equilibrium price. Emphasize that a price floor holds up a price that would otherwise fall to the equilibrium wage.

Students have not been formally exposed to a labor market graph yet and may confuse the product market with the labor market. Make clear that the demand curve represents employer demand for labor, and the supply curve represents the willingness of employees to offer their labor. The wage is the equivalent of the price of labor.

Presenting the Material
Consider this concrete example to illustrate a price floor.

Wage	Quantity of labor demanded	Quantity of labor supplied
$6.75	300	500
$6.00	400	400
$5.75	500	300
$5.50	550	200
$5.00	600	100
$4.75	650	50

1. What is the equilibrium wage rate? ($6.00)

2. If a price floor is set at $6.75 (minimum wage), how much of a surplus of unemployed workers will be created? (200)

Using the Case Study in the Text

'Black Labor' in Southern Europe (text pages 94–95)
Illustrate on two supply and demand diagrams the differences between European and U.S. minimum wage laws incorporating these facts:

1. Higher productivity of labor in the United States relative to Europe.

2. A larger unemployment effect in Europe. (The demand for labor will be higher in the United States, and the minimum wage in the United States is closer to the equilibrium wage.)

In the News

Divide the class in half. Assign reading 1 to half the students and reading 2 to the other half. In the next class, pair students who have read the same article. Ask them to summarize the main arguments. Pairs then must find another pair in the room who have the opposite article. Students explain the arguments to the other pair. Then ask for a few pairs to report to the whole class.

Reading 1: States Move on Minimum Wage

Economic Policy Institute, June 11, 2003, Issue Brief #195
www.epinet.org/content.cfm/issuebriefs_ib195 by Jeff Chapman

The President and Congress are poised to beat an embarrassing record currently held by their predecessors of the 1980s—eight years without raising the minimum wage. Each year the federal government fails to act, minimum wage workers pay the price, as the rising cost of living erodes the value of their paycheck.

The need for a minimum wage increase is clear: a stagnant minimum wage has a significant impact on the earnings of low-wage workers. The last time the federal government failed so badly to meet its responsibility—in the 1980s—states stepped in. Between 1979 and 1989, a period in which the purchasing power of the federal minimum wage fell every year, the number of states with minimum wages higher than the federal level went from 1 to 15.

Because the earnings of low-wage women are particularly tied to the minimum wage, the decline in real (i.e., inflation-adjusted) wages was particularly pronounced among female workers. Women made up 58.2% of the workers directly affected by the 1996–97 increase in the minimum wage, but only constituted 47.7% of the total workforce. While the inflation-adjusted median wage of female workers ages 18 to 64 grew by 8.4% from 1979 to 1989, the wages of the bottom 20% of women fell dramatically.

The minimum wage is unusual among federal policies in that its value is not held constant over time. For example, since 1975 Social Security benefits have been adjusted for changes in the cost of living. Were Social Security benefits like the minimum wage, the living standards of survivors, and the retired and disabled persons would rise and fall according to congressional action (or inaction)?

In Washington state and Oregon, annual increases in the minimum wage are tied to increases in the cost of living. For example, if prices rise by 2% from 2002 to 2003, then the minimum wage in the two states will be 2% higher in 2004 than it was in 2003. This keeps the actual purchasing power of the minimum wage constant.

Reading 2: Minimum Wage Redux

(Opposition to a raise in the minimum wage)
by Doug Bandow, November 1, 1999
www.cato.org/dailys/11-01-99.html

With control of the House in the balance, congressional Democrats are pushing for a big minimum wage hike. The Republicans, desperate to defuse a potential political issue, are doing what they do best: preparing to surrender.

No serious economist doubts that the minimum wage destroys jobs. The only question is how many. Economists Richard Burkhauser, Kenneth Couch and David Wittenberg estimate that every 10 percent increase in the minimum reduces employment by between 2 percent and 6 percent. They figure Congress' 1996 minimum wage hike cost between 153,000 and 457,000 teens their jobs.

These ill consequences have been moderated by America's booming economy. But those with the least education, experience and training would be most harmed by any new increase. Particularly vulnerable are welfare recipients attempting to become self-sufficient.

The 1996 welfare reform law has helped to dramatically cut the welfare rolls. However, recipients with the best employment prospects have already found jobs. The National Governors' Association warns that remaining beneficiaries face "significant challenges to workplace success."

Unfortunately, many of those on welfare are effectively illiterate.

According to the National Adult Literacy Survey, nearly half of welfare recipients have trouble performing basic arithmetic, reading and writing tasks. The Educational Testing Service says one of three has only "minimal skills," essentially the level of high school dropouts. Yet, just 10 percent of new jobs are open to people with so little expertise.

Companies do help train welfare recipients. Indeed, Michael Weinstein of The New York Times warns that even those who find work might find themselves trapped in low-paying jobs "unless work and training are combined." However, firms can't afford to do as much when the minimum wage rises.

Peter Brandon of the Institute for Research on Poverty has found that minimum-wage hikes draw new workers, particularly teens and students, into the labor force, who in turn displace those on welfare. As a result, welfare recipients in states that hiked their minimum wages remained on welfare 44 percent longer than those in states that did not increase their minimums.

Quantity Controls

Creating Student Interest

Ask students why New York City would want to have a law to limit the quantity of taxi licenses issued. What are the pros and cons of such a law? Give other examples of quantity controls, such as fishing catch limits and quotas on imported goods.

Common Student Misunderstandings

Students may be unfamiliar with quotas or quantity controls. Make clear that this limitation is holding down the quantity sold below what the equilibrium quantity would be.

Presenting the Material

Consider this concrete example to illustrate quantity controls.

Sugar market (U.S. domestic market without sugar quotas)

Price (per pound)	Quantity demanded (thousands of pounds)	Quantity supplied (thousands of pounds)
$3.00	600	1,400
$2.75	700	1,300
$2.50	800	1,200
$2.00	900	1,100
$1.75	1,000	1,000
$1.50	1,500	900

In the absence of a quota, the equilibrium quantity will be 1,000,000 pounds. Let's say the government restricts the quantity of imported sugar and the quantity limitation is now set at 900,000 pounds. The effect of the quota is shown in the following graph.

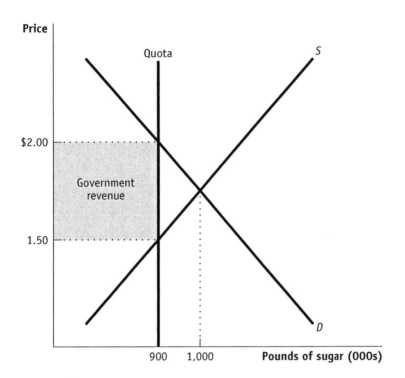

With the quota, 900,000 pounds will be sold at a price of $2.00. $2.00 is the demand price for 900,000 pounds. Domestic producers of sugar get a quota rent of $.50 per pound of sugar. Ask students to brainstorm who wins and who loses from the quota.

Using the Case Study in the Text

The Clams of New Jersey (text page 100)

Ask students:

1. Why did New Jersey institute a clam quota? (Excessive fishing threatened to wipe out the clam beds.)
2. What were the consequences of the clam quota? (Fishing was reduced as licenses became necessary to fish. Some boat owners make more from renting out their licenses than using them to fish.)

Activity

Quantity Control of Sugar Imports (5–10 minutes)

Divide the class into two parts. Explain that the United States has quantity limits on the amount of sugar that can be imported into the United States. The purpose of the limit is to protect U.S. sugar growers. Ask half the class to write down the benefits of the quantity control and the other to brainstorm the opportunity costs of the control. Then ask students to find another student in the room to discuss the pros and cons. Ask a few of the pairs to report.

Excise Taxes

Creating Student Interest

Ask students to think about products that have excise taxes on them. (Many are aware of gasoline, alcohol, and cigarette taxes.) What is the purpose of the tax?

Common Student Misunderstandings

Students may confuse who pays a tax with the incidence of a tax. Explain that we are not looking at who actually writes the check for the tax but how much buyers or sellers "pay" for the tax in the form of a higher price (buyers) or a smaller profit (sellers).

Students may not understand why a tax shifts the supply curve upward by the amount of the tax. Explain that in order to supply a specific quantity, sellers will ask for a higher price to cover the tax. This higher price is represented by a point vertically above the original supply curve at that same quantity.

Presenting the Material

Use the example of a $20 excise tax on the sale of motorcycles, as illustrated in the graph below. The tax causes the supply curve to shift to S_2 by the amount of the tax. The new equilibrium price is now $1,010. The effect of the excise tax is to push up the equilibrium price to $1,010, from $1,000. This means that buyers are paying $10 more than before, and because sellers are paying the government $20, they are now netting just $990 for each bike sold. Buyers and sellers are bearing an equal burden of the tax: buyers have to pay $10 more than before and sellers net $10 less than before.

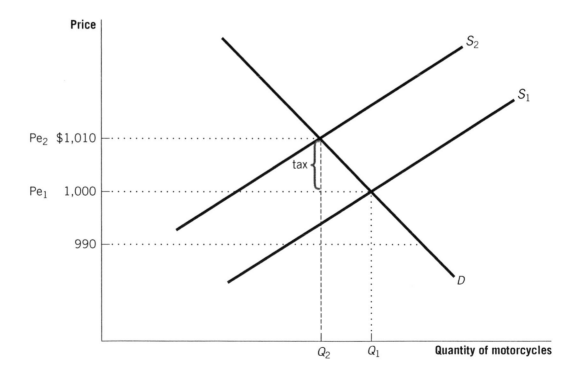

Activity

The Impact of Taxes (15–20 minutes)

Organize teams of four students each. In each team, one student plays the role of business groups, one student plays the role of an environmental group, one plays the role of government, and the last plays the role of U.S. consumers. Give students a copy of the following two unlabeled graphs.

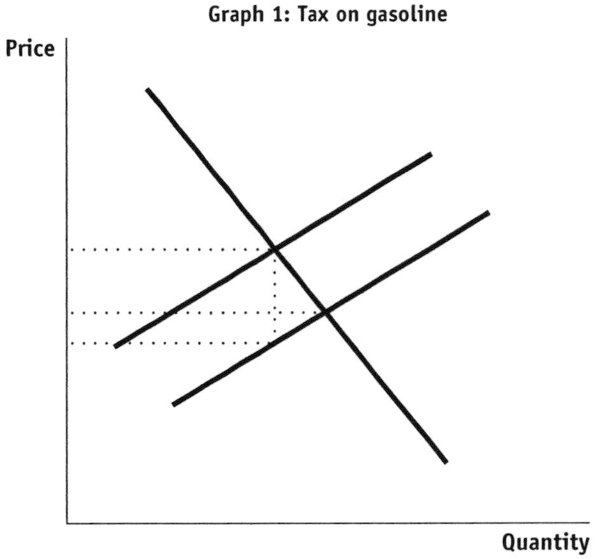

Graph 1: Tax on gasoline

Price

Quantity

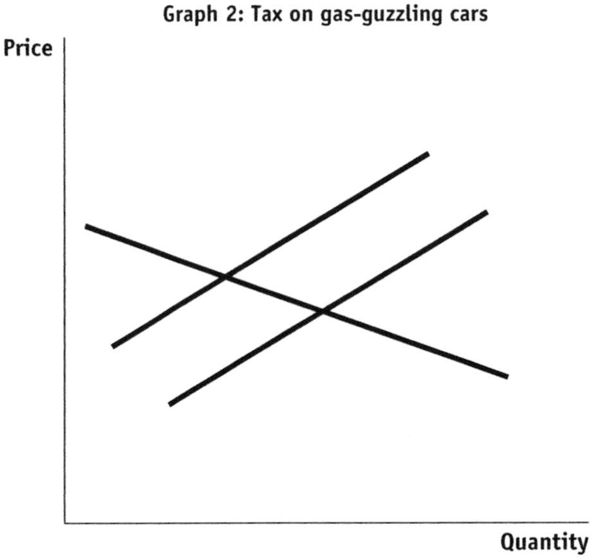

Graph 2: Tax on gas-guzzling cars

Price

Quantity

1. Ask teams to label each diagram to show the impact of the tax on the group they are representing. (The tax on gasoline hits consumers harder—the equilibrium price rises more. However, gasoline and gas guzzling cars are complementary goods and the higher price on gasoline will reduce the popularity of large cars. Businesses absorb more of the tax in the case of the tax on gasoline. Environmental groups may favor the tax on gas-guzzling cars because it results in a large drop in the quantity demanded. Governmental views may vary: the gasoline tax will affect more buyers, but depending on the amount of the tax, the higher price on the cars may generate higher revenues.)

2. Based on the roles they are playing, ask students to determine if they prefer a tax on gasoline or a tax on gas-guzzling cars.

3. As a team, have students answer the following:
   a. Agree on which type of the two taxes each group, government, environmental, business, and consumer groups would favor.
   b. If you had in mind the welfare of the entire society, which tax do you think is better?

chapter 5

Elasticity

Chapter Objectives

Students will learn in this chapter:
- The definition of elasticity, a measure of responsiveness to changes in prices or incomes.
- The importance of the price elasticity of demand, which measures the responsiveness of the quantity demanded to price.
- The meaning and importance of the income elasticity of demand, a measure of the responsiveness of the quantity demanded to income.
- The significance of the price elasticity of supply, which measures the responsiveness of the quantity supplied to price.
- What factors influence the size of the various elasticities.
- How elasticity affects the incidence of a tax, the measure of who bears its burden.

Chapter Outline

Opening Example: If OPEC raises the price of oil, will this affect people's driving habits in the short run and the long run? It all depends on elasticity.

I. Defining and Measuring Price Elasticity of Demand

  A. *Definition:* The **price elasticity of demand** is the ratio of the percentage change in quantity demanded to the percentage change in the price as one moves along the demand curve.

$$\frac{\% \text{ change in quantity demanded}}{\% \text{ change in price}} = \text{price elasticity of demand}$$

  B. Using the midpoint method to calculate elasticities

    1. *Definition:* The **midpoint method** is a technique for calculating the elasticity of demand. In this approach, one calculates percent changes in price and quantity compared with the average or "midpoint" of the initial and final values.

    2. Midpoint formula: Used when you have information about quantity demanded for widely separated prices.

$$\left| \frac{\dfrac{Q_2 - Q_1}{(Q_1 + Q_2)/2}}{\dfrac{P_2 - P_1}{(P_1 + P_2)/2}} \right| = E$$

$E > 1$: elastic demand

$E < 1$: inelastic demand

$E = 1$: unit-elastic demand

II. Interpreting the Price Elasticity of Demand

    A. How elastic is elastic?

        1. *Definition:* Demand is **perfectly inelastic** when the quantity demanded does not respond at all to changes in the price. When demand is perfectly inelastic, the demand curve is a vertical line.

        2. *Definition:* Demand is **perfectly elastic** when any price increase will cause the quantity demanded to drop to zero. When demand is perfectly elastic, the demand curve is a horizontal line.

        3. *Definition:* Demand is **elastic** if the price elasticity of demand is greater than 1, **inelastic** if the price elasticity of demand is less than 1, and **unit-elastic** if the price elasticity of demand is exactly 1. These are illustrated in text Figure 5-3, shown below.

Unit-Elastic Demand, Inelastic Demand, and Elastic Demand

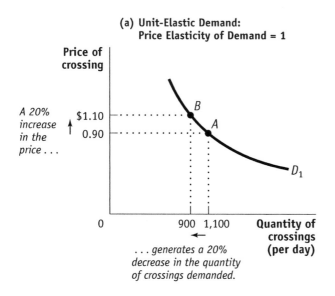

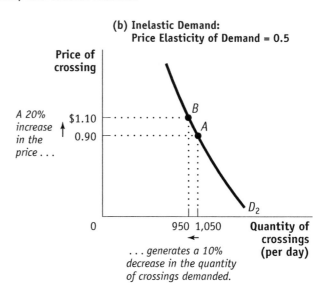

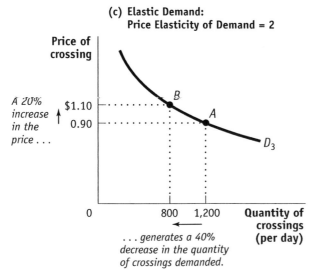

B. What factors determine the price elasticity of demand?
1. The availability of close substitutes
   a. The price elasticity of demand will tend to be high if there are close substitutes.
   b. The price elasticity of demand will tend to be low if there are no close substitutes.
2. Whether the good is necessary or a luxury
   a. The price elasticity of demand tends to be low if the good is a necessity.
   b. The price elasticity of demand tends to be high if the good is a luxury.
3. Time
   a. The long-run price elasticity of demand is often higher than the short-run elasticity.

C. Elasticity affects total revenue.
1. *Definition:* The **total revenue** is the total value of sales of a good. It is equal to the price of a good multiplied by the quantity sold.
2. Except in the rare case of a good with perfectly elastic or perfectly inelastic demand, when a seller raises the price of a good, two effects are present.
   a. A **price effect:** After a price increase, each unit sold sells at a higher price, which tends to raise revenue. The price effect is the change in price times the new quantity.
   b. A **sales effect:** After a price increase, fewer units are sold, which tends to lower revenue. The sales effect is the change in quantity sold times the original price.
3. The price elasticity of demand determines which effect predominates and therefore, indicates what happens to total revenue when price changes.
   a. If demand for a good is *elastic,* an increase in the good's price reduces total revenue; a fall in price increases total revenue. In this case, the sales effect is stronger than the price effect.
   b. If demand for a good is *inelastic,* a higher price increases total revenue; a fall in price results in a decrease in total revenue. The price effect in this case is stronger than the sales effect.
   c. If demand for a good is *unit-elastic,* an increase or a decrease in the good's price does not change total revenue. Here, the sales effect and the price effect exactly offset each other.
4. Total revenue is illustrated as an area below a demand curve: price times quantity sold.

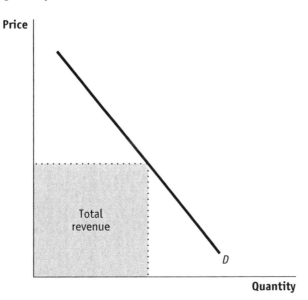

III. Other Demand Elasticities

A. The cross-price elasticity of demand

    1. *Definition:* The **cross-price elasticity of demand** between two goods measures the effect of the change in one good's price on the quantity demanded of the other good. It is equal to the percent change in the quantity demanded of one good divided by the percent change in the other good's price.

    2. The sign on the cross-price elasticity number is important; it indicates whether the two goods are complements or substitutes.

      a. When the cross-price elasticity is positive, the two goods are substitutes.

      b. When cross-price elasticity is negative, the two goods are complements.

B. The income elasticity of demand

    1. *Definition:* The **income elasticity of demand** is the percent change in the quantity demanded of a good when a consumer's income changes, divided by the percent change in income.

      a. Normal goods have a positive income elasticity (examples: cars, new homes).

      b. Inferior goods have negative income elasticity (example: macaroni and cheese).

    2. *Definition:* The demand for a good is **income-elastic** if the income elasticity of demand for that good is greater than 1.

    3. *Definition:* The demand for a good is **income-inelastic** if the income elasticity of demand for that good is positive but less than 1.

IV. The Price Elasticity of Supply

A. *Definition:* The **price elasticity of supply** is a measure of the responsiveness of the quantity supplied of a good to changes in the price of that good. It is the ratio of the percent change in the quantity supplied to the percent change in the price as one moves along the supply curve.

B. *Definition:* There is **perfectly inelastic supply** when the price elasticity of supply is zero, so that changes in the price of the good have no effect on the quantity supplied. A perfectly inelastic supply curve is a vertical line.

C. *Definition:* There is **perfectly elastic supply** when even a tiny increase or reduction in the price will lead to very large changes in the quantity supplied, so that the price elasticity of supply is infinite. A perfectly elastic supply curve is a horizontal line.

D. What factors determine the price elasticity of supply?

    1. The availability of inputs: When inputs are easily available, the price elasticity of supply will tend to be large; when the inputs are difficult to obtain, the price elasticity of supply will tend to be small.

    2. Time: The price elasticity of supply tends to be larger the longer the period of time that producers have to respond to a price change. Long-run price elasticity of supply is often greater than short-run elasticity.

V. Elasticity and Tax Incidence

A. The incidence of a tax is a measure of who bears the burden of the tax, regardless of who actually writes the check to the government.

B. Elasticity determines the incidence of an excise tax.

1. When the price elasticity of supply is high and the price elasticity of demand is low (supply is elastic and demand is inelastic), the burden of an excise tax falls mainly on consumers (text Figure 5-7, shown below).

An Excise Tax Paid Mainly by Consumers

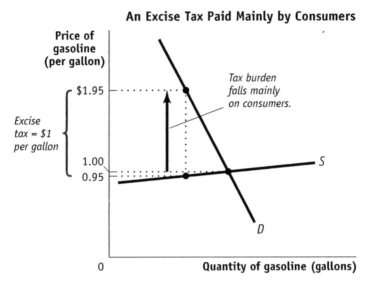

2. When the price elasticity of demand is high and the price elasticity of supply is low (demand is elastic and supply is inelastic), the burden of an excise tax falls mainly on producers (text Figure 5-8, shown below).

An Excise Tax Paid Mainly by Producers

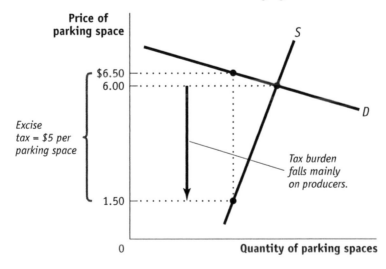

Teaching Tips

Price Elasticity of Demand

Creating Student Interest

Choose a student in class and say, "Let's assume that we both have the same hair stylist or barber. What would you do if he raised the price of a hair cut by $10.00?" If the student changes hair stylists, she is demonstrating "responsiveness" to a price change. Indicate that you would not change stylists, and so your response is less sensitive to a price change. This can lead to a definition of the difference between inelastic and elastic demand.

Parking space on campus is limited. Is your demand for a guaranteed space on campus sensitive to price or not? Would you pay "anything" for it?

Ask students if the demand for college textbooks is very responsive to price increases. How many substitutes are available? Have they checked online for textbooks?

Common Student Misunderstandings

The discussion of price elasticity follows that of supply and demand, and students may still be thinking in terms of shifting the demand or supply curves. With price elasticity we are examining the effects of a change in price only, so the focus is now on a movement along a demand curve or supply curve.

Often, students are not clear what "sensitivity" or "responsiveness" to a price change means. Provide a concrete example of consumers changing their behavior as a result of a price increase. Do consumers buy a little bit less (inelastic demand) or a lot less (elastic demand) of the product?

Students need to be clear that the elasticity coefficient is a number and not a percentage.

Students may need to review how to calculate a basic percent change, and then you can introduce the midpoint formula for larger price changes.

Often, students will say or write that a particular product is "elastic." They need to be clear that elasticity refers to the demand for that product, not to the product itself.

Presenting the Material

First, review the law of demand. The law states that as price rises, *ceteris paribus,* the quantity demanded falls. The question now is: by how much? Are consumers very sensitive to a price change or not? If consumers respond a lot to a price change, demand is elastic. If consumers do not respond very much to a price change, demand is inelastic.

Use the elasticity estimates in the text to illustrate various products and the price elasticities:

Inelastic Demand	Elastic Demand
Eggs = 0.1	Housing = 1.2
Beef = 0.4	Restaurant Meals = 2.3
Stationery = 0.5	Airline Travel = 2.4
Gasoline = 0.5	Foreign Travel = 4.1

Use a simple example to illustrate the basic elasticity formula. If price rises by 10% and quantity demanded falls by 20%, then elasticity = –2. |–2 | = 2, elastic demand. If price rises by 10% and quantity demanded falls by 5%, then elasticity is –0.5. |–0.5 | = 0.5 which indicates inelastic demand. Point out that quantity demanded is still dropping, but not by very much. And last, if price rises by 10% and quantity demanded falls by 10%, then elasticity is -1.0. |–1.0 | = 1.0, and demand is unit elastic.

Using the Case Study in the Text

Estimating Elasticities (text page 113)

Ask students:

1. Why is it so difficult to estimate the price elasticity of demand? (Other factors affect the quantity demanded at any particular price, such as changes in income, population, and tastes. Economists have to use statistical devices to isolate just the response to a change in price.)

Activities

Elasticity and the Demand for CDs (10 minutes)

Do a quick survey to determine if the demand for CDs is price elastic or price inelastic. Write on the board or overhead the following prices for CDs: $22.00, $20.00, $18.00, $16.00, $14.00, $12.00, and $10.00. Next ask 10 students to tell you how many CDs they would purchase at each price. Then, using their answers, construct a demand curve. Is it fairly steep (inelastic) or relatively flat (elastic)? Have them speculate how the Internet has changed the price elasticity of demand for CDs.

Ranking Goods by Their Price Elasticity (5–10 minutes)

Pair students and put the following six goods in order of most elastic to least elastic:

> Salt
> Audi A4 car
> A doctor's visit
> T Bone steaks
> A luxury room at the Crowne Plaza hotel
> Electricity

The order will be close to:

> Audi A4 car
> A luxury room at the Crowne Plaza hotel
> T Bone steaks
> Salt
> A doctor's visit
> Electricity

Why Do Business Travelers Pay More? (3–5 minutes)

Here is a concrete example to illustrate the difference between elastic and inelastic demand.

The elasticity of demand for airline travel differs when we look at business travelers versus vacation travelers.

Vacation travelers	Business travelers
$P_1 = \$200$	$P_1 = \$200$
$P_2 = \$220$	$P_2 = \$220$
$Q_1 = 10{,}000$ tickets	$Q_1 = 10{,}000$ tickets
$Q_2 = 8{,}000$ tickets	$Q_2 = 9{,}500$ tickets

The response of vacation travelers to an increase in the price of airline tickets from $200 to $220 results in a fall in quantity demanded from 10,000 tickets to 8,000 tickets. The same increase in price for business travelers causes the quantity demanded to fall a little; from 10,000 tickets to 9,500 tickets.

Ask students to calculate the price elasticity of demand for vacation travelers and for business travelers, using the midpoint formula.

For vacation travelers: $\left| \dfrac{\dfrac{10{,}000 - 8{,}000}{(10{,}000 + 8{,}000)/2}}{\dfrac{200 - 220}{(200 + 220)/2}} \right| = 2.33$

For business travelers: $\left| \dfrac{\dfrac{10{,}000 - 9{,}500}{(10{,}000 + 9{,}500)/2}}{\dfrac{200 - 220}{(200 + 220)/2}} \right| = 0.54$

Work It Out

Price Elasticity of Demand (text page 119)

This numerical example asks students to compute the value of price elasticity of demand for two goods. Afterward, students must use the computed values of elasticity of demand to determine which good has more elastic demand and what impact an increase in the price of these goods will have on a store's total revenue.

Total Revenue and Price Elasticity of Demand

Creating Student Interest

Ask: "Will a firm increase its revenues when it raises its price?" Students will come up with some circumstances in which this strategy may not work well, especially when consumers have many substitutes. Or, would a supermarket increase its revenues from salt sales by lowering its price? How many consumers will respond to this type of sale? If very few consumers respond, what will happen to total revenues?

Common Student Misunderstandings

Students may confuse total revenues with a firm's profits. Clarify that revenues are income from sales; deducting costs results in the firm's total profit.

Students have difficulty understanding how a decrease in price lowers total revenues when demand is inelastic. Explain that if each item is priced lower and the same quantity is sold, then the price effect dominates the sales effect, causing revenues to fall.

Presenting the Material

Elasticity is an important concept because it influences a firm's total revenues and thus profits. Since the focus now has shifted from the consumer to the firm, make sure students understand the definition of total revenue. Emphasize that the success of a price change for a firm will depend on consumers' response.

Using the Case Study in the Text

America's a Nice Place to Live, but We Can't Afford to Visit
(text pages 119–120)
Ask students:

1. How was American tourism to Canada affected by the depreciation of the Canadian dollar? (Prices in Canada were 20% cheaper, causing more Americans to take vacations in Canada.)
2. Why is the price elasticity of demand for foreign travel about 4.1? (There are many substitutes for foreign travel.)

Activity

Calculating Total Revenue (5 minutes)
Use the previous example involving the demand for airline tickets to calculate the change in total revenue resulting from the price increase from $200 to $220. Have students calculate the price effect and the sales effect of the price change, and then use that information to determine if demand is elastic or inelastic.

For vacation travelers:
- Total revenue before the price change is: $200 × 10,000 tickets = $2 million
- Total revenue after the price change is $220 × 8,000 tickets = $1.76 million
- Price effect is $20 × 8,000 tickets = $160,000
- Sales effect is $200 × (–2,000 tickets) = –$400,000
- The sales effect dominates the price effect. Total revenues will fall after a price increase, so demand is price elastic.

For business travelers:
- Total revenue before the price change is: $200 × 10,000 tickets = $2 million
- Total revenue after the price change is $220 × 9,500 tickets = $2.09 million
- Price effect is $20 × 9,500 tickets = $190,000
- Sales effect is $200 × (–500 tickets) = –$100,000
- The price effect dominates the sales effect. Total revenues will rise after a price increase, so demand is price inelastic.

Determinants of Price Elasticity

Creating Student Interest

Ask students why demand for cars is more price elastic in the long run than in the short run.

Common Student Misunderstandings

Sometimes students are not clear what the term "determinants" means. Explain that the determinants of price elasticity of demand are factors that cause consumer demand to be very sensitive to changes in price or not.

Presenting the Material

Use the table on the next page to ask students which determinant of demand explains the elasticity number.

Product	Price elasticity of demand	Determinants of elasticity
Eggs	0.1	a small part of the consumer's budget
Beef	0.4	large category: not as many substitutes as T-bone steak
Stationery	0.5	small part of the consumer's budget
Gasoline	0.5	a necessity
Housing	1.2	a large proportion of a consumer's budget
Restaurant meals	2.3	there are substitutes
Airline travel	2.4	there are many substitutes
Foreign travel	4.1	there are many substitutes

Activity

Determining Elasticity (3–5 minutes)

Form pairs of students and ask them to calculate the percent change in quantity demanded for each of the goods above if the price of the product rises by 10%.

Income and Cross-Price Elasticity

Creating Student Interest

Ask students to think of products that do not sell well in economic downturns, or recessions. (Some goods with high-income elasticity are cars, houses, and luxury goods.) Have students contrast those products with products whose sales do not suffer much during a downturn.

Common Student Misunderstandings

Students have just mastered price elasticity of demand and are now confronted with two new elasticities. Take the time to put all three up on the board and review the differences for price elasticity, income elasticity, and cross-price elasticity.

Presenting the Material

You can use these two additional numerical examples to illustrate cross-price elasticity.

1. If the quantity demanded for housing rises 5% for every 1% reduction in the price of a home loan, then the cross-price elasticity of demand will be:

   +5%/–1% = –5

   The negative sign indicates that these two goods, houses and home loans, are complementary goods.

2. If the quantity demanded for Gateway computers falls by 2% for every price reduction of 10% for Dell computers, then the cross-price elasticity of demand will be:

–2%/–10% = +0.2

The positive sign indicates that these two brand name computers are substitute goods.

Using the Case Study in the Text

Spending It (text pages 122–123)

Ask students:

1. What do studies indicate about the income elasticity for "Meals eaten at home." (It is considerably less than 1. As a family's income rises, the share of its income spent on meals at home falls.)

2. What do the studies tells us about income elasticity of "Meals eaten away from home"? (Income elasticity is closer to 1. This means that wealthier families eat away from home more often and at fancier places.)

Activities

What's a Complement? (3–5 minutes)

Pair students and ask them to think of as many examples as they can of firms using complementary goods to boost sales. (Cameras and film sold by Kodak, for example.)

Ranking Income Elasticity (5–10 minutes)

Ask students to rank the following products by their income elasticities—from high income elasticity to negative income elasticity:

> Bus Trips
>
> Gum
>
> New Home
>
> New Car
>
> Used Car
>
> Restaurant meals
>
> Powdered milk
>
> A can of Pepsi

The ranking should look something like:

> New Home (high income elasticity)
>
> New Car (high income elasticity)
>
> Restaurant meals (high income elasticity)
>
> A can of Pepsi (lower income elasticity)
>
> Gum (lower income elasticity)
>
> Used Car (lower income elasticity or possibly negative income elasticity)
>
> Bus Trips (may be negative income elasticity)
>
> Powdered milk (probably negative income elasticity)

Elasticity of Supply

Creating Student Interest

Ask students how the supply curve would look for beachfront property in exclusive Malibu, California. (The supply curve will be almost perfectly vertical—very inelastic supply.)

Common Student Misunderstandings

Students may confuse price elasticity of demand with price elasticity of supply because both involve a movement along the curve. Explain that elasticity of supply refers to how much sellers or producers will change their production in response to a change in price.

Presenting the Material

Students may find it difficult to envision the constraints or lack of constraints on a production process. Try this example. In response to a change in the price of pizza, a pizza restaurant can easily supply 20 more pizzas even in the short run; supply of pizzas is price elastic. In contrast, the quantity of beachfront property in Malibu, California, is limited, so the supply of beachfront property is inelastic.

Using the Case Study in the Text

European Farm Surpluses (text page 125)

Ask students:

1. How did the Europeans underestimate the price elasticity of supply for farm goods? (They thought that the supply of farm goods was less elastic than it actually turned out to be. Because the supply of farm goods is very elastic, the surpluses caused by price floors increased even more than expected.)

2. What were the consequences? (Huge surpluses of farm goods.)

3. Show graphically why the food surpluses were much larger than they anticipated. (The supply curve for farm goods should be very elastic—not very steep.)

Activity

What's a Baseball Card Worth? (5 minutes)

Inform students that there is only one "mint condition" Honus Wagner (he was a shortstop for the Pittsburgh Pirates in the early 1900s) baseball card in existence. What would the supply curve for this baseball card look like?

Price Elasticity and Tax Incidence

Creating Student Interest
Ask students who they think pays most of the gasoline excise tax?

Common Student Misunderstandings
Students may be unclear about the meaning of the term *tax incidence*. Explain that it refers to who bears the burden of the tax. In some situations, sellers can pass the tax onto the buyers; in others, they cannot. For example, if the equilibrium price rises from $2.00 to $2.15, after a tax increase of $.20, then the seller had to pay $.05 of the tax, and $.15 of the tax was paid by consumers.

Presenting the Material
Review the idea that the tax on the seller is an additional cost. At each quantity, sellers will supply that quantity of the product only at a price that is higher by the amount of the tax. Show the students that graphically this causes the supply curve to shift upward by a vertical distance equal to the amount of the tax.

Using the Case Study in the Text

So Who Does Pay the FICA? (text page 129)
Ask students:
1. On paper, half the payroll tax is paid by workers and half paid by employers. But who really "pays" this tax? (Most economists agree that workers pay most of this tax.)
2. Why do workers have most of the burden of this tax? (Because the elasticity of the supply of labor is very low.)
3. Why do you think the supply of labor is relatively inelastic? (As wages rise, workers can afford to cut back on hours of work.)

Activities

Who Pays the Tax? (2–3 minutes)
Pair students and ask them to think of circumstances when a seller can pass the full amount of an excise tax on to consumers. (Most students will understand that the more inelastic the demand, the more the tax can be pushed on to consumers. However supply elasticity is also relevant here: The more elastic the supply is, the more sellers can transfer the tax to consumers.) Ask students if they think their state excise tax on gasoline is completely passed on to consumers.

Those Pesky Excise Taxes (2–3 minutes)
List the following products on the board and ask: If these products had an excise tax placed on them, who would wind up paying the tax and why?
- Gasoline (inelastic demand and inelastic supply in the short run—the buyer will pay more of the tax)
- Super Bowl tickets (inelastic supply, elastic demand—the seller pays more of the tax)
- Luxury cars (elastic supply and elastic demand)

Drive We Must (3–5 minutes)

Use the opening case study "Drive we must" on textbook page 109 for this activity. Or assign it as individual homework.

The text chapter opening story describes a meeting between oil ministers from Mexico and Saudi Arabia in which they discuss how much to restrict the supply of oil to increase their total revenues. The tricky issue for them is: by how much? By how much will quantity demanded fall when they raise the price? This will depend on the price elasticity of demand. This is a good summary activity for students. Pair students and ask them to graph two possible scenarios: inelastic demand and very elastic demand. Under which circumstance will the oil ministers be able to increase their revenues with an increase in oil prices?

In the News

Four Biggest Cigarette Makers Can't Raise Prices As They Did

From: *The Wall Street Journal*, October 25, 2002.

Since 1999, cigarette companies have raised prices seven times. The profit on each pack of Philip Morris cigarettes sold in the United States has jumped 38% between 1997 and 2001, before the current round of discounting in 2002. Raising prices helped smokers quit. The number of cigarettes smoked in the United States has fallen continuously 1% to 2% for decades. But faced with $246 billion in lawsuit settlements, the cigarette makers raised prices by 49% in 1997. These sharp price increases caused the quantity demanded to fall by 7% in 1997.

Ask students the following questions:

1. Given the data, what is the elasticity of demand for cigarettes? (.07/.49 = .14, indicating inelastic demand.)
2. Will a tax on cigarettes raise a state's revenues? (Generally yes because demand is inelastic. However, smokers can cross state lines to avoid the tax, and cheaper cigarettes can be smuggled in through a black market.)
3. Why might the price elasticity of demand for cigarettes by younger smokers be different from the price elasticity of demand for cigarettes by older smokers? (Because younger smokers are not as addicted to nicotine as older smokers are.)

chapter **6**

Consumer and
Producer Surplus

Chapter Objectives
Students will learn in this chapter:
- The meaning of consumer surplus and its relationship to the demand curve.
- The meaning of producer surplus and its relationship to the supply curve.
- The meaning and importance of total surplus and how it can be used both to measure the gains from trade and to evaluate the efficiency of a market.
- Why the **deadweight loss** of a tax means that its true cost is more than the amount of tax revenue collected.
- How to use changes in total surplus to measure the deadweight loss of taxes.

Chapter Outline

Opening Example: The used textbook market is given as an example of consumer and producer surplus. This example then appears throughout this chapter.

I. Consumer Surplus and the Demand Curve

    A. *Definition:* A consumer's **willingness to pay** for a good is the maximum price at which he or she would buy that good.

    B. Willingness to pay and consumer surplus

        1. *Definition:* **Individual consumer surplus** is a net gain to an individual buyer from the purchase of a good. It is equal to the difference between what the buyer would have been willing to pay and what the buyer actually pays.

        2. *Definition:* **Total consumer surplus** is the sum of the individual consumer surpluses of all the buyers of a good.

        3. *Definition:* The term **consumer surplus** is often used to refer both to individual and to total consumer surplus.

        4. The total consumer surplus generated by purchases of a good at a given price is equal to the area under the demand curve but above the price. This is illustrated in text Figure 6-3, shown on the next page.

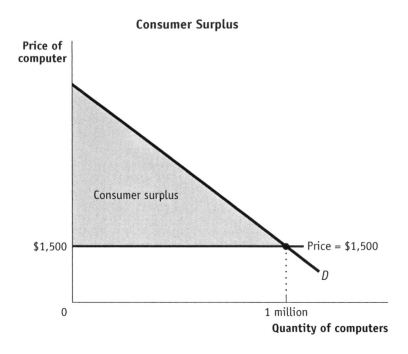

Consumer Surplus

C. How changing prices affect consumer surplus

1. When the price of a good falls, the total consumer surplus increases through two channels: a gain to consumers who would have bought at the original price, and a gain to consumers who are persuaded to buy at the lower price. When the price of a good increases, the total consumer surplus decreases in a similar fashion.

2. During World War II rationing, many consumers bought coupons on the black market and were in effect paying for the right to get their consumer surplus.

II. Producer Surplus and the Supply Curve

A. Cost and producer surplus

1. *Definition:* A potential seller's **cost** is the lowest price at which he or she is willing to sell a good.

2. *Definition:* **Individual producer surplus** is the net gain to a seller from selling a good. It is the difference between the market price and the seller's cost.

3. *Definition:* **Total producer surplus** in a market is the sum of the individual producer surpluses of all the sellers of a good. Economists use the term **producer surplus** to refer both to individual and to total producer surplus.

4. The total producer surplus from sales of a good at a given price is the area above the supply curve but below that price. This is illustrated in text Figure 6-8, shown on the next page.

B. Changes in producer surplus

1. If the price of a good rises, producers will experience an increase in producer surplus through two channels: the gains of those who would have supplied the good even at the original, lower price and the gains of those who are induced to supply the good at the higher price. A fall in the price similarly leads to a fall in the producer surplus.

Producer Surplus

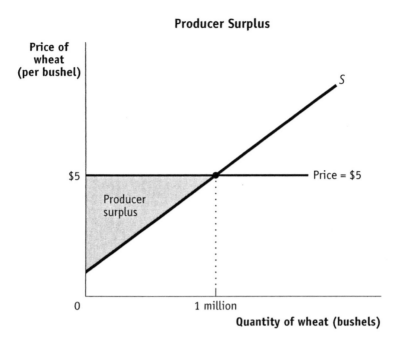

Quantity of wheat (bushels)

III. Consumer surplus, producer surplus, and the gains from trade

A. The gains from trade

1. *Definition:* The **total surplus** generated in a market is the total net gain to consumers and producers. It is the sum of the producer and the consumer surplus.

2. Both consumers and producers gain in a specific market—there are gains from trade. This is why everyone is better off participating in a market economy than they would be if each individual tried to be self-sufficient. This is illustrated in text Figure 6-10, shown below.

Total Surplus

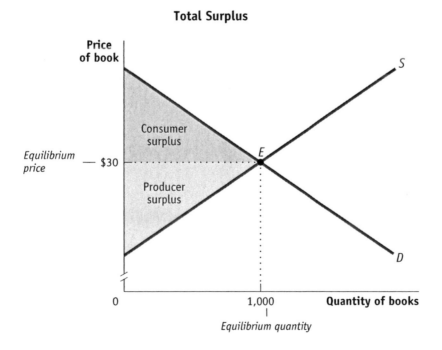

Equilibrium quantity

B. The efficiency of markets: a preliminary view
  1. Markets are usually efficient. Typically, there is no way to make anyone better off without making someone else worse off.
  2. The market equilibrium achieves the maximum possible total surplus. It does this because the market
     a. Allocates the good to potential buyers who value it the most, indicated by the willingness to pay.
     b. Allocates sales to the potential sellers who value the right to sell the good the most, as indicated by the fact that they have the lowest cost.
     c. Ensures that every consumer who makes a purchase has a value of the good greater than every seller who makes a sale, so that all transactions are mutually beneficial.
     d. Ensures that every potential buyer who doesn't make a purchase has a value of the good lower than that of every potential seller who doesn't make a sale, so that no mutually beneficial transactions are missed.

IV. Applying the Concept of Consumer and Producer Surplus: The Efficiency Cost of a Tax

  A. *Definition:* The **excess burden** or **deadweight loss** from a tax is the extra cost in the form of inefficiency that results because the tax discourages mutually beneficial transactions.
  B. Consumers and producers both lose when an excise tax is imposed. The impact of a tax on consumer and producer surpluses is modeled in text Figure 6-14, shown below.

A Tax Reduces Consumer and Producer Surplus

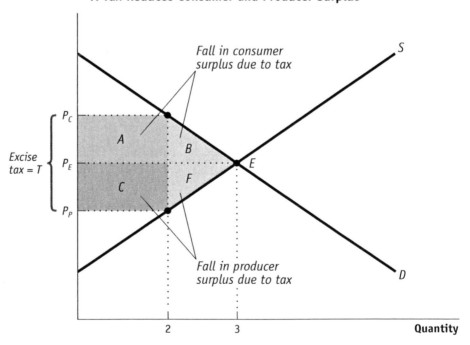

C. The deadweight loss is the monetary value of consumer and producer surplus lost from unrealized market exchanges.

    1. The general rule for economic policy is that other things being equal, you want to choose the policy that produces the smallest deadweight loss.

D. Deadweight loss and elasticities

    1. A tax imposed on a good for which either demand or supply is elastic, or both, will experience a relatively large decrease in the quantity transacted and a large deadweight loss. This is illustrated in text Figure 6-16, shown below.

Deadweight Loss and Elasticities

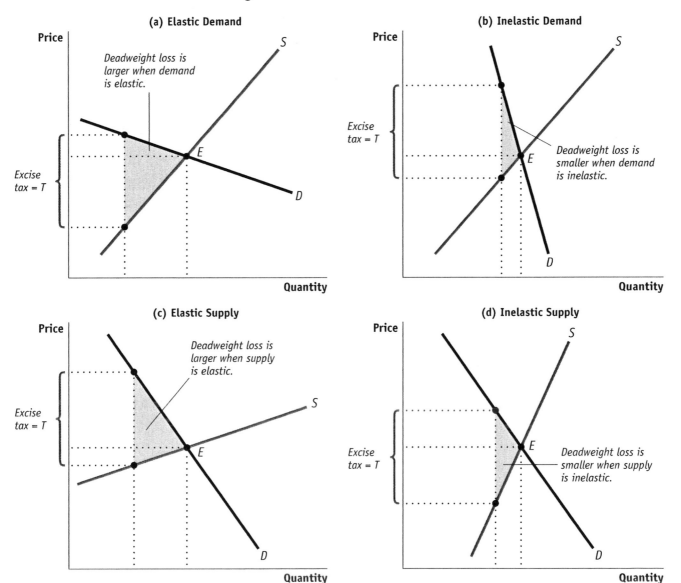

    2. To lessen efficiency costs of taxation, excise taxes should fall on goods for which demand or supply is relatively inelastic.

E. The Yacht Tax of 1990 (text page 156) is used as an example of an inefficient tax. The demand and supply in this market turned out to be relatively elastic.

Teaching Tips

Consumer Surplus

Creating Student Interest

- Talk about Adam Smith's statement in *The Wealth of Nations* that it is in people's nature to want to "truck and barter." Ask students why people like to think they "got a steal" when buying a good.

Common Student Misunderstandings

- Students may be unclear about the term *willingness to pay*. Explain that it is the maximum price they would pay to buy a good.
- Students may be confused in calculating the total consumer surplus on a graph, after looking at the derivation of individual consumer surplus. Explain that in a market as a whole, with many buyers, the total of all of these individual surpluses fills up the entire area of the consumer surplus triangle.
- Students may have forgotten the formula for calculating the area of a triangle. Remind them that it is one-half the length of the base × the length of the height ($1/2bh$).

Presenting the Material

Use a simple example of calculating consumer surplus. Explain that it is the difference between the market price of a good and the willingness of an individual to buy a good.

Willingness to pay for 1 hour of math tutoring	Actual market price for one hour of math tutoring	Consumer surplus
Jack's willingness to pay = $24	Price = $10	$14
Karla's willingness to pay = $21	Price = $10	$11
Harold's willingness to pay = $18	Price = $10	$8
Kathy's willingness to pay = $15	Price = $10	$5
Chester's willingness to pay = $10	Price = $10	$0

The total consumer surplus is the sum of the individual consumer surpluses, in this case, $38.

Show the areas under the demand curve that represent each individual's consumer surplus. This is shown in the graph on the next page.

Explain that in a larger market, with many buyers, the sum of the individual consumer surpluses is known as the total consumer surplus in the market.

Change the price of tutoring in the example above and show how it reduces the consumer surplus.

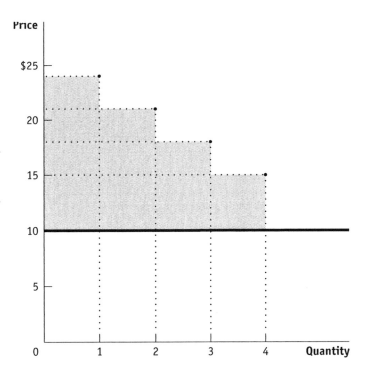

Using the Case Study in the Text

I Want a New Drug. . . (text page 141)

Ask students:

1. How should we calculate the value to society from the introduction of a new drug? (By estimating the gain to consumer welfare.)

2. Why did penicillin, the first antibiotic, add more to consumer welfare than the introduction of a new painkiller, which is a slight improvement on aspirin? (Because it cures a disease that was previously incurable, many people would be willing to pay a lot more than the market price.)

3. Why is just calculating how much was actually spent on each drug an inadequate measure of consumer welfare? (Because many consumers would be willing to pay more than the market price to get the drug.)

Activities

What's Your Bid? (3–5 minutes)

Ask for five volunteers and have them write down on a piece of paper the maximum price they would be willing to pay for a textbook. Then have the students share this with the whole class. Tell them that the used price for their text is $35 (or a representative price). Compute each individual's consumer surplus.

What's a New Drug Worth? (3–5 minutes)

Pair students and ask them how they would go about assigning a monetary value to the benefit of a new drug on the market which cures autoimmune diseases. Ask a few pairs to report their calculations. (The benefits of the drug may be much larger than what is actually spent on it, because people may be willing to pay more than the actual price of the good. To measure the gains of the drug, we have to figure out what people would be willing to pay for the drug and subtract what they actually pay.)

Producer Surplus

Creating Student Interest

Ask students what determines the lowest price a seller is willing to sell a good for. Help students see that this price will be equivalent to the seller's cost. The cost in this case represents all the opportunity costs of the seller.

Common Student Misunderstandings

Students may be unclear about the "cost"of a used textbook they plan to sell. Explain that the true cost is their opportunity cost: They are giving up the ability to use the textbook for other purposes, such as a reference for upper division microeconomics.

Presenting the Material

Use a specific example of how producer surplus is calculated. Make clear that we are now looking at tutors and their willingness to sell their services. The opportunity cost of using their time in tutoring is equal to the forgone value of that time in other activities.

Seller's minimum price to sell (= the seller's opportunity cost)	Actual market price for tutoring	Producer surplus
Dora's price = $10	$10	$0
Lee's price = $8	$10	$2
Sam's price = $6	$10	$4
Kathy's price = $4	$10	$6

The total producer surplus is the sum of the individual seller's producer surplus. Here it is equal to $12. Again, you can change the price to show the effect on the total producer surplus. Show the entire area of both the producer and consumer surplus, which is the total area of both the consumer and producer surplus, as illustrated below.

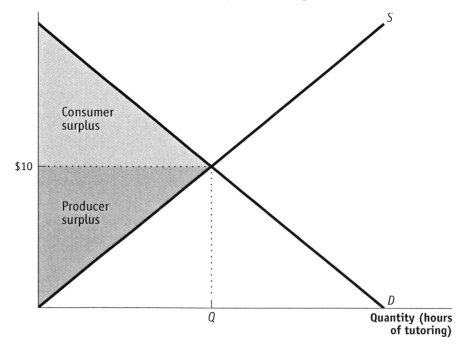

Using the Case Study in the Text

Gaining from Disaster (text page 146)

Ask students:

1. Construction workers flocked to work in Florida after Hurricane Andrew. How should we calculate their producer surplus? (By their net gain: take their money salary and subtract all costs, both direct and opportunity costs.)

2. Why is counting what these workers were paid not an accurate measure of their producer surplus? (It does not take into account the costs of going to Florida to work.)

Activities

What's Your Minimum Offer Price? (2–3 minutes)

Ask students to write down a minimum price they would accept to sell their textbook at the end of the semester. Ask them to share how they estimated its dollar value to them. Put four or five responses on the board and given the bookstore's repurchase price, form students into pairs, then have each pair calculate the producer surplus.

What's an Internship Worth? (2–3 minutes)

Give the class the following scenario: You have the opportunity of doing a summer internship abroad for 3 months for a fixed salary of $800 per month, but the costs of rent, food, and travel expenses are not included. What is your producer surplus? (Students will have to subtract their estimated rent, food, and travel expenses from their salary.)

Gains from Trade/Market Efficiency

Creating Student Interest

Ask students to summarize the gains from the used textbook market for students who are buying and selling texts. What would they lose if this market did not exist?

Common Student Misunderstandings

Review the meaning of efficiency: Once a market has produced its gains from trade, there is typically no way to make anyone better off without making someone else worse off. Emphasize that competitive market equilibrium achieves the maximum total surplus, but *this does not mean that it is the best outcome for every buyer and seller in the market.*

Students may be unclear about all the various triangles that represent the gains and losses from trade. Clearly mark the gains from trade and then show the changes from an excise tax or price ceiling/price floor on a separate graph.

Presenting the Material

Using the math tutoring example, indicate that the college has set an $8 price ceiling on tutoring. This is shown in the graph on the next page.

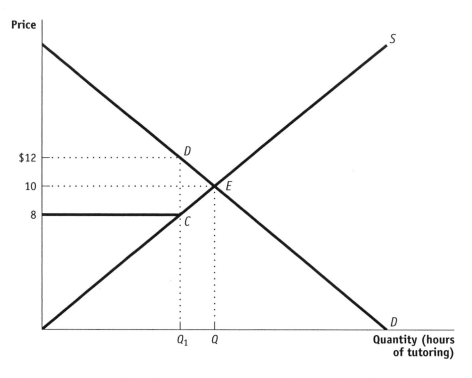

Buyers gain somewhat from the lower price but lose from the cutback in the hours of tutoring offered. Tutors definitely lose from the lower price they earn. The area *CDE* on the graph represents the deadweight loss from the price ceiling.

Use an example of an excise tax on the sale of CDs. The demand and supply schedules for CDs are:

Price of CDs	Quantity of CDs demanded (000s)	Quantity of CDs supplied (000s)
$20	0	6
$18	1	5
$16	2	4
$14	3	3
$12	4	2
$10	5	1
$8	6	0
$6	7	0
$4	8	0
$2	9	0

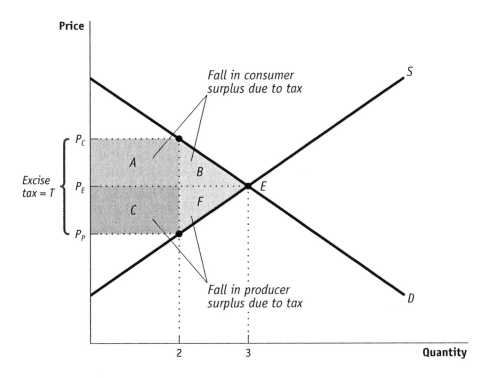

Suppose an excise tax of $4 is implemented. Before, sellers were willing to sell 1 at $10, but now with the excise tax will require $14 for that quantity. The new supply schedule, along with the original demand schedule is:

Price	Quantity supplied	Quantity demanded
$24	6	0
$22	5	0
$20	4	0
$18	3	1
$16	2	2
$14	1	3

The new equilibrium price is $16, and the equilibrium quantity is 2. Sellers were able to pass $2 of the tax on to consumers. The deadweight loss is equal to B and F on the graph.

Using the Case Study in the Text

eBay and Efficiency (text page 151)

Ask students:

1. Why is eBay far more efficient than local garage sales? (It brings a huge quantity of buyers and sellers together. Sellers can easily find a buyer, and buyers can quickly find the items they want to buy.)

2. How does eBay help to enlarge the total surplus? (eBay adds to both consumer and producer surplus.)

Work It Out

Calculating Deadweight Loss (text pages 155–156)

In this numerical exercise, students are asked to use the market equilibrium quantity and price information presented in a graph to calculate the values of consumer surplus, producer surplus, and deadweight loss.

Activity

Gains in the CD Market (5–10 minutes)

Pair students and give them the example above regarding the excise tax on CDs. Ask students:

1. What is the equilibrium price and quantity before the excise tax is imposed? ($14 and 3)

2. What areas on the graph represent the consumer and producer surplus before the tax? (Area *A* + *B* is the area for consumer surplus, and area *C* + *F* represents producer surplus.)

3. An excise tax is imposed on each CD of $4 per CD.

4. What is the new supply schedule? (See above.)

5. What is the equilibrium quantity of CDs bought and sold after the tax? (The equilibrium quantity is 2.)

6. What is the price paid by consumers? What is the price received by the sellers? (Buyers now pay $16, and sellers net $16 – $4 = $12.)

7. How much of the excise tax is paid by consumers and producers? ($2 is paid by consumers and $2 is paid by producers.)

8. Show on the graph the deadweight loss from the tax. (area *B* and *F*)

chapter 7

Behind the Supply Curve: Inputs and Costs

Chapter Objectives

Students will learn in this chapter:
- The importance of the firm's production function, the relationship between quantity of inputs and quantity of output.
- Why production is often subject to diminishing returns to inputs.
- The various forms of a firm's costs and how they generate the firm's marginal and average cost curves.
- Why a firm's short-run costs may differ from its long-run costs.
- How the firm's technology of production can generate economies of scale.

Chapter Outline

Opening Example: The example describes why European farmers are more productive than U.S. farmers in producing wheat: European government policies provide incentives for using more inputs, and with more inputs comes increased productivity.

I. The Production Function

A. *Definition:* A **production function** is the relationship between the quantity of inputs a firm uses and the quantity of output it produces.

B. Inputs and outputs

1. *Definition:* A **fixed input** is an input whose quantity is fixed and cannot be varied.

2. *Definition:* A **variable input** is an input whose quantity the firm can vary.

3. *Definition:* The **long run** is the time period in which all inputs can be varied.

4. *Definition:* The **short run** is the time period in which at least one input is fixed.

5. *Definition:* The **total product curve** shows how the quantity of output depends on the quantity of the variable input, for a given amount of the fixed input.

6. The slope of the total product curve is not constant. The slope of the total product curve is equal to the marginal product of the variable input.

    a. *Definition:* The **marginal product** of an input is the additional quantity of output that is produced by using one more unit of that input.

    b. Marginal product of labor $= \dfrac{\text{Change in quantity of output}}{\text{Change in quantity of labor}} =$

                    $=$ Change in quantity of output generated by one additional unit of labor,

  or $MPL = \Delta Q/\Delta L$

  7. *Definition:* There are **diminishing returns to an input** when an increase in the quantity of that input, holding the levels of all other inputs fixed, leads to a decline in the marginal product of that input.

    a. Diminishing returns only holds if the quantity of all other inputs is fixed.

    b. Frederick P. Brooks Jr.'s book, *The Mythical Man-Month,* is discussed to illustrate the concept of diminishing returns.

C. From the production function to cost curves

  1. *Definition:* An **explicit cost** is a cost that involves actually laying out money.

  2. *Definition:* An **implicit cost** does not require an outlay of money; it is measured by the value, in dollar terms, of the benefits that are forgone.

  3. *Definition:* A **fixed cost** is a cost that does not depend on the quantity of output produced. It is the cost of the fixed input.

  4. *Definition:* A **variable cost** is a cost that depends on the quantity of output produced. It is the cost of the variable input.

  5. *Definition:* The **total cost** of producing a given quantity of output is the sum of the fixed cost and the variable cost of producing that quantity of output.

  6. Total Cost = Fixed Cost + Variable Cost, or $TC = FC + VC$

  7. *Definition:* The **total cost curve** shows how total cost depends on the quantity of output.

    a. The total cost curve becomes steeper as more output is produced due to diminishing returns. This is illustrated in text Figure 7-4, shown below.

Total Cost Curve

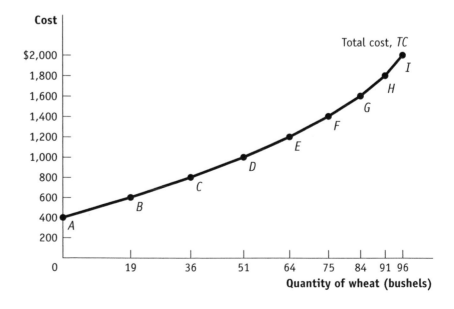

II. Two Key Concepts: Marginal Cost and Average Cost

A. Marginal cost

1. *Definition:* The **marginal cost** of an activity is the additional cost incurred by doing one more unit of that activity.

2. $$\text{Marginal cost} = \frac{\text{Change in total cost}}{\text{Change in quantity of output}}$$

   $$= \text{Change in total cost generated by one additional unit of labor}$$

   or $MC = \Delta TC / \Delta Q$

3. *Definition:* There is **increasing marginal cost** from an activity when each additional unit of the activity costs more than the previous unit.

4. *Definition:* The **marginal cost curve** shows how the cost of undertaking one more unit of an activity depends on the quantity of that activity that has already been done.

5. Marginal cost rises because there are diminishing returns to inputs when a variable input is increased as quantities of the other inputs are fixed.

B. Average cost

1. *Definition:* **Average total cost,** often referred to simply as **average cost,** is total cost divided by quantity of output produced.

   $$ATC = \frac{\text{Total cost}}{\text{Quantity of output}} = \frac{TC}{Q}$$

2. Average total cost is important because it tells the producer how much the average or typical unit of output costs to produce. Marginal cost tells the producer how much the *last* unit of output costs to produce.

3. *Definition:* A **U-shaped average total cost curve** falls at low levels of output, then rises at higher levels.

4. *Definition:* **Average fixed cost** is the fixed cost per unit of output.

   $$AFC = \frac{\text{Fixed cost}}{\text{Quantity of output}} = \frac{FC}{Q}$$

5. *Definition:* **Average variable cost** is the variable cost per unit of output.

   $$AVC = \frac{\text{Variable cost}}{\text{Quantity of output}} = \frac{VC}{Q}$$

6. Average fixed cost falls as more output is produced. Another way to think of this is that as more output is produced, the fixed cost is spread over more units of output. This is illustrated in text Figure 7-8, shown below.

Marginal Cost and Average Cost Curves

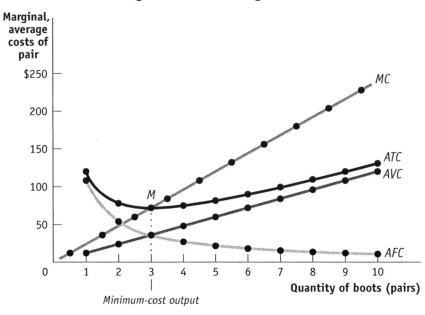

7. Average total cost is the sum of average fixed cost and average variable cost. It has a U-shape because these components move in opposite directions as output rises.
   a. When the U-shaped average total cost curve slopes downward, the "spreading effect" dominates: Fixed cost is spread over more units of output.
   b. When the U-shaped average total cost curve slopes upward, the "diminishing returns effect" dominates: An additional unit of output requires more variable inputs.

C. Minimum average total cost
   1. *Definition:* The **minimum-cost output** is the quantity of output at which average total cost is lowest—the bottom of the U-shaped average total cost curve.

2. Falling marginal cost pulls the average total cost downward, and rising marginal cost pulls the average total cost upward. This is illustrated in text Figure 7-9, shown below.

The Relationship Between the Average Total Cost and the Marginal Cost Curves

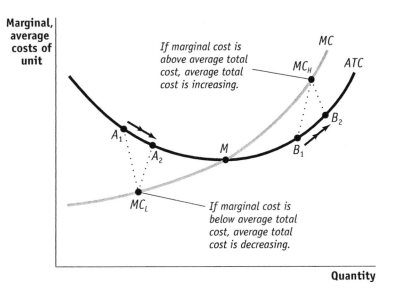

3. Therefore, the minimum point on the average total cost curve intersecting with the marginal cost curve reflects general principles that are always true.
   a. At minimum-cost output, average total cost is equal to marginal cost.
   b. At output less than the minimum-cost output, marginal cost is less than average total cost and average total cost is falling.
   c. At output greater than the minimum-cost output, marginal cost is greater than average total cost and average total cost is rising.

D. Does the marginal cost curve always slope upward?
   1. Marginal cost curves often slope down as a firm increases its production from zero up to some low level; they slope upward only at higher levels of production.

E. Hydroelectric power in the Western United States is used to illustrate the consequences of confusion between marginal cost and average total cost.

III. Short-Run Versus Long-Run Costs

A. *Definition:* The **long-run average total cost curve** shows the relationship between output and average total cost when fixed cost has been chosen to minimize total cost for each level of output. This is illustrated in text Figure 7-12, shown below.

Short-Run and Long-Run Average Total Cost Curves

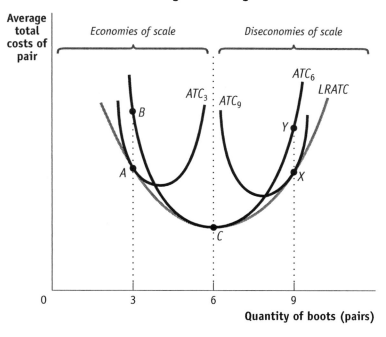

1. In the long run, when a producer has had time to choose the fixed cost appropriate for its desired level of output, that producer will be on some point on the long-run average total cost curve.

2. If the output level is altered, the firm will no longer be on its long-run average total cost curve and will instead be moving along its current short-run average total cost curve.

3. Once the firm has adjusted its fixed cost, it will operate on a new short-run average total cost curve and on the long-run average total cost curve.

B. Economies and diseconomies of scale

1. *Definition:* There are **economies of scale** when long-run average total cost declines as output increases.

2. *Definition:* There are **diseconomies of scale** when long-run average total cost increases as output increases.

3. *Definition:* There are **constant returns to scale** when long-run average total cost is constant as output increases.

4. Scale effects depend on the technology of production.

Teaching Tips

The Production Function

Creating Student Interest

A good starting point is to talk about the costs of owning a car. Assume that the car is a fixed input while it is in the garage and a variable input when you drive it. Ask students to think about the fixed cost of owning a car (as it sits in the garage) and the variable costs of owning a car (as you drive the car). The fixed costs are depreciation and registration fees, and the variable expenses are gasoline and maintenance.

Ask students to brainstorm the fixed and variable inputs used at a fast-food restaurant or at the student bookstore. List them on the board.

Common Student Misunderstandings

Students often confuse diminishing marginal product with a fall in total production. Explain that diminishing marginal product occurs when total output rises at a slower rate, versus a fall in total production.

Students may not fully understand why the text discusses production and cost separately. The chapter examines the inputs that are necessary to *physically* produce the product first, and then the cost of these inputs.

Presenting the Material

Use this example of a fast-food restaurant to illustrate the concept of a production function. Use the size of the store as the fixed input and the number of workers as the variable input.

Quantity of labor (workers)	Total production of hamburgers per hour	Marginal product of labor
0	0	
1	55	55
2	120	65
3	190	70
4	230	40
5	240	10
6	245	5

This example of a production function shows the total output of hamburgers given the addition of workers. Diminishing marginal product occurs after the third worker. The total production function rises at an increasing rate through the third worker and rises at a slower rate after the third worker. Explain that this happens due to crowding. Plot the total product curve and the marginal product curves on two separate graphs.

Using the Case Study in the Text

The Mythical Man-Month (text pages 167–168)
Ask students:

1. How does the law of diminishing marginal product apply to the writing of software? (It was found that doubling the number of programmers did not proportionately reduce the time necessary to complete a project.)

2. How did the title of the book *The Mythical Man-Month* originate? (It was found that a project that was possible for one programmer to produce in 12 months could not be accomplished by 12 programmers in one month.)

3. How does the nature of programming lead to diminishing returns? (Programmers must coordinate their work with all the other programmers: A greater quantity of programmers leads to an increase in the time spent communicating with everyone instead of writing code.)

Activities

Producing Successful College Students (3–5 minutes)
Pair students or form into teams of four. Ask them to list all the inputs on a college campus which are used to "produce" successful college students. In the "short run," which inputs are "fixed"? which inputs are "variable"? (Plant size, such as the number of classrooms, is the fixed input. As the number of registered students increases, the number of instructors needed—a variable input—increases.)

Production at a Fast-Food Restaurant (3–5 minutes)
Ask students to list the fixed and variable inputs at a typical fast-food restaurant. How has the company attempted to produce efficiently during busy times of the day? What technological changes has the company added to achieve a more efficient production? For a follow-up assignment ask students to interview a manager of a fast-food restaurant and ask what production problems occur. Ask the manager what amount of hamburger production is efficient and what quantity would be highly inefficient to produce.

Grow Rice on a Chalkboard" (10–20 minutes)
(Adapted from *Classroom Activities* by Charles Stull, Dryden Press, 2001.)

"Grow Rice on a Chalkboard" is a short simulation that illustrates the principle of diminishing marginal product. On the board, draw two rectangles, 2 × 3 feet each. Select two volunteers to act as farm managers and draw two equal-sized rectangular areas on the chalkboard, approximately 2 × 3 feet. These rectangles are the farm on which they will "grow" rice by writing the word RICE. Before they start producing, they must run to the back of the class to get a slip of paper from you that says LOAN on it. They then run to the board and start writing RICE in the same size, in a 30-second period. In the next round, the managers can hire one worker from the class. The game is played repeatedly, adding another student each period. Track total output and the quantity of labor on the board as the game proceeds. It becomes increasingly too crowded to produce the rice efficiently. A typical result might be as follows:

Labor	Total Output
0	0
1	3
2	15
3	25
4	32
5	33

Have the class calculate the marginal product and determine when diminishing marginal product began.

The Cost of Having a Child (5–10 minutes)

In her book *The Price of Motherhood*, Ann Crittenden claims the total cost for a college-educated couple to have a child is $1 million over the child's lifetime. She discusses the following items as the costs of an educated woman having a child. Pair students and ask them to classify these as explicit or implicit costs of having a child.

1. Unearned social security credits (implicit cost)
2. Forgone promotions (implicit cost)
3. Salary while not working (implicit cost)
4. Expenses for baby's room (explicit cost)
5. Loss of experience at work (implicit cost)
6. Depreciation of work skills (implicit cost)
7. Food and clothing for the child (explicit cost)
8. Loss of pension benefits (implicit cost)
9. Awards given for excellence in your paid job (implicit cost)
10. Babysitting fees (explicit cost)
11. Preschool expenses (explicit cost)
12. Earnings from paid work contributed by an employer to a retirement account (implicit cost)
13. Doctor visits/medical expenses (explicit cost)
14. Costs of decorating child's room (explicit cost)
15. Lost training opportunities at work (implicit cost)

Marginal Cost and Average Cost

Creating Student Interest

Ask students to estimate McDonald's cost per Big Mac. (The average total cost is about 16 cents.) Why is it important for a firm to know the cost per hamburger?

Online grocery delivery services charge a flat fee to deliver groceries. Ask students: Why do customers have an incentive to order a lot of groceries? (They want to "spread" the fixed costs over many items, so that average fixed cost falls.)

Common Student Misunderstandings

Students are often unclear about the difference between average total cost and marginal cost. Give the example of an airline company's decision to fly the next flight. What are the additional costs of flying the plane? (Salaries of pilots and crew, cost of jet fuel, food, landing fee.) What costs don't change even if they fly the plane? (administrative salaries,

Web site maintenance, marketing costs.) Explain that average total cost, or cost per passenger per mile, is calculated by dividing the total costs of the airline (administrative salaries, cost of jets, crew salaries, Web site maintenance, marketing costs, jet fuel, insurance costs, etc.) by the number of passenger-miles flown.

In plotting average and marginal cost curves, remind students that marginal quantities are plotted between the two quantities.

Presenting the Material

Try the following sequence to explain marginal cost and average cost.

- Use a simple example of total costs first. Here are some concrete examples of both fixed and variable costs of production for a toy manufacturing firm. The fixed cost of this company is $30. The variable input is labor; as more toys are produced, variable costs rise as more labor is hired. Point out that total cost always rises as more toys are produced.

Quantity of toys produced	Variable costs of production	Fixed costs of production (per hour)	Total costs of production
0	0	$30	$30
1	$10	30	40
2	25	30	55
3	45	30	75
4	70	30	100
5	100	30	130
6	135	30	165

- Now introduce average costs. To calculate these we just divide total costs by quantity produced.

Quantity of toys produced (in thousands)	Variable costs of production	Fixed costs of production (per hour)	Total costs of production	Average variable cost (VC/Q)	Average fixed cost (FC/Q)	Average total cost (TC/Q)
0	0	$30	$30	—	—	—
1	$10	30	40	10	30	40
2	25	30	55	12.5	15	27.5
3	45	30	75	15	10	25
4	70	30	100	17.5	7.50	25
5	100	30	130	20	6	26
6	135	30	165	22.5	5	27.5

1. At what rate of production is average total cost at a minimum? (Between 3000 and 4000 toys. You will need to point out that the *ATC* is not flat between 3,000 and 4,000 but without further information—a marginal cost curve—we don't know the precise minimum of *ATC*.)

2. Why is it important for a company to know what its average total cost per item is? (Because firms calculate their profit per unit from that amount and often price their products in relation to average total cost.

3. Why does average fixed cost always fall? (Because you are dividing a fixed dollar amount by an increasing quantity. You are "spreading" the fixed costs over more toys produced.)

- Once you have explained average cost, introduce and define marginal cost. Take the time to give specific examples of marginal cost for a specific firm (such as the toy manufacturing firm).

Quantity of toys produced	Total costs of production	Marginal cost of production $\Delta TC/\Delta Q$
0	$30	
1	40	$10
2	55	15
3	75	20
4	100	25
5	130	30
6	165	35

Using the Case Study in the Text

The Cost of Power (text page 176)

Ask students:

1. What type of power generation was abundant in the West? (Hydroelectric power.)
2. Why, despite the ample supplies of water in the West, did power companies ask for an increase in price? (They had confused the difference between the average cost of power and the marginal cost of generating more power. Because of the inability to build new dams, the marginal cost of adding to productive capacity was quite high.)
3. As new customers came into the area, what type of power had to be utilized? (Power from fossil fuels and nuclear power.)

Activities

Average Total Cost (15 minutes)

Pair students and have them brainstorm average total cost for three specific products they buy. (For example, a Big Mac's *ATC* is 16 cents, a CD is reported to be $1.00.) Why is it important for a firm to know what its average total cost is? Have a few pairs report.

Coca-Cola and the Price of Sugar (15 minutes)

Pair students and give them the following case study: In 1985, the Coca-Cola Company was faced with soaring prices for cane sugar. A 1-cent increase in the price of cane sugar raised its total cost by $20 million. Rather than raise price, the company looked for a cheaper input and replaced cane sugar with corn sugar. Because corn was more plentiful in the United States, it was cheaper to produce.

Ask students the following questions:

1. Why couldn't the Coca-Cola Company simply raise price? (Demand was too price elastic.)
2. Is sugar a fixed or variable input? (It is a variable input.)
3. Did the switch in the input lower *TC*? (Yes) *VC*? (Yes) *FC*? (No) *ATC*? (Yes) *AFC*? (No) *AVC*? (Yes)

Short-Run versus Long-Run Costs

Creating Student Interest

Ask students what advantages Wal-Mart has over its competitors. What are the advantages in producing on a large scale? (Wal-Mart is known as a firm that owes its success to economies of scale—it buys in bulk.)

Common Student Misunderstandings

Students often confuse diminishing marginal product with diseconomies of scale. Explain that diminishing marginal product occurs when only one input is varied and all other inputs are fixed; diseconomies of scale occur when a firm is in a planning horizon in which *all* inputs can be varied. You might give the example of General Motors building an auto plant that was the size of four football fields. One side of the plant could not communicate properly with the other side. The firm closed the large plant because of diseconomies of scale.

Students are not clear about the meaning of long-run in terms of the production period. Explain that it does not refer to a specific time period (i.e., 3 years), but occurs when managers can vary the size and scale of all inputs used by the firm. Give examples of different local firms or industries and speculate with your students as to how long each firm's long run might be. A hair salon may have a long run that is just 30 days long, if they have a month-to-month lease. A car manufacturer has a long run that is years long.

Presenting the Material

- Try this specific example of an auto company. Auto Nation is a small car maker, and it can vary the size of the plant it is considering building. The table below shows Auto Nation's long-run average total cost.

Quantity of Cars	*LRATC* (per car)
1	$ 40,000
2	30,000
3	20,000
4	15,000
5	13,000
6	13,000
7	15,000
8	20,000

1. For which levels of output does Auto Nation experience economies of scale? (from 1–5 cars)

2. For which levels of output does Auto Nation experience diseconomies of scale? (from 6–8 cars)

- This example, which gives specific average total cost amounts for three firms, helps to differentiate between economies of scale and constant returns to scale.

Quantity	Firm A TC	Firm A ATC	Firm B TC	Firm B ATC	Firm C TC	Firm C ATC
1	$60	$60	$11	$11	$21	$21
2	70	35	24	12	34	17
3	80	26.7	39	13	49	16.3
4	90	22.5	56	14	66	16.5
5	100	20	75	15	85	17
6	110	18.7	96	16	106	17.7
7	120	17.1	119	17	129	18.4

1. Which firm has economies of scale as output increases? (Firm A)

2. Which firm has diseconomies of scale as output increases? (Firm B)

3. Which firm has economies of scale first, and then diseconomies of scale, as output increases? (Firm C)

Using the Case Study in the Text

There's No Business like Snow Business (text page 181)
Ask students:

1. Why does snowfall in Washington D.C. create chaos, while the same snowfall is no big deal in Chicago? (Washington D.C. has fewer snowplows because snowstorms are much more infrequent there than in Chicago.)

2. What is the output in this case? (Snow removal)

3. Why did Washington D.C. choose a lower level of fixed cost? (Because it snows less in Washington D.C., it has invested in fewer snowplows. This makes sense most of the time but creates problems when the snow is heavy.)

Activity

Cost per Page (15–20 minutes)
Organize students into teams of six, and then have them divide up into three subgroups, with each subgroup assuming a different technology to produce printed pages. Ask each subgroup to calculate the average total cost for producing printed pages, using its technology.

Subgroup 1: You have purchased a Level One scanner for $100. It costs you $3 a page in paper.

Number of pages	FC (machine)	VC (supplies)	TC ($)	ATC ($ per page)
30				
50				
100				
500				
1000				
2000				

Subgroup 2: You have purchased a Level Two scanner for $200. It costs you $1.50 per page in paper.

Number of pages	FC (machine)	VC (supplies)	TC ($)	ATC ($ per page)
30				
50				
100				
500				
1000				
2000				

Subgroup 3: You have purchased a Level Three scanner for $1000. It costs you $.75 cents per page in paper.

Number of pages	FC (machine)	VC (supplies)	TC ($)	ATC ($ per page)
30				
50				
100				
500				
1000				
2000				

As a Team: After each subgroup has completed their calculations, students get together as a team to complete the following table.

Number of pages	Which scanner is least expensive?	Average total cost?
30		
50		
100		
500		
1000		
2000		

In this case, were there economies of scale, diseconomies of scale, or constant returns to scale as you progressed from one technology to a more sophisticated technology?

chapter **8**

Perfect Competition and the Supply Curve

Chapter Objectives

Students will learn in this chapter:
- The meaning of perfect competition, and the characteristics of a perfectly competitive industry.
- The difference between accounting profit and economic profit, and why economic profit is the correct basis for decisions.
- How a price-taking producer determines its profit-maximizing quantity of output.
- How to assess whether or not a producer is profitable and why an unprofitable producer may continue to operate in the short run.
- Why industries behave differently in the short run and the long run.
- What determines the industry supply curve in both the short run and the long run.

Chapter Outline

Opening Example: High prices for organic foods eventually will lead to an increase in the quantity of organic foods supplied.

I. Perfect Competition

A. *Definition:* A **price-taking producer** is a producer whose actions have no effect on the market price of the good it sells.

B. *Definition:* A **price-taking consumer** is a consumer whose actions have no effect on the market price of the good he or she buys.

C. Defining perfect competition
1. *Definition:* A **perfectly competitive market** is a market in which all market participants are price-takers.
2. The model of a perfectly competitive market is representative of some but not all markets.
3. *Definition:* A **perfectly competitive industry** is an industry in which producers are price-takers.

D. Two necessary conditions for perfect competition
1. For an industry to be perfectly competitive, it must contain many producers, none of whom has a large market share.
   a. *Definition:* A producer's **market share** is the fraction of the total industry output represented by that producer's output.

2. An industry can be perfectly competitive only if consumers regard the products of all producers as equivalent.
   a. *Definition:* A good is a **standardized product,** also known as a **commodity,** when consumers regard the products of different producers as the same good.

E. Free entry and exit
   1. Most perfectly competitive industries are also characterized by free entry and exit.
   2. *Definition:* There is **free entry and exit** into and from an industry when new producers can easily enter into or leave that industry.

F. An example of the expiration of drug patents is used to illustrate an industry becoming perfectly competitive.

II. Production and Profits

A. *Definition:* **Profit** is the difference between revenue and cost.

B. Profit is measured mathematically as Profit = $TR - TC$.

C. *Definition:* The **principal of marginal analysis** says that the optimal quantity of an activity is the quantity at which marginal benefit is equal to marginal cost.

D. Using marginal analysis to choose the profit-maximizing quantity of output
   1. *Definition:* **Marginal revenue** is the change in total revenue generated by an additional unit of output.

   $$\text{Marginal revenue} = \frac{\text{Change in total revenue}}{\text{Change in output}}$$

   $$= \text{Change in total revenue generated by one additional unit of output}$$

   or $MR = \Delta TR / \Delta Q$

   2. *Definition:* The **optimal output rule** says that profit is maximized by producing the quantity of output at which the marginal revenue of the last unit produced is equal to its marginal cost.
      a. $MR = MC$ at the optimal quantity of output.
   3. *Definition:* The **price-taking firm's optimal output rule** says that a price-taking firm's profit is maximized by producing the quantity of output at which the marginal cost of the last unit produced is equal to the market price.
      a. For a perfectly competitive industry, $P = MC$ at the price-taking firm's optimal quantity of output. This is illustrated in text Figure 8-1, shown on the next page.
   4. *Definition:* The **marginal revenue curve** shows how marginal revenue varies as output varies.
   5. Whenever a firm is a price-taker, its marginal revenue curve (MR) is a horizontal line at the market price.

E. Accounting versus Economic Profit

   1. *Definition*: The **accounting profit of a business** is the business's revenue minus the explicit cost and depreciation.

   2. *Definition:* The **economic profit** of a business is the business's revenue minus the opportunity cost of its resources. It is usually less than the accounting profit.

   3. *Definition*: The **capital** of a business is the value of its assets—equipment, buildings, tools, inventory, and financial assets.

   4. *Definition:* The **implicit cost of capital** is the opportunity cost of the capital used by a business—the income the owner could have realized from that capital if it had been used in its next best alternative way.

F. When is production profitable?

   1. If $TR > TC$, the firm is profitable. If $TR = TC$, the firm breaks even. If $TR < TC$, the firm incurs a loss.

The Price-Taking Firm's Profit-Maximizing Quantity of Output

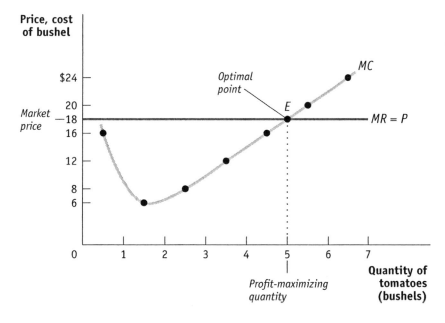

   2. For profit per unit of output, Profit/Q = TR/Q – TC/Q
     a. TR/Q is average revenue, or the market price.
     b. TC/Q is average total cost.

   3. If $P > ATC$, the firm is profitable. If $P = ATC$, the firm breaks even. If $P < ATC$, the firm incurs a loss.

   4. Total profit can be expressed in terms of profit per unit.
     a. Profit = TR – TC = $(TR/Q$ – $TC/Q) \times Q$.
     b. Equivalently, Profit = $(P$ – $ATC) \times Q$.

   5. *Definition:* The **break-even price** of a price-taking firm is the market price at which it earns zero profits. This is illustrated in text Figure 8-2, shown on page 94.

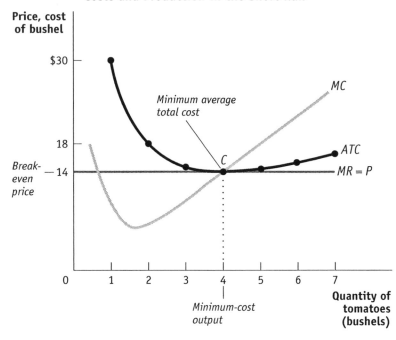

Costs and Production in the Short Run

6. The rule for determining whether a producer of a good is profitable depends on a comparison of the market price of the good to the producer's break-even price—its minimum average total cost.
    a. Whenever market price exceeds minimum average total cost, the producer is profitable.
    b. Whenever the market price equals minimum average total cost, the producer breaks even.
    c. Whenever market price is less than minimum average total cost, the producer is unprofitable.

G. The short-run production decision
    1. Fixed cost is irrelevant to the firm's optimal short-run production.
    2. *Definition:* A firm will cease production in the short run if the market price falls below the **shut-down price,** which is equal to minimum average variable cost.
    3. When market price exceeds a firm's minimum average variable cost, the price-taking firm produces the quantity of output at which marginal cost equals price.
    4. *Definition:* A **sunk cost** is a cost that has already been incurred and is nonrecoverable. A sunk cost should be ignored in decisions about future actions.
    5. *Definition:* The **short-run individual supply curve** shows how an individual producer's optimal output quantity depends on the market price, taking fixed cost as given.
        a. The short-run individual supply curve corresponds to the marginal cost curve at market prices above the shut-down price.

H. Changing fixed cost

   1. Fixed cost matters in the long run.

   2. In most perfectly competitive industries, the number of producers, although fixed in the short run, changes in the long run as firms enter or leave an industry.

   3. In the long run, a firm will exit the industry if price is less than minimum average total cost. If price exceeds minimum average total cost, a firm will remain in the industry; in addition, other firms will enter.

I. The California electricity crisis is used to illustrate economists applying marginal analysis.

III. The Industry Supply Curve

A. *Definition:* The **industry supply curve** shows the relationship between the price of a good and the total output of the industry as a whole.

B. The short-run industry supply curve

   1. *Definition:* The **short-run industry supply curve** shows how the quantity supplied by an industry depends on the market price, given a fixed number of producers.

   2. *Definition:* There is a **short-run market equilibrium** when the quantity supplied equals the quantity demanded, taking the number of producers as given.

C. The long-run industry supply curve

   1. *Definition:* A market is in **long-run market equilibrium** when the quantity supplied equals the quantity demanded, given that sufficient time has elapsed for entry into and exit from the industry to occur.

     a. In the long-run market equilibrium, no producer has an incentive to enter or exit.

   2. *Definition:* The **long-run industry supply curve** shows how the quantity supplied responds to the price once producers have had time to enter or exit the industry.

     a. The long-run industry supply curve is often horizontal, although it may be upward sloping when a necessary input is in limited supply.

     b. The long-run industry supply curve is always more elastic than the short-run industry supply curve because of the entry and exit of producers.

   3. In practice, we see that an increase in demand initially leads to a large price increase. However, if the long-run industry supply curve is horizontal, prices return to their initial level once new firms have entered the industry.

   4. In reverse, a fall in demand reduces prices in the short run. If the long-run industry supply curve is horizontal, prices return to their initial level as producers exit the industry.

D. The cost of production and efficiency in long-run equilibrium

   1. In a perfectly competitive industry in equilibrium, the value of marginal cost is the same for all firms.

   2. In a perfectly competitive industry with free entry and exit, each firm will have zero economic profits in long-run equilibrium.

   3. The long-run market equilibrium of a perfectly competitive industry is efficient.

E. The California wine industry is used to illustrate the effects of the industry supply curve.

Teaching Tips

Perfect Competition

Creating Student Interest

Ask students if they have ever tried to sell a product and had to take the existing market price.

Ask students what markets have identical products among sellers.

In what industries have students noticed considerable entry of new firms?

Common Student Misunderstandings

Students may be unclear about the meaning of "price taker." Give a specific example of a wheat farmer who has to turn on the radio or financial programs to find out the market price of wheat. Wheat also is useful for illustrating a standardized product.

Students may be unclear as to the difference between a firm and an industry. Make it clear that an industry is a collection of individual firms.

Presenting the Material

Introduce the characteristics of perfect competition and give a few examples of industries that fit this structure.

Market Structure:
  Perfect Competition
    1. Many sellers, each with a small market share
    2. Consumers see all the products in the market as identical
    3. Easy entry and exit of firms
  Examples:
    Agricultural markets such as dairy farming, organic tomato farming

To illustrate market shares, use the U.S. fast-food market. Ask students why this industry is *not* perfectly competitive. (Buyers do not see the products as identical.)

Firms in the U.S. fast-food industry	Market share
McDonalds	20%
Burger King	9%
Wendy's	5%
Kentucky Fried Chicken	5%
Hardees	4%
Pizza Hut	4%

Using the Case Study in the Text

The Pain of Competition: Generic Drugs (text page 189)

Ask students:

1. Why are the prices of generic drugs so much cheaper after they come off a patent? (The entry of new producers shifts the supply curve to the right, causing the market price to fall.)

2. Pharmaceutical firms often attempt to extend a patent period for a specific good. Why? (To maintain positive profits.)

Activity

A Perfectly Competitive Industry? (10–15 minutes)

After covering the basic characteristics of perfect competition, list the following industries on the board and discuss with your students whether they would meet the two necessary conditions for an industry to be classified as perfectly competitive: (1) there are many sellers, with each having a small market share, and (2) consumers regard the products of all sellers in the industry as the same.

- Fast-food industry (There are many sellers, but consumers view each seller's product as unique.)
- Cellular telephone service (There are a few sellers in this market.)
- The U.S. stock market (There are thousands of sellers of a particular company's common stock, and each share of a company's common stock is the same, so the market is perfectly competitive.)
- Wholesale flowers (The market is perfectly competitive because there are many sellers, and buyers view the products as identical.)
- eBay (eBay is one firm among other online auction sites and is therefore not an industry. It allows sellers to auction off a variety of products for a fee. Within most product categories, the items have distinguishing features.)

Production and Profits

Creating Student Interest

A restaurant does most of its business at the dinner meal. Ask students under what conditions should it also stay open for lunch. Point out that the restaurant is making a "how much" decision.

How does an organic tomato farmer decide how many tomatoes to grow? (This may stimulate a discussion of factors such as demand and price. Students may ignore the farmer's cost conditions.)

Common Student Misunderstandings

Students may be unclear about the three separate issues in this section. The first is how firm profitability is determined. The second issue is whether a firm should stay in business or shut down in the short run, even if facing a loss. The last issue is whether a firm should enter or exit a specific industry in the long run, when a firm can choose a level of fixed costs.

Students may be confused by the way in which marginal quantities are graphed in the book. The *MC* of producing the third unit, for instance, is plotted halfway between quantities of 2 and 3. As a result, the *MC* that is plotted directly above $q = 3$ will be the average of the *MC* of the third and fourth units. Review text Figure 8-3 with students, being careful in choosing your numerical examples.

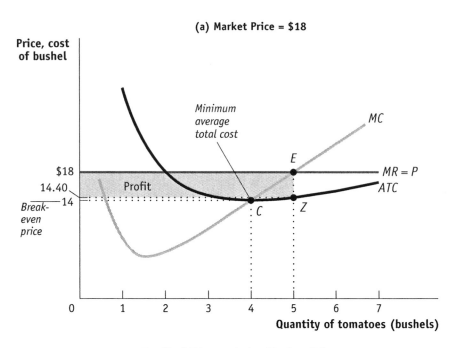

(a) Market Price = $18

Profitability and the Market Price

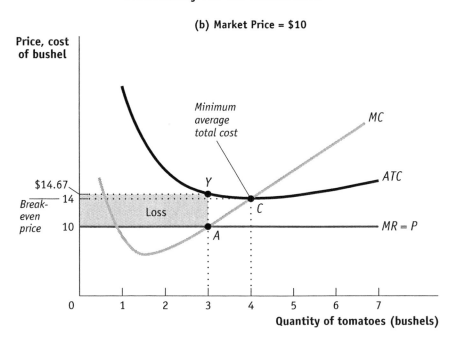

(b) Market Price = $10

Students often memorize the $MR = MC$ optimal output rule but do not really understand its underlying logic. Review the idea that the optimal amount of any activity is when the marginal benefits are equal to the marginal costs.

Students may wonder why a firm will stay in business at all if price falls below minimum average cost. Explain that in this case, price greater than AVC produces revenue that covers all variable costs and some fixed costs, so in the short run the firm will have a smaller loss if it produces than if it shuts down. In the long run, the firm will exit the industry.

Students are often unclear in determining the profitability of a firm from a MR, MC graph. Explain that the graph shows price and marginal cost and profit per unit. Total profit is shown on the graph as the area of the rectangle where the width is the optimal quantity and the height is the profit per unit.

Presenting the Material

You can use the following data from a flower business to illustrate the concepts of production and profit. Ask students how profit is calculated. In this example, the quantity that will maximize profit is four bunches of flowers.

Quantity of flowers (in bunches)	Price	Total revenue	Total cost	Profit	
0	$10	0	$10	−$10	
1	$10	$10	$15	−$5	
2	$10	$20	$18	+$2	
3	$10	$30	$27	+$3	
4	$10	$40	$36	+$4	***max profit
5	$10	$50	$47	+$3	

Explain how marginal revenue is calculated. Use the table below to explain why, for perfectly competitive firms, price equals marginal revenue.

Quantity of flowers (in bunches)	Price	Total revenue (Price × quantity)	Marginal revenue $\Delta TR/\Delta Q$
1	$10.00	$10.00	
2	$10.00	$20.00	$10.00
3	$10.00	$30.00	$10.00
4	$10.00	$40.00	$10.00

Explain that as long as marginal revenue is greater than marginal cost, the firm can add to profits by increasing output.

A firm maximizes profit at an output level at which

1. Total revenue exceeds total cost by the greatest amount.
2. Marginal revenue equals marginal cost.

Quantity (of flowers in bunches)	Price	Total revenue	Marginal Revenue	Total Cost	Marginal Cost	Profit	
0	$10	0	—	$10	—	−$10	
1	$10	$10	$10	$15	$5	−$5	
2	$10	$20	$10	$17	$8	+$3	
3	$10	$30	$10	$26	$9	+$3	
4	$10	$40	$10	$36	$10	+$4	***max profit
5	$10	$50		$47	$17	+$3	

In the graph below, the maximum profit quantity is shown where marginal cost is equal to price.

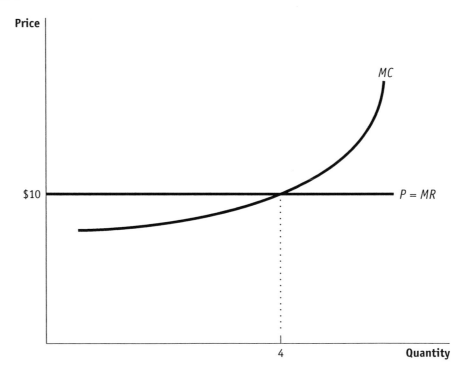

Work It Out

Profit-Maximizing Quantity of Output (text page 201)

This exercise asks students to use graphical information for a firm operating in the short run to determine the following:

- The firm's profit maximizing level of output
- The level of output at which the firm earns zero economic profit
- The range of prices over which the firm earns economic losses
- The firm's shut-down price

Using the Case Study in the Text

California Screaming (text pages 201–202)

Ask students:

1. Cite evidence to support the notion that the California energy market was not perfectly competitive during the energy crisis. (Energy producers were receiving a price greater than their marginal cost.)
2. How can we tell if electricity firms are behaving as price-takers? (We would have to determine if they are producing a quantity of electricity at which price equals marginal cost.)

Activities

Maximizing Profit (20–30 minutes)

Before the class, pass out the following worksheets on separate pieces of paper. Organize students into teams of at least six people each. Give each team a copy of the worksheets for Parts 1, 2, and 3. Have the teams divide into three subgroups, of at least two people each, to complete these worksheets. When they are done, give each team the "Team Gets Together" worksheet to answer as a group.

Part 1

(Note to instructor: Leave the Total profit column blank for the students' worksheet.)

Q	TR	TC	Total profit
0	0	20	−20
1	30	40	−10
2	60	56	+4
3	90	76	14
4	120	105	19
5	150	130	20
6	180	170	10

1. What do the abbreviations of Q, TR, and TC stand for?
2. How much is the company's fixed cost?
3. Calculate total profits at every output level.
4. What quantity will maximize profits?

Part 2

(Note to instructor: Leave all columns filled in for the students' worksheet.)

Q	MR	MC
0	—	—
1	30	20
2	30	16
3	30	20
4	30	29
5	30	30
6	30	40

1. What do the abbreviations Q, MR, and MC stand for?
2. Define MR and MC.
3. Based on the optimal output rule, what quantity will maximize profits?
4. Are there any conditions for which this will not be true?

Part 3

(Note to instructor: Leave the MR and MC columns blank in the students' worksheets.)

Q	TR	MR	TC	MC
0	0	—	20	—
1	30	30	40	20
2	60	30	56	16
3	90	30	76	20
4	120	30	105	29
5	150	30	130	30
6	180	30	170	40

1. What do the abbreviations Q, TR, MR, TC, and MC stand for?
2. Define MR and MC.
3. Calculate MR and MC to complete the table.

Team Gets Together

1. Share your results. Does everyone agree on the definitions of Q, TR, MR, TC, and MC?
2. What are two ways for finding the profit-maximizing quantity? (Where TR exceeds TC by the largest amount, and where MR = MC.)
3. What do both of these ways assume about minimum average variable cost? (The price the firm receives is greater than the minimum average variable cost at the quantity level.)

Accounting Profit Versus Economic Profit (3–5 minutes)

Pair students and have them calculate the accounting profit and economic profit for the following case study. The owner of Crested Butte Ski Rentals purchased $150,000 worth of skis for rentals. The revenue from the rentals is $300,000. Utilities are $20,000 per year and wages are $50,000. There is an outstanding loan, and the interest owing per year is $12,000. If the skis had not been purchased, the owner could earn $11,500 in annual interest income on the $150,000 otherwise used to buy the skis. The owner was offered another managerial position at another ski shop for $40,000 a year.

Accounting profit		Economic profit	
Revenues	+$300,000	Revenues	+$300,000
Costs:		Costs:	
Cost of skis	-$150,000	Cost of skis	-$150,000
Cost of utilities	-$20,000	Cost of utilities	-$20,000
Wages	-$50,000	Wages	-$50,000
Interest owed	-$12,000	Interest owed	-$12,000
		Forgone interest on money used to buy skis	-$11,500
		Forgone salary opportunity	-$40,000
Total cost	-$232,000	Total cost:	-$283,500
Total accounting profit	+$68,000	Total economic profit	$16,500

Match the Graph (5–10 minutes)

Hand out the following graphs and have students match them with the following labels:

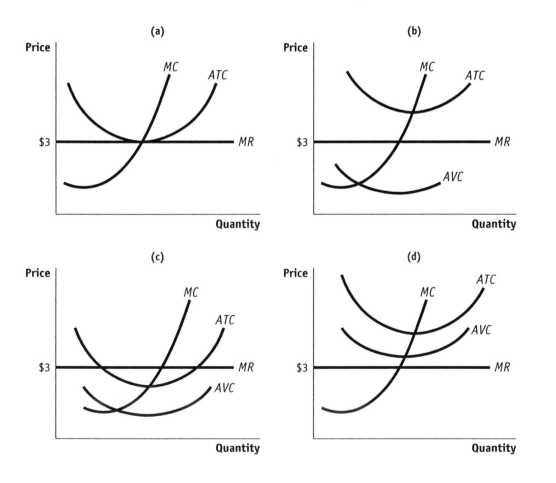

(a)

(b)

(c)

(d)

1. Shut down (answer: graph D)
2. Loss (answer: graph B)
3. Break-even (answer: graph A)
4. Economic profit (answer: graph C)

Ask a few pairs to report and explain their answers.

The Industry Supply Curve

Creating Student Interest
Ask students what industries are experiencing the entry of new firms.

Common Student Misunderstandings
Students may confuse "short-run production" with the short-run industry supply curve. Explain that short-run production refers to a condition in which one input of a firm is fixed. In the context of this chapter, short-run also indicates that the number of firms in the industry is fixed.

Presenting the Material
- Explain that in the long run, firms can choose to enter or exit an industry (and therefore there are no fixed costs in the long run). The conditions are as follows:
    1. If price is sustained above the market price, firms will enter.
    2. If price is sustained below the market price, firms will exit.
- Entry of new firms causes the industry supply curve to shift to the right, causing the equilibrium price to fall. As more firms are now in the industry, equilibrium output rises.

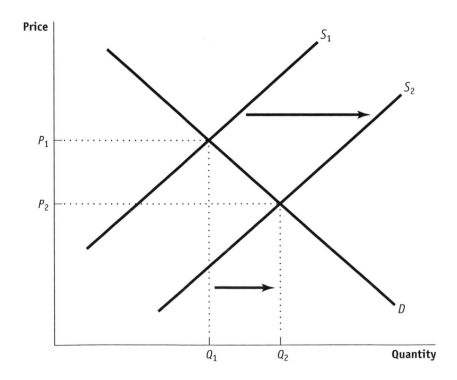

• Point out that the long-run industry supply curve is more elastic than the short-run industry supply curve, because more firms have entered and added more output at every possible price.

Using the Case Study in the Text

A Crushing Reversal (text page 208)
Ask students:

1. How did an increase in the demand for wine affect existing growers? (They increased their production.)
2. After the increase in demand, growers were making positive profits. What happened next? (New growers entered.)
3. Show the short-run and long-run effects of the increase in demand for the existing wine growers and the long-run effects on the industry. (Initially, wine growers will increase production, but too much entry and a fall in market price causes producers to cut back production. The long-run effect was a shift in supply of grapes to the right and a fall in the market price.)

Activities

Graphing a Fall in Price (10–15 minutes)
Pair students and ask them to show graphically the effects of a fall in the demand for wine on the initial growers and on the industry as a whole. (This is the opposite from the case illustrated in the chapter.)

Constructing an Industry Supply Curve (15–20 minutes)
A competitive firm has the following short-run total cost.

Quantity	Total cost	Marginal cost	Variable cost	Average variable cost
0	$10			
1	20			
2	26			
3	36			
4	50			
5	68			
6	90			

The market demand for this product is as follows:

Price	Quantity demanded
$12	200
10	300
8	400
6	500
4	600

1. Complete the table on costs.
2. What is the firm's break-even price? ($5.30)
3. How much is the fixed cost? ($10)
4. There are 100 firms in this industry and all have identical costs. Construct the short-run industry supply curve. In the same diagram, draw in the demand curve.
5. What is the market price? Equilibrium quantity? ($10, 300)
6. Will there be entry or exiting of firms? (Firms will exit because each firm earns a loss of $2 per unit: $10 minus *ATC* of $12 per unit.)

chapter 9

Factor Markets and the Distribution of Income

Chapter Objectives

Students will learn in this chapter:
- How the factors of production—resources such as land, labor, and both physical and human capital—are traded in factor markets, determining the factor distribution of income.
- How the demand for factors leads to the marginal productivity theory of income distribution.
- An understanding of the sources of wage disparities and the role of discrimination.
- The way in which a worker's decision about time allocation gives rise to labor supply.

Chapter Outline

Opening Example: Higher education pays.

I. The Economy's Factors of Production

A. Factors of production are bought and sold in factor markets, and the price for these resources is known as factor prices.

B. *Definition:* **Physical capital** consists of manufactured resources such as buildings and machines. Often referred to simply as "capital."

C. *Definition:* **Human capital** is the improvement in labor created by education and knowledge that is embodied in the workforce.

D. Factor prices play a key role in allocating resources among producers.

E. Demand for a factor is a *derived demand:* The demand for the factor is derived from the demand for the firm's output.

F. *Definition:* The **factor distribution of income** is the division of total income among labor, land, and capital.

II. Marginal Productivity and Factor Demand

A. Most factor markets in the modern U.S. economy are perfectly competitive, meaning that buyers and sellers of a given factor are price-takers.

B. An employer's marginal cost of hiring an additional worker is simply the worker's wage rate.

C. The marginal cost of hiring one additional worker must be weighed against the marginal benefit of that additional worker.

D. *Definition:* The **value of the marginal product** of a worker is the value of the additional output generated from hiring one more unit of labor.

E. The formula for the value of the marginal product of labor, assuming perfectly competitive labor markets, is:

$VMPL = MPL \times$ price per unit of output.

F. *Definition:* The **marginal benefit** from an activity is the additional benefit derived from undertaking one more unit of that activity.

G. The hiring rule for labor is to hire up until

$VMPL = W$,

where W is the wage.

H. The hiring rule applies to any factor of production: A profit-maximizing price-taking producer employs each factor of production up to the point at which the value of the marginal product of the last unit of the factor employed is equal to that factor's price.

I. *Definition:* The **value of the marginal product curve** of a factor shows how the value of the marginal product of that factor depends on the quantity of the factor employed.

J. The value of the marginal product curve is equal to the firm's demand for labor curve. This is illustrated in text Figure 9-3, shown below.

The Value of the Marginal Product Curve

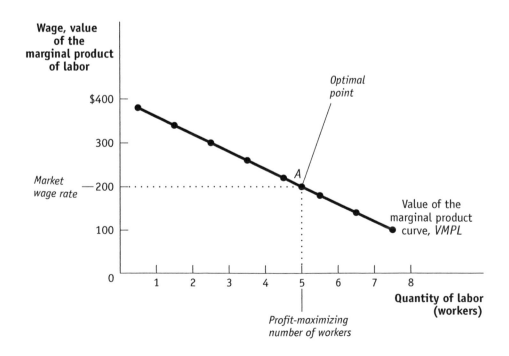

K. Shifts in the factor demand curve occur as a result of

1. Changes in prices of goods: An increase in the price of the good shifts the *VMPL* curve upward.

2. Changes in supply of other factors: An increase in the supply of a complementary input increases the MPL, shifting the VMPL curve upward.

3. Changes in technology: An improvement in technology that increases *MPL* shifts the *VMPL* curve upward.

L. The same logic of marginal productivity for labor applies to other factors of production such as capital or land.

1. *Definition:* The **rental rate** of either land or capital is the cost, implicit or explicit, of using a unit of that asset for a given period of time.

2. *Definition:* The **equilibrium value of the marginal product** of a factor is the additional value produced by the last unit of that factor employed in the factor market as a whole.

3. *Definition:* According to the **marginal productivity theory of income distribution,** every factor of production is paid its equilibrium value of the marginal product.

4. In a perfectly competitive market economy, the market price of each factor is equal to its equilibrium value of the marginal product. This determines the distribution of factor income.

III. Is the Marginal Productivity Theory of Income Distribution Really True?

A. There are two main objections to the marginal productivity theory of income distribution.

1. In the real world, we see large disparities of income that may not be due to productivity differences.

2. Some people wrongly believe that the marginal productivity theory of income gives a moral justification for the distribution of income. In turn, this sometimes leads people who believe that the current distribution of income is unfair to reject marginal productivity theory.

B. Wage disparities in practice

1. There are wage disparities across gender and ethnicity: White males have the highest earnings, while women (averaging across all ethnicities) earn only about 67 percent as much; African-American workers (male and female combined) earn only 69% as much; and Hispanic workers, only 58 percent as much. (Data are from text Figure 9-7.)

2. A large part of the observed inequality in wages can be explained by considerations that are consistent with the marginal productivity theory of income distribution.
   a. *Definition:* **Compensating differentials** are wage differences across jobs that reflect the fact that some jobs are less pleasant than others. Dangerous and hazardous jobs pay more.
   b. Individuals differ in talent and abilities.
   c. Individuals differ in the amount of human capital they have.

3. *Definition:* **Unions** are organizations of workers that try to raise wages and improve working conditions for their members.

4. However, marginal productivity theory does not explain all the inequality in wages. There are three major additional explanations.
   a. Market power: Factor markets are not perfectly competitive. Employees (in the form of **unions**) and employers can have market power in bargaining for wages.

    b. *Definition:* According to the **efficiency-wage model**, some employers pay an above-equilibrium wage as an incentive for better performance.

    c. Discrimination: Although market forces tend to work against discrimination, employers may have the ability to discriminate without hurting their profits when labor markets don't work well. Also, sometimes discrimination has been institutionalized in government policy—for example, apartheid in South Africa, which was abolished in 1994.

IV. The Supply of Labor

    A. Work versus leisure

        1. In the labor market, labor is demanded by firms and supplied by households.

        2. *Definition:* Decisions about labor supply result from decisions about **time allocation,** how many hours to spend on different activities. Individuals choose between market work and leisure activities.

        3. *Definition:* **Leisure** is time available for purposes other than earning money to buy marketed goods. This includes spending time with family or pursuing hobbies.

        4. The opportunity cost of leisure is the forgone income that could have been earned.

        5. The opportunity cost of work is the forgone leisure activities that could have been engaged in.

        6. *Definition:* **Utility** is a measure of the satisfaction a consumer derives from the consumption of goods, services, and leisure.

        7. Individuals decide on how much leisure to consume by making a marginal comparison: They compare the marginal utility of an additional hour of leisure with the marginal utility they get from the income earned from an additional hour of work.

        8. The *optimal labor supply* choice occurs when the marginal utility of one hour of leisure is equal to the marginal utility one gets from the goods that one's hourly wage can purchase.

    B. Wages and labor supply

        1. *Definition:* The **substitution effect** of a change in the price of a good is the change in the quantity consumed of that good as the consumer substitutes the good that has become relatively cheaper in place of the good that has become relatively more expensive.

        2. The **income effect** of a change in the price of a good is the change in the quantity consumed of the good that results from a change in the consumer's purchasing power due to the change in the price of the good.

        3. If an individual chooses to work more hours as a result of a wage increase, the *substitution effect* dominates. This is shown graphically as an upward sloping labor supply curve.

        4. If an individual chooses to work fewer hours as a result of a wage increase, the *income effect* dominates. This is shown graphically as a backward-bending, or downward-sloping, labor supply curve.

        5. *Definition:* The **individual labor supply curve** shows how the quantity of labor supplied by an individual depends on that individual's wage rate.

        6. Americans' increasing consumption of leisure over the past century indicates the income effect is stronger than the substitution effect.

C. Shifts in the labor supply curve
   1. The labor supply curve can shift due to
      a. Changes in preferences and social norms.
      b. Changes in population.
      c. Changes in opportunities for workers.
      d. Changes in wealth; an increase in wealth can increase the ability to consume more leisure and shift the labor supply curve to the left.

Teaching Tips

Factors of Production and the Demand for Labor

Creating Student Interest

Ask students to brainstorm about the factors that influence what an individual earns. Then ask if they think employers are wage-takers.

Common Student Misunderstandings

Students may not understand the difference between the marginal product of labor and the value of the marginal product of labor. Give a specific example of a baseball pitcher: His marginal product is how many games he wins; his *VMP* is how many extra ticket sales he generates from being on the field.

Presenting the Material

Give some specific examples of the demand for labor that is derived from the sale of the following products.

> Computers (computer assembly workers)
>
> Autos (car salesmen, auto manufacturers, auto workers)
>
> Health care (doctors, nurses)

Use a specific example of how the marginal product and the value of the marginal product of labor are calculated, given a product price of $5.00.

Quantity of labor	Quantity of widgets	Marginal product of labor ($\Delta TP/\Delta Q$)	Value of the marginal product (marginal product × product price)
0	0	—	
1	38	38	$190
2	72	34	170
3	102	30	150
4	128	26	130
5	150	22	110
6	168	18	90
7	182	14	70
8	192	10	50

If the equilibrium wage rate for these workers is $100, then the firm will hire 5 workers; if the wage is $80, the firm will hire 6 workers; if the wage rate is $60, the firm hires 7 workers.

Construct the individual firm's demand curve from the value of the marginal product data.

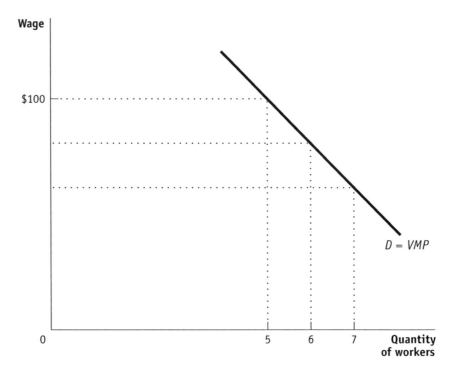

Using Case Study in the Text

The Factor Distribution in the United States (text pages 215–216)
Ask students:

1. Why don't wages measure the full return to labor? (Labor also receives compensation in the form of health insurance. In addition, a large number of people own their own businesses and earn sole proprietor income.)

2. Why is human capital the most important factor of production in a modern economy? ? (The product of skilled labor raises the standard of living in an economy.)

Activity

The Marginal Product of Labor (10–15 minutes)
Using the preceding table and graph related to widgets and workers, ask pairs of students to answer the following:

1. The product price increases from $5 to $6. Given wage rates of $100, $80 and $60, how many workers will each firm hire?

2. Draw the value of the marginal product curve.

3. The marginal product of each worker doubles; how many workers will the firm now hire at the same wage rates? (Assume a product price of $6.)

4. Draw the new marginal product curve. What could have caused this doubling of marginal product? (The firm could have done on-the-job training or added new technology that boosted the value of the marginal product of each worker.)

The Marginal Productivity Theory of Income and Wage Disparities

Creating Student Interest

Ask students what the following statistics tell us:

1. Women on average earn 77 cents for each dollar a man earns.
2. Hispanic men with a college degree earn on average about 90 percent more than Hispanic men who do not have a high school diploma.

Get students thinking about the differences between their answers to (1) and (2).

Common Student Misunderstandings

Students often think that the wage of a worker should equal that individual's marginal product, but that is not what the marginal productivity theory of income says. In equilibrium, wages for all workers in a market will equal the marginal product of the *last worker* hired.

Students may assume that all wages are determined by the marginal productivity of labor in that market. Explain that other factors are involved as well: compensating wage differentials, labor unions, and discrimination, for example.

Presenting the Material

Cite research on wage disparities between men and women as an example. Ask students which of the explanations below are about differences in *VMPL* between men and women. Wage disparities by gender can be due to

- Compensating wage differentials: Men may be employed in more dangerous or "dirty" jobs that pay more.
- Choice of college major and choice of career.
- Time constraints: Mothers may have only limited time to pursue career advancement.
- The differing negotiating skills of men and women.
- Number of years of experience.
- Number of years in continuous employment.
- Number of hours of work.
- Employer discrimination.
- Customer discrimination.

Using the Case Studies in the Text

Star Power (text page 224)

Ask students:

1. Why do a few top musicians earn so much more than other musicians? (They have a high value of marginal product—they sell lots of CDs and concert tickets.)
2. How does a global music market affect the demand for their services? (It increases the demand for their product.)

The Economics of Apartheid (text pages 229–230)

Ask students:

1. In this case, how was wage discrimination established? (It was put in place by the white-dominated government.)

2. Why, when apartheid has been abolished, do large wage disparities exist between white and black workers? (There is a legacy of differences in human capital investments between white and black workers.)

Activity

The Gender Pay Gap (5-10 minutes)

Pair students and have them brainstorm possible reasons for the pay gaps between men and women in the occupations shown in the table (www.aflcio.org/yourjobeconomy/women/equalpay/ThePayGapByOccupation.cfm (July 20, 2004).

Ask a few pairs to list their responses on the board. Then ask students to identify which reasons are in accord with marginal productivity theory and which are not.

Occupation	Men's weekly earnings*	Women's weekly earnings*	Weekly pay gap
Accountants, Auditors— Management-Related	$954	$687	$267
Adjusters, Examiners and Investigators, Insurance	$662	$546	$116
Administrators, Education and Related Fields	$1,189	$819	$370
Advertising and Related Sales	$782	$663	$119

*These are median weekly earnings of full-time wage and salary workers.

In The News

Ask students if the following article is in accord with marginal productivity theory of income.

Women Fall Behind When They Don't Hone Their Negotiation Skills

by JOANN S. LUBLIN
The Wall Street Journal, November 11, 2004.

In most workplaces, it still pays to be a man. Women often are less adroit at winning better salaries, assignments and jobs — either because they don't ask or because they cave in when they do.

Skipping or bungling a single negotiation can inflict a huge penalty. A 22-year-old woman who fails to get her first job offer of $25,000 boosted by $5,000 stands to lose more than $568,000 by age 60, says Linda Babcock, a Carnegie Mellon University economics professor. Men are eight times as likely as women to bargain over starting pay. "It's the accumulation of disadvantage," she says.

A growing flurry of books, online courses and executive-education programs aim to fix this situation by teaching women to be more effective advocates. I attended one such workshop in Boston last week. The three-day "Negotiation Edge" was run by Deborah M. Kolb, a Simmons School of Management professor.

Eighteen women overcame their negotiation jitters by discussing case histories, role playing a few scenarios and videotaping simulations of their own pending negotiations, such as a bid for severance.

Dr. Kolb's bottom line: If a woman develops good negotiating skills, she can enhance her career in many ways. She cited a senior vice president of a major corporation who repeatedly accepted better-paying positions without question. Officials recently passed her over for an important assignment requiring negotiation skills because they didn't know she had those talents. ...

Workshop participants learned to make their value visible and to avoid sabotaging themselves. Setting goals too low "is likely to become a self-fulfilling prophecy," Dr. Kolb warned. "Backbone really is about preparation."

In salary talks, for instance, she told the women to gather data about pay rates, jot down their strongest attributes and rehearse explanations for weaknesses. "I give up too easily," grumbled a 40-year-old computer saleswoman as she completed a self-assessment. "I don't set my expectations high enough."

The woman explained how she wrangled a signing bonus of stock options, only to discover later that equally qualified new hires had won bigger grants.

If a potential employer insists times are tough, swap a hefty raise for an unusual perquisite, Dr. Kolb proposed. Consider "trading things that have value for you for things that have value for others."

The collaborative strategy worked well for participant Terry Regan. In hiring the human-resources manager, a suburban Boston biotech concern balked at giving her more than its promised 10% raise. But the company agreed to immediately pay all expenses so she could complete graduate school. Official policy partly covered tuition after six months' service. She also got time off to study. "It was a mutual gain for both of us," said Ms. Regan, now 39.

Some women tend to accept extra work without negotiating fewer regular duties or higher pay because they don't want to appear pushy, Dr. Kolb observed. "Never make a unilateral concession," she suggested. "Say, 'At what price?'" ...

The Supply of Labor

Creating Student Interest
Ask students: If they received a raise at work, would they want to work more hours or less? Why?

Common Student Misunderstandings
Students may think that leisure refers to time relaxing, having fun, or traveling. Explain that in economics the umbrella term *leisure* includes any activity other than paid work—educational pursuits, time spent with family and in raising children, etc.

Students may not understand how the supply of labor curve can be downward sloping. Explain that at a high wage, a lawyer, for example, may have enough income to enjoy more leisure and choose to work fewer hours. The supply of labor curve above that wage will start to bend backward.

Presenting the Material
- Explain that individuals make choices about how many hours to devote to paid market work and how many hours to spend in leisure. Time is scarce in this case, and the opportunity cost of leisure is the loss of money from paid work.
- Ask students to write down how many hours they will work at the following wage rates (this is the same supply curve we derived in Chapter 3): $16, $14, $12, $10, $8, $6, $4. Ask three or four students to construct a labor supply curve on the board from the data. Ask students if any of them had an income effect: They want to work less hours for pay if the wage rises. (They may want to devote more time

to their education.) Ask them what their reservation wage is: What is the lowest wage they will accept to work for pay?

Using the Case Study in the Text

The Decline of the Summer Job (text page 234)

Ask students:

1. In what way did the income effect cause a decline in the number of teenagers willing to work as lifeguards? (The stock market boom of the late 1990s increased the wealth of many families, and they could afford to have their teenagers not working in the summer.)

2. Use the text to come up with another explanation for the lifeguard shortage. (Compensating differentials—perhaps the work is viewed as dangerous, other jobs could be viewed as more desirable.)

Activity

Substitution and Income Effects (5–10 minutes)

Pair students and ask them to apply the concepts of income effects and substitution effects to the following data:

Men's labor participation rate

1950	86.4%
2002	72.2%

Women's labor participation rate

1950	59.2%
1998	67.1%

(Source: http://www.bls.gov/opub/mlr/1999/12/art1full.pdf [for individuals 16 and older].)

(For women, rising wages over this period caused them to enter the labor market, and the substitution effect dominated. For men, they may have been able to afford to retire earlier; in that case, the income effect dominated. Younger men were also staying in school longer than they did in earlier periods.)

chapter 10

Efficiency, Inefficiency, and Equity

Chapter Objectives

Students will learn in this chapter:
- How the overall concept of efficiency can be broken down into three components: efficiency in consumption, efficiency in production, and efficiency in output levels.
- Why an economy consisting of many perfectly competitive markets is typically, but not always, efficient.
- Why it is easier to determine if an economy is efficient than to determine if it is fair or equitable.
- What externalities are and why they can lead to inefficiency in a market economy and support for government intervention.
- What public goods are and why markets fail to supply them efficiently.

Chapter Outline

Opening Example: When the Berlin Wall came down in 1989 and West and East Germany reunified, West Germany provided huge amounts of financial aid to the former East Germans. Germans thought this fair. But it may be that this aid reduced incentives for the former East Germany to become more efficient. Here was a clear efficiency versus equity trade-off.

I. Efficiency

 A. *Definition:* A **competitive market economy** is an economy in which all markets, for goods and for factors, are perfectly competitive.

 B. *Definition:* An economy is in **general equilibrium** when the quantity supplied is equal to the quantity demanded in all markets.

 C. An economy is efficient if it does not pass up any opportunities to make some people better off without making other people worse off.

 D. To achieve efficiency an economy must meet three criteria.

  1. *Definition:* An economy is **efficient in consumption** if there is no way to redistribute goods among consumers that makes some consumers better off without making others worse off. This is the first criterion.

  2. *Definition:* An **economic signal** is any piece of information that helps people make better economic decisions.

3. *Definition:* An economy is **efficient in production** if there is no way to produce more of some goods without producing less of other goods. This is the second criterion.

4. *Definition:* An economy has an **efficient allocation of resources** if there is no way to reallocate factors of production among producers to produce more of some goods without producing less of others.

5. *Definition:* An economy is **efficient in output levels** if there isn't a different mix of output that would make some people better off without making others worse off. This is the third criterion.

   a. To achieve efficiency in output levels, market prices act as signals to producers.

   b. This assumes that producers face a common labor market and that labor can easily be transferred from producing one product to another.

   c. As the demand for one product rises, the value of the marginal product of labor in that market rises. This causes firms to demand more labor in this industry; as more labor is utilized, the value of the additional output eventually falls. The value of the additional output across the two labor markets eventually will reach equilibrium.

   d. The markets for goods and services are interconnected with the factor markets.

   e. Efficiency in output levels can be illustrated using a circular-flow diagram that shows the demand and supply for goods and services in the product markets and the demand and supply of the factors of production.

II. Efficiency and Equity

A. What's fair?

1. An outcome can be efficient without being desirable and can be desirable without being efficient.

2. As explained in Chapter 1, *equity* means that the distribution of utility among individuals is fair.

3. There is no agreed-on definition of fairness.

B. The utility possibilities frontier

1. *Definition:* A **utility possibility frontier** shows how well-off one individual or group could be for each given total utility level of another individual or group.

2. Efficiency is not a goal in itself, to be pursued at the expense of other goals. It is only a way to achieve our goals more effectively—whatever those goals may be.

III. Market Failure: The Case of Externalities

A. *Definition:* **Market failure** occurs when a market fails to be efficient.

1. Two examples of market failure are externalities and public goods.

B. Externalities

1. *Definition:* An **external cost** is an uncompensated cost that an individual or firm imposes on others.

2. Air pollution generated by electric utilities is an example of an external cost.

3. *Definition:* An **external benefit** is a benefit that an individual or firm confers on others without receiving compensation.

4. *Definition:* External costs and external benefits are known as **externalities.**

   5. *Definition:* External costs are **negative externalities.**
   6. *Definition:* External benefits are **positive externalities.**
   7. Externalities can lead to individual decisions that are not optimal.
   8. *Definition:* The **marginal social cost of a good or activity** is equal to the marginal cost of production plus its marginal external cost.

C. Economic Policy
   1. Taxes can be used to lead to an efficient level of production of a good or service that generates a negative externality.
   2. *Definition:* Taxes designed to reduce external costs are known as **Pigouvian taxes.**
   3. In 1960, Nobel laureate Ronald Coase theorized that in an ideal world the private sector could deal with externalities.
   4. *Definition:* According to the **Coase theorem,** even in the presence of externalities an economy can always reach an efficient solution as long as **transaction costs**—the costs to individuals of making a deal—are sufficiently low.
   5. Transaction costs include:
      • The costs of communication among interested parties
      • The costs of making legally binding agreements
      • Costly delays involved in bargaining
   6. *Definition:* When individuals take external costs or benefits into account, they **internalize the externality.**

D. Private versus Social Benefits
   1. Not all externalities are negative—some economic activities generate external benefits.
   2. An example of an external benefit is the creation of knowledge in one industry that can also be used to enhance production in another industry.
   3. *Definition:* A **technology spillover** is an external benefit that results when knowledge spreads among individuals and firms.
   4. The informal exchange of information at social events among people working in Silicon Valley is used as an example of technology spillover.
   5. *Definition:* The **marginal social benefit of a good or activity** is equal to the marginal benefit that accrues to consumers plus its external benefit.
   6. *Definition:* A **Pigouvian subsidy** is a payment designed to encourage activities that yield external benefits.
   7. *Definition:* An **industrial policy** is a policy that supports industries believed to yield positive externalities.

IV. Market Failure: The Case of Public Goods

A. Private Goods
   1. *Definition:* A good is **excludable** if the supplier of that good can prevent people who do not pay from consuming it.
   2. *Definition:* A good is **rival in consumption** if the same unit of the good cannot be consumed by more than one person at a time.
   3. *Definition:* A good that is both excludable and rival in consumption is a **private good.**

B. Public Goods
   1. *Definition:* When a good is **nonexcludable,** the supplier cannot prevent consumption by people who do not pay for it.

2. *Definition:* A good is **nonrival in consumption** if more than one person can consume the same unit at the same time.

3. *Definition:* A **public good** is both nonexcludable and nonrival in consumption.

4. Some examples of public goods include:
   - Disease prevention: When doctors act to stamp out the beginnings of an epidemic before it can spread, they protect people around the world.
   - National defense: A strong military protects all citizens.
   - Scientific research: More knowledge benefits everyone.

5. *Definition:* Goods that are nonexcludable suffer from the **free-rider problem:** individuals have no incentive to pay for their own consumption and instead will take a "free ride" on anyone who does pay.

6. In most cases public goods must be provided by the government, where the efficient quantity of a public good is the quantity at which marginal social benefit equals marginal cost.

7. *Definition:* Governments engage in **cost-benefit analysis** when they estimate the social costs and social benefits of providing a public good.

Teaching Tips

Efficiency

Creating Student Interest

Ask students if efficiency is a desirable goal. What is more important to them: efficiency or equity?

Why can't economists define efficiency as a positive achievement rather than the absence of something: Nobody can be made better off without making someone worse off?

Common Student Misunderstandings

The idea of general equilibrium is very abstract for students. Explain that this assumes that each and every product market as well as every factor market is in equilibrium. The quantity demanded for chicken, for example, equals the quantity supplied, and the quantity demanded for chicken processors equals the quantity supplied, and so on across all markets.

Presenting the Material

A general rule is: An economy is efficient if it does not pass up opportunities to make someone better off without making someone else worse off.

Review the three criteria for an efficient economy.

1. Efficiency in consumption: There is no way to redistribute the goods among consumers without making someone worse off.

2. Efficiency in production: It is not possible to produce more of some goods without producing less of others.

3. Efficiency in output levels: There is not a different mix of output that would make some people better off without making others worse off.

Explain that all markets will be in equilibrium when the quantity of *each good* and the *factor demanded* is equal to the quantity of *each good and factor supplied*. This is the general economy counterpart to an individual market in equilibrium.

Using the Case Study in the Text

A Great Leap Backward (text page 246)

Ask students:

1. Why did the Chinese "Great Leap Forward" fail? (It allocated resources to their most inefficient uses.)

2. Was it inefficient in production or consumption? (Both, because it transferred production to workers who were ill-equipped for it, and because there was no way in the system for consumers to register their demand for goods.)

3. Illustrate the effects of this program on a production possibilities frontier. (Overall production of both industrial goods and farm goods fell; this is represented by a point inside the production possibility frontier.)

Activity

Changing the Mix (5–10 minutes)

Ask pairs of students to consider the following scenario: In a perfectly competitive market economy that is in equilibrium, consumers decide that they prefer more chicken and less red meat. Have students explain in words and in the following four graphs how an efficient economy will adjust so that total surplus is maximized. (This assumes that all producers face a common labor market and that there are no market failures.)

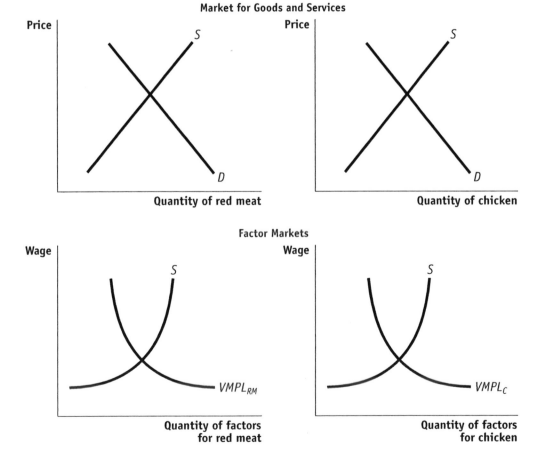

(Students should shift the demand for chicken to the right and the demand for beef to the left in the product markets. In the factor markets, student should shift the demand for chicken processors to the right and shift the demand for red meat workers to the left.)

(Because of this change in consumer tastes, a greater demand for chicken will cause an increase in the price of chicken, P_C. $VMPL_C = P_C \times MPL_C$ will therefore rise, with the result that $VMPL_C >$ wage rate. A lower demand for red meat will cause a fall in the price of red meat, Pr. $VMPL_r = P_r \times MPL_r$ will fall, with the result that $VMPL_r <$ wage rate. Red meat producers will let some of their workers go, and these workers will move to chicken producers who are hiring additional workers. As labor moves from the red meat industry to the chicken industry, MPL_C and $VMPL_C$ fall, while MPL_r and $VMPL_r$ rise.)

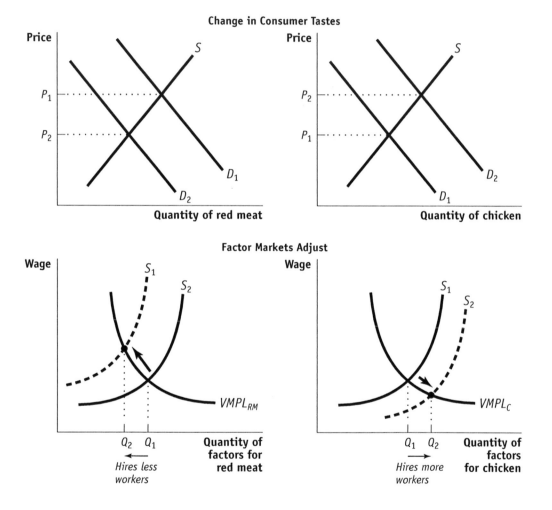

Change in Consumer Tastes

Factor Markets Adjust

Efficiency and Equity

Creating Student Interest

Ask students if the incomes of the rich are rising, while the incomes of the poor are not. By what definition(s) of "fair" is this unfair? (According to John Rawls, this situation would not be fair.)

Is efficiency a goal in itself? An economy under a dictator may be efficient, but is it desirable?

Ask students if it is fair for the rich to pass on their wealth to their children while other children in the same community are born into abject poverty.

Common Student Misunderstandings

Students may be unclear about the meaning of "fairness" in economics. Explain that there are many valid definitions of what constitutes a "fair" economic outcome.

Students may also have difficulty understanding the meaning of the term *equity* in economics. Using the definition provided in Chapter 1 in the context of this chapter, equity refers to whether an economic outcome is fair and/or the distribution of income (utility) is fair.

The utility frontier graph is abstract and may be difficult for students to understand. Explain that any point on the frontier has maximized total surplus. Any point inside is inefficient in the sense that one group can be made better off without the other group being made worse off.

Presenting the Material

Give students a concrete example of how efficiency and equity may be in conflict. For example:

Pharmaceutical companies are given patents to encourage the development of very costly drugs. During the patent period, however, the prices of these drugs for the uninsured are prohibitive.

The efficiency issue is: How do we provide enough incentives to encourage the production of new drugs?

The equity issue is: How do we distribute medicines in a way that is fair?

(Emphasize that efficiency is not the only consideration in evaluating the desirability of economic outcomes.)

Use text Figure 10-6, shown below, to illustrate allocative efficiency. If you could only choose between an efficient point *A* and the inefficient point *C*, is point *A* always preferable? (Not necessarily. Point *C* may be fairer to Easterners because it gives them more total utility, even though it is a point of inefficiency.)

Efficiency versus Equity

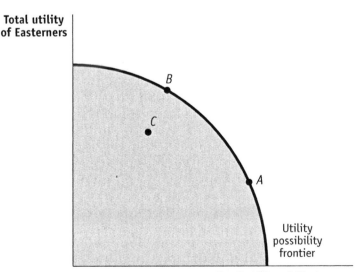

Total utility of Easterners

Total utility of Westerners

Utility possibility frontier

Using the Case Study in the Text

Death and Taxes (text page 250)
Ask students:

1. Give opposing definitions of fairness with regard to inheritance. (One is to argue for equal opportunity or the same starting line for all children in society, and so be against the ability of the rich to pass on wealth to their children. The second emphasizes the right of people to do what they want with their money.)

2. What does the use of the terms *inheritance tax* and *death tax* tell you about the frame of reference of writers on this issue? (Inheritance tax emphasizes the assets children will be inheriting. If you feel that all children should start out in life on the same starting line, you emphasize the unfairness of the inheritance tax. Politicians who argue for the free choice of the parents in disposing of their assets refer to death taxes.)

Activities

The Veil of Ignorance (20–30 minutes)
Organize students into teams of four or five each. Have each group set up an entirely new economy (from Rawls's *Theory of Social Justice*). Tell them: You no longer know what your nationality, age, gender, and social class is now or will be in the new society. What kind of an efficient and fair economy will you set up?

(Rawls argued that in this situation people run the risk of being poor, so they will set up an economy that is fair to the poor. He argued that a market economy with private property, profits, and incentives will be productive and innovative and should be preserved as much as possible. *But it is fair only* if as the rich get richer, the poor also advance. Rawls advocated a redistribution of income from the rich to the poor.)

Are Taxes Theft? (5–10 minutes)
Robert Nozick, in his book *Anarchy, State and Utopia* (1974), argued that taxes are theft and violate a person's basic property rights. In other words, taxes by their very nature are unfair. Ask pairs of students to develop arguments for and against this proposition. Ask a few students to report.

To Each According . . . (5-10 minutes)
Pair students and ask them to evaluate the famous quote from Karl Marx: "From each according to their ability, to each according to their need." What does this statement mean? If an economy were organized this way, would it be efficient? Why or why not? Would it be fair?

What Is Economic Justice? (5–10 minutes)
Ask students to write down on a piece of paper how they would define the term *economic justice*. Ask some students to volunteer to read their definitions aloud. (These definitions will range from equal opportunity to economic freedom.)

Market Failure: The Case of Externalities

Creating Student Interest
In an effort to stimulate student interest in the topic of externalities, ask students if their college should provide free flu shots for everyone on campus. On another issue, would they favor a ban on cell phone use while driving?

Common Student Misunderstandings

It is often difficult for students to understand that the existence of pollution has benefits. Explain that reducing pollution is costly, so polluting allows firms to save the cost of purchasing pollution-reducing equipment. As a result firms won't have to pass the cost of this equipment on to consumers in the form of higher prices of goods and services.

Presenting the Material

Begin teaching this topic by explaining the key terms used in this section. This will give students a working vocabulary with which to study externalities. Whenever possible provide real world examples of positive and negative externalities. The appropriate use of taxes to correct for negative externalities, and subsidies to correct for positive externalities is demonstrated graphically in Figures 10-7 and 10-8, respectively. It is important that students understand that while government policies, such as taxes and subsidies, are most commonly used to deal with externalities, it is also possible, under certain circumstances, for market forces to achieve an efficient outcome.

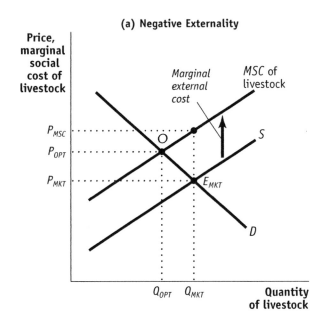

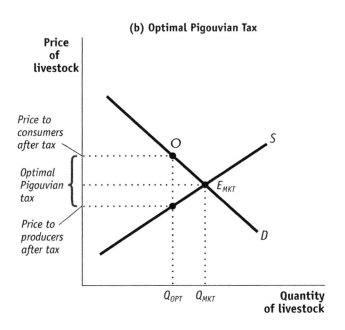

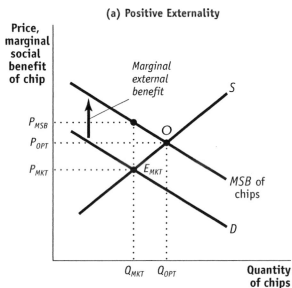

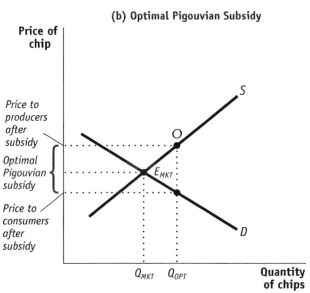

Using the Case Studies in the Text

Talking and Driving (text page 253)
Ask students the following questions:

1. In what way is cell phone use while driving a negative externality? (Distracted drivers pass on the risk of an accident to other drivers.)
2. What are the consequences of the negative externalities of cell phone use while driving in the United States? (There are 600 or more traffic deaths per year.)
3. Should driving while using a cell phone be made illegal as it is in Japan? (Students can debate this decision.)

Spillovers in Silicon Valley (text page 257)
Ask students the following questions:

1. What kinds of positive externalities were explored by author Tom Wolfe? (He explored technological innovation in the semiconductor industry.)
2. How were the externalities spread? (They were spread by concentrating the development of the semiconductor industry in one locale—Silicon Valley—and allowing the young men and women in the industry to meet and share knowledge after work in informal settings such as restaurants.)

Activities

Should Smoking be Banned on Campus? (3–5 minutes)
Pair students and ask them to debate the pros and cons of banning all smoking on campus. Ask them to consider the case that a small amount of smoking is preferable to a complete ban. Have a few pairs present their pro and con arguments. Extend this issue by asking if the Coase theorem can be used in this case. Could students themselves, without the intervention of student government, reach an agreement among the smokers and nonsmokers on campus?

Is It Positive or Negative? (5–8 minutes)
Pair students and ask them to classify each of the following as an example of a positive or negative externality.
- Smoking on campus exposes students to secondhand smoke. (Negative externality)
- College graduates add to the nation's supply of skilled workers and add to productivity. (Positive externality)
- Biotech firms invent new medicines. (Positive externality)
- Using energy-saving lightbulbs reduces the pollution from electricity-generating plants. (Positive externality)
- Crowded freeways with heavy truck usage expose the surrounding communities to increased health risks. (Negative externality)
- Restoring the Amazon forest can reduce global levels of pollution. (Positive externality)

Work It Out

Externality and Optimal Pigouvian Tax (text page 256)
Students are asked to use a graph to mathematically determine the value of the optimal tax that a government should impose on firms that generate a negative externality. In addition, students are also asked to mathematically determine the following:
- Post-tax equilibrium price and quantity of the good
- Burden of the tax paid by the producers

- Burden of the tax paid by the consumers
- Effect on the negative externality (i.e., amount of litter)

Market Failure: The Case of Public Goods

Creating Student Interest

In the past, fire departments charged a fee to homeowners for fire protection. What are the problems with that approach? What's the marginal cost of one more download of an MP3 file? Why do firms charge per download?

Common Student Misunderstandings

Students may be unclear about the meaning of the term *rival in consumption*. Give a specific example of a student eating an apple. No one else can eat the apple at the same time. The free-rider problem is another difficult concept for students. Explain that this problem exists for public goods. If a private producer cannot exclude those customers who do not pay for the good, then consumers have an incentive to free-ride while someone else pays for the good. Students often point out apparent exceptions to the free-rider problem: donations to religious institutions, National Public Radio, PBS (ask about *Sesame Street*), and charitable organizations. Point out that the free-rider problem assumes that people operate in their own self-interest. Not everyone whose children watch *Sesame Street* contributes to Public Television; most families free-ride on the generosity of others.

Presenting the Material

Emphasize the characteristics that distinguish private goods from public goods. Specifically, public goods are nonexcludable and nonrival in consumption, while private goods are excludable and rival in consumption. Provide students with real world examples of both types of goods. Point out the free-rider problem that is associated with public goods. Also explain to students that public goods are typically provided by governments, while private goods are usually provided by a market system.

Using the Case Study in the Text

Old Man River (text page 264)

Ask students:

1. In what way is the Old River Control structure a public good? (It is impossible to exclude residents from the benefits of preventing flooding—Old River Control is nonrival in consumption.)
2. Why is it difficult for government to determine the marginal benefit to each individual resident from the flood control system? (Each resident is likely to overstate the benefits.)

Activities

Are These Public Goods? (5 minutes)

Pair students and ask why the following goods are public goods. How do they suffer from the free-rider problem?

- Highways (Toll roads do exclude drivers. If a highway is very crowded, consumption is rival in nature.)
- National Defense (Once national defense is provided, no person can be excluded from its benefits.)

Why is TV a Public Good in the U.K.? (3–5 minutes)

Pair students and ask them to discuss, based on the example on text page 260, why and how broadcast television is considered a public good in the U.K. Is it really excludable? How does the government attempt to exclude viewers? Which approach do students prefer: the U.S. system of TV as a private good financed through advertising or the U.K. system where television is funded via a yearly license fee?

Is Voting a Public Good? (5–10 minutes)

Pair students and divide the class in half. One side takes the pro position and the other, the con position on the following statement: Because voting suffers from a free-rider problem, voting should be made mandatory.

chapter **11**

Monopoly

Chapter Objectives

Students will learn in this chapter:
- The significance of monopoly, an industry in which a single monopolist is the only producer of a good.
- How a monopolist determines its profit-maximizing output and price.
- The difference between monopoly and perfect competition, and the effects of that difference on society's welfare.
- How policy makers address the problems posed by monopoly.
- What price discrimination is, and why it is so prevalent when producers have market power.

Chapter Outline

Opening Example: DeBeers, the world's main supplier of diamonds, is a successful monopolist that limits the quantity of diamonds supplied to the market. By so doing, DeBeers drives up the price of diamonds.

I. Types of Market Structure

    A. There are four principal models of market structure: perfect competition, monopoly, oligopoly, and monopolistic competition.

    B. Economists use these four models of market structure to develop principles and make predictions about markets and how producers will behave in them.

    C. Market structure is based on two dimensions: the number of producers in the market (one, few, or many) and whether the goods offered are identical or *differentiated*.

        1. In *perfect competition*, many producers sell an identical product.

        2. In *monopoly*, a single producer sells a single, undifferentiated product.

        3. In *oligopoly*, a few producers—more than one but not a large number—sell products that may be identical or may be differentiated.

        4. In *monopolistic competition*, many producers each sell a differentiated product.

II. The Meaning of Monopoly

A. *Definition:* A **monopolist** is a firm that is the only producer of a good that has no close substitutes. When an industry is controlled by a monopolist, it is known as a **monopoly.**

B. Monopoly: Our first departure from perfect competition

    1. True monopolies are hard to find in the economy because of legal obstacles: Antitrust laws help to prevent monopolies from emerging.

    2. Monopolies play an important role in some sectors of the economy, such as pharmaceutical markets.

C. What monopolists do

    1. Monopolies raise price above the perfectly competitive price and restrict output.

    2. *Definition:* **Market power** is the ability of a firm to raise prices.

    3. Under perfect competition, economic profits normally vanish in the long run. This is not the case for monopolists.

D. Why do monopolies exist?

    1. *Definition:* To earn monopoly profits, a monopolist must be protected by a **barrier to entry,** something that prevents other firms from entering the industry.

    2. The four principal types of barriers to entry are:
        a. Control of a scarce resource or input.
        b. Economies of scale: Large firms with lower unit costs drive out smaller firms.
            (1) *Definition:* A **natural monopoly** exists when economies of scale provide a large cost advantage to having all of an industry's output produced by a single firm.
        c. Technological superiority: Monopolies can be created by *network externalities* whereby the value of a good for a consumer rises as more people use it (such as Microsoft's Windows program).
        d. Government-created barriers, such as patents and copyrights.

III. How a Monopolist Maximizes Profit

A. The monopolist's demand curve and marginal revenue

    1. The demand curve for a monopolist is downward sloping, whereas the demand curve for a perfectly competitive firm is horizontal.

    2. For a monopolist, the demand curve is the market demand curve.

    3. The additional revenue a monopolist earns as output is increased by one unit less than the price at which the unit is sold.

    4. For a monopolist, an increase in production has two opposing effects on revenue.
        a. The quantity effect: As one more unit is sold, it increases total revenue by the price at which the unit is sold.
        b. The price effect: In order to sell the last unit, the monopoly must cut the price on all units sold.
        c. At low levels of output, the quantity effect is larger than the price effect; at higher output levels, the price effect is stronger than the quantity effect.

    5. For a firm with market power, the marginal revenue curve always lies below its demand curve. This is illustrated in text Figure 11-5, shown on the next page.

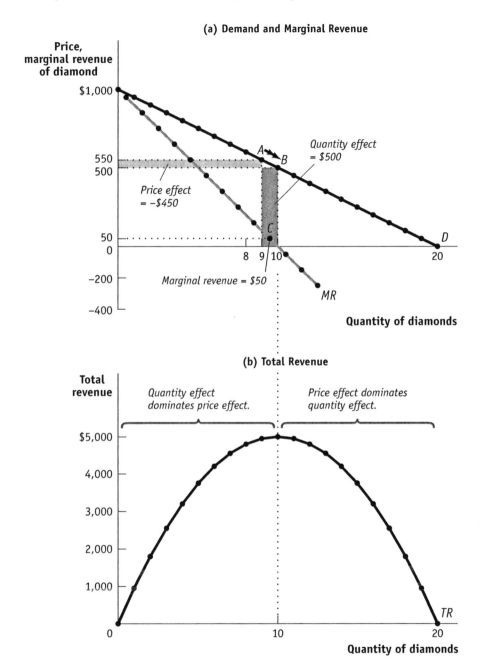

A Monopolist's Demand, Total Revenue, and Marginal Revenue Curves

(a) Demand and Marginal Revenue

(b) Total Revenue

B. The monopolist's profit-maximizing output and price

1. A monopolist maximizes profit at an output level where $MR = MC$.

2. The price a monopolist charges is what consumers are willing to pay for that output level. This price is found on a graph by going vertically up from the optimal output level to the demand curve and then left to the price axis, as illustrated in text Figure 11-6, which is shown on the next page.

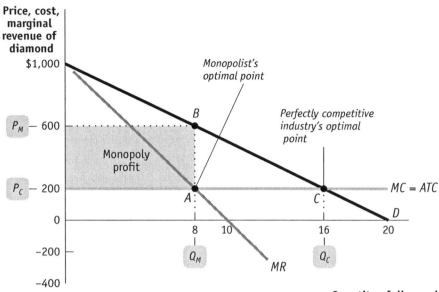

The Monopolist's Profit-Maximizing Output and Price

C. Monopoly versus perfect competition

1. For a perfectly competitive firm, $P = MC$ at the profit-maximizing quantity of output.
2. $P > MR = MC$ for a monopolist at the profit-maximizing quantity of output.
3. Compared to a firm in perfect competition, a monopolist produces a smaller quantity, charges a higher price, and earns a positive profit.
4. A monopolist that faces a market with very elastic demand will behave more like a perfectly competitive firm.

D. Monopoly: The general picture

1. Generally, a monopolist will have an upward-sloping marginal cost curve.
2. The total profit for a monopolist $= (P_M \times Q_M) - (ATC_M \times Q_M)$

$$= (P_M - ATC_M) \times Q_M.$$

3. Monopolies can earn profits in the short run and the long run. The monopolist's profit is illustrated in text Figure 11-7, shown below.

The Monopolist's Profit

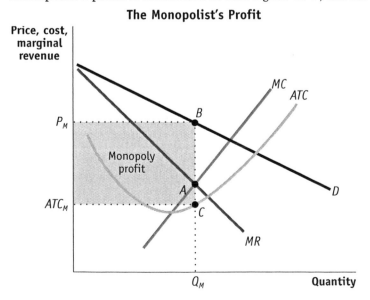

IV. Monopoly and Public Policy

A. Welfare effects of monopoly

  1. There are welfare losses from monopoly; the loss to consumers is greater than the gain in profits for the monopoly.

  2. Total surplus is less under monopoly than under perfect competition.

B. Preventing monopoly

  1. If the monopoly is not a natural monopoly, it is best to prevent its existence or break it up.

  2. Antitrust laws prevent or eliminate monopolies.

C. Dealing with natural monopoly

  1. There are two major public policies toward natural monopolies: public ownership or regulation.

  a. *Definition:* In **public ownership** of a monopoly, the good is supplied by the government or by a firm owned by the government.

  b. *Definition:* **Price regulation** limits the price that a monopolist is allowed to charge.

  c. Price regulation of natural monopolies does not lead to shortages as long as price is above marginal cost.

V. Price Discrimination

A. *Definition:* A **single-price monopolist** offers its product to all consumers at the same price.

B. *Definition:* Sellers engage in **price discrimination** when they charge different prices to different consumers for the same good.

C. The logic of price discrimination

  1. Most monopolists can increase their profits by engaging in price discrimination. This is illustrated in text Figure 11-11, shown below (see the next page for part [c]).

Price Discrimination

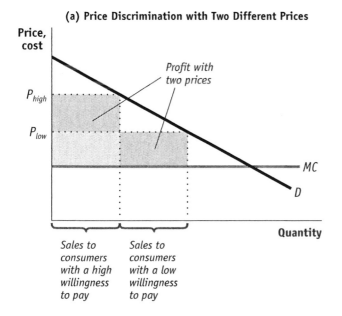

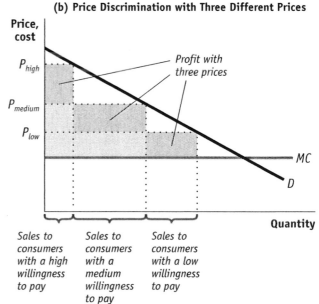

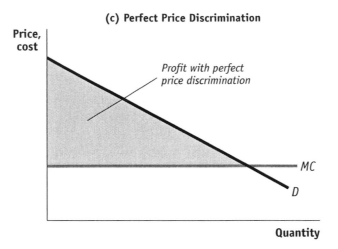

(c) Perfect Price Discrimination

Price, cost

Profit with perfect price discrimination

MC

D

Quantity

D. Price discrimination and elasticity

    1. If a monopoly can identify two separate customer groups that have differing price elasticities of demand, it can engage in price discrimination.

        a. A firm with market power will raise price on customers who have inelastic demand and lower price on customers who have elastic demand.

E. Perfect price discrimination

    1. *Definition:* **Perfect price discrimination** takes place when a monopolist charges each consumer his or her willingness to pay—the maximum that the consumer is willing to pay.

    2. The greater the number of prices the monopolist charges, the lower the lowest price; that is, some consumers will pay prices that approach marginal cost.

    3. The greater the number of prices the monopolist charges, the more money it can extract from consumers.

    4. Monopolies try to achieve perfect price discrimination by

        a. Advance purchase restrictions.

        b. Volume discounts.

        c. Two-part tariffs.

Teaching Tips

Types of Market Structure

Creating Student Interest
Ask students to classify the music industry in terms of the degree of competition. (Students are often surprised to learn that six global music companies produce and sell most of the music they buy.)

Common Student Misunderstandings
Students may confuse monopoly with monopolistic competition because of the similarities in names. Explain that the term monopolistic is used in monopolistic competition to indicate that firms in the industry, of which there are many, try to convince consumers that they are the only brand with a particular unique feature.

Presenting the Material

Use the chart in text Figure 11-1 to illustrate the differences between the types of market structure.

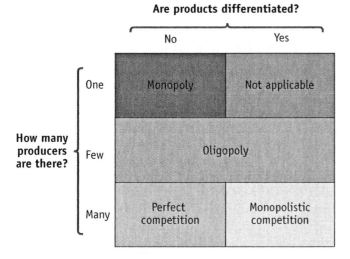

Types of Market Structure

Give specific examples of industries that fit each classification.

Monopoly (pharmaceutical companies with drugs under patent)

Oligopoly (autos, airlines, photographic film, colas)

Monopolistic competition (fast food, retail clothing stores, sports clubs)

Perfect competition (wheat, corn, soybeans, stock market)

Using the Case Study in the Text

Are Diamonds Monopolies Forever? (text pages 276–277)

Ask students:

1. How did De Beers create its monopoly position in diamonds? (Initially, the diamond mines in South Africa were larger than other sources in the world. With new sources in other countries, De Beers bought up the mines or entered into exclusive licenses with local governments to be the sole distributor.)

2. Why is De Beers losing some market power over the diamond market? (More diamond mines have been found, and the production of synthetic diamonds has increased.)

Activities

Classifying Markets (2–3 minutes)

Ask students to classify the following products as being in monopoly, oligopoly, monopolistically competitive, or perfectly competitive industries. What is the source of their market power?

Microsoft's Windows operating system (near monopoly, patents)

Kodak's 35 mm film (oligopoly, patents and copyrights)

Burrows Welcome's drug for AIDS patients (oligopoly, patents)

McDonald's Big Mac (monopolistic competition, brand loyalty)

A regional electric company (monopoly, economies of scale, government license)

Monopoly: Output and Pricing

Creating Student Interest

Ask students whether the college bookstore is a monopoly. Has the Internet reduced the monopoly power of college bookstores?

Common Student Misunderstandings

- Students often think that a monopolist can "charge whatever price it wants to." Explain that the downward-sloping demand curve for the industry's product means that if the monopoly charges too high a price, it will have no customers. Therefore, because the firm is the industry, the industry demand curve is downward sloping.
- Students may not understand what a natural monopoly is. Explain that one firm will emerge as dominant because it has unit cost advantages that allow the company to keep price low enough to drive out less efficient competitors.
- Students may be confused by the practice of plotting marginal quantities between two quantities. For instance, the MC of producing the third unit is plotted midway between quantities 2 and 3. As a result, numerical examples must be constructed carefully.

Presenting the Material

Explain that the goal of a monopoly is to maximize profits by producing the quantity where MR = MC. At the profit-maximizing quantity, the monopolist has lower output and charges a higher price than in perfect competition. Give a specific numerical example for a monopoly firm, such as De Beers' diamonds.

Quantity of diamonds	Price of diamonds	Total revenue	Marginal revenue	Total cost	Marginal cost	Profit
0	$200	0		100		-100
			180		10	
1	$180	$180		110		70
			140		30	
2	$160	$320		140		180
			100		60	
3	$140	$420		200		220
			60		100	
4	$120	$480		300		180
			20		150	
5	$100	$500		450		50

Point out that the first two columns of the table constitute the demand curve for the monopolist. Also note that marginal revenue is less than price at each output level. The maximizing output level is 3, and the most profitable price is $140.

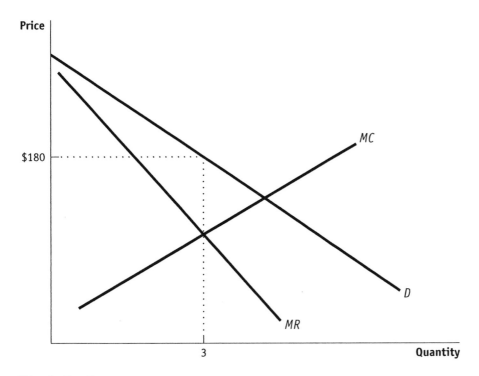

Work It Out

Profit Maximization for a Monopolist (text page 284)

This numerical example asks students to determine a monopolist's profit maximizing output level, price, and associated profit using information provided in a graph. In addition, students are asked to compare the optimal output level and price for a monopolist with those that would prevail if the same market was perfectly competitive.

Using the Case Study in the Text

California Power Play (text pages 284–285)

Ask students:

1. What caused the blackouts in California in 2000? (El Paso Corporation, which had a monopoly over the pipelines, restricted output.)

2. How was price manipulated when it was controlled by federal regulators? (El Paso used its monopoly over a pipeline to drive up prices received by its own natural gas subsidiary.

Activities

The Only Concert on Campus (10–15 minutes)

Organize students into teams of four or five and describe the following scenario: You are organizing a concert on campus with a band that is *extremely* popular with students. This will be the *only concert of its kind* for the next 5 years. The auditorium holds 1,000 students. It will cost you $20,000 to hire the band. There are no marginal costs.

Teams do the following:

Step 1: Brainstorm three prices for concert tickets.

Step 2: Students should now complete the following table.

Price	Quantity demanded	Total revenue	Total cost	Total profit

Step 3: Now show students the actual demand curve for the concert, given below. (Point out that while a monopolist can control the supply of the product, it is not in control of the demand for it. The more price elastic the demand, the less control a monopolist has over demand.)

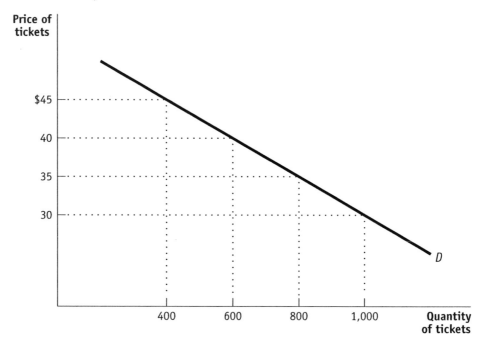

A price of $30 is the most profitable price (*TR* = $30,000; profit + $10,000). Did students choose the most profitable price?

Point out that there are substitutes for the concert: Students have other entertainment options. Point out that in general monopolies may control supply but cannot control demand. Even at the height of De Beers' monopoly power, the demand for diamonds was not perfectly inelastic.

Monopolies and Public Policy

Creating Student Interest

Ask students how many regulated monopolies serve their individual homes.

Common Student Misunderstandings

Students may think that monopolies emerge by predatory behavior. Explain that a natural monopoly may emerge because it has unit cost advantages. This presents policy makers with a dilemma: how to preserve the low price for consumers but allow only one company to serve the entire market.

Presenting the Material

Use the example of a natural gas company that emerges as a natural monopoly. If it is able to serve the entire market, it can spread the high fixed costs of the pipelines over more customers and enjoy economies of scale. If two or more firms serve the market, customers will not enjoy low prices. A regulated price is set to cover the firm's unit costs.

Regulated Natural Monopoly

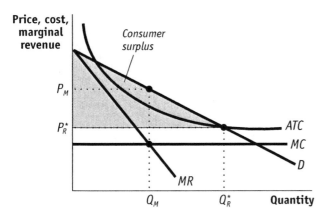

Using the Case Study in the Text

Cable Dilemmas (text page 290)

Ask students:

1. Why is cable TV a natural monopoly? (It enjoys economies of scale if it serves a large geographic area.)

2. Why was cable TV regulated, deregulated, and re-regulated? (It was thought to be a natural monopoly and in need of regulation, then there was intense lobbying by cable firms for deregulation. After deregulation, rates rose, customers complained, and cable companies were
re-regulated.)

Activities

Regulate it? (5–10 minutes)

Ask students if the companies below should be subject to price regulation. (Are they natural monopolies? Would price regulation give enough incentive to the firm to innovate? Would price regulation protect consumers?)

> Your local electricity company
>
> Your local cable TV company
>
> The theme park in your area
>
> Your trash pickup company

Price Discrimination

Creating Student Interest

Ask students why a movie theater charges two prices: one for children and one for adults.

Common Student Misunderstanding

Because price discrimination is covered in this chapter, students may think that only monopolies price discriminate. Explain that any firm with market power and with distinct customer groups with differing elasticities can engage in price discrimination.

Presenting the Material

Use the example of airline travel by business and vacation travelers that was described in Chapter 5 of this instructor's manual. The price elasticity of demand for business travelers was calculated to be .54, or very inelastic. The price elasticity of demand for vacation travelers was 2.33, or very elastic. Airlines have a clear opportunity to practice price discrimination by raising prices on business travelers, and charging a lower price for vacation travelers.

Use text Figure 11-10 to illustrate the profits from two different groups of customers. (This is another airline ticket example.)

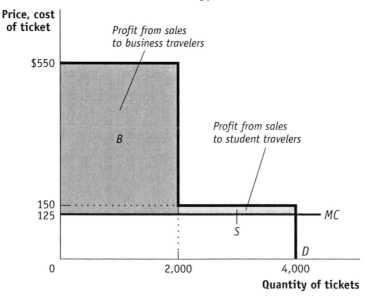

Two Types of Airline Customers

Using the Case Study in the Text

Sales, Factory Outlets, and Ghost Cities (text pages 295–296)

Ask students:

1. Why do stores put goods on sale? (To increase revenues by appealing to their customers who have high price elasticity of demand.)

2. What two different types of customers is the store catering to? (Customers who will shop regardless of price and customers who will buy only if the item is on sale.)

3. Why are outlet stores on the outskirts of towns? (These appeal to customers who are willing to take the time to drive to enjoy lower prices; the time spent driving is an opportunity cost. These customers also have high price elasticity of demand.)

Activity

Price Discrimination on Campus (5–10 minutes)

Pair students and tell them that they represent the student government on campus. Can they engage in profitable price discrimination on the following services?

> Parking spaces
>
> Theater productions
>
> Sports events

Ask a few pairs to report. Make sure that they were able to determine whether there are separate groups with differing price elasticities.

chapter 12

Oligopoly, Monopolistic Competition, and Product Differentiation

Chapter Objectives

Students will learn in this chapter:
- The meaning of oligopoly, and why it occurs.
- How our understanding of oligopoly can be enhanced by game theory, especially the concept of the prisoners' dilemma.
- How repeated interactions among oligopolists can help them achieve tacit collusion.
- How oligopoly works in practice, under the legal constraints of antitrust policy.
- How prices are determined in monopolistic competition in the short run and the long run.
- Why oligopolists and monopolistically competitive firms differentiate their products.
- The economic significance of advertising and brand names.

Chapter Outline

Opening Example: The opening example deals with collusion between Archer Daniels Midland and Ajinomoto to carve up the market for lysine, an additive in animal feed. Collusion is illegal in the United States, and these companies were caught red-handed. This example is used throughout the chapter.

I. Oligopoly

    A. *Definition:* An **oligopoly** is an industry with only a small number of producers. A producer in such an industry is known as an **oligopolist.**

        1. The number of firms determines whether or not a specific market is an oligopoly, not the size of each firm.

        2. Each oligopolist has some market power.

    B. *Definition:* When no one firm has a monopoly, but producers nonetheless realize that they can affect market prices, an industry is characterized by **imperfect competition.**

    C. The most important source of oligopoly is the existence of economies of scale, which gives bigger producers a cost advantage over smaller ones.

D. Duopoly Example

    1. *Definition:* An oligopoly consisting of only two firms is a **duopoly.** Each firm is known as a **duopolist.**

E. *Definition:* Sellers engage in **collusion** when they cooperate to raise each others' profits. A **cartel** is an agreement by several producers that increases their combined profits by telling each one how much to produce.

    1. OPEC is the most famous of the world's cartels.

    2. Cartels among firms are illegal in the United States and many other jurisdictions.

    3. Individual firms in a cartel have an incentive to cheat.

    4. *Definition:* When the decisions of two or more firms significantly affect each others' profits, they are in a situation of **interdependence.**

    5. *Definition:* The study of behavior in situations of interdependence is known as **game theory.**

F. The prisoners' dilemma

    1. *Definition:* The reward received by a player in a game, such as the profits earned by an oligopolist, is that player's **payoff.**

    2. *Definition:* A **payoff matrix** shows how the payoff to each of the participants in a two-player game depends on the actions of both. This is illustrated in text Figure 12-1, shown below.

A Payoff Matrix

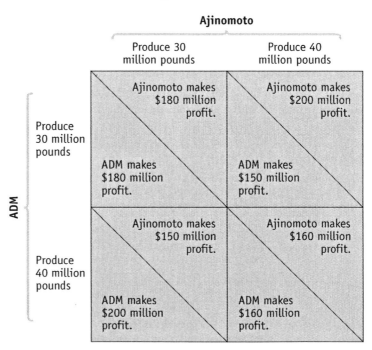

    a. *Definition:* **Prisoner's dilemma** is a game based on two premises: (1) Each person has an incentive to choose an action that benefits him or herself at the other player's expense. (2) When both players act in this way, both are worse off than if they had chosen different actions.

    b. When both players in the prisoners' dilemma cheat, both are worse off than they would have been if neither had cheated.

    c. *Definition:* An action is a **dominant strategy** when it is a player's best action regardless of the action taken by the other player.

    d. *Definition:* A **Nash equilibrium,** also known as a **noncooperative equilibrium,** is the result when each player in a game chooses the action that maximizes his or her payoff given the actions of the other players, ignoring the effects of that action on the payoffs received by those other players.

G. Overcoming the prisoners' dilemma: Repeated interaction and tacit collusion

    1. Oligopolists in the real world play repeated games.

    2. *Definition:* A firm engages in **strategic behavior** when it attempts to influence the future behavior of other firms.

    3. *Definition:* A strategy of **tit for tat** involves playing cooperatively at first, then doing whatever the other player did in the previous period.

    4. *Definition:* When firms limit production and raise prices in a way that raises each others' profits, even though they have not made any formal agreement, they are engaged in **tacit collusion.**

    5. When oligopolists expect to compete with each other over an extended period of time, each individual firm will often find it in its own best interests to help other firms in the industry, and so there will be tacit collusion.

II. Oligopoly in Practice

A. The legal framework

    1. Before 1890 in the United States, cartels were legal but legally unenforceable.

    2. *Definition:* **Antitrust policy** refers to the efforts of the government to prevent oligopolistic industries from becoming or behaving like monopolies.

    3. The Sherman Antitrust Act was passed in 1890; its goal was to prevent the creation of monopolies and to break up existing ones.

        a. One of the first actions taken under the Sherman Antitrust Act was the breakup of Standard Oil.

B. Tacit collusion and price wars

    1. Oligopolists do succeed in keeping prices above their noncooperative level.

    2. Tacit collusion is a normal state for an oligopoly.

    3. However, four major factors make it hard for an industry to coordinate on high prices.

        a. Large numbers: The more firms in an oligopoly, the less incentive for firms to behave cooperatively.

        b. Complex products and pricing schemes: In the real world, oligopolists produce many products, which makes it difficult for a firm to track what its competitors are doing.

        c. Differences in interests: Firms differ in what they perceive as fair and what strategies are in their real interests.

        d. Bargaining power of buyers: Often, oligopolists sell to large buyers who can bargain for lower prices.

        e. *Definition:* A **price war** occurs when tacit collusion breaks down and prices collapse.

III. Monopolistic Competition

A. *Definition:* **Monopolistic competition** is a market structure in which there are many competing producers in an industry, each producer sells a differentiated product, and there is free entry into and exit from the industry in the long run.

B. In a monopolistically competitive industry, each producer has some ability to set the price of her differentiated good. Exactly how high she can set it is limited by the competition she faces from other existing and potential producers that produce close, but not identical, products.

C. Monopolistic competition in the short run

    1. Like a monopolist, a monopolistically competitive firm faces a downward-sloping demand curve for its good and its marginal revenue curve is also downward-sloping.

    2. In the short run a monopolistically competitive firm can be profitable, as shown in panel (a) of Figure 12-5 in the text, or it can be unprofitable as shown in panel (b) of Figure 12-5 in the text.

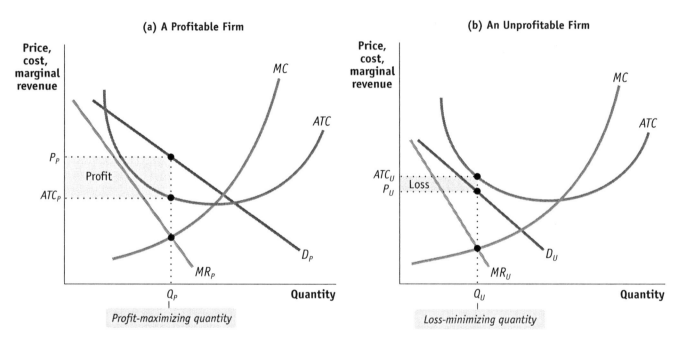

D. Monopolistic competition in the long run

    1. Entry of new firms into a monopolistically competitive industry will occur in the long run when existing firms are profitable, thus causing each existing firm's demand curve and marginal revenue curve to shift to the left, as shown in panel (a) of Figure 12-6 in the text. Each firm will receive a lower price for every unit of output that it sells and profit will fall. Entry will cease when firms earn zero profit.

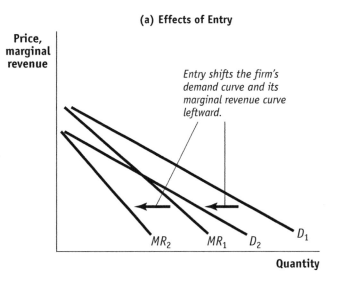

(a) Effects of Entry

2. Firms in a monopolistically competitive industry will exit from the industry in the long run when existing firms are unprofitable, thereby causing each remaining firm's demand curve and marginal revenue curve to shift to the right, as shown in panel (b) of Figure 12-6 in the text. Each remaining firm will receive a higher price for every unit it sells, and profit rises. Exit will cease when all remaining firms earn zero profit.

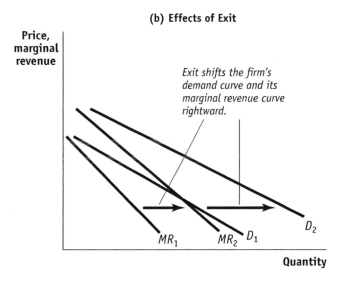

(b) Effects of Exit

3. *Definition*: In the long run, a monopolistically competitive industry ends up in **zero-profit equilibrium:** each firm makes zero profit at its profit-maximizing quantity.

4. A monopolistically competitive industry will be in long-run equilibrium when all firms in the industry earn zero profit, as illustrated in Figure 12-7 in the text.

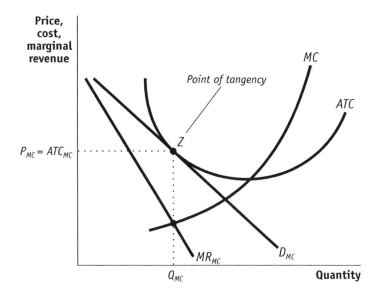

5. In the long run, when a monopolistically competitive industry is in zero-profit equilibrium, each firm's demand curve is tangent to its average total cost curve at its profit-maximizing quantity.

IV. Product Differentiation

A. *Definition*: Firms engage in **product differentiation** when they try to convince buyers that their product is different from the products of other firms in the industry.

B. Three important types of product differentiation include:
   - differentiation by style or type
   - differentiation by location
   - differentiation by quality

C. Product differentiation can occur in oligopolies that fail to achieve tacit collusion, as well as in monopolistic competition.

D. In industries with product differentiation, firms advertise their products in order to increase demand for their good or service.

E. When advertising gives consumers useful information, it is not considered a waste of resources. However, advertising that simply touts a good is explained by the fact that either consumers are irrational, or expensive advertising conveys to consumers that the firm's products are of higher quality.

F. *Definition*: A **brand name** is a name owned by a particular firm that distinguishes its products from those of other firms.

G. Brand names can convey real information when they assure consumers of the quality of a product.

Teaching Tips

Oligopoly

Creating Student Interest

Ask students to identify industries that are dominated by a few firms. Ask them if the college textbook market is an oligopoly.

Common Student Misunderstandings

Students may assume that because there are only a few firms in an oligopoly, firms do not compete fiercely. Remind students that the goal of any firm is to maximize profits. Firms in oligopolies can compete intensely in price wars, retaliatory pricing, and product differentiation.

Presenting the Material

Use OPEC as an example of a cartel that restricts the quantity of oil produced. In the graph below, without a cartel in the market, the equilibrium price is P_e, and the equilibrium quantity of oil is Q_e. If cartel members agree to collude and restrict output, then the cartel supply is represented by the vertical supply line, set at a fixed quantity Q_c. Show students that P_c is the cartel price with a fixed agreed-on quota of oil.

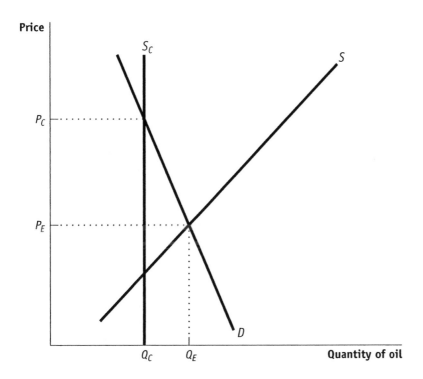

Use the payoff matrix on the next page. In this game, there are two airlines, Sky World and Bay City Airlines, and they have the choice of pricing high or low. Each company's profit depends on how the other company responds to its pricing strategy. If both firms collude and agree on a high price, they each earn $30 in profit. If one prices low and the other prices high, the low-price firm earns $50 (grabbing market share), while the high price firm earns only $4. Because of the risk of retaliation, the likely outcome is that both firms will price low and earn only $10 each. The dominant strategy in this game is to choose a low price.

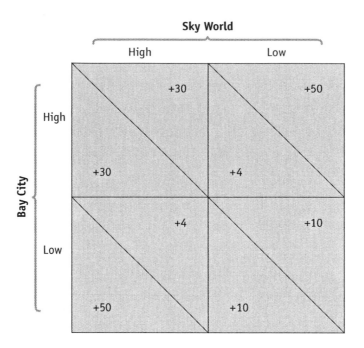

Using the Case Study in the Text

The Rise and Fall and Rise of OPEC (text pages 308–309)

Ask students:

1. How successful is OPEC as a cartel? (In 1974 and 1978, OPEC was successful as a cartel. In the mid-1980s, a glut of oil and cheating by cartel members reduced cooperation. In the late 1990s, OPEC's clout increased when Mexico, a nonmember, agreed to follow output reductions.)

2. Does OPEC meet in public? (Yes, the cartel meets frequently outside the United States.)

Activities

Tit for Tat? (30–45 minutes)

Organize students into teams of three, with each team representing a specific oligopoly industry. Each student represents a specific company within the oligopoly. Make this clear by standing by one team and indicating that one student may play the role of Kellogg's, the second Quaker Oats, and the third student General Mills. The goal of each company is to maximize profits for their corporation.

Explain that during this experiment, each firm must decide whether to choose a high price for their product (H = $8) or a low price (L = $6). (In this game, oligopolists are competing on price alone, not on quantities.) If a student is operating as the price leader, she will signal a high price by thumbs up and a low price by thumbs down.

Before the experiment begins, distribute the following chart for students to fill out.

Prices (possible outcomes of each round)	Total sales in the market	Price	Firm's sales (quantity)	Total revenue (P x Q)	Total cost ($110 fixed and $2 variable)	Profit
HHH 60,60,60	180	H = $8				
HHL 20,20,160	200	H = $8 L = $6				
HLL 10,100,100	210	H = $8 L = $6				
LLL 72,72,72	216	L = $6				

During the game, students track their pricing and profits with the form below:

Profit or Loss Statement form (extend this form to show 15 rounds):

Round	Industry situation (HHH,HHL,HLL,LLL)	Your firm's price (H or L)	Profit	Loss
1				
2				
3				
4				
5				

- Tell students that any verbal discussion on pricing strategy during the game will be punished under antitrust laws: a team can be thrown out into the hall. Optional: Remind students that the most profitable strategy for the industry as a whole is to collude.
- To start the experiment, ask each team to choose a price leader for the first round; the student taking this role changes each round. Ask the price leader to choose a high or low price and signal to the team his or her choice. Then have the two other students choose their prices and secretly record them on the firm's profit sheet, covering their prices with their hands. Now it is time for them to reveal their pricing decisions to the industry. The oligopoly determines the outcome: HHH, HHL, HLL, LLL, etc. Then each firm records its individual profit or loss for this first round.
- Teams continue this process until they have played all 15 rounds: The new price leader shows the choice of his or her firm's price, and the two other firms secretly respond. The two firms show their choice, the oligopoly determines the outcome, and individual firms record their profit or loss for that round.
- Observe the teams during the game to see if any are able to achieve tacit collusion and agree on a high price. Because leading with a high price risks rivals undercutting the price, the least risky strategy is to lead with a low price. Students tend to use a tit for tat strategy in this game.

To Collude or Not? (5–10 minutes)

Use the payoff matrix shown previously for the two airlines to play the following game. Pair students and tell them that each student in a pair represents an airline in a duopoly. On the count of three, each student chooses a high or a low price by signaling thumbs up or thumbs down. Students then record their profits based on the payoff matrix.

Round	Your price	Your payoff
1		
2		
3		
4		
5		
6		
Profit		

Debrief the game by pointing out that the dominant strategy in this game is to choose a low price.

Oligopoly in Practice

Creating Student Interest

Ask students if they are aware of antitrust proceedings against a specific firm. What type of behavior was found to be illegal?

Common Student Misunderstandings

Students may think that the marketplace is a "free for all" in which there are no rules of the game. Explain that United States antitrust laws lay out the rules of the game, and certain types of practices are illegal, such as predatory pricing and price setting.

Presenting the Material

Use the examples of Standard Oil and AT&T as monopolies that were broken up under antitrust laws. Then present the following article as a current example of antitrust enforcement: (Department of Justice, Antitrust Division 2004).

Infineon Technologies AG Agrees to Plead Guilty to Participating in DRAM Price-Fixing Conspiracy

Also Agrees to Pay $160 Million Fine—Third Largest In Antitrust History

WASHINGTON, D.C. — Infineon Technologies AG (Infineon), a German manufacturer of dynamic random access memory (DRAM), has agreed to plead guilty and to pay a $160 million fine for participating in an international conspiracy to fix prices in the DRAM market, the Department of Justice announced.

DRAM is the most commonly used semiconductor memory product, providing high-speed storage and retrieval of electronic information for a wide variety of computer, telecommunication, and consumer electronic products. DRAM is used in personal computers, laptops, workstations, servers, printers, hard disk drives, personal digital assistants, modems, mobile phones, telecommunication hubs and routers, digital cameras, video recorders and televisions, digital set top boxes, game consoles, and MP3 digital music players. There are more than $5 billion in DRAM sales annually in the United States.

According to the one-count felony charge filed today in the U.S. District Court in San Francisco, from July 1, 1999 to June 15, 2002, Infineon conspired with unnamed DRAM manufacturers to fix the prices of DRAM sold to certain computer and server manufacturers. Under the plea agreement, which must be approved by the court, Infineon has agreed to cooperate with the government in its ongoing investigation of other DRAM producers.

"This case sends the message that high-tech price-fixing cartels will not be tolerated—a message reinforced by the largest criminal fine levied in a Department of Justice case in the past three years," said Attorney General John Ashcroft. "Vigorous antitrust enforcement is important to our nation's economy. We are committed to pursuing illegal price-fixing cartels that harm American consumers, regardless of whether they are at home or abroad."

The computer makers directly affected by the price-fixing conspiracy were: Dell Inc., Compaq Computer Corporation, Hewlett-Packard Company, Apple Computer Inc., International Business Machines Corporation, and Gateway Inc.

Using the Case Study in the Text

Air Wars (text page 313)
Ask students:

1. What tactics did Robert Crandall, then CEO of American Airlines, use to get a cooperative agreement among the major airlines? (He talked directly to the competition about raising price, and he tried price leadership, which failed.)

2. Why are airlines prone to price wars? (Companies compete on price and availability, so competition is fierce. In addition, airline pricing is complex, and it is difficult to determine if a rival is violating the tacit agreement.)

Activities

Guilty or Not? (3–5 minutes)
Ask students to go to the Justice Department's web page (www.usdoj.gov/) and look under Antitrust Division to find an interesting case of price fixing. Have them bring the case in and present it to the class.

Microsoft's Monopoly (5–10 minutes)
Ask students to research the Microsoft antitrust case. What specific business practices of Microsoft were in violation of antitrust laws? Pair students and ask them to share their findings with their partners. Ask a few students to report.

Monopolistic Competition

Creating Student Interest
Ask students what type of market power a nail salon or local restaurant has.

Common Student Misunderstandings
Students may confuse monopolistic competition with monopoly. Explain that the "monopolistic" aspect of monopolistic competition means that firms attempt to convince consumers that they have a unique product.

Presenting the Material

Make clear that the most important feature of monopolistic competition is many sellers, which makes it clearly different from monopoly. Give some examples of markets that fit this type of market structure: cosmetics, fast food, retail clothing stores, restaurants, coffee houses, hair salons, and nail salons.

Explain that firms in monopolistic competition have some market power because they can differentiate their product, and they also face a downward-sloping demand curve. Give a concrete example of a monopolistically competitive firm in the *short run* and have students determine the output level and price at which profits will be maximized. Use the following table.

Quantity	Price	Total revenue	Marginal revenue	Total cost	Average total cost	Marginal cost	Profit
0	$17	$0		$10	—	—	−$10
			16			8	
1	$16	16		18	18		−$2
			14			5	
2	$15	30		23	11.5		+$7
			12			2	
3	$14	42		25	8.3		+$17
			10			2	
4	$13	52		27	6.8		+$25
			8			3	
5	$12	60		28	5.6		+$32
			6			4	
6	$11	66		32	5.3		+$34
			4			6	
7	$10	70		38	5.4		+$32
			2			10	
8	$9	72		48	6		+$24
			0			14	
9	$8	72		62	6.9		+$10

The profit-maximizing price is $11, and the output is 6. Total profits at this level of production are $34. Point out that the first two columns represent the demand curve; the fourth column is the downward-sloping marginal revenue curve.

Work It Out

Monopolistic Competition (text page 319)

In this numerical exercise students are asked to refer to a graph depicting a monopolistically competitive firm to determine the following:

- the profit-maximizing level of output for the firm in the short run
- the price charged by the firm when it produces its profit-maximizing level of output
- the maximum amount of profit earned by the firm
- the graph of the long-run outcome for this firm

Using the Case Study in the Text

Bagels from Boom to Bust (text page 319)

Ask students:

1. Why is the bagel market an example of monopolistic competition? (There are many sellers and products are differentiated. There are no barriers to entry and exit.)

2. Why did sales boom in the 1990s? (A change in consumer tastes or perhaps the popularity of New York-based TV shows.)

3. What happened to profits of previously existing bagel firms? (They were eroded due to the entry of new firms.)

Activities

Classifying Industries (3–5 minutes)

Ask pairs of students to classify the following markets into monopoly, oligopoly, monopolistic competition, or perfect competition.

Cosmetics (monopolistic competition)

Quick Lube service stations   (monopolistic competition)

Gasoline stations   (monopolistic competition)

Wheat (perfect competition)

Oil industry   (oligopoly)

Clothing shops   (monopolistic competition)

Colas   (oligopoly)

Film   (oligopoly)

Wholesale flower market (perfect competition)

Pharmacies (monopolistic competition)

Stock market (perfect competition)

Computer operating systems (Windows is a near monopoly.)

Homework assignment: To prepare for the next class session, ask students to go to www.lasvegas.com and click on Dining. How many restaurants are there? How do they differentiate their product? Why is this market an example of monopolistic competition? Ask a few students to report.

Who's Profitable? (3–5 minutes)

Put the following three graphs on the board or on an overhead. Ask students to characterize the firm as earning economic profits, having break-even profit, or bearing losses.

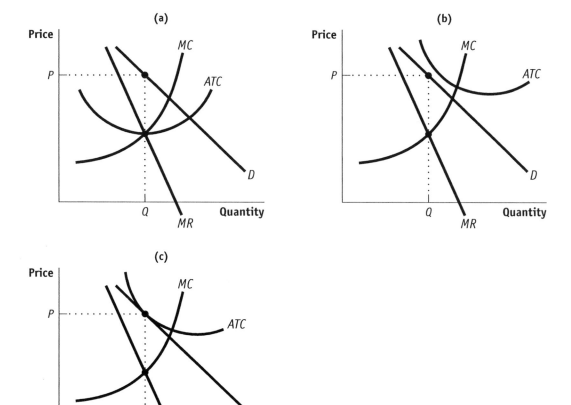

(a. economic profit; b. loss; c. break-even profit)

Product Differentiation

Creating Student Interest

Ask students to think of three recent purchases. To what extent did advertising or brand names influence their decision? What was it about the advertising that influenced them? Why do some consumers say that they are not influenced by advertising?

Ask students how much they think a domain name on the web is worth to a business. For example, how much is a website such as www.lasvegas.com worth?

Ask students whether the quality of a Nike athletic shoe is really superior to that of a store brand purchased at Wal-Mart.

Ask students if they think they can tell the difference in taste between Sam's Club cola and Coca-Cola.

Common Student Misunderstandings

Students may be confused about whether an ad actually conveys useful information. Explain that an ad can tell a consumer about product availability, location, and features. But an ad also may contain no useful information, as some students suspect.

Presenting the Material

Advertising attempts to make the demand curve for a product more inelastic in order to convince buyers that there are few substitutes. In addition, advertising causes the demand curve to shift to the right.

Use the following article to illustrate the powerful effect of a brand name on consumer demand. Indicate to students that Chanel No. 5 is one of the oldest brand names in perfumes.

Famous Early Perfumes—Chanel No. 5

Ernest Beaux created Chanel No. 5 for *Coco Chanel* in 1921. It has a floral top note of ylang-ylang and neroli, with a heart of blends of jasmine and rose all above a woody base of sandalwood and vetiver. Chanel believed that women should wear perfume wherever they hoped to be kissed. Today Chanel No. 5 sells a bottle every 30 seconds. Recently, it has been marketed as a spray with two refills in an effort to have it recognized as an essential everyday finishing touch rather than a precious scent to be used sparingly.

Using the Case Study in the Text

Any Color, So Long as It's Black (text page 325)

Ask students:

1. Why did Henry Ford offer only one style of cars in the early 1900s? (He wanted to maximize the firm's economies of scale and reduce per unit cost.)
2. How was General Motors able to challenge Ford's dominance? (By offering cars of differing styles and colors, which appealed to customer tastes.)

Activity

What's in a Name? (3–5 minutes)

Pair students and ask them to write down what comes to mind when they hear the following brand names. Ask whether the products are worth their higher price. Why do consumers buy brand names?

> Tiffany jewelry
>
> Porsche car
>
> Nike athletic shoes
>
> Häagen-Dazs ice cream
>
> Tommy Hilfiger clothing

In the News

Use the following table to provoke a discussion about the value of a brand name.

The World's Ten Most Valuable Brands

Rank	Brand	2003 brand value (US$ in billions)
1	Coca-Cola	70.45
2	Microsoft	65.17
3	IBM	51.77
4	GE	42.34
5	Intel	31.11
6	Nokia	29.44
7	Disney	28.04
8	McDonald's	24.70
9	Marlboro	22.18
10	Mercedes	21.37

(Source: http://strategis.ic.gc.ca/sc_mrksv/cipo/tm/whtname-e.html#3.)

chapter 13

International Trade

Chapter Objectives

Students will learn in this chapter:
- The sources of international comparative advantage.
- Who gains and loses from international trade, and why the gains exceed the losses.
- How tariffs and import quotas cause inefficiency and reduce total surplus.
- Why governments often engage in trade protection to shelter domestic industries from imports, and how international trade agreements counteract this.

Chapter Outline

Opening Example: Roses sold for Valentine's Day in the United States are produced almost exclusively in Colombia and flown in. This example emphasizes the importance of international trade for all nations. It also hints at the question of whether trade benefits everyone.

I. Comparative Advantage and International Trade

   A. Imports, exports, and comparative advantage

      1. *Definition:* Goods and services purchased from other countries are **imports;** goods and services sold to other countries are **exports.**

      2. A country has a comparative advantage in producing a good if the opportunity cost of producing the good is lower for that country than for other countries.

      3. International trade allows each country to specialize in producing the good in which it has a comparative advantage. That leads to gains for both when they trade.

      4. The Pitfalls on text page 332 deals with the pauper labor fallacy: the argument that importing goods produced by "pauper labor" reduces the standard of living in the United States. The key to this misconception is the confusion between comparative advantage and absolute advantage.

   B. Sources of comparative advantage

      1. Differences in climate. For example, tropical countries grow and export tropical products such as coffee, sugar, and bananas, whereas countries in temperate zones export crops such as wheat and corn.

      2. Differences in factor endowments

         a. *Definition:* The **factor intensity** of production of a good is a measure of which factor is used in relatively greater quantities than other factors in production.

         b. *Definition:* According to the **Heckscher–Ohlin model,** a country has a comparative advantage in a good whose production is intensive in the factors that are abundantly available in that country.

c. The opportunity cost of a given factor is low for a country that possesses an abundance of that factor.

d. International specialization of production is often incomplete: Countries often maintain some domestic production of a good that they import.

3. Differences in technology. Superior production techniques can lead to comparative advantages, though it is somewhat mysterious why technology differs between countries.

II. Supply, Demand, and International Trade

A. The effects of imports

1. *Definition:* The **domestic demand curve** shows how the quantity of a good demanded by domestic consumers depends on the price of that good.

2. *Definition:* The **domestic supply curve** shows how the quantity of a good supplied by domestic producers depends on the price of that good.

3. *Definition:* **Autarky** is a situation in which a country cannot trade with other countries.

4. In autarky, the equilibrium in a market is determined by the intersection of the domestic demand and domestic supply curves.

5. *Definition:* The **world price** of a good is the price at which that good can be bought or sold abroad.

6. As a result of imports, domestic consumers gain and domestic producers lose, but the gain to consumers exceeds the loss to producers. This is illustrated in text Figure 13-4, shown on the next page.

7. Note that although a country as a whole gains from trade, some groups lose.

B. The effects of exports

1. Exports also lead to an overall gain in total surplus for the exporting country.

The Effects of Imports on Surplus

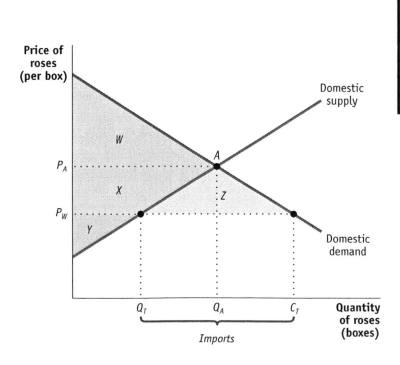

	Changes in surplus	
	Gain	Loss
Consumer surplus	$X + Z$	
Producer surplus		$- X$
Change in total surplus	**+Z**	

2. As a result of exports, domestic consumers lose and domestic producers gain, but the gain to producers exceeds the loss to consumers. This is illustrated in text Figure 13-6, shown below.

C. International trade and factor markets

1. International trade tends to raise the prices of factors that are abundantly available and reduce the prices of factors that are scarce.

The Effects of Exports on Surplus

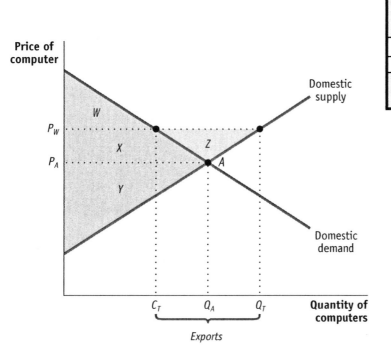

	Changes in surplus	
	Gain	Loss
Consumer surplus		– X
Producer surplus	X + Z	
Change in total surplus	**+Z**	

2. *Definition:* **Exporting industries** produce goods and services that are sold abroad.

3. *Definition:* **Import-competing industries** produce goods and services that are also imported.

4. U.S. exports tend to be human-capital-intensive and U.S. imports tend to be unskilled-labor-intensive. This suggests that international trade raises the wage rate of highly-educated workers and reduces the wage rate of unskilled workers in the United States.

III. The Effects of Trade Protection

A. The effects of a tariff

1. *Definition:* An economy has **free trade** when the government does not attempt either to reduce or to increase the levels of exports and imports that occur naturally as a result of supply and demand.

2. *Definition:* Policies that limit imports are known as **trade protection** or simply as **protection.**

3. *Definition:* A **tariff** is a tax levied on imports.

4. In the past, tariffs were an important source of government revenue because they were relatively easy to collect.

5. Today, tariffs are usually intended to discourage imports and protect import-competing domestic producers.

6. Tariffs raise both the price received by domestic producers and the price paid by domestic consumers.

7. With a tariff, producers gain, consumers lose, and the government gains, but consumer losses are greater than the sum of producer and government gains. There is a net reduction in total surplus. This is illustrated in text Figure 13-8, shown below.

A Tariff Reduces Total Surplus

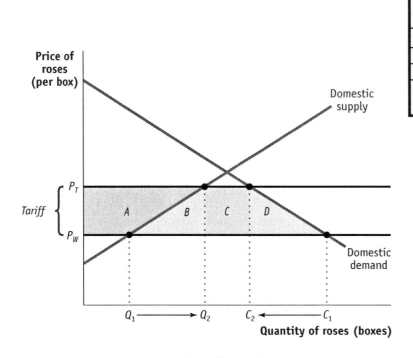

	Changes in surplus	
	Gain	Loss
Consumer surplus		$-(A + B + C + D)$
Producer surplus	A	
Government revenue	C	
Change in total surplus		$-(B + D)$

B. The effects of an import quota

1. *Definition:* An **import quota** is a legal limit on the quantity of a good that can be imported.

2. Import quotas are similar to tariffs, except that the money that would otherwise have been government revenue becomes quota rents to license-holders.

IV. The Political Economy of Trade Protection

A. Arguments for Trade Protection

1. There are three common arguments for trade protection.
   a. *National security:* Overseas sources of crucial goods such as oil are vulnerable to disruption, so a country should be self-sufficient in these goods.
   b. *Job creation:* Import-competing industries create jobs.
   c. *Infant industry argument:* New industries need a temporary period of trade protection to become established.

B. The politics of trade protection

1. Much trade protection has little to do with the above arguments.

2. Trade protection usually reflects the political influence of import-competing producers.

3. Producers are usually a smaller and more cohesive body than the consumers who lose from trade restrictions. Thus, producers wield more political influence.

C. International trade agreements and the World Trade Organization

1. Trade protection hurts domestic consumers and foreign export industries. Therefore, countries care about each others' trade policies.

2. *Definition:* **International trade agreements** are treaties in which a country promises to engage in less trade protection against the exports of other countries in return for a promise by other countries to do the same for its own exports.

3. *Definition:* The **World Trade Organization** oversees international trade agreements and rules on disputes between countries over those agreements.

Teaching Tips

Comparative Advantage and International Trade

Creating Student Interest

Ask students if they are aware of how many imports they purchase.

Ask students why they did not grow and produce their own breakfast. Why does it make sense to purchase a product from someone who specializes in the production of that product?

Common Student Misunderstandings

Students are often confused about the difference between absolute advantage and comparative advantage. Explain that absolute advantage refers to which country has the ability to produce more of a good with the same amount of inputs, and comparative advantage refers to which country has the lower opportunity costs of producing a product.

Presenting the Material

Ask students to recall the real world example regarding the production of computers in the United States, the production of roses in Colombia, and trade of these goods between these countries. Explain that this scenario illustrates the concept of comparative advantage. Also emphasize the various sources of comparative advantage:

- differences in climate
- differences in factor endowments
- differences in technology

Using the Case Study in the Text

The Comparative Advantage of the United States (text pages 334–335)

Ask students:

1. What was the "Leontief paradox"? (Many economists assumed that because the United States is capital intensive in its production of goods, its exports would be capital intensive. Leontief found that this was not true; U.S. exported goods had a slightly lower capital-to-labor ratio than the goods it imported.)

2. How is this paradox explained? (It depends on the definition of capital. U.S. exports use more human capital than physical capital in their production.)

Activity

Who Has the Comparative Advantage? (10 minutes)

For this activity, ask students to bring extra sheets of white paper and a textbook. Pair students and tell them you are going to test for comparative advantage in their ability to turn pages and fold paper with one hand only. Tell students that you are going to set the timer for 1 minute; during that time, one student in the pair folds as many sheets of paper as he or she can with one hand. Then set the timer for the same student to turn book pages with one hand. Finally, time the other student on both tasks.

Ask students to set up a table that will help them calculate which of them has the comparative advantage in paper folding and which has the comparative advantage in page turning (the quantities in the table are hypothetical).

Student	Paper folding per minute	Page turning per minute
Student A	5	10
Student B	7	15

Supply, Demand, and International Trade

Creating Student Interest

Ask students why Americans buy so many clothing items produced in China. What have these imports done to the price of clothing generally?

Common Student Misunderstandings

Students may be unclear about what the autarky price means in the context of this section of the chapter. Explain that this is the domestic price that prevails in the absence of trade.

Students may be confused about adding up the areas of consumer and producer surplus and deriving total surplus, as in text Figure 13-4 and shown in this manual's Outline. Use the graph and the table in Figure 13-4 to show how this is done.

Students may not understand why there are the welfare gains to trade, as described in this section. In the case of imports, the gains to consumer surplus exceed the welfare losses to domestic producers. In the case of exports, producer surplus gains exceed the loss of domestic consumer surplus.

Presenting the Material

To explain the *impact of imports* on domestic supply and demand, guide students through the logical steps below. Assuming that the world price is below the domestic price, ask:
- If the world price is below the domestic price, what do imports do to the domestic supply of roses? (The domestic supply decreases but the total supply increases)
- What does the increased supply of imported roses do to the domestic price of roses? (It causes it to fall.)
- What does the lower price do to domestic producers' incentive to produce? (They have less incentive to produce.)
- What does a lower price do to the quantity demanded by domestic consumers? (The quantity demanded increases.)

- Does the amount of consumer surplus increase or decrease? (It increases.)
- What happens to domestic producer surplus? (It falls.)

To explain the *impact of exports* on domestic supply and demand, guide students through the logical steps below. Assuming that the world price is higher than the domestic price, ask:
- If the world price is higher than the domestic price, what will domestic producers want to do? (Export and earn the world price.)
- What does the quantity exported do to the domestic price? (It increases the domestic price.)
- What does a higher domestic price do to the quantity consumed domestically? (Quantity demanded will fall.)
- What has happened to the domestic consumer surplus? (It has fallen.)
- What has happened to the domestic producer surplus? (It has increased.)

Work It Out

Imports and Total Surplus (text page 340)
In this numerical example students are asked to use graphs depicting a domestic market for grapes to determine the value of the following:

- consumer surplus in autarky
- producer surplus in autarky
- total surplus in autarky
- imports
- domestic consumer surplus with world trade
- domestic producer surplus with world trade
- change in domestic total surplus as a result of world trade

Using the Case Study in the Text

Trade, Wages, and Land Prices in the Nineteenth Century (text page 341)
Ask students:
1. What triggered the explosion of international trade after the 1870s? (The invention of the steam engine and the expansion of railroads.)
2. What happened to the price of agricultural products in land intensive countries? (Agricultural exports reduced the domestic supply and caused the price to rise.)
3. What happened to the price of land in England? (It fell as agricultural imports increased.)
4. Who were the winners and losers from this change? (Workers in Europe enjoyed cheaper food and landowners were hurt by falling land prices.)

Activities

What Jobs Are Lost? (5–10 minutes)
Trade negatively affects import-competing industries and helps exporting industries. Pair students and ask them to identify three import-competing industries and three exporting industries in the United States. (Import-competing industries include textiles, shoes, and toy production. Exporting industries include computers, telecommunications equipment, and software.)

Imported Sweets? (3–5 minutes)

Pair students and tell them to assume that the world price of sugar is lower than the domestic price of sugar. Assume that there are no barriers to trade. What will happen to consumers and producers of sugar in the domestic market? (Buyers of sugar will import the cheaper sugar from abroad. Domestic producers of sugar will have less incentive to produce sugar as the domestic price falls to world levels.)

Effects of Trade Protection

Creating Student Interest

Ask students: If free trade has so many advantages, why do countries impose tariffs?

Common Student Misunderstandings

Students think that protectionist measures do not have reciprocal effects. Explain that U.S. tariffs can trigger retaliation from its trading partners. Trade wars can reduce exports and hurt economic growth.

Presenting the Material

Before illustrating the impact of a tariff with a supply and demand graph, ask students to track the impact of a tariff. Assume that the world price of steel is lower than the domestic price of steel.

A tariff will:
- Decrease the quantity of imported steel.
- Raise the domestic price of the steel.
- Reduce the quantity demanded by steel buyers.
- Increase the profits of domestic producers of steel.
- Increase employment in the domestic steel industry.
- Generate consumer losses that exceed producer and government gains.

Using the Case Study in the Text

Trade Protection in the United States (text pages 344–345)

Ask students:

1. On what two markets does the United States enact trade barriers? (Agricultural products and textiles.)
2. Does the United States have a comparative advantage in these industries? (No.)
3. How do foreign producers earn quota rents? (The United States awards import quota rights, and these rights are resold to other countries.)

Activities

A Sugar Quota (5–10 minutes)

Pair students and ask them to brainstorm the effects of one of the oldest protectionist measures in the United States: sugar quotas. Explain that Caribbean countries have a comparative advantage in the production of sugar, yet we block their imports. Ask students to consider the impact of the quota on sugar on consumers and producers in the United States. (Sugar prices in the United States are twice the world level.) How would doing away with sugar quotas help poor countries? (They gain income from exporting products for which they have a comparative advantage.)

What's the Price of a Tariff? (3–5 minutes)
Pair students and present the following scenario: The United States imposes a tariff on imported Canadian lumber on the grounds that Canadian firms "dumped" lumber in the United States below unit costs. Ask the pairs of students how the tariff will affect consumers and producers in the United States.

The Political Economy of Trade Protection

Creating Student Interest
Ask students why there are protests at every meeting of the World Trade Organization.

Workers in the flower market in Colombia are exposed to 27 different types of pesticides. Ask students if we can improve their working conditions by refusing to buy imported flowers.

Common Student Misunderstandings
Students think that trade hurts all American jobs. Make the distinction between import-competing industries, where jobs are lost, and exporting industries, where jobs are added as a result of trade.

Many students believe that global corporations exploit labor in the countries where they hire labor. The text argues that most of these jobs pay relatively higher wages than the prevailing domestic wages.

Presenting the Material
Discuss the rationale for trade protection and talk about the weaknesses of each of these arguments.

Arguments for protection	Problems with protectionist arguments
1. *National security*. The United States does not want to depend on an import that is necessary for national defense.	Some industries, such as sugar, have argued for protection based on national security grounds, a clearly spurious argument.
2. *Job Creation*. The United States wants to limit the number of jobs lost to trade.	Jobs lost in import-competing industries are offset by job gains in export-competing industries. Countries often retaliate against a tariff by enacting tariffs on American goods.
3. *Infant industries*. Some industries need protecting until they are more fully developed and ready to compete in global trade.	It is difficult to determine when an industry emerges from an "infant" position.

Using the Case Study in the Text

Declining Tariffs (text page 347)
Ask students:
1. When did U.S. tariffs peak? (They peaked in the 1930s after the passage of the Smoot-Hawley law in 1930.)
2. What has happened to U.S. tariffs since the 1930s? (They have fallen continuously.)
3. In terms of global trade, what types of products still have high tariffs on them? (Agricultural goods reflecting the lobbying clout of farmers.)

Activities

Pick a Trade Dispute (5–10 minutes)

Ask students to visit the World Trade Organization's website at www.wto.org (on the left of the screen under "Trade Topics" click on "Disputes") and investigate a current trade dispute. What countries and products are involved in the dispute? Pair students and ask them to share their findings with their partner and ask a few to report to the whole class.

Sweatshop Labor (5–10 minutes)

Cooperative Controversy (Warning: this can be a very controversial issue, and you may want to caution students to be open to all opinions): Divide the class in half and have one side take the pro position and the other take the con position on the following proposition: Should your college or university sell imported clothing items made in unhealthy and unsafe working environments? Assume that these clothing items are priced cheaper than comparable items produced in the United States. Then form pairs on each side of the issue. Have a pro pair join a con pair to share their arguments.

chapter 14

Macroeconomics:
The Big Picture

Chapter Objectives

Students will learn in this chapter:

- The definition of macroeconomics and get an overview of the economy as a whole.
- How macroeconomics differs from microeconomics and that what is good for the part is not necessarily good for the whole.
- The importance of the business cycle and why policy makers seek to diminish the severity of business cycles.
- The difference between nominal and real variables.
- How unemployment rates are calculated.
- The definitions of inflation and deflation.
- Why policy makers and economists prefer price stability in the macroeconomy.

Chapter Outline

Opening Example: A comparison of starting salaries of new MBA graduates from top business schools in 2000, 2002, and 2004 reveals the effect the business cycle had on the job market. Starting salaries for new MBAs were highest in 2000, when the economy was expanding, and lowest in 2002, when the economy was considerably weaker.

I. Microeconomics Versus Macroeconomics

    A. *Definition:* **Macroeconomics** is the area of economics that focuses on the behavior of the economy as a whole.

    B. *Definition:* **Microeconomics** is concerned with the production and consumption decisions of consumers and producers and with the allocation of scarce resources among industries.

    C. In the short run—a period consisting of several years but typically less than a decade—the combined effect of individual (microeconomic) decisions can have effects on the macroeconomy that are very different from what any one individual intended. Thus, macroeconomics is not simply the aggregate outcome of all microeconomic choices.

    D. Most economists agree that, except for a very limited number of specific cases, government intervention in markets at the microeconomic level usually leaves society worse off.

    E. Economists typically believe there is a much wider role for the government to play in the macroeconomy, especially in managing short-term fluctuations and adverse events in the economy. This view dates back to the Great Depression of the 1930s.

    F. *Definition:* **Economic aggregates** are economic measures that summarize data across different markets for goods, services, workers, and assets.

II. **The Business Cycle**

    A. *Definition:* The **business cycle** is the short-run alternation between economic downturns, known as recessions, and economic upturns, known as expansions.

        1. The average length of time of the business cycle, from the beginning of a recession to the beginning of the next recession, has been 5 years and 7 months.

        2. Since World War II there have been 10 recessions in the United States, with the average recession lasting 10 months and the average expansion lasting 57 months.

    B. *Definition:* A **depression** is a very deep and prolonged economic downturn.

    C. *Definition:* **Recessions** are periods of economic downturns when output and employment are falling.

    D. *Definition:* **Expansions**, or recoveries, are periods of economic upturns when output and employment are rising.

    E. Employment and unemployment

        1. *Definition:* **Employment** is the number of people currently employed in the economy.

        2. *Definition:* **Unemployment** is the number of people who are actively looking for work but aren't currently employed. The monthly unemployment rate from 1948 to 2004 is illustrated in Figure 14-2 on page 358 of the text.

        3. *Definition:* The **labor force** is equal to the sum of employment and unemployment.

        4. *Definition:* **Discouraged workers** are nonworking people who are capable of working but have given up looking for a job.

        5. *Definition:* The **unemployment rate** is the percentage of the total number of people in the labor force who are unemployed.

$$\text{Unemployment rate} = \frac{\text{Number of unemployed workers}}{\text{Number of unemployed workers} + \text{Number of employed workers}} \times 100$$

        6. *Definition:* **Underemployment** is the number of people who work during a recession but receive lower wages than they would during an expansion due to fewer number of hours worked, lower-paying jobs, or both.

    F. *Definition:* **Aggregate output** is the economy's total production of final goods and services for a given period.

    G. Taming the business cycle

        1. *Definition:* Policy efforts undertaken to reduce the severity of recessions and rein in excessively strong expansions are called **stabilization policy.**

2. *Definition*: **Monetary policy** is a type of stabilization policy that involves changes in the quantity of money in circulation or in interest rates, or both.

3. *Definition*: **Fiscal policy** is a type of stabilization policy that involves changes in taxation, or in government spending, or both.

4. Policy makers have developed methods for preventing another Great Depression from occurring; however, they have not been able to completely control the business cycle.

III.   Inflation and Deflation

A. *Definition*: A **nominal** measure is a measure that has not been adjusted for changes in prices over time.

B. *Definition*: A **real** measure is a measure that has been adjusted for changes in prices over time.

C. *Definition*: The **aggregate price level** is the overall price level for final goods and services in the economy.

D. *Definition*: **Inflation** is a rising aggregate price level.

E. *Definition*: **Deflation** is a falling aggregate price level.

F. *Definition*: The economy has **price stability** when the aggregate price level is changing only slowly.

G. *Definition*: The **inflation rate** is the annual percent change in the aggregate price level. The annual rate of change in the CPI from 1929 to 2004 is illustrated in Figure 14-6 on page 364 in the text.

Teaching Tips

Microeconomics Versus Macroeconomics

Creating Student Interest

Ask students why they chose to enroll in this course, Macroeconomics, rather than in a Microeconomics class. Afterward, ask those students who have not previously taken any economics classes if they know the difference between microeconomics and macroeconomics and the topics covered in each. List their responses on the board.

Common Student Misunderstandings

Students may feel that a course in microeconomics is a prerequisite for the study of macroeconomics. Emphasize that, especially in the short run, the combined effect of individual (microeconomic) decisions can have effects on the macroeconomy that are very different from what any one individual intended. Thus, macroeconomics is more than simply the aggregate outcome of all microeconomic choices, and one's understanding of macroeconomics does not rely on a prior understanding of microeconomics.

Presenting the Material

Direct students' attention to the Microeconomic Versus Macroeconomic Questions listed in Table 14-2 on page 354 in the text. Have them compare their earlier responses regarding the differences between microeconomics and macroeconomics with the specific questions listed in this table.

Microeconomic Versus Macroeconomic Questions

Microeconomic Questions	Macroeconomic Questions
Should I go to business school or take a job right now?	How many people are employed in the economy as a whole this year?
What determines the salary offered by Citibank to Cherie Camajo, a new Columbia MBA?	What determines the overall salary levels paid to workers in a given year?
What determines the cost to a university or college of offering a new course?	What determines the overall level of prices in the economy as a whole?
What government policies should be adopted to make it easier for low-income students to attend college?	What government policies should be adopted to promote employment and growth in the economy as a whole?

Using the Case Study in the Text

The Great Depression (text pages 356–357)

Ask students:

1. When did the Great Depression occur and which countries were affected by this event? (Answer: The Great Depression began in 1929 and lasted through the 1930s. The impact of the Great Depression was felt in virtually all of the world's market economies.)

2. What impact did the Great Depression have on the development of macroeconomic theory? (Answer: Modern macroeconomic theory developed in response to the economic events of the Great Depression, in particular, focusing on how the business cycle can be controlled to prevent such an event from happening again.)

3. How did the Great Depression affect people living in the United States at that time? (Answer: The unemployment rate rose to nearly 25%, which caused many people to lose their homes and rely on soup kitchens and other forms of charity to survive.)

4. Who is John Maynard Keynes and what influence did he have in the development of modern macroeconomic theory? (Answer: John Maynard Keynes was a British economist whose seminal work, *The General Theory of Employment, Interest, and Money* was published in 1936. In his book, Keynes advocated an active role for government in maintaining economic stability and growth. His theories have greatly influenced countless economists and policy makers over the decades.)

Activity

Thinking Like an Economist (10 minutes)

Explain to students that three important topics of interest to economists are:

- employment
- prices
- output

Pair students and ask them to develop one microeconomic statement and one macro-economic statement dealing with each of the three topics just listed. Possible answers may include:

- Microeconomic Employment Statement: Steve worked at the local General Motors plant for 20 years, but he was recently laid off from his job.
- Macroeconomic Employment Statement: The unemployment rate in the United States rose to 24.9% during the Great Depression.
- Microeconomic Price Statement: When the price of a gallon of gasoline reached $3.00, Randy started to carpool with his friend to school.
- Macroeconomic Price Statement: The rate of inflation in the United States rose to 3.9% in September 2005 due to higher energy prices.
- Microeconomic Output Statement: An Iowa soybean farmer saw his output drop due to a severe drought.
- Macroeconomic Output Statement: Following the Great Depression, total output did not rise above its 1929 level until 1937.

The Business Cycle

Creating Student Interest

Ask students if they have ever heard of the term recession. Afterward, ask any responders if they can describe what occurs during a recession. Finally, ask students if the economy is currently in a recession. On what evidence did they base their answer to this question?

Common Student Misunderstandings

Students may think that all recessions (or expansions) are the same in terms of duration and severity. This misconception can be displaced by referring to Figure 14-2 on page 358 in the text which shows differently sized shaded bands for periods during which the U.S. economy was in a recession and, hence, the unemployment rate was rising.

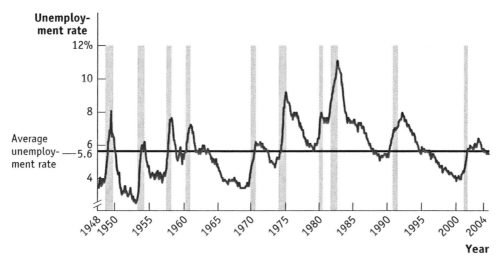

The Unemployment Rate and Recessions Since 1948

Presenting the Material

Begin teaching this section using the following hypothetical figure of the business cycle. By your starting the discussion with this relatively simple graph, students will be more inclined to absorb all of the associated definitions, i.e., recession, depression, expansion, and peak.

Hypothetical Business Cycle

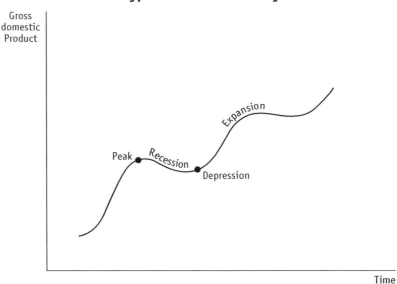

Using the Case Study in the Text

Has the Business Cycle Been Tamed? (text pages 361–362)

Ask students:

1. What tools can policy makers use to affect the state of the business cycle? (Answer: Policy makers can use either monetary or fiscal policies to affect the state of the business cycle.)

2. How successful have policy makers been in controlling the U.S. business cycle since the Great Depression? (Answer: Policy makers have been very successful in controlling the U.S. business cycle so that no economic downturn as severe as the Great Depression has occurred. However, occasional recessions, such as the one in 2001, still do take place.)

Activities

Numbers Game (5–10 minutes)

Provide students with the following data:

Number of people employed	120,500
Number of people unemployed	4,050

Ask students to compute:

1. The number of people in the labor force.
   (Answer: 4,050 + 120,500 = 124,550)

2. The unemployment rate.
   (Answer: (4,050/(4,050+120,500) $\times$ 100) = 3.25%)

What Can Policy Makers Do? (15 minutes)

Pair students and ask them to answer the following questions.

1. What are stabilization policies?
2. Describe two types of stabilization policy.

Answers:

1. Stabilization policies are efforts undertaken to reduce the severity of recessions and to rein in the excessively strong expansions in the economy.
2. Two types of stabilization policies are fiscal policy, which involves changes in government spending and/or taxes to affect the state of the macroeconomy, and monetary policy, which involves changes in the quantity of money in circulation and/or changes in interest rates to affect the state of the macroeconomy.

Inflation and Deflation

Creating Student Interest

Ask students if their grandparents (or even parents) are surprised by the cost of things that students buy today, e.g., tuition, books. Similarly, relate to students how much you paid for your first car and when you bought it. Compare this amount with the cost of a similar car today. Indicate that the difference in price of these comparable cars is largely due to inflation.

Common Student Misunderstandings

Since it is far more common for people to relate to the effects inflation, some students are not aware that the average price level can actually fall. You can dispel this myth by directing students' attention to Figure 14-6 on page 364 in the text which shows periods of deflation during the late 1920s and early 1930s.

Presenting the Material

First define the terms inflation and deflation and the negative impacts each can have on an economy. Also stress that these are measures of changes in the *aggregate* level of prices in the economy, and not necessarily reflective of the changes in the price of any one specific good. Afterward, discuss the importance of price stability in an economy for achieving long-run economic growth.

Using the Case Study in the Text

A Fast (Food) Measure of Inflation (text page 364)

Students will enjoy discussing this case study because it relates the concept of inflation to one of their most common purchases. Ask students why McDonald's chose to cut the price of their hamburgers in 1997. (Answer: This was in response to decreases in the rate of inflation, which undoubtedly led to lower costs for McDonald's, thus justifying the choice to lower the price of their hamburgers.)

Activity

Differences in Price Changes (10–15 minutes)

Pair students and ask if the nominal prices of the following goods or services have increased or decreased over the past 10 years.

Personal Computer	(Answer: decreased)
First Class Postage Stamp	(Answer: increased)
Internet Service	(Answer: decreased)
College Tuition	(Answer: increased)
T.V. Guide Magazine	(Answer: increased)

chapter 15

Tracking the Macroeconomy

Chapter Objectives

Students will learn in this chapter:

- How economists use aggregate measures to track the performance of the economy.
- What gross domestic product, or GDP, is and the three ways of calculating it.
- The difference between real GDP and nominal GDP and why real GDP is the appropriate measure of real economic activity.
- The significance of the unemployment rate and how it moves over the business cycle.
- What a price index is and how it is used to calculate the inflation rate.
- What some of the specific price indexes are and how economists use them.

Chapter Outline

Opening Example: Using an historical perspective of the tumultuous Portuguese economy in the mid-1970s, the example illustrates the importance of collecting and analyzing accurate data on the macroeconomy before instituting any economic or social policy measures.

I. The National Accounts

  A. In the United States, the Bureau of Economic Analysis—a division of the Commerce Department—collects and calculates various types of economic data and compiles them in the national product and income accounts.

  B. *Definition*: The **national income and product accounts,** or **national accounts,** keep track of the flow of money between different sectors of the economy.

  C. The expanded circular flow diagram, shown in Figure 15-1 on page 369 in the text, illustrates the flow of funds through the four sectors of the economy—households, firms, government, and the rest of the world—via three types of markets—factor markets, markets for goods and services, and financial markets.

  D. Households

   1. *Definition*: **Consumer spending** is household spending on goods and services.

   2. Most households receive the majority of their income from wages. However, some households also receive income from the ownership of stocks and bonds, which generate profit and interest income, respectively.

3. *Definition:* A **stock** is a share in the ownership of a company held by a shareholder.

4. *Definition:* A **bond** is borrowing in the form of an IOU that pays interest.

5. *Definition:* **Government transfers** are payments by the government to individuals for which no good or service is provided in return.

6. *Definition:* **Disposable income,** equal to income plus government transfers minus taxes, is the total amount of household income available to spend on consumption and savings.

7. *Definition:* **Private savings,** equal to disposable income minus consumer spending, is disposable income that is not spent on consumption.

8. The total sum of flows of money out of households—the sum of taxes paid, consumer spending, and private savings—must equal the total flow of money into households—the sum of wages, profits, interest, rent, and government transfers.

E. *Definition:* The banking, stock, and bond markets, which channel private savings and foreign lending into investment spending, government borrowing, and foreign borrowing, are known as the **financial markets.**

F. Government

1. *Definition:* **Government borrowing** is the amount of funds borrowed by the government in the financial markets.

2. *Definition:* **Government purchases of goods and services** are government expenditures on goods and services.

G. International Sector

1. *Definition:* **Exports** are goods and services sold to residents of other countries.

2. *Definition:* **Imports** are goods and services purchased by residents of other countries.

3. *Definition:* **Net exports** are the difference between the value of exports and the value of imports.

H. Business Investment

1. *Definition:* **Investment spending** is spending on productive physical capital, such as machinery and construction of structures, and on changes to inventories.

I. Final Goods Versus Intermediate Goods

1. *Definition:* **Final goods and services** are goods and services sold to the final, or end, user.

2. *Definition:* **Intermediate goods and services** are goods and services—bought from one firm by another firm—that are inputs for production of final goods and services.

J. Gross Domestic Product

1. *Definition:* **Gross domestic product,** or **GDP,** is the total value of all final goods and services produced in the economy during a given year.

2. GDP is used as a measure of the size of an economy and can also be used to compare the economic performance in other countries.

3. In 2004, the GDP of the United States was $11,734 billion.

4. There are three ways to measure GDP:
   - As the value of production of final goods and services.
   - As spending on domestically produced final goods and services.
   - As factor income earned from firms in the economy.

5. *Definition*: **Aggregate spending,** the sum of consumer spending, investment spending, government purchases, and exports minus imports, is the total spending on domestically produced final goods and services in the economy.

K. Measuring GDP as the value of production of final goods and services

1. GDP is calculated by summing the value of all final goods and services produced in an economy in a given year.

2. The value of intermediate goods is omitted from this calculation of GDP. This is because if the value of intermediate goods is included, this would result in double-counting or more, since the value of intermediate goods is already included in the value of final goods. For example, the value of the steel produced that is used in an automobile is not counted in GDP since this is an intermediate good. However, the value of this steel adds to the value of the automobile, a final good, which is included in GDP.

3. *Definition*: The **value added** of a producer is the value of its sales minus the value of its purchases of inputs.

4. An alternative approach to computing GDP is to sum the value added by all firms.

5. To avoid double-counting, only each producer's value added is counted in the calculation of GDP.

L. Measuring GDP as spending on domestically produced final goods and services

1. GDP is calculated by summing spending on all final goods and services by all sectors of the economy—households (C), businesses (I), governments (G), and foreigners (X)—are added together and spending on imports (IM) is subtracted.

2. Mathematically stated:

$$GDP = C + I + G + X - IM$$

M. Measuring GDP as factor income earned from firms in the economy

1. GDP is calculated by adding all of the income earned by factors of production from firms in the economy. This includes:
   - Wages earned by labor
   - Interest earned by those who lend their savings to firms and the government
   - Rent earned by those who lease their land or structures to firms
   - Profit earned by the owners of capital

N. The components of GDP spending in 2004 included:

1. Consumer spending: $8,229 billion, or 70.1% of GDP

2. Government spending: $2,184 billion, or 18.6% of GDP

3. Investment spending: $1,927 billion, or 16.4% of GDP

4. Net Exports: –$607 billion, or –5.2% of GDP

   The components of GDP are illustrated in Figure 15-3 on page 376 in the text.

III. Real GDP and Aggregate Output

A. *Definition*: **Real GDP** is the total value of all final goods and services produced in the economy during a given year, calculated using the prices of a selected base year.

B. *Definition*: **Nominal GDP** is the value of all final goods and services produced in the economy during a given year, calculated using the prices current in the year in which the output is produced.

C. To determine the actual growth in aggregate output, we calculate the change in real GDP using prices from some given base year, as in the following:

$$\text{Growth in real GDP} = \frac{\text{Real GDP in year 2} - \text{Real GDP in year 1}}{\text{Real GDP in year 1}}$$

D. *Definition*: **GDP per capita** is GDP divided by the size of the population; it is equivalent to the average GDP per person.

$$\text{GDP per capita} = \frac{\text{GDP}}{\text{size of the population}}$$

E. Real per capita GDP is not a sufficient measure of human welfare or the quality of life, which also depends on how the GDP is spent.

III.   The Unemployment Rate

A. The unemployment rate is an indicator of the state of the labor market.

B. The unemployment rate can overstate the true level of unemployment because it is normal for workers to spend some time searching for a job even when jobs are plentiful.

C. The unemployment rate can also understate the true level of unemployment because it doesn't include the percentage of frustrated workers who can't find jobs, also known as discouraged workers.

D. The unemployment rate can vary widely across different age, gender, and racial groups. This is shown in Figure 15-5 on page 382 of the text.

E. There is a strong inverse relationship between growth in real GDP and changes in the unemployment rate. This inverse relationship is illustrated using actual data shown in Figure 15-6 on page 383 in the text.

IV.   Price Indexes and the Aggregate Price Level

A. *Definition*: A **market basket** is a hypothetical set of consumer purchases of goods and services.

B. *Definition*: A **price index** measures the cost of purchasing a given market basket in a given year, where that cost is normalized so that it is equal to 100 in the selected base year.

C. Formula for price index:

$$\text{Price index in a given year} = \frac{\text{(Cost of market basket in a given year)}}{\text{(Cost of market basket in base year)}} \times 100$$

D. *Definition*: The **inflation rate** is the percent change per year in a price index— typically, the consumer price index.

E. The inflation rate from year 1 to year 2 is computed as:

$$\text{Inflation rate} = \frac{\text{(Price index in year 2)} - \text{(Price index in year 1)}}{\text{(Price index in year 1)}} \times 100$$

F. There are three measures of prices in the macroeconomy including:
- The Consumer Price Index, or CPI
- The Producer Price Index, or PPI
- The GDP Deflator

G. *Definition*: The **consumer price index,** or **CPI,** measures the cost of the market basket of a typical urban American family.

H. *Definition*: The **producer price index,** or **PPI,** measures changes in the prices of goods purchased by producers.

I. *Definition*: The **GDP deflator** for a given year is 100 times the ratio of nominal GDP to real GDP in that year.

Teaching Tips

The National Accounts

Creating Student Interest

Ask students if they have heard the term Gross Domestic Product and if they know what is included in GDP. Since the term is quite specific regarding what is counted in GDP, immediately correct any errors presented by students and write the exact definition of this term on the board. Explain that GDP is generally used as a measure of aggregate economic activity, especially in developed countries.

Common Student Misunderstandings

Because GDP can be calculated three different ways—summing income earned, summing expenditures, and summing the value of production—students may mistakenly believe that these three methods yield different values for GDP in a given period. Emphasize to students that this is not the case, because ultimately the value of all final goods and services produced must equal the value of income earned in the production of all final goods and services in a given year.

Presenting the Material

Figure 15-1 on page 369 of the text, The Expanded Circular-Flow Diagram: The Flows of Money through the Economy, demonstrates the manner in which money flows from producers to households, governments, and the rest of the world, and vice versa. Since this figure is quite complex at first glance to students, break up the elements in the diagram and describe them individually. First, identify the major economic agents—households, firms, governments, and the rest of the world—and the markets—product markets, factor markets, and financial markets. Afterward, concentrate on the flows of money, using the arrows in the diagram on the next page.

**An Expanded Circular-Flow Diagram:
The Flows of Money Through the Economy**

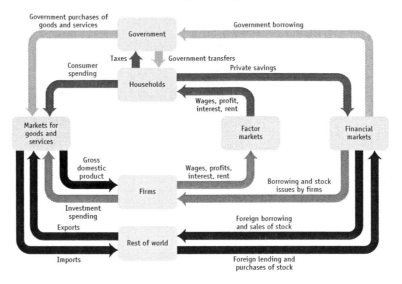

Using the Case Study in the Text

Creating the National Accounts (text page 377)

Ask students the following questions:

1. Who created the original national income accounts and when did this occur? (Answer: Russian-born economist Simon Kuznets, working with the U.S. Department of Commerce, developed the national income accounts following the Great Depression and presented the first version of these data in 1937.)

2. How were the original national income accounts later revised? (Answer: During World War II, policy makers had a greater need for more comprehensive production data. Thus, the national income accounts were expanded to provide estimates of gross domestic product and gross national product in 1942.)

Activities

What's In and What's Out? (15 minutes)

Pair students and ask them to categorize the following items as either included in the calculation of GDP or excluded from it. Also ask students to indicate the reason for their choice in each case.

- Hamburger buns bought by McDonald's Corporation for making Big Macs (Answer: Excluded from GDP since they constitute an intermediate good.)
- A used macroeconomics textbook (Answer: Excluded from GDP since it is not a newly produced good.)
- A new pair of Levi's jeans (Answer: Included in GDP since it is a newly produced good.)
- Newly purchased shares of Google stock (Answer: Excluded from GDP since they are not a good or service that is produced.)
- A new Chrysler P.T. Cruiser automobile (Answer: Included in GDP since it is a newly produced good.)

- A new Lexus SUV (Answer: Excluded from GDP since it is not a domestically produced good.)
- A newly purchased $10,000 U.S. Treasury Bill (Answer: Excluded from GDP since it is not a good or service that is produced.)
- A cup of coffee purchased at Starbucks (Answer: Included in GDP as it is a newly produced good.)

Who's Spending? (10 minutes)

Ask students to rank, from highest to lowest, the following types of spending comprising GDP:

- Government spending
- Consumer spending
- Business spending
- Net exports

Answer:

- Largest: Consumer spending comprises 70.1% of GDP
- ⠀⠀⠀⠀⠀⠀⠀⠀⠀⠀Government spending comprises 18.6% of GDP
- ⠀⠀⠀⠀⠀⠀⠀⠀⠀⠀Investment spending comprises 16.4% of GDP
- Smallest: Net exports comprises -5.2% of GDP

Real GDP and Aggregate Output

Creating Student Interest

Ask students if the number of goods and services produced per year changes. (Answer: Yes) Ask students if the prices of goods and services change each year. (Answer: Yes) So if, for example, GDP is increasing from one year to another, how can we tell if the reason GDP is rising is due to higher prices or a greater amount of output being produced? Explain to students that this is why we must look at real measures of monetized economic variables, such as GDP, when we compare their values over time.

Common Student Misunderstandings

Since students often think of output in physical terms rather than in monetized terms, they may not immediately see the need for measuring real GDP. Emphasize that all goods and services are measured in monetized terms, so the value of production of all goods and services can be summed together when calculating GDP.

Presenting the Material

Using the data presented in Table 15-1 on page 378 of the text, first show students how to compute nominal GDP for year 1. Next, ask students to compute nominal GDP for year 2 independently. Follow a similar process when computing real GDP for years 1 and 2, assuming year 1 is the base year. Point out the differences in value in nominal and real GDP for year 2.

Calculating GDP and Real GDP in a Simple Economy

	Year 1	Year 2
Quantity of apples (billions)	2,000	2,200
Price of apple	$0.25	$0.30
Quantity of oranges (billions)	1,000	1,200
Price of orange	$0.50	$0.70
GDP (billions of dollars)	$1,000	$1,500
Real GDP (billions of year 1 dollars)	$1,000	$1,150

Using the Case Study in the Text

Good Decades, Bad Decades (text pages 380–381)

Ask students the following questions:

1. What effect did deflation in the period 1929–1939 have on GDP in nominal and real terms? (Answer: During this decade nominal GDP fell by 11%, but real GDP rose by 9.9%.)

2. Why was there a large difference between the rate of growth of real and nominal GDP over the period 1969–1979? (Answer: The large difference in the rates of growth of real and nominal GDP was due to the high rate of inflation that characterized this decade.)

Activities

Calculating Nominal and Real GDP (20 minutes)

Ask students to use the data in the following table, where it is assumed that only two goods, bread and cake, are produced in an economy, and 2004 is the base year.

	2004	2005
Quantity of bread (billions)	5,000	6,000
Price of bread	$2.50	$2.25
Quantity of cake (billions)	1,200	1,150
Price of cake	$4.00	$3.80

Calculate the following:

1. Nominal GDP in 2004 and 2005
2. Real GDP in 2004 and 2005

Answers:

1. Nominal GDP in 2004 = (5,000 × $2.50) + (1,200 × $4.00) = $17,300 billion
   Nominal GDP in 2005 = (6,000 × $2.25) + (1,150 × $3.80) = $17,870 billion
2. Real GDP in 2004 = (5,000 × $2.50) + (1,200 × $4.00) = $17,300 billion
   Real GDP in 2005 = (6,000 × $2.50) + (1,150 × $4.00) = $19,600 billion

Per Capita GDP in LDCs (10 minutes)

Explain to students that a persistent problem plaguing less-developed countries is low per capita GDP. Ask students for ways this problem can be alleviated.

Answers may include:

- Increasing labor productivity, which will lead to greater output and hence higher levels of GDP
- Controlling population growth rates
- Improving the capital stock, which will lead to greater output and hence higher levels of GDP
- Improving the state of technology

In the News

Use this article regarding revised GDP figures to stimulate discussion on the actual measurement of GDP by the U.S. Commerce Department.

Third-Quarter GDP Revised Sharply Higher

By Andrea Hopkins

U.S. economic growth was much stronger in the third quarter than first thought as consumers and businesses spent more than estimated, but Gulf Coast hurricanes sideswiped corporate profits, a government report showed on Wednesday.

U.S. gross domestic product, a measure of all goods and services produced within U.S. borders, grew at a revised 4.3 percent annual rate in the July-to-September period, the fastest pace since the first three months of 2004, the Commerce Department said.

In its first snapshot a month ago, the department had put third-quarter growth at 3.8 percent and Wall Street economists had expected the rate to be revised up more modestly, to 4.0 percent. The sharp upward bump took growth a full point above the second-quarter's 3.3 percent rate.

"Clearly the economy had a good head of steam on it right through the hurricane period," said Alan Ruskin, research director at 4CAST Ltd in New York.

Inflation was a bit lower than first reported, the report showed. The core consumer price index, which strips out volatile food and energy prices and is the Federal Reserve's favored inflation measure, moved up just 1.2 percent, down from the 1.3 percent pace originally reported.

That was the lowest rate of core inflation in more than two years. Economists had expected the price index to be revised higher, and the surprise downward revision suggests Fed policymakers have little to be concerned about on the inflation front.

The dollar gained against the euro on the unexpectedly strong upward revision to growth, while the price of U.S. Treasury bonds rose as the tame inflation data reassured investors the extra spending had not stoked price rises.

SLOWER GROWTH AHEAD

Overall, the report reinforced the view that the U.S. economy is on a solid footing, with tame inflation and strong consumer and business spending. Economists expect growth to cool in the fourth quarter and into 2006, however, as the housing market starts to fade and consumers pull back.

"We still think that the growth rate will slow substantially in the fourth quarter, in part because the housing sector is softening which will tend to soften consumer spending as well. That is one factor that will probably help the Federal Reserve eventually conclude its monetary tightening cycle," said Patrick Fearon, senior economist at A.G. Edwards & Sons in St. Louis.

The Fed has raised short-term interest rates 12 times since mid-2004 in a bid to keep price rises in check, but many analysts suspect the rate-hike campaign is nearing an end.

The report offered the first look at corporate profits in the third quarter. Profits after tax fell 3.7 percent, the largest decline in four years, after a 5.3 percent rise in the second quarter. The Commerce Department said profits were reduced by $151.2 billion at an annual rate because of Hurricanes Katrina and Rita, as insurance companies made huge benefits payments and uninsured corporate property was lost.

The stronger-than-expected GDP growth in the third quarter was attributed to higher spending by both businesses and consumers.

Consumer spending advanced at a robust 4.2 percent pace, above the 3.9 percent rate first reported. While growth in spending on big-ticket items was softer than initially thought, though at a still-booming 10.5 percent pace, purchases of nondurable goods grew 3.6 percent — stronger than the 2.6 percent pace first reported.

Spending on housing, too, was stronger than initially thought. Residential fixed investment grew at an 8.4 percent pace, up from the 4.8 percent growth first reported, after a 10.8 percent growth surge in the second quarter.

Business spending was also robust. Non-residential fixed investment rose at an 8.8 percent pace, above the initially estimated 6.2 percent growth, as spending on equipment and software rose at a 10.8 percent rate, just below the second-quarter's 10.9 percent clip.

While businesses reduced inventories in the third quarter, the drawdown was not as sharp as first thought. Stocks of unsold goods dropped at a $13.4 billion annual rate, slower than the $16.6 billion pace reported a month ago. That was still the largest drop since the fourth quarter of 2001 — after the Sept 11. attacks in New York and on the Pentagon.

Source: Hopkins, Andrea, "Third-Quarter GDP Revised Sharply Higher," online by Reuters News Limited, November 30, 2005.

Questions for Discussion:

1. What is the core consumer price index? (Answer: The core consumer price index is measured by removing any changes in the prices of food and energy from the CPI.)

2. What factors contributed to third-quarter GDP being revised sharply higher in 2005? (Answer: There was stronger than expected growth in consumer spending and business investment during this period, which boosted GDP.)

The Unemployment Rate

Creating Student Interest

Ask students if any have ever been unemployed. Ask any of those who responded "yes" what they had to do to file for unemployment benefits, i.e., the unemployment office representative will ask if the applicant is ready, willing, and able to work, and whether he/she has sought employment. Explain that all these questions are used to categorize an individual as being either unemployed, and therefore eligible for unemployment benefits, employed, or out of the labor force.

Common Student Misunderstandings

Since most students have never filed for unemployment benefits, they may erroneously believe that individuals can collect unemployment whenever they are not working, regardless of the reason. Explain that this is not the case since, for example, workers who are on strike, or are away from their job due to illness or bad weather cannot collect unemployment benefits.

Presenting the Material

The unemployment rate is an indicator of how easy it is for individuals to find a job. It also indicates the potential for lost output, since GDP will generally fall when the unemployment rate rises. This inverse relationship is illustrated in Figure 15-6 on page 383 of the text with a scatter plot of historical data on the real GDP growth rate and the unemployment rate.

The Relationship between Real GDP and Unemployment, 1949–2004

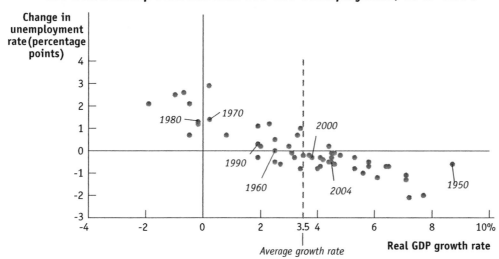

There are some limitations associated with the reported unemployment rate. They include:

- It can overestimate the actual rate of unemployment because some people intentionally do not take the first job they are offered but rather take additional time to search for a job.
- It can underestimate the actual rate of unemployment because discouraged workers cease looking for a job and thus are no longer counted as unemployed, even though they would really like to work.
- The unemployment rate can vary widely across age, gender, and racial groups. These differences are not reflected in the most commonly reported overall unemployment rate. These differences are illustrated in Figure 15-5 on page 382 in the text.

Using the Case Study in the Text

Jobless Recoveries (text page 384)

Ask students the following:

- Does the unemployment rate always fall during an economic expansion? (Answer: The unemployment rate doesn't always fall during an economic expansion. It will actually rise during periods when there is slow but positive growth in real GDP. This is known as a jobless recovery, the most recent of which occurred from 2001 to 2003.)

Activity

Describing Situations (10 minutes)

Pair students and ask them to develop a real-world scenario for each of the following terms:

- Discouraged worker
- Overstatement of the unemployment rate

Possible answers:

- Discouraged worker: Bob wants to work as a sports announcer. After losing his previous job, he looked for employment for 18 months with no luck. He finally gave up looking for a job last month.
- Overstatement of the unemployment rate: Connie received her M.B.A. She has been interviewing for jobs for the past 6 weeks and has been offered a job. Yet she has continued to go on additional interviews and has not accepted a position.

Price Indexes and the Aggregate Price Level

Creating Student Interest

Ask students if they are paying more to fill the gasoline tanks of their vehicles. Since their vehicle's gasoline tank capacity hasn't changed (assuming they haven't traded in their vehicle), then the reason they are spending more to fill up is due to rising gasoline prices.

Common Student Misunderstandings

Students may mistakenly believe that a reported increase in the CPI means that all prices of goods and services in the economy are increasing at the same stated rate. Emphasize that the CPI, or any price index, indicates the rate of change for the average of all prices included in the index.

Presenting the Material

Explain the notion of a market basket and how it is used in the computation of price indexes. Afterward, use the data in Table 15-3 of the text to compute the pre-frost cost of a market basket of citrus fruit on the board. Ask students to compute the cost of the post-frost market basket independently. After ensuring that students have completed their calculations correctly, compute the following as a class:

- The price index
- The rate of inflation

Calculating the Cost of a Market Basket

	Pre-frost	Post-frost
Price of orange	$0.20	$0.40
Price of grapefruit	$0.60	$1.00
Price of lemon	$0.25	$0.45
Cost of market basket (200 oranges, 50 grapefruit, 100 lemons)	(200 x $0.20) + (50 x $0.60) + (100 x $0.25) = $95.00	(200 x $0.40) + (50 x $1.00) + (100 x $0.45) = $175.00

It is also important that students understand the differences in the three measures of prices—the consumer price index, the producer price index, and the GDP deflator—as well as the appropriate uses of each.

Using the Case Study in the Text

Indexing to the CPI (text pages 388–389)

Ask students the following:

1. What does the term "indexing" mean? (Answer: When monetary payments are indexed this means that their values are tied or adjusted to some measure of price changes in an economy, such as the CPI. The process of indexing allows payments to keep pace with inflation, so no loss in purchasing power occurs.)

2. What payments are indexed in the United States? (Answer: In the United States, Social Security payments are indexed each January with the value of the CPI in the previous September. In addition, some wages are indexed using Cost of Living Adjustments, or COLAs, as are federal income tax brackets.)

Activity

Which One? (20 minutes)

Pair students and ask them to determine the most appropriate price index to use in each of the following situations and provide justification for each answer.

1. Chris is writing a research paper on the automobile industry. She needs to include a discussion of how higher costs of production have affected American auto producers. What price index should she use? (Answer: Chris should use the Producer Price Index to measure changes in prices paid by producers of goods.)

2. Charles works as an economist for the United Mine Workers. He is developing the justification for the pay raise the union is seeking from management in its new contract. What price index should he use? (Answer: Charles should use the Consumer Price Index to demonstrate that the union members' wages should rise by at least the same rate as the increase in consumer prices.)

3. William is a television reporter. He is preparing a documentary on the status of the U.S. economy. His documentary will focus on all sectors of the economy. What price index should he use? (Answer: William should use the GDP deflator, since it measures inflation as it affects all sectors of the economy.)

4. In November, Lucy volunteered to compute the value of her grandmother's Social Security payments for the following year. What price index should she use? (Answer: Lucy should use the CPI, since this is the measure used to index Social Security payments for inflation each year.)

chapter 16

Aggregate Supply and Aggregate Demand

Chapter Objectives

Students will learn in this chapter:
- How the aggregate supply curve illustrates the relationship between the aggregate price level and the quantity of aggregate output supplied in the economy.
- Why the aggregate supply curve is different in the short run as compared to the long run.
- How the aggregate demand curve illustrates the relationship between the aggregate price level and the quantity of aggregate output demanded in the economy.
- The importance of the multiplier, which determines the total change in aggregate output arising from a shift of the aggregate demand curve.
- How the *AS–AD* model is used to analyze economic fluctuations.
- How the economy tends to self-correct in the long run.
- How monetary policy and fiscal policy can be used to try to stabilize the economy in the short run.

Chapter Outline

Opening Example: The events leading up to the recession of 1979-1982 are compared to the factors which led to the Great Depression. The important distinction is made that the recession of 1979-1982 was largely due to supply shocks affecting the production and price of oil, while the Great Depression was caused by a loss of business and consumer confidence, exacerbated by a banking crisis.

I. Aggregate Supply

    A. *Definition*: The **aggregate supply curve** shows the relationship between the aggregate price level and the quantity of aggregate output supplied.

    B. The Short-Run Aggregate Supply Curve

        1. *Definition*: The **nominal wage** is the dollar amount of the wage paid.

        2. Nominal wages are assumed to be "sticky" or inflexible due to the fact that they are determined by either labor contracts or informal wage agreements that businesses are reluctant to change in response to short-run economic fluctuations.

3. *Definition*: The **short-run aggregate supply (SRAS) curve** shows the relationship between the aggregate price level and the quantity of aggregate output supplied that exists in the short run, the period when many production costs can be taken as fixed.

4. The short-run aggregate supply curve is positively sloped indicating that as the aggregate price level increases, the quantity of aggregate output supplied increases in the short run, as illustrated in Figure 16-1 on page 397 in the text.

5. The reason the short-run aggregate supply curve is positively sloped is that, as the aggregate price level increases and wages remain sticky, it becomes more profitable for firms to supply more output.

6. During the Great Depression, the economy moved down the short-run aggregate supply curve, with deflation causing the quantity of aggregate output supplied to decrease.

C. Shifts of the Short-Run Aggregate Supply Curve

   1. Short-run aggregate supply increases when producers increase the quantity of aggregate output they are willing to supply at any given price level.

   2. Short-run aggregate supply increases when:
      • Commodity prices fall
      • Nominal wages fall
      • Any other factors change that decrease firms' costs of production
      • Productivity rises

   3. An increase in short-run aggregate supply is demonstrated by a rightward shift of the short-run aggregate supply curve.

   4. Short-run aggregate supply decreases when producers decrease the quantity of aggregate output they are willing to supply at any given price level.

   5. Short-run aggregate supply decreases when:
      • Commodity prices rise
      • Nominal wages rise
      • Any other factors change that increase firms' costs of production
      • Productivity falls

   6. A decrease in short-run aggregate supply is demonstrated by a leftward shift of the short-run aggregate supply curve.

D. The Long-Run Aggregate Supply Curve

   1. *Definition*: The **long-run aggregate supply (LRAS) curve** shows the relationship between the aggregate price level and the quantity of aggregate output supplied that would exist if all prices, including nominal wages, were fully flexible.

   2. The long-run aggregate supply curve, *LRAS*, is vertical because changes in the aggregate price level have no effect on aggregate output in the long run.

   3. *Definition*: **Potential output** is the level of real GDP the economy would produce if all prices, including nominal wages, were fully flexible.

   4. The long-run aggregate supply curve is vertical at the level of potential output, as shown in Figure 16-3 on page 400 in the text.

   5. U.S. potential output has risen over time due to increases in physical and human capital, and technological progress.

6. An increase in long-run aggregate supply is shown by a rightward shift of the long-run aggregate supply curve.

7. A decrease in long-run aggregate supply is shown by a leftward shift of the long-run aggregate supply curve.

E. From the Short Run to the Long Run

    1. At any point in time, the economy is either operating on a short-run aggregate supply curve or on the long-run aggregate supply curve.

    2. It is possible for the economy to be operating on both a short-run aggregate supply curve and the long-run aggregate supply curve simultaneously by being at that level of output where the short-run aggregate supply curve and the long-run aggregate supply curve intersect.

    3. If actual aggregate output exceeds potential aggregate output, nominal wages will eventually rise in response to low unemployment, and aggregate output will fall, represented by a leftward shift of the short-run aggregate supply curve. This adjustment process is shown in panel (a) in Figure 16-5 on page 402 in the text.

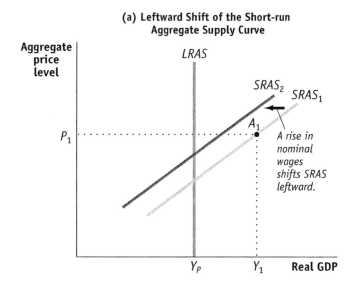

(a) Leftward Shift of the Short-run Aggregate Supply Curve

    4. If potential aggregate output exceeds actual aggregate output, nominal wages will eventually fall in response to high unemployment, and aggregate output will rise, represented by a rightward shift of the short-run aggregate supply curve. This adjustment process is shown in panel (b) in Figure 16-5 on page 402 in the text.

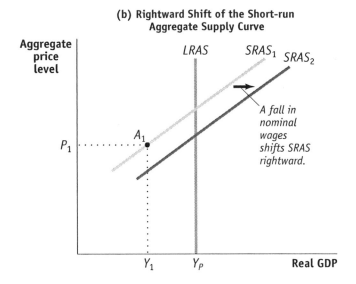

(b) Rightward Shift of the Short-run Aggregate Supply Curve

II. Aggregate Demand

A. *Definition*: The **aggregate demand (AD) curve** shows the relationship between the aggregate price level and the quantity of aggregate output demanded by households, businesses, the government, and the rest of the world.

B. The aggregate demand (*AD*) curve is negatively sloped since the aggregate price level is inversely related to the quantity of aggregate output demanded. This is shown in Figure 16-7 on page 404 in the text.

C. *Definition*: The **wealth effect of a change in the aggregate price level** is the effect on consumer spending caused by the effect of a change in the aggregate price level on the purchasing power of consumers' assets.

D. *Definition*: The **interest rate** is the price, calculated as a percentage of the amount borrowed, charged by the lender to a borrower for the use of their savings for one year.

E. *Definition*: The **interest rate effect of a change in the aggregate price level** is the effect on investment spending and consumer spending caused by the effect of a change in the aggregate price level on the purchasing power of consumers' and firms' money holdings.

F. There are two reason for the negative slope of the aggregate demand curve:
- The wealth effect of a change in the aggregate price level—a higher aggregate price level reduces the purchasing power of households' wealth and reduces consumer spending.
- The interest rate effect of a change in the aggregate price level—a higher aggregate price level reduces the purchasing power of households' and firms' money holdings, leading to a rise in interest rates and a fall in investment spending.

G. Shifts of the Aggregate Demand Curve
1. An increase in aggregate demand means that the quantity of aggregate output demanded increases at any given aggregate price level.
2. An increase in aggregate demand is shown by the rightward shift of the aggregate demand curve, as illustrated in panel (a) in Figure 16-8 on page 406 in the text.

3. Aggregate demand increases when:
   - Consumers and firms have optimistic expectations regarding the future
   - Households' wealth rises, due to reasons other than a decrease in the aggregate price level
   - Firms increase investment spending on physical capital

4. A decrease in aggregate demand means that the quantity of aggregate output demanded decreases at any given aggregate price level.

5. A decrease in aggregate demand is shown by the leftward shift of the aggregate demand curve, as illustrated in panel (b) in Figure 16-8 on page 406 in the text.

6. Aggregate demand decreases when:
   - Consumers and firms have pessimistic expectations regarding the future
   - Households' wealth decreases, for reasons other than an increase in the aggregate price level
   - Firms reduce investment spending on physical capital

H. Government Policies and Aggregate Demand

1. Fiscal policy affects aggregate demand directly through government purchases, and indirectly through changes in taxes or government transfers.

2. Monetary policy affects aggregate demand indirectly through changes in the interest rate.

3. Expansionary fiscal policies and expansionary monetary policies cause aggregate demand to increase, or shift to the right.

4. Contractionary fiscal policies and contractionary monetary policies cause aggregate demand to decrease, or shift to the left.

III. The Multiplier

A. *Definition*: The **marginal propensity to consume (MPC)** is the increase in consumer spending when disposable income rises by $1.

$$MPC = \frac{\Delta \text{Consumer Spending}}{\Delta \text{Disposable Income}}$$

B. *Definition*: The **marginal propensity to save (MPS)** is the increase in household savings when disposable income rises by $1.

$$MPS = \frac{\Delta \text{Household Savings}}{\Delta \text{Disposable Income}}$$

In addition,

$$MPS = 1 - MPC$$

C. *Definition*: An **autonomous change in aggregate spending (AAS)** is an initial change in the desired level of spending by firms, households, or government at a given level of real GDP.

D. *Definition*: The **multiplier** is the ratio of the total change in real GDP caused by an autonomous change in aggregate spending to the size of that autonomous change.

$$\text{Multiplier} = \frac{1}{1-MPC} = \frac{\Delta Y}{\Delta AAS}$$

E. The change in GDP arising from an autonomous change in aggregate spending is calculated as:

$$\Delta Y = \frac{1}{1-MPC} \times \Delta AAS$$

IV. The *AS–AD* Model

A. *Definition*: The **AS–AD model** uses the aggregate supply curve and the aggregate demand curve together to analyze economic fluctuations.

B. Short-Run Macroeconomic Equilibrium

1. *Definition*: The economy is in **short-run macroeconomic equilibrium** when the quantity of aggregate output supplied is equal to the quantity demanded. This is illustrated in Figure 16-11 on page 413 in the text.

2. *Definition*: The **short-run equilibrium aggregate price level** is the aggregate price level in the short-run macroeconomic equilibrium.

3. *Definition*: **Short-run equilibrium aggregate output** is the quantity of aggregate output produced in the short-run macroeconomic equilibrium.

C. Shifts of the *SRAS* Curve

1. *Definition*: An event that shifts the short-run aggregate supply curve is a **supply shock.**

2. A negative supply shock, which increases firms' cost of production, shifts the *SRAS* curve to the left, resulting in an increase in the equilibrium aggregate price level and a decrease in the equilibrium level of aggregate output. This is illustrated in panel (a) in Figure 16-12 on page 415 in the text.

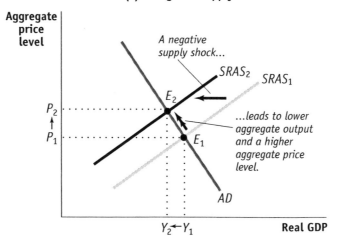

(a) A Negative Supply Shock

3. A positive supply shock, which decreases firms' costs of production, shifts the *SRAS* curve to the right, resulting in a decrease in the equilibrium aggregate price level and an increase in the equilibrium level of aggregate output. This is illustrated in panel (b) in Figure 16-12 on page 415 in the text.

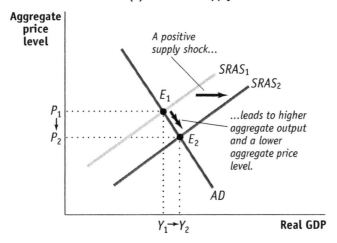

4. *Definition*: **Stagflation** is the combination of inflation and falling aggregate output.

D. Shifts of Aggregate Demand: Short-Run Effects

1. *Definition*: An event that shifts the aggregate demand curve is a **demand shock.**

2. A negative demand shock, such as the collapse of business or consumer confidence, shifts the aggregate demand curve to the left, resulting in a decrease in the aggregate price level and a decrease in the equilibrium level of aggregate output. This is illustrated in panel (a) in Figure 16-13 on page 416 in the text.

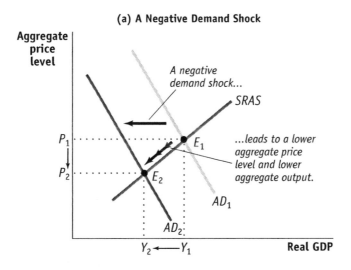

3. A positive demand shock, such as an increase in consumer spending, shifts the aggregate demand curve to the right, resulting in an increase in the aggregate price level and an increase in the equilibrium level of aggregate output. This is illustrated in panel (b) in Figure 16-13 on page 416 in the text.

(b) A Positive Demand Shock

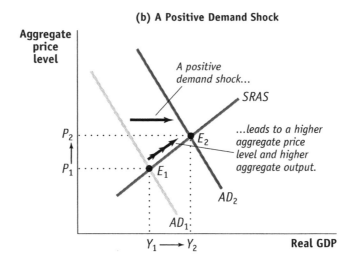

E. Long-Run Macroeconomic Equilibrium

1. *Definition*: The economy is in **long-run macroeconomic equilibrium**
when the point of short-run macroeconomic equilibrium is on the long-
run aggregate supply curve. Specifically, long-run macroeconomic equilibrium occurs where the *AD*, *SRAS*, and *LRAS* curves intersect. This is illustrated in Figure 16-14 on page 417 in the text.

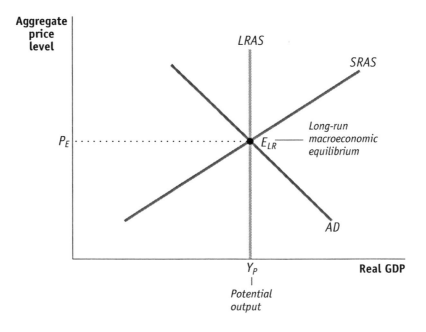

2. *Definition*: There is a **recessionary gap** when aggregate output is below
potential output. This is illustrated in Figure 16-15 on page 417 in the text.

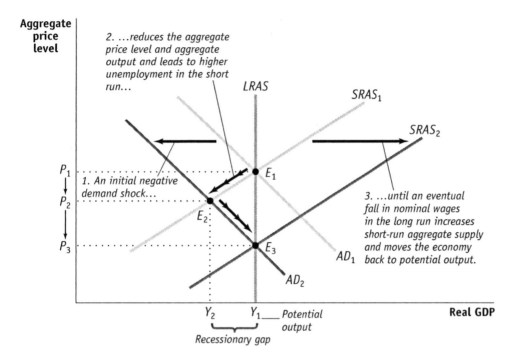

3. *Definition*: There is an **inflationary gap** when aggregate output is above potential output. This is illustrated in Figure 16-16 on page 418 in the text.

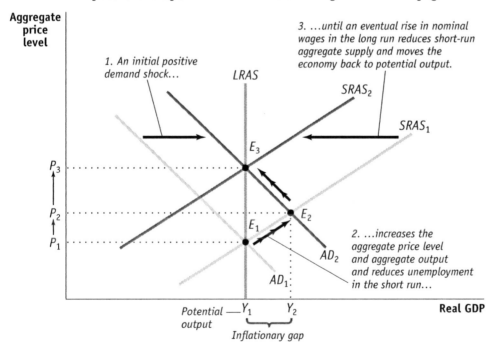

4. *Definition*: In the long run, the economy is **self-correcting:** shocks to aggregate demand affect aggregate output in the short run but not in the long run.

V. Macroeconomic Policy

A. Stabilization policy is the use of monetary or fiscal policy to offset demand shocks.

B. Stabilization policy can lead to a long-term rise in the budget deficit and lower long-run growth from crowding out.

C. Macroeconomic policies that are used to counteract a fall in aggregate output, caused by a negative supply shock, will lead to higher inflation, while a policy that counteracts inflation, caused by a positive supply shock, by reducing aggregate demand will deepen a recession or depression.

Teaching Tips

Aggregate Supply

Creating Student Interest

Remind students of the devastation wrought by Hurricanes Katrina and Rita in 2005. This is a great example of a supply shock. The physical capital that was destroyed by these hurricanes diminished productive capacity and reduced oil production in this area of the country, and hence decreased aggregate supply.

Common Student Misunderstandings

It's important to emphasize to students that the long-run period referred to in this chapter with respect to long-run aggregate supply is the same period that was analyzed in Chapter 8 in the context of long-run economic growth. Both concepts relate to an extended period during which the economy's rate of economic growth will correspond to the rate of growth of potential output in the economy in the long run.

Presenting the Material

The short-run adjustment process demonstrated in panels (a) and (b) in Figure 16-5 on page 402 can be explained in a somewhat less abstract manner by selecting specific values for potential output as well as specific output. By assigning these values within these graphs, students should be able to better understand the effects on unemployment, nominal wages, and the *SRAS* curves in these graphs. Specifically, in panel (a), let Y_P = $11,000 billion and Y_1 = $12,500 billion, and in panel (b), let Y_P = $11,000 billion and Y_1 = $8,000 billion. Also tell students to assume that the initial nominal wage is $15 per hour in each scenario.

Using the Case Study in the Text

Prices and Output During the Great Depression (text pages 403–404)
Ask students:

1. Describe the movement along the economy's short-run aggregate supply curve during the period 1929–1933. (Answer: The economy was moving down along the short-run aggregate supply curve during this period of time, as both aggregate output and the aggregate price level fell.)

2. Describe the movement along the economy's short-run aggregate supply curve during the period 1933–1937. (Answer: The economy was moving up along the

short-run aggregate supply curve during this period of time, as both aggregate output and the aggregate price level rose.)

3. Over the period 1929–1942, how did the short-run aggregate supply curve shift, and why did it shift? (Answer: Over the period 1929–1942, the short-run aggregate supply curve shifted to the right due to technological progress during this time.)

Activities

Which Way Does *SRAS* Shift? (15 minutes)

Ask students to work in pairs to determine the effect on the short-run aggregate supply (*SRAS*) curve for each of the following scenarios. Also ask students to demonstrate their graphical analysis in each case. Remind students to accurately label all lines, points, and axes when drawing the graphs for these exercises.

1. Labor productivity increases in the macroeconomy. (Answer: The *SRAS* curve will shift to the right.)

2. An earthquake destroys a significant amount of infrastructure in the economy. (Answer: The *SRAS* curve will shift to the left.)

3. Technological progress occurs in the economy. (Answer: The *SRAS* curve will shift to the right.)

Understanding *LRAS* (10 minutes)

Pair students and ask them to answer the following thought questions.

1. Why is the *LRAS* curve vertical? (Answer: The *LRAS* curve is vertical because despite any changes in the aggregate price level, aggregate output cannot change from its fixed level, known as potential output. This is due to the fact that all prices, including nominal wages are fully flexible in the long run.)

2. Can the *LRAS* curve shift? (Answer: Due to long-run economic growth, the level of potential output can increase over time, resulting in a rightward shift of the *LRAS*.)

Aggregate Demand

Creating Student Interest

Ask students what happens to the purchasing power of their checking accounts when the average level of prices rises. Explain that from a macroeconomic perspective, an increase in the aggregate price level diminishes all buyers' purchasing power. Thus, as the aggregate price level rises, the quantity of aggregate output demanded decreases, as illustrated by the downward-sloping aggregate demand curve.

Common Student Misunderstandings

Students may be confused about why a change in wealth has the potential to cause both a shift of the aggregate demand curve as well as movement along the aggregate demand curve. Explain that a change in wealth, independent of a change in the aggregate price level, results in a shift of the aggregate demand curve. However, movement along the aggregate demand curve will occur when wealth is changed, due to a change in the aggregate price level. Emphasize that the source of the change in wealth is an important factor in distinguishing whether there is movement along, or a shift of, the aggregate demand curve.

Presenting the Material

It is critical that students can translate their understanding of the factors that shift the aggregate demand curve to representing these concepts graphically. When discussing the factors that will shift the *AD* curve, draw graphs to illustrate these concepts, such as those shown in Figure 16-8 on page 406 in the text.

Using the Case Study in the Text

Movement Along the Aggregate Demand Curve, 1979–1980
(text pages 408–409)
Ask students:

1. How did the oil crisis of 1979 affect consumers' purchasing power? (Answer: The oil crisis of 1979 resulted in a sharp increase in the aggregate price level, thereby diminishing consumers' purchasing power.)

2. What effect did the oil crisis of 1979 have on the aggregate demand curve? (Answer: The decrease in consumers' purchasing power, arising from the oil crisis in 1979, led to movement up along the aggregate demand curve, with the quantity of aggregate output falling as the aggregate price level rose.)

Activity

What Is the Effect on *AD*? (20 minutes)
Pair students and ask them to determine the effect on the short-run aggregate demand (*AD*) curve for each of the following scenarios and sketch a graph to illustrate each answer.

1. A decrease in consumer wealth occurs due to a plunge in stock prices. (Answer: The *AD* curve will shift to the left.)

2. Households and businesses have more optimistic expectations regarding future economic performance. (Answer: The *AD* curve will shift to the right.)

3. There are higher levels of investment spending by businesses. (Answer: The *AD* curve will shift to the right.)

4. The government cuts taxes for households and businesses. (Answer: The *AD* curve will shift to the right.)

5. The Fed decreases the money supply. (Answer: The *AD* curve will shift to the left.)

The Multiplier

Creating Student Interest

Ask students to assume that they get a raise in their pay. Then ask, "What will you do with this extra money?" Students will obviously state that they will both save and spend this extra money. Explain that the extra money they are spending will foster additional production of goods and services, which in turn will generate additional income for the producers of these goods and services. Some of the additional income earned by the producers of these goods and services will also be spent, which will create additional spending rounds in the macroeconomy. This process is known as the multiplier effect.

Common Student Misunderstandings

Students may not immediately see the connection between an increase in investment spending (*I*) and the impact on consumer spending (*C*). This is likely due to the fact that students see *C* and *I* as separate entities. Explain that new investment (i.e., plant and equipment) is created by workers who are members of households. Some of the income earned by these workers is spent, which creates the subsequent rounds of consumer spending that follow the initial increase in investment spending.

Presenting the Material

A great way to explain the multiplier process is with a numerical example, such as the one outlined on pages 411 and 412 in the text. By carrying out the calculations of the additional consumer spending rounds arising from an initial increase in investment spending, students will have a better understanding of the multiplier process. Note that prices are being held constant during this analysis.

Work It Out

The Multiplier (text page 412)

In this numerical example, students are asked to compute the value of the marginal propensity to consume and the amount by which consumption spending will change, given a $100 billion increase in disposable income. In addition, students are also asked to compute the value of the multiplier and determine the total change in real GDP resulting from an increase in government spending.

Activities

Spending Round by Round (15 minutes)

Pair students and ask them to complete the following exercises.

1. Assume the MPC is 0.75. What is the value of the multiplier?
2. Assume investment spending increases by $20 billion and the MPC is 0.75. Calculate the first through the fourth rounds of spending in the economy.
3. Assume investment spending increases by $20 billion and the MPC is 0.75. Calculate the total change in GDP arising from this increase in investment spending.

Answers:

1. $$\text{Multiplier} = \frac{1}{1 - MPC} = \frac{1}{1 - 0.75} = 4$$

2. Round 1: Increase in investment spending= $20 billion
   Round 2: Increase in consumer spending= 0.75 x $20 billion= $15 billion
   Round 3: Increase in consumer spending= $(0.75)2$ x $20 billion= $11.25 billion
   Round 4: Increase in consumer spending= $(0.75)3$ x $20 billion= $8.4375 billion

3. Total increase in GDP arising from $20 billion increase in investment spending

$$= \$20 \text{ billion} \times \frac{1}{1 - MPC} = \$20 \text{ billion} \times \frac{1}{1 - 0.75} = \$80 \text{ billion}$$

You Be the Policy Maker (15 minutes)

Pair students and ask them to answer the following question.

Assume you are an economist working on the President's Council of Economic Advisors. The President wants U.S. GDP to increase by $160 billion. If the MPC is 0.80, by how much must government spending, G, increase to achieve the desired change in GDP?

Answer:

Use the formula:

$$\Delta Y = \frac{1}{1-MPC} \times \Delta AAS = \frac{1}{1-MPC} \times \Delta G$$

In this case, ΔY = $160 billion, MPC = 0.80, and ΔAAS represents the change in autonomous aggregate spending. To determine the value of ΔAAS, substitute the known values into the above formula.

$$\$160 \text{ billion} = \frac{1}{1-0.80} \times \Delta AAS$$

$$\$160 \text{ billion} = 5 \times \Delta AAS$$

$$\Delta G = \Delta AAS = \frac{\$160 \text{ billion}}{5} = \$32 \text{ billion}$$

The *AS–AD* Model

Creating Student Interest

Remind students that, thus far, aggregate demand and aggregate supply have been discussed in isolation from each other. However, a market is defined by bringing supply and demand together. Therefore in this section aggregate demand and aggregate supply are analyzed together.

Common Student Misunderstandings

Students may erroneously think that a change in investment spending (I) shifts the aggregate supply curve. Explain that since I is a component of aggregate spending or the demand for GDP, a change in I will result in a change in the demand for GDP, which is shown as a shift in the aggregate demand curve.

Presenting the Material

It is important for students to first see an initial equilibrium indicated in each graph, followed by the effects of a change in AS or AD on equilibrium aggregate output, and the aggregate price level. This should be done from the following perspectives:

- Effect of a supply shock on *AD*, *SRAS*, equilibrium aggregate output, and equilibrium aggregate price level.

- Effect of a supply shock on *AD*, *LRAS*, equilibrium aggregate output, and equilibrium aggregate price level.

- Effect of a demand shock on *AD*, *SRAS*, equilibrium aggregate output, and equilibrium aggregate price level.

Using the Case Study in the Text

Supply Shocks versus Demand Shocks in Practice (text pages 419–420)

Ask students:

1. Is it possible for supply shocks or demand shocks to cause recessions? (Answer: Both supply shocks and demand shocks are capable of causing recessions. Historical data indicate that seven of the nine postwar recessions have been due to demand shocks and two were attributed to supply shocks.)

2. How did the Arab–Israeli war of 1973 affect the U.S. economy? (Answer: The Arab–Israeli war disrupted oil supplies, resulting in a supply shock that shifted the *SRAS* curve to the left.)

Activities

Shifting *AS* and *AD* (20 minutes)

Ask students to work in pairs to complete the following exercises.

1. Draw a short-run *AS–AD* graph showing the effect of a severe drop in stock prices which decreases households' and businesses' wealth. Indicate the effect on the equilibrium aggregate price level and equilibrium aggregate output.

2. Draw a short-run *AS–AD* graph showing the effect of a significant decrease in the world supply of oil. Indicate the effect on the equilibrium aggregate price level and equilibrium aggregate output.

3. Draw an *AS–AD* graph showing a recessionary gap.

4. Draw an *AS–AD* graph showing an inflationary gap.

Answers:

1.

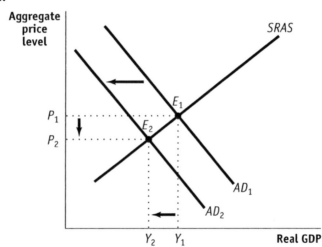

2.

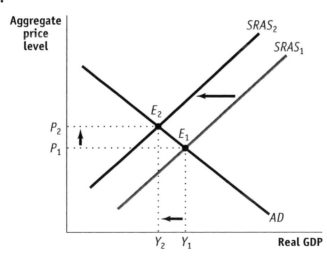

3.

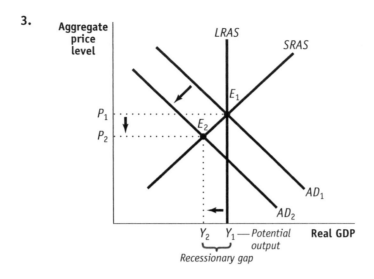

4.

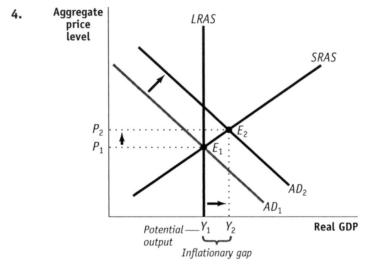

All About Equilibrium (10 minutes)

Ask students to complete the following exercises.

   1. Draw a graph illustrating short-run macroeconomic equilibrium.
   2. Draw a graph illustrating long-run macroeconomic equilibrium.

Answers:

1.

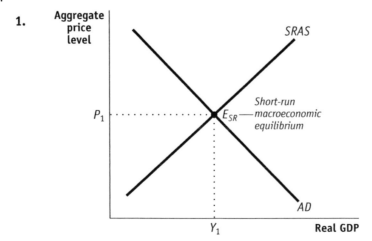

2.

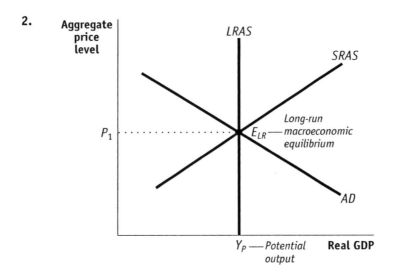

Macroeconomic Policy

Creating Student Interest

To stimulate discussion, ask students if there would ever be a situation in which policy makers advocate a tax increase. From an economic perspective, some policy makers would push for a tax increase if they felt the funds would be used to pay down the government budget deficit. However, from a political perspective, such a policy may have few advocates as constituents may reach aversely to a tax hike.

Common Student Misunderstandings

Students may overestimate the control the President has over fiscal policy in the economy. It is important to remind students that while the President may propose, say a tax cut or an increase in government spending, such a request must be approved by Congress.

Presenting the Material

It is extremely important that both the short-run and long-run impacts of demand and supply shocks are examined. This should be done both verbally and graphically. It is also important to explain to students why policy leaders may choose to implement a fiscal policy which will have a desired economic impact in the short run but an undesired effect in the long run.

Using the Case Study in the Text

The End of the Great Depression (text page 422)

Ask students:

1. How did World War II affect production in the U.S. economy? (Answer: World War II greatly affected production in the U.S. economy. Specifically, even before the United States entered the war, the United States exported military equipment and other goods to Britain. After the United States entered the war, U.S. government spending on military equipment escalated.)

2. What affect did World War II have on U.S. aggregate demand? (Answer: The increase in U.S. military and other exports to Britain along with the increase in U.S. government spending on military equipment contributed significantly to increasing U.S. aggregate demand.)

Activity

Debating the Usefulness of Macroeconomic Policies (20 minutes)

Divide the class into two groups: one in favor of government intervention in the economy and the other against it. Ask each group to create a list of talking points to defend their position. Leave sufficient time for students to present their ideas as well as engage in well-placed counterarguments.

In the News

To stimulate discussion, ask students to read the following article by Jonathan Weisman: "House Passes 3 Tax Cuts, Plans a 4th," *The Washington Post Online*, December 8, 2005, p. AO1. Direct them to: http://www.washingtonpost.com/wp-dyn/content/article/2005/12/07/AR2005120702608.html. This article discusses some tax cuts recently passed by the U.S. House of Representatives as well as their expected impacts.

Questions for discussion:

1. To whom are the three tax cuts approved by the House in December 2005 directed? (Answer: These tax cuts are targeted toward U.S. troops serving in Iraq, those citizens living along the Gulf Coast who suffered losses due to hurricanes, and taxpayers who otherwise would have had to pay the alternative minimum tax.)
2. How much tax revenue is the U.S. government foregoing by instituting these tax cuts? (Answer: The U.S. government will forego $94.5 billion over five years.)

chapter 17

Fiscal Policy

Chapter Objectives

Students will learn in this chapter:
- What fiscal policy is and why it is an important tool in managing economic fluctuations.
- Which policies constitute an expansionary fiscal policy and which constitute a contractionary fiscal policy.
- Why fiscal policy has a multiplier effect and how this effect is influenced by automatic stabilizers.
- Why tax and transfer multipliers are less than the government purchases multiplier.
- Why governments calculate the cyclically adjusted budget balance.
- Why a large public debt may be a cause for concern.
- Why implicit liabilities of the government are also a cause for concern.

Chapter Outline

Opening Example: The excessive level of spending by the Japanese government in the 1990s on bridges, dams, roads, and other infrastructure, in an effort to move its economy out of a slump, is used as an example of discretionary fiscal policy.

I. Fiscal Policy: The Basics

  A. Sources of government tax revenue in the United States in 2004 included:
  - Personal income taxes: 35%
  - Social insurance taxes: 28%
  - Corporate profit taxes: 8%
  - Other taxes mainly collected at the state and local level: 29%

  B. Total government spending in the United States in 2004 included:
  - Education: 17%
  - Medicare and Medicaid: 16%
  - National defense: 15%
  - Social Security: 14%
  - Other goods and services: 29%
  - Other government transfers: 9%

  C. *Definition*: **Social insurance** programs are government programs intended to protect families against economic hardship.

D. The government directly controls government spending (G), and indirectly influences consumer spending (C) with transfer payments and taxes, and sometimes influences investment spending (I) through its tax policies.

E. Expansionary Fiscal Policy

    1. Expansionary fiscal policies include:

- Increases in government purchases of goods and services
- Decreases in taxes
- Increases in government transfer payments

    2. Expansionary fiscal policies increase aggregate demand and thereby shift the aggregate demand curve to the right.

F. Contractionary Fiscal Policy

    1. Contractionary fiscal policies include:

- Decreases in government purchase of goods and services
- Increases in taxes
- Decreases in government transfer payments

    2. Contractionary fiscal policies decrease aggregate demand and thereby shift the aggregate demand curve to the left.

G. Due to the long period needed to implement fiscal policies and the sometimes long period before these policies effects are felt, it is often difficult to accurately implement fiscal policy at the right time.

II. Fiscal Policy and the Multiplier

A. Multiplier Effects of a Change in Government Purchases of Goods and Services

    1. An increase or decrease in government spending changes real GDP by a larger amount than the initial change in government spending due to the multiplier effect.

    2. The magnitude of the shift of the aggregate demand curve, due to a change in government spending, is determined by the value of the multiplier.

    3. The multiplier associated with changes in government spending is expressed mathematically as:

$$\frac{1}{1-MPC}$$

B. Multiplier Effects of Changes in Government Transfers and Taxes

    1. An increase or decrease in transfer payments or taxes changes real GDP by a larger amount than the initial change in transfer payments or taxes due to the multiplier effect.

    2. The size of the multiplier effect associated with a change in either transfer payments or taxes is smaller than the multiplier effect associated with a change in government spending, because part of any change in taxes or transfers is absorbed by savings in the first round of spending.

    3. The magnitude of the shift of the aggregate demand curve, due to a change in transfer payments or taxes, is determined by the value of the multiplier.

    4. The multiplier associated with changes in transfer payments or taxes is expressed mathematically as:

$$\frac{MPC}{1-MPC}$$

5. *Definition:* A **lump-sum tax** does not change when real GDP changes.
6. *Definition:* A **proportional tax** increases when real GDP increases and decreases when real GDP decreases.
7. *Definition:* **Automatic stabilizers** are government spending and taxation rules that cause fiscal policy to be expansionary when the economy contracts and contractionary when the economy expands.
8. *Definition:* **Discretionary fiscal policy** is fiscal policy that is the result of deliberate actions by policy makers rather than rules.

III. The Budget Balance

A. The Budget Balance as a Measure of Fiscal Policy

1. *Definition:* The **budget balance** is the difference between tax revenue and government spending.
2. The budget balance is expressed mathematically as:

$$\text{Budget Balance} = T - G - TR$$

where T represents tax revenue, G denotes government purchases, and TR represents government transfers.

3. *Definition:* The **budget surplus** is the difference between tax revenue and government spending when tax revenue exceeds government spending.
4. *Definition:* The **budget deficit** is the difference between tax revenue and government spending when government spending exceeds tax revenue.
5. Increases in government purchases on goods and services, increases in government transfers, or lowering taxes reduce the budget balance, thereby making a budget surplus smaller or a budget deficit larger, for that year, *ceteris paribus.*
6. Decreases in government purchases of goods and services, decreases in government transfers, or increases in taxes increase the budget balance, thereby making a budget surplus bigger or a budget deficit smaller, for that year, *ceteris paribus.*
7. Two different changes in fiscal policy that have equal effects on the budget balance may have quite unequal effects on aggregate demand.

B. The Business Cycle and the Cyclically Adjusted Budget Balance

1. The budget deficit tends to rise during recessions and fall during expansions due, in part, to the business cycle.
2. *Definition:* The **cyclically adjusted budget balance** is an estimate of what the budget balance would be if real GDP were exactly equal to potential GDP. The cyclically adjusted budget deficit is shown in Figure 17-9 on page 441 in the text.
3. Most economists believe that governments should run budget surpluses during expansionary periods in the business cycle and budget deficits during contractionary periods in the business cycle.
4. Some economists believe that laws requiring a balanced budget would undermine the role of automatic stabilizers in the economy.

IV. Long-Run Implications of Fiscal Policy

A. Deficits, Surpluses, and Debt

1. *Definition:* **Fiscal years** run from October 1 to September 30 and are named by the calendar year in which they end.
2. U.S. government budget accounting is calculated on the basis of fiscal years.

3. *Definition:* **Public debt** is government debt held by individuals and institutions outside the government.

4. Persistent budget deficits result in increases in the public debt.

5. *Definition:* **Crowding out** is the negative effect of budget deficits on private investment.

6. Rising public debt can lead to crowding out of private investment or, in extreme situations, government default.

B. Deficits and Debt in Practice

1. *Definition:* The **debt–GDP ratio** is government debt as a percentage of GDP.

2. A country with rising GDP can have a stable debt–GDP ratio, even if it runs budget deficits, if GDP is growing faster than the debt.

3. *Definition:* **Implicit liabilities** are spending promises made by governments that are effectively a debt despite the fact that they are not included in the usual debt statistics.

4. Social Security, Medicare, and Medicaid represent large implicit liabilities of the U.S. government.

Teaching Tips

Fiscal Policy: The Basics

Creating Student Interest

Since the topic of fiscal policy was introduced in a previous chapter, ask students to recall the definition of fiscal policy and to provide an example. List the students' responses on the board. Explain that this chapter will explore the topic in much greater depth.

Common Student Misunderstandings

Students sometimes don't understand why transfer payments are discussed separately from government spending on goods and services. Explain that transfer payments are somewhat unique relative to other forms of government spending. Specifically, transfer payments made by the government are not in direct exchange for any goods or services received by the government.

Presenting the Material

It is important to point out the sources of tax revenue as well as the major spending areas for governments. These data are displayed in Figures 17-2 and 17-3 on pages 428 and 429, respectively, in the text.

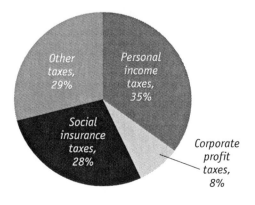

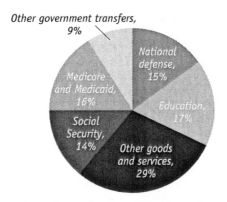

In addition, demonstrate the effect of contractionary and expansionary fiscal policies on the *AS-AD* model from both the long-run and short-run perspectives. Emphasize the manner in which fiscal policy can be used to close a recessionary gap or an inflationary gap as shown in Figures 17-4 and 17-5 on page 431 in the text.

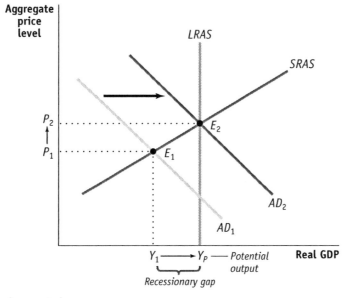

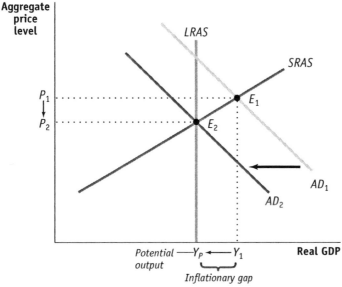

Using the Case Study in the Text

Expansionary Fiscal Policy in Japan (text pages 432–433)

Ask students:

1. Why did economists refer to the Japanese economy in the 1980s as the "bubble economy"? (Answer: Economists referred to the Japanese economy in the 1980s as the "bubble economy" because consumer spending rose during this period due to rising stock and real estate prices, which were not justified by rational calculations. After stock and real estate values fell in the late1980s, the Japanese economic bubble burst.)

2. What actions were taken to move the Japanese economy out of its recession during the late 1980s and 1990s? (Answer: Policy makers in Japan used vast increases in government spending, largely on construction of roads, bridges, and other infrastructure, to increase aggregate demand and move the Japanese economy out of recession.)

Activity

Filling in the Gaps (10 minutes)

Ask students to work in pairs on the following exercises.

1. Describe a policy measure the government can use to close a recessionary gap.
2. Illustrate your response to question 1 in a graph.
3. Describe a policy measure the government can use to close an inflationary gap.
4. Illustrate your response to question 3 in a graph.

Answers:

1. To close a recessionary gap the government can use expansionary fiscal policies such as decreasing taxes paid by businesses or households, or increasing government spending on, say, public schools or roads.

2.

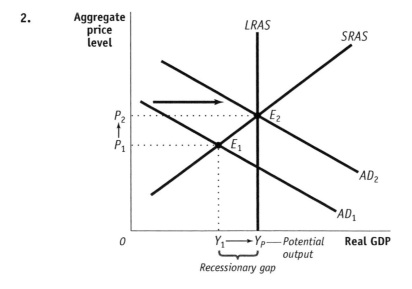

3. To close an inflationary gap, the government can use contractionary fiscal policies such as increasing taxes paid by businesses or households, or decreasing government spending on, say, public hospitals and the military.

4.

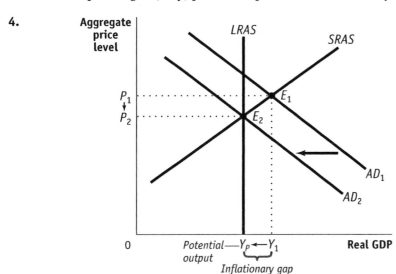

Fiscal Policy and the Multiplier

Creating Student Interest

Ask students what effect they think a $50 billion increase in government spending will have on the economy. Students should be able to draw some connections to the previous discussion of the multiplier in Chapter 16, regarding the effect a change in investment has on the economy. Indicate that, in a similar way, a change in government will have a direct impact on the economy as well as subsequent indirect impacts on consumer spending. Also mention that the effect of a change in government spending or taxes on the macroeconomy can be measured using the government spending or tax multiplier, respectively.

Common Student Misunderstandings

Students may not immediately understand why the multiplier effect associated with a change in taxes or transfer payments is smaller than the multiplier effect associated with an equivalent change in government spending. Explain to them that since the *MPC* is less than 1, the size of the multiplier effect associated with a change in either transfer payments or taxes is smaller than the multiplier effect associated with a change in government spending, because part of any change in taxes or transfers is absorbed by savings in the first round of spending.

Presenting the Material

Perhaps the most effective way for students to understand the relative differences between the effect of a change in government spending on real GDP and the effect of a change in taxes or transfer payments on real GDP is to carry out mathematical examples of each. First, present the generalized formulas for measuring a change in real GDP in each case. Afterward, choose a value for the *MPC* and a value by which government spending increases, which is the same as the value by which taxes decrease or transfer payments increase, and carry out the computations in front of the class. Follow up these calculations with the graphical analysis of the effect on aggregate demand, as shown in

Figure 17-6 on page 434 in the text. It is also important to discuss the notions of automatic stabilizers and discretionary fiscal policy.

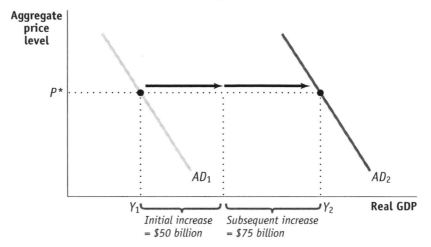

Work It Out
Fiscal Policy Multiplier (text page 435)

In this numerical example, students are given the value of the marginal propensity to consume and are asked to determine the value of the multiplier as well as the amount by which government spending or transfer payments must rise in order for the government to achieve its goal of increasing aggregate demand by $500 billion per year. Afterward, students are instructed to solve this problem again assuming a different value for the marginal propensity to consume.

Using the Case Study in the Text
How Much Bang for the Buck? (text pages 437–438)

Ask students:

1. What specific type of fiscal policy was used to move the U.S. economy out of the recession in the early 2000s? (Answer: Tax cuts and increased government spending were used between 2001 and 2003 to move the U.S. economy out of a recessionary phase.)

2. According to economist Mark Zandi, what specific types of fiscal policy would have the greatest expansionary impact on the macroeconomy? (Answer: Mark Zandi has estimated that extending emergency federal unemployment benefits, reducing the marginal tax rate from 15% to 10% on some sources of income, and providing federal aid to state and local governments would have some of the greatest expansionary impacts on the economy.)

Activities
Defining Terms (15 minutes)

Pair students and ask them to define the following terms and assess the importance of each in maintaining macroeconomic stability.

1. Automatic stabilizers
2. Discretionary fiscal policy

Answers:

1. Automatic stabilizers are government spending and taxation rules that cause fiscal policy to be expansive when the economy contracts and contractionary when the economy expands. Most economists agree that expansionary and contractionary fiscal policies that are the result of automatic stabilizers are helpful in maintaining macroeconomic stability.

2. Discretionary fiscal policy is fiscal policy that is the result of deliberate actions by policy makers rather than rules. It is important to note that economists are not in agreement regarding the effectiveness of discretionary fiscal policy.

Working with Multipliers (15 minutes)

Pair students and ask them to complete the following exercises.

1. Assume the MPC is 0.80 and the government increases spending on cancer research by $15 billion. What is the value of the initial impact on real GDP? What is the value of the total impact on real GDP?

2. Assume the MPC is 0.80 and policy makers have targeted real GDP to increase by $200 billion. By how much must taxes be reduced to achieve this goal?

Answers:

1. Initial change in real GDP = change in government spending = $15 billion
   Total change in real GDP computed as:

$$\Delta \text{real GDP} = \frac{1}{1-MPC} \times \Delta G$$
$$= \frac{1}{1-0.80} \times \$15 \text{ billion}$$
$$= 5 \times 15 \text{ billion}$$
$$= \$75 \text{ billion}$$

2.

$$\$200 \text{ billion} = \frac{MPC}{1-MPC} \times \Delta T$$
$$\$200 \text{ billion} = \frac{0.80}{1-0.80} \times \Delta T$$
$$\$200 \text{ billion} = 4 \times \Delta T$$
$$\Delta T = \frac{\$200 \text{ billion}}{4} = \$50 \text{ billion (meaning } T \text{ must decrease by } \$50 \text{ billion)}$$

The Budget Balance

Creating Student Interest

Ask students if they know whether the U.S. government budget is in balance or in surplus or deficit. Afterward ask students if they know the value of the government budget deficit. Record the students' responses on the board and compare them to the actual value of the budget deficit. Refer to the website www.globalpolicy.org/socecon/crisis/tradedeficit/tables/budgetdeficit.htm for information regarding the government budget deficit prior to class for the data needed for this exercise.

Common Student Misunderstandings

Students may erroneously think that the U.S. budget must be balanced each year by law. Explain that while there have been attempts in the past to pass legislation requiring the federal government to balance the budget each year, no such law exists to date.

Presenting the Material

Begin by reviewing the definition for the budget balance as follows:

$$\text{Budget Balance} = T - G - TR$$

where T represents tax revenue, G denotes government purchases, and TR represents government transfers. Afterward, discuss the relationship between the business cycle and the cyclically adjusted budget balance. Figure 17-7 on page 439 in the text provides a great illustration of the close ties between the U.S. federal budget deficit and the business cycle. Also provide a balanced presentation of pros and cons of a legally mandated balanced federal government budget.

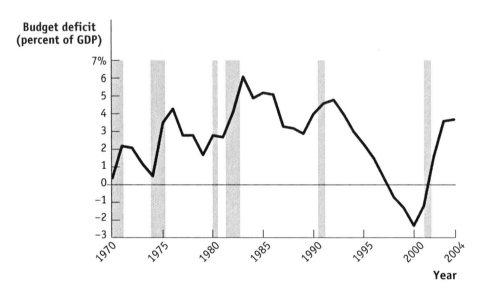

Using the Case Study in the Text

Stability Pact—or Stupidity Pact? (text pages 441–442)

Ask students:

1. Describe the stability pact that members of the euro zone agreed to in 1999. (Answer: The stability pact required each European government in the euro zone to keep its actual budget deficit below 3% of its GDP or else face fines.)

2. Why was the stability pact rewritten in 2005? (Answer: The stability pact was rewritten in March 2005 because two of the most powerful nations in the euro zone, France and Germany, were unable to keep their government budget deficits below 3% of their GDP. Furthermore, these governments were unwilling to raise taxes or cut government spending to be compliant with the stability pact, as these actions would exacerbate the recessions going on in these countries at that time.)

Activities

What the Budget Balance Can't Tell Us (15 minutes)

Pair students and ask them to explain why changes in the budget balance cannot be used as an accurate measure of the effectiveness of fiscal policy in the macroeconomy.

Answer: Changes in the budget balance cannot be used as an accurate measure of the effectiveness of fiscal policy in the macroeconomy because:

- Two different changes in fiscal policy that have equal effects on the budget balance may have quite unequal effects on aggregate demand.

- Changes in the budget balance can be the result, not the cause, of fluctuations in the economy.

Debate Time (20 minutes)

Divide the students into two groups: one, for a constitutional amendment guaranteeing a balanced government budget each year, and the other against such an amendment. Provide students with sufficient time to appoint representatives to engage in the debate and to record points supporting their side. Also allow sufficient time to both carry out and assess the outcome of the debate with the students.

Long-Run Implications of Fiscal Policy

Creating Student Interest

Ask students if they know the value of the U.S. government debt. Note students' responses on the board. Afterward, inform students of the actual value of the government debt, which can be found at the website www.publicdebt.treas.gov/opd/ opd.htm, and compare it with the students' responses.

Common Student Misunderstandings

Students often use the terms deficit and debt interchangeably. Emphasize that the two terms are indeed different measures. Specifically, the deficit indicates the difference between what the government spends and the amount it receives in tax revenue in a given period. By contrast, the debt is a cumulative measure indicating the sum of money that a government owes at a particular point in time.

Presenting the Material

It is important to distinguish between the government deficit and the government debt, as well as to identify the holders of the federal debt. The debt to GDP ratio is an effective tool for measuring the relative magnitude of the debt in the economy over time. Panels (a) and (b) in Figure 17-11 on page 445 in the text provide historical data on the federal budget deficit as well as the federal debt–GDP ratio.

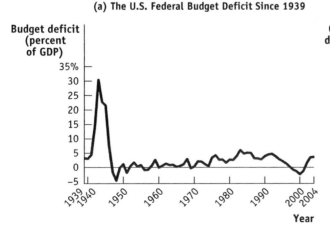

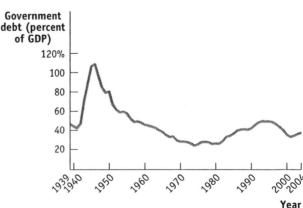

In addition, it is also important to point out the effect that a growing debt can have on the macroeconomy, in terms of higher interest rates in the future, crowding out of private investment, and increasing the possibility of the government defaulting on its debt.

Using the Case Study in the Text
Argentina's Creditors Take a Haircut (text page 448)
Ask students:

1. What type of deal was negotiated by the government of Argentina with its creditors, after Argentina defaulted on its debt in late 2001? (Answer: The government of Argentina negotiated an agreement by which it issued new bonds for holders of this nation's debt at just 32% of their original value.)

2. How did Argentina's slide into default affect the economy of this country? (Answer: Argentina's default on its debt triggered soaring rates of unemployment and poverty, as well as public unrest due to the depressed state of the economy.)

Activity
Computing Surpluses, Deficits, and the Debt (15 minutes)
Provide students with the following data from the government of Macroland. Ask students to work in pairs to complete the following exercises. Note: All data are in billions of dollars.

Year	Tax Revenue (T)	Government Spending on Goods & Services (G)	Transfer Payments (TR)
1998	$2,000	$1,200	$600
1999	$1,600	$1,500	$900
2000	$1,700	$1,400	$700
2001	$2,200	$1,000	$500
2002	$2,400	$1,600	$800

1. Determine the value of the budget balance and indicate whether there is a government surplus, deficit, or balance for each year.
2. Determine the value of the government debt for the period 1998–2002.

Answers:

1. In general, the budget balance is computed for any year as:

$$\text{Budget Balance} = T - G - TR$$

Year	Budget Balance (billions)	Status of Government Budget
1998	$200	Surplus
1999	$–800	Deficit
2000	$–400	Deficit
2001	$700	Surplus
2002	$0	Balanced

2. Debt = Sum of the budget balance for the years 1998–2002

Debt = $200 + $–800 + $–400 + $700 + $0 = $–300 billion

In the News

Use the following article featuring a question and answer regarding ownership of the U.S. government debt to stimulate further discussion on this topic.

Ask David Wessel
David Wessell

Q: One hears a lot about which foreign countries own the most U.S. debt. How much of the government debt do U.S. citizens and corporations own?

A: As of the end of June 2005, the latest period for which detailed data are reported in the December 2005 issue of the government's "Treasury Bulletin," the federal government had debt outstanding of $7.8 trillion. Of this total, though, slightly more than $4 trillion was held in the Social Security trust fund and other government accounts or by the Federal Reserve; that's essentially money one arm of the government owes to another arm of the government.

That leaves about $3.8 trillion. Of this amount, the Treasury said, about $2 trillion, roughly 53%, was held by foreigners of all sorts, from individual investors to foreign central banks.

That leaves roughly $1.8 trillion held by Americans. The biggest chunk of that—nearly $850 billion—is owned by pension funds, insurance companies, mutual funds and banks. They are in the business of taking savings from those who have them and lending that money to those, including the federal government, who need it.

An additional $430 billion in U.S. government debt is held by state and local governments. And there is more than $200 billion in oldfashioned savings bonds. The rest of the money is held by various investors, largely Americans although sometimes foreigners hold U.S. Treasury bonds in U.S. accounts.

Not included in any of these figures is the amount of U.S. currency held outside the country, often by foreigners who trust the dollar more than their own currencies. According to the Federal Reserve, recent estimates show that between one-half and two-thirds of the $780 billion worth of U.S. currency in circulation is held abroad.

Estimated Ownership of U.S. Debt
Figures are in billions

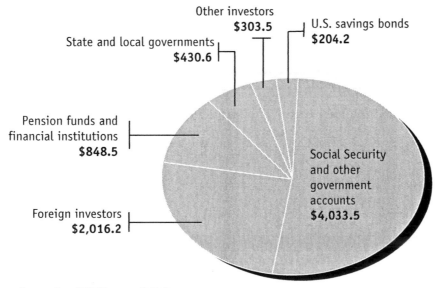

Source: Dec. 2005 Treasury Bulletin

Source: Wessel, David, "Ask David Wessel," *The Wall Street Journal Sunday* supplement appearing in *Sunday Patriot-News*, Harrisburg, PA, January 15, 2006, p. C-5.

Questions for Discussion:

1. How much of the U.S. government debt was owned by foreigners at the end of June 2005? (Answer: As of the end of June 2005, $2 trillion of U.S. government debt was held by foreign banks, individuals, and governments.)

2. How much of the U.S. government debt was held by Americans at the end of June 2005? (Answer: At the end of June 2005, $1.8 trillion of U.S. government debt was held by Americans.)

3. How much of the U.S. government debt was held in the form of U.S. savings bonds at the end of June 2005? (Answer: At the end of June 2005, $204.2 billion of the U.S. government debt was held in U.S. savings bonds.)

chapter **18**

Money, the Federal Reserve System, and Monetary Policy

Chapter Objectives

Students will learn in this chapter:
- The various roles money plays and the many forms it takes in the economy.
- The difference between commodity-backed money and fiat money.
- How the Federal Reserve System is structured and the various roles it plays.
- How the actions of private banks and the Federal Reserve determine the money supply.
- How the Federal Reserve uses open-market operations to change interest rates.
- How monetary policy affects aggregate output in the short run.

Chapter Outline

Opening Example: The statements made by the Federal Open Market Committee, eight times a year, are carefully analyzed by policy makers to discern the Fed's future stance on monetary policy.

I. The Meaning of Money

    A. What Is Money?

        1. *Definition:* A household's **wealth** is the value of its accumulated savings.

        2. *Definition:* **Money** is an asset that can easily be used to purchase goods and services.

        3. *Definition:* An asset is **liquid** if it can be quickly converted into cash without much loss of value.

        4. *Definition:* **Currency in circulation** is cash held by the public.

        5. *Definition:* **Checkable bank deposits** are bank accounts on which people can write checks.

        6. *Definition:* The **money supply** is the total value of financial assets in the economy that are considered money.

        7. The narrowest definition of the money supply—M1—is the most liquid as it includes only currency in circulation, traveler's checks, and checkable bank deposits.

8. A broader definition of the money supply—M2—includes currency in circulation, traveler's checks, checkable bank deposits, as well as other assets that are "almost" checkable, such as savings account deposits that can easily be transferred into a checking account.

9. An even broader definition of the money supply—M3—includes currency in circulation, traveler's checks, checkable bank deposits, savings accounts, and other deposits that come with larger penalties for early withdrawal.

B. Roles of Money

1. *Definition*: A **medium of exchange** is an asset that individuals acquire for the purpose of trading rather than for their own consumption.

2. *Definition*: A **store of value** is a means of holding purchasing power over time.

3. *Definition*: A **unit of account** is a measure used to set prices and make economic calculations.

4. Money plays three main roles in the economy:
    *   Medium of exchange
    *   Store of value
    *   Unit of account

C. Types of Money

1. *Definition*: **Commodity money** is a good used as a medium of exchange that has other uses.

2. *Definition*: A **commodity-backed money** is a medium of exchange with no intrinsic value whose ultimate value is guaranteed by a promise that it can be converted into valuable goods.

3. *Definition*: **Fiat money** is a medium of exchange whose value derives entirely from its official status as a means of payment.

4. *Definition*: A **monetary aggregate** is an overall measure of the money supply.

5. *Definition*: **Near-moneys** are financial assets that can't be directly used as a medium of exchange but can be readily converted into cash or checkable bank deposits.

6. Panels (a) and (b) in Figure 18-1 on page 456 in the text illustrate the components of M1 and M2, respectively.

II. The Monetary Role of Banks

A. *Definition*: A **bank** is a financial intermediary that provides liquid assets in the form of bank deposits to lenders and uses those funds to finance the illiquid investments or investment spending needs of borrowers.

B. *Definition*: A **financial intermediary** is an institution that transforms the funds it gathers from many individuals into financial assets.

C. *Definition*: A **bank deposit** is a claim on a bank that obligates the bank to give the depositor his or her cash when demanded.

D. *Definition*: **Bank reserves** are the currency banks hold in their vaults plus their deposits at the Federal Reserve.

E. *Definition*: An **asset** is a claim that provides income in the future.

F. *Definition*: A **liability** is a requirement to pay in the future.

G. *Definition*: The **reserve ratio** is the fraction of bank deposits that a bank holds as reserves.

H. A summary of a bank's financial position:

    1. A bank's assets include its reserves as well as any loans it has issued.

    2. A bank's liabilities include the deposits it holds.

I. *Definition*: A **bank run** is a phenomenon in which many of a bank's depositors try to withdraw their funds due to fears of a bank failure.

J. *Definition*: **Deposit insurance** guarantees that a bank's depositors will be paid even if the bank can't come up with the funds, up to a maximum per account.

K. Most banks in the United States are members of FDIC—the Federal Deposit Insurance Corporation—which currently guarantees the first $100,000 held in each account at a bank.

L. *Definition*: **Reserve requirements** are rules set by the Federal Reserve that determine the minimum reserve ratio for a bank.

M. *Definition*: **Excess reserves** are a bank's reserves over and above its required reserves.

N. When currency is deposited into a bank, the bank can lend excess reserves out, which leads to new deposits in the banking system and an increase in the money supply.

III. The Federal Reserve System

A. The Fed: America's Central Bank

    1. *Definition*: A **central bank** is an institution that oversees and regulates the banking system and conducts monetary policy.

    2. The Federal Reserve, established in 1913, is the central bank of the United States.

    3. The Federal Reserve system consists of two parts:
- The Board of Governors
- The 12 regional Federal Reserve Banks that provide various banking and supervisory services to commercial banks.

    4. The seven members of the Board of Governors are appointed by the president with Senate approval and serve 14-year terms.

    5. The chairman of the Fed is appointed by the president with Senate approval and serves a 4-year term with possible reappointment.

    6. Federal Open Market Committee comprised of the:
- Board of Governors
- President of the New York Federal Reserve Bank plus five other regional Federal Reserve Bank presidents.

    7. Federal Open Market Committee makes decisions regarding monetary policy.

B. What the Fed Does: Reserve Requirements and the Discount Rate

    1. *Definition*: The **federal funds market** allows banks that fall short of the reserve requirement to borrow funds from banks with excess reserves.

    2. *Definition*: The **federal funds rate** is the interest rate determined in the federal funds market.

    3. *Definition*: The **discount rate** is the rate of interest the Fed charges on loans to banks.

C. Open-Market Operations

    1. *Definition*: An **open-market operation** is a purchase or sale of government debt by the Fed.

   2. The Federal Reserve's assets include government debt, mainly in the form of U.S. Treasury bills.

   3. The Federal Reserve's liabilities include the currency in circulation plus bank reserves.

   4. Monetary policy is most often conducted using open-market operations.

   5. An open-market purchase of Treasury bills increases the money supply, while an open-market sale of Treasury bills decreases the money supply.

IV. Monetary Policy and Aggregate Demand

   A. Expansionary and Contractionary Monetary Policy

   1. *Definition*: The **target federal funds rate** is the Federal Reserve's desired federal funds rate.

   2. *Definition*: **Expansionary monetary policy** is monetary policy that increases aggregate demand.

   3. Expansionary monetary policy reduces the interest rate, causing the aggregate demand curve to shift to the right, and so is used to eliminate a recessionary gap.

   4. *Definition*: **Contractionary monetary policy** is monetary policy that reduces aggregate demand.

   5. Contractionary monetary policy increases the interest rate, causing the aggregate demand curve to shift to the left, and so is used to eliminate an inflationary gap.

   B. Monetary Policy and the Multiplier

   1. An expansionary monetary policy, which reduces interest rates, leading to an initial increase in investment spending, and a subsequent rise in consumer spending, shifts the aggregate demand curve to the right.

   2. Assuming a fixed price level, and no taxes or foreign trade, an expansionary monetary policy which reduces interest rates, increases planned investment spending, I, and induces an increase in consumer spending, C. Thus, the total amount by which real GDP increases, ΔY, due to an expansionary monetary policy is measured using the multiplier as follows:

$$\Delta Y = \Delta I \times \frac{1}{1 - MPC}$$

Teaching Tips

The Meaning of Money

Creating Student Interest

Ask students, "What is money?" It is likely that someone will respond that it is something used to purchase goods and services. Ask students if they can name some forms of money. Indicate that, in addition to U.S. coins and bills, gold, silver, tobacco, and shells have all been used as money at one time in this country.

Common Student Misunderstandings

It is important to point out the different effects two very commonly used methods of payment have on the money supply. Specifically, debit cards immediately deduct the value of a purchase from the card owner's bank account, say, his checking account. As a result, debit cards which enable the cardholder to access his or checking account balance, which is a part of M1, do have an impact on the money supply. However, credit card purchases do not affect the money supply, since the balance on a credit card is considered a liability of the cardholder, which is not part of the money supply.

Presenting the Material

Begin by defining the term money, and discussing the various roles money serves in an economy. Panels (a) and (b) in Figure 18-1 on page 456 in the text provide very useful information when delineating the various components of M1 and M2.

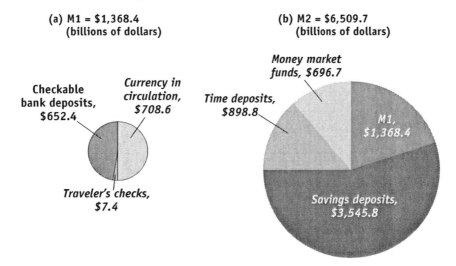

Using the Case Study in the Text

The History of the Dollar (text pages 457–458)

Ask students:

1. Was money issued in the United States always fiat money as it is today? (Answer: Not all money used in the United States has been fiat money. For example, during colonial times tobacco and shells were used as money. In addition, historically, private banks issued paper currency that was backed by silver or gold.)

2. When did the United States stop linking its currency to gold? (Answer: The United States stopped linking its currency to gold briefly in the 1930s; however, it made a more permanent move away from gold backing in 1971.)

Activity

What Goes Where? (10 minutes)

Pair students and ask them to accurately allocate each of the following being as part of M1 and/or M2.

• Currency held by individuals

• Checking accounts

• Savings accounts

• Certificates of deposit

• Traveler's checks

• Money market accounts

Answers:

- Currency held by individuals   Part of M1 and M2
- Checking accounts   Part of M1 and M2
- Savings accounts   Part of M2
- Certificates of deposit   Part of M2
- Traveler's checks   Part of M1 and M2
- Money market accounts   Part of M2

The Monetary Role of Banks

Creating Student Interest

Ask students to assume that they each have $100 in a checking account at a local bank. Subsequently, ask students whether the bank holds on to all of this money. Explain that banks are required to hold in reserve only a small fraction of deposits. The particular amount banks must hold in reserve is determined by the Fed.

Common Student Misunderstandings

Some students may think that a run on the banks, similar to the one they read about during the Great Depression, could happen today. Indicate to them that, due to extensive regulations and auditing of commercial banks today, along with the existence of deposit insurance on accounts of up to $100,000 issued by the Federal Deposit Insurance Corporation (FDIC), such a run on banks is not a worry in today's economy.

Presenting the Material

Begin by discussing the meaning of the key terms, **bank reserves** and the **reserve ratio,** along with the significance of each. Also identify the assets and liabilities of a bank. Finally, discuss the various forms of banking regulation—deposit insurance, capital requirements, and reserve requirements—and how they have vastly reduced the probability of bank runs today.

Using the Case Study in the Text

It's a Wonderful Banking System (text pages 461–462)
Ask students:

1. When have runs on banks in the United States occurred? (Answer: During late 1930, the spring of 1931 and early 1933, there were runs on banks in the United States By 1933, nearly one-third of the nation's banks had failed.)

2. What steps were taken to restore faith in the U.S. banking system in the 1930s? (Answer: On entering office, President Franklin Roosevelt declared a bank holiday and closed the banks for one week to assess their solvency and calm anxious investors. In addition, many regulations were imposed on commercial banks, along with FDIC insurance on accounts in order to regain and maintain the confidence of the banking public.)

Activities

Setting Up a T-Account (10 minutes)
Pair students and ask them to complete the following exercises.

1. Construct a general T-account for a bank.

2. What must be true of the total values on each side of the T-account?

Answers:

1.

ASSETS	LIABILITIES
Loans	Deposits
Reserves	

2. Both sides of the T-account must be equal.

Be a Bank's Accountant (15 minutes)

Pair students and ask them to complete the following exercises.

1. The A&Z Bank has $250,000 in deposits. If the reserve ratio is 10%, how much of these deposits must the bank hold in reserve?

2. How much in loans can the A&B Bank issue in the given situation?

3. Construct the T-account for the A&B Bank.

Answers:

1. In general, Reserves = Reserve Ratio × Deposits.

Reserves = (0.10) × $250,000 = $25,000

2. In general, Loans = Deposits − Reserves

Loans = $250,000 − $25,000 = $225,000

3.

ASSETS	LIABILITIES
Loans $225,000	Deposits $250,000
Reserves $ 25,000	

In the News

Use the following article, published by a researcher at the regional Federal Reserve bank in Cleveland, Ohio, to stimulate discussion on the topic of bank failures.

What Caused High Bank Failure Rates in 2002?

Bruce Wedel, Examiner Specialist

On December 18, 2002, the Louisiana state banking authorities closed Farmers Bank and Trust of Chenyville, making it the eleventh federally insured financial institution to have failed in 2002. Based on publicly available information, the bank's demise does not seem particularly headline worthy: At $37 million in assets, it was relatively small and well established, having been founded in 1946. Because it was not subject to formal enforcement action by federal banking supervisors and there was no widespread media coverage, the cause of the bank's failure is not evident. But what makes this bank failure noteworthy is that it pushed the number of Bank Insurance Fund-insured failures into double digits for the year, and it was the eleventh failure handled by the FDIC (one institution covered by the Savings Association Insurance Fund also closed).

Last year saw more bank failures than any year since 1994, when 15 federally insured banks and thrifts were closed or otherwise resolved. Both numbers seem insignificant compared to 1984–92, when approximately 2,600 institutions were closed — an average of more than 300 each year. Nonetheless, the current spike warrants analysis to determine whether any common themes are present. Because publicly available information is harder to come by as time passes, here we use "current" to refer to the period after December 31, 1996, and we use "banks" to mean banks and thrifts.

It is commonly believed that newer enterprises have higher failure rates — and for that reason, regulators pay close attention to de novo banks (in business for under five years). Over the past seven years, however, only two of the 34 institutions that failed were de novo banks. In fact, the median age of failed banks over the period was 39 years, with 16 banks over 50 years old at the time of failure. On the surface, it appears that a bank's age has little to do with its chance of failure.

Failures do seem to be more common among smaller banks. Since the end of 1996, only eight banks with assets over $100 million have closed and, of those eight, only three had assets over $1 billion. The median bank size was $42 million.

Because of the small sample size (34 of 7,933 banks) that exists, the federal regulatory agency does not seem to make a difference. More banks regulated by the FDIC (13) and the Office of the Comptroller of the Currency (10) failed, but their constituencies are much larger than either the Federal Reserve (7) or the Office of Thrift Supervision (4).

Although the locations of the failed banks were geographically distributed, they tend to be concentrated in the Southern and Midwestern states. Failures in the New England and eastern states were rare.

With little evidence that age, location, or regulator have much to do with bank failure, we are still left with the question of what does cause banks to fail. Although the hard evidence is not in the public domain, reasonably informed estimates can be made by assuming that formal regulatory actions (cease-and-desist or written formal agreements) in place at the time of the bank closure addressed the weaknesses leading to the failure. These agreements, however, require some speculation because they are not written as explicit instructions. Further, several failed banks were not subject to formal agreements.

Despite all of the new (or newly identified) risks in the banking industry, the majority of bank failures over the past six years can be attributed to two causes. Loan quality—often resulting from poor underwriting practices—was the culprit in nearly half the cases. Fraud, embezzlement, and insider abuse was evident in another one-third of the cases. Of the remaining failures, most had causes that were not evident, though a few seemed to result from problems with internal routines or controls, meaning the fraud or embezzlement occurred after the supervisory action was put in place.

Two factors relating to credit quality are subprime lending and improper accounting related to the securitizing of assets. In some cases, these two issues were intertwined. Given the media attention and regulatory scrutiny given to subprime lending and asset securitization, there should be few, if any, surprises resulting from these practices.

Source: Wedel, Bruce "What Caused High Bank Failure Rates in 2002?" *Fourth District Conditions*, Federal Reserve Bank of Cleveland, Vol. 4, No. 1.

Questions for Discussion:

1. According to the results of this research, is there a negative relationship between the length of time a bank has been open to the probability of a bank's failure? (Answer: No such correlation was found in this study.)

2. Is the size of a bank's assets related to its probability of failure? (Answer: According to the findings in this study, it was found that banks with lesser assets did have a higher rate of failure than banks with greater assets.)

3. What were the most commonly cited causes of bank failure between 1996 and 2002? (Answer: The most common causes of bank failures during this time period were: poor loan quality due to inadequate underwriting of loans, fraud, embezzlement, and insider abuse.)

The Federal Reserve System

Creating Student Interest

Bring some one dollar bills to class. Inform students that there are twelve Federal Reserve Banks, each serving a distinct region of the country. Every one dollar bill bears a seal with a letter in the center. The letters range from A through L, representing each of the regional Federal Reserve Banks. After revealing which letters you have on your bills, ask students to check their one dollar bills in a similar fashion.

Common Student Misunderstandings

Students may confuse the Federal Reserve with the regional Federal Reserve Banks. Indicate that the institution known as the Federal Reserve is comprised of two entities—the Board of Governors, and the 12 regional Federal Reserve Banks. Further, it is the responsibility of the regional Federal Reserve Banks to audit the books of private-sector banks to ensure the banks' solvency, and act as a clearing house for checks drawn from accounts in banks in their district. The regional Federal Reserve Banks also print money.

Presenting the Material

Begin by presenting the organization of the Federal Reserve System, as well as the duties of each functional group. Afterward, discuss the various policy tools of the Fed and the manner in which a change in each affects the money supply.

Using the Case Study in the Text

Building Europe's Fed (text page 465)

Ask students:

1. How does the European Central Bank compare to the Federal Reserve? (Answer: The European Central Bank is comparable to the Fed's Board of Governors, as it is charged with formulating monetary policy for the 11 European nations that adopted the euro as their currency.)

2. What role do the former central banks of the 11 nations that adopted the euro as their currency currently have? (Answer: These former central banks now act in the same way as do the regional Federal Reserve Banks in the United States. They provide various financial services to commercial banks and businesses. In addition, like the New York Federal Reserve Bank, they also carry out open-market operations.)

Activity

Which of the Fed's Policy Tools...? (15 minutes)

Pair students and ask them to identify an appropriate tool at the Fed's disposal, as well as the appropriate action to be taken by the Fed, to deal with the following economic situations.

1. Significant decreases in real GDP for three straight quarters

2. Increases in the unemployment rate over the past six months

3. Monthly increases in the producer price index for the past four months

4. A severe depression

5. Significant increases in the CPI over the past six months

Possible Answers:

1. Decrease the required reserve ratio

2. Purchases of U.S. Treasury bills by the Fed

3. Sales of U.S. Treasury bills by the Fed

4. Decreasing the discount rate

5. Increasing the federal funds rate by selling U.S Treasury bills

Monetary Policy and Aggregate Demand

Creating Student Interest

Ask students why the Fed initiates monetary policy. Undoubtedly, someone will respond that the Fed initiates monetary policy to affect the state of the macroeconomy. Explain to students that in this section of the chapter they will learn how to graphically illustrate the effect of monetary policy on aggregate output and the aggregate price level, using the AS–AD model that was developed in the previous chapter.

Common Student Misunderstandings

Students may mistakenly think that changes in the money supply affect aggregate supply. This misperception is most likely due to their seeing the word *supply* in each phrase. Emphasize to students that a change in the money supply affects key interest rates in the economy, such as the prime rate of interest paid by very large business borrowers, and mortgage interest rates paid by consumers. As a result, changes in the money supply affect consumer spending and business investment and, therefore, shift the aggregate demand curve, not the aggregate supply curve.

Presenting the Material

Use the *AS-AD* model, shown in Figure 18-5 and Figure 18-4 on pages 466 and 467 in the text, respectively, to illustrate the manner in which a recessionary gap can be closed using expansionary monetary policy, and the manner in which contractionary monetary policy can be used to close an inflationary gap.

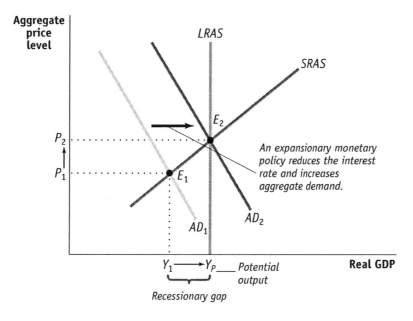

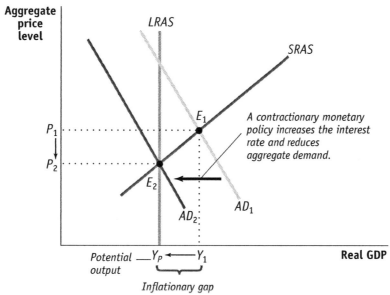

The multiplier impact of a change in the money supply on the aggregate demand curve can be introduced intuitively. Afterward, the multiplier effect can be developed both mathematically and graphically, as shown in Figure 18-6 on page 468 in the text.

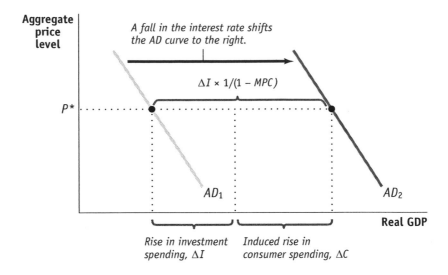

Using the Case Study in the Text

The Fed and the Output Gap, 1985-2004 (text pages 469–470)

Ask students:

1. For the time period 1985–2004, what was the relationship between the federal funds rate and the output gap? (Answer: Data for this period indicate that there was a direct or positive relationship between the federal funds rate and the output gap. This means that, as the output gap rose, the Federal Open Market Committee increased the federal funds rate to slow the economy down and lessen inflationary pressure on wages and prices.)

2. Why do the data indicate that there was often a lag in terms of the Federal Open Market Committee adjusting the target federal funds rate to changes in the output gap? (Answer: The Fed has been known to act cautiously and wait until it is certain that a policy change is necessary in response to changes in the output gap. Therefore, the data on the federal funds rate and the output gap do indicate a slight lag in terms of the Fed's changes in the federal funds rate compared with changes in the value of the output gap.)

Activity

Monetary Policy and the Multiplier (20 minutes)

Pair students and ask them to complete the following exercises.

1. How can changes in monetary policy affect the aggregate demand curve?
2. Explain the multiplier effect associated with expansionary monetary policy that shifts the aggregate demand curve.
3. Draw a graph to illustrate your answer to question 2.

Answers:

1. Changes in the money supply cause the interest rate to change, which in turn cause the level of investment spending to change. Since investment spending, *I*, is a component of aggregate demand, a change in *I* will cause the aggregate demand curve to shift. Contractionary monetary policies will result in a higher interest rate, which will cause investment spending to fall, thereby shifting the aggregate demand curve to the left. Conversely, expansionary monetary policies will result in a lower interest rate, which will cause investment spending to rise, thereby shifting the aggregate demand curve to the right.

2. Expansionary monetary policy will reduce the interest rate and thereby cause investment spending to rise. In addition, this increase in investment spending will cause disposable income to rise which, in turn, will cause consumer spending to increase. In summary, expansionary monetary policy has a multiplier effect, which first results in an increase in investment spending and then, subsequently, a rise in consumer spending.

3.

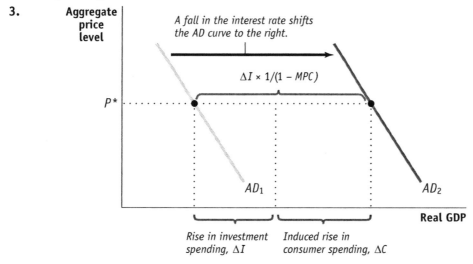

A fall in the interest rate shifts the AD curve to the right.

$\Delta I \times 1/(1 - MPC)$

Rise in investment spending, ΔI

Induced rise in consumer spending, ΔC

Work It Out

Monetary Policy (text page 468)

In this numerical example, students are presented with the value of the marginal propensity to consume, and the estimate that for every 0.25 % decrease in interest rates, investment spending rises by $50 billion. They are asked to determine the following:

- the value of the investment multiplier
- the amount by which investment spending must change in order to increase aggregate demand by $500 billion
- the amount by which the Fed must lower interest rates in order to increase aggregate demand by $500 billion
- the appropriate conduct by the FOMC to achieve an increase in aggregate demand
- the impact on the money supply

First Principles

1. In each of the following situations, identify which of the nine principles is at work.

   a. You choose to shop at the local discount store rather than paying a higher price for the same merchandise at the local department store.

   b. On your spring vacation trip, your budget is limited to $35 a day.

   c. The student union provides a website on which departing students can sell items such as used books, appliances, and furniture rather than giving them away to their room-mates as they formerly did.

   d. You decide how many cups of coffee to have when studying the night before an exam by considering how much more work you can do by having another cup versus how jittery it will make you feel.

   e. There is limited lab space available to do the project required in Chemistry 101. The lab supervisor assigns lab time to each student based on when that student is able to come.

   f. You realize that you can graduate a semester early by forgoing a semester of study abroad.

   g. At the student union, there is a bulletin board on which people advertise used items for sale, such as bicycles. Once you have adjusted for differences in quality, all the bikes sell for about the same price.

   h. You are better at performing lab experiments, and your lab partner is better at writing lab reports. So the two of you agree that you will do all the experiments, and she will write up all the reports.

   i. State governments mandate that it is illegal to drive without passing a driving exam.

1. a. People usually exploit opportunities to make themselves better off. In this case, you make yourself better off by buying merchandise at a lower price.

   b. Resources are scarce. Since you have only $35 a day, your resources are limited (scarce).

   c. Markets usually lead to efficiency. The market here is represented by the buyers and sellers who use the student union website to trade goods, in contrast to the "nonmarket" of simply giving items away to one's roommate. The market is efficient because it enables people who want to sell items to find those who want to buy those items. This is in contrast to a system in which items are simply left with a roommate, who may have little or no desire to have them.

   d. "How much?" is a decision at the margin. Your decision is one of "how much" coffee to consume, and you evaluate the trade-off between keeping yourself awake and becoming more jittery from one more cup of coffee.

   e. Resources should be used as efficiently as possible to achieve society's goals. Allocating scarce lab space according to when each student can use that space is efficient.

   f. The real cost of something is what you must give up to get it. The real cost of a semester abroad is giving up the opportunity to graduate early.

   g. Markets move toward equilibrium. Any bicycle a buyer chooses will leave him or her equally well off. That is, a buyer who chooses a particular bicycle cannot change actions and find another bicycle that makes him or her better off. Also, no seller can take a different action that makes him or her better off: no seller can charge a higher price for a bicycle of similar quality, since no one would buy that bicycle.

h. There are gains from trade. If each person specializes in what he or she is good at (that is, in comparison with others that person has an advantage in producing that good), then there will be gains from specialization and trade.

i. When markets don't achieve efficiency, government intervention can improve society's welfare. Unsafe drivers don't take into account the dangers they impose on others and often on themselves. So when unsafe drivers are allowed to drive, everyone is made worse off. Government intervention improves society's welfare by assuring a minimum level of competence in driving.

2. Describe some of the opportunity costs when you decide to do the following.

a. Attend college instead of taking a job

b. Watch a movie instead of studying for an exam

c. Ride the bus instead of driving your car

2. a. One of the opportunity costs of going to college is not being able to take a job. By choosing to go to college, you give up the income you would have earned on the job and the valuable on-the-job experience you would have acquired. Another opportunity cost of going to college is the cost of tuition, books, supplies, and so on. On the other hand, the benefit of going to college is being able to find a better, more highly paid job after graduation in addition to the joy of learning.

b. Watching the movie gives you a certain benefit, but allocating your time (a scarce resource) to watching the movie also involves the opportunity cost of not being able to study for the exam. As a result, you will likely get a lower grade on the exam—and all that that implies.

c. Riding the bus gets you where you need to go more cheaply, but probably not as conveniently, as driving your car. That is, some of the opportunity costs of taking the bus involve having to walk from the bus stop to where you need to go rather than parking your car right outside the building, waiting for the bus, and probably a slower journey. If the opportunity cost of your time is high (your time is valuable), these costs may be prohibitive.

3. Liza needs to buy a textbook for the next economics class. The price at the college bookstore is $65. One online site offers it for $55 and another site for $57. All prices include sales tax. The accompanying table indicates the typical shipping and handling charges for the textbook ordered online.

a. What is the opportunity cost of buying online?

b. Show the relevant choices for this student. What determines which of these options the student will choose?

Shipping method	Delivery time	Charge
Standard shipping	3–7 days	$3.99
Second-day air	2 business days	$8.98
Next-day air	1 business day	$13.98

3. a. The opportunity cost of buying online is whatever you must give up to do so. That is, you give up the money for the shipping charges, and there is also an opportunity cost of your time: You have to wait for the book to be delivered (at the bookstore you get the book right away). But, of course, you save the difference in the price of the book between the bookstore and the online retailer.

b. Below is a list of all of Liza's options and their purely monetary costs:

Buy from bookstore	$65
Buy from first site (price $55), 1-day delivery	$55 + $13.98 = $68.98
Buy from first site (price $55), 2-day delivery	$55 + $ 8.98 = $63.98
Buy from first site (price $55), 3- to 7-day delivery	$55 + $ 3.99 = $58.99
Buy from second site (price $57), 1-day delivery	$57 + $13.98 = $70.98
Buy from second site (price $57), 2-day delivery	$57 + $ 8.98 = $65.98
Buy from second site (price $57), 3- to 7-day delivery	$57 + $ 3.99 = $60.99

It is clear that Liza would never buy from the second site, where the book costs $57: For each delivery time, she is better off buying the book from the first site, where the book costs $55. It is also clear that she would never buy the book from the first site and have it delivered the next business day: it costs more that way ($68.98) than getting it from the bookstore (assuming that it is costless to get to and from the bookstore). But it is not clear whether she will buy the book from the bookstore or the first site with delivery times of 2 or 3–7 days: This depends on her opportunity cost of time. The higher the cost of waiting, the more likely she is to buy the book from the bookstore, where she does not need to wait.

4. Use the concept of opportunity cost to explain the following.

   a. More people choose to get graduate degrees when the job market is poor.

   b. More people choose to do their own home repairs when the economy is slow.

   c. There are more parks in suburban areas than in urban areas.

   d. Convenience stores, which have higher prices than supermarkets, cater to busy people.

   e. Fewer students enroll in classes that meet before 10:00 A.M.

4. **a.** The worse the job market, the lower the opportunity cost of getting a graduate degree. One of the opportunity costs of going to graduate school is not being able to work. But if the job market is bad, the salary you can expect to earn is low or you might be unemployed—so the opportunity cost of going to school is also low.

   b. When the economy is slow, the opportunity cost of people's time is also lower: the salary they could earn by working longer hours is lower than when the economy is booming. As a result, the opportunity cost of spending time doing your own repairs is lower—so more people will decide to do their own repairs.

   c. The opportunity cost of parkland is lower in suburban areas. The price per square foot of land is much higher in urban than in suburban areas. By creating parkland, you therefore give up the opportunity to make much more money in cities than in the suburbs.

   d. The opportunity cost of time is higher for busy people. Driving long distances to supermarkets takes time that could be spent doing other things. Therefore busy people are more likely to use a nearby convenience store.

   e. Before 10:00 A.M. the opportunity cost of time for many students is very high—it means giving up an extra hour's sleep. That extra hour is much more valuable before 10:00 A.M. than later in the day.

5. In the following examples, state how you would use the principle of marginal analysis to make a decision.

   a. Deciding how many days to wait before doing your laundry

   b. Deciding how much library research to do before writing your term paper

   c. Deciding how many bags of chips to eat

   d. Deciding how many lectures of a class to skip

5. a. Each day that you wait to do your laundry imposes a cost: You have fewer clean clothes to choose from. But each day that you wait also confers a benefit: You can spend your time doing other things. You will wait another day to do your laundry if the benefit of waiting to do the laundry that day is greater than the cost.

   b. The more research you do, the better your paper will be. But there is also an opportunity cost: every additional hour you spend doing research means you cannot do other things. You will weigh the opportunity cost of doing one more hour of research against the benefit gained (in terms of an improved paper) from doing research. You will do one more hour of research if the benefit of that hour outweighs the cost.

   c. Each bag of chips you eat gives you a benefit: it satisfies your hunger. But it also has a cost: the money spent for each bag (and if you are weight-conscious, the additional calories). You will weigh the cost against the benefit of eating one more bag. If the cost is less than the benefit, you will eat that one more bag of chips.

   d. Each lecture that you skip implies a cost: getting further behind with the material and having to teach it to yourself just before the exam. But each skipped lecture also means you can spend the time doing other things. You will continue to skip lectures if the cost of skipping is lower than the benefit of spending that time doing other things.

6. This morning you made the following individual choices: you bought a bagel and coffee at the local café, you drove to school in your car during rush hour, and you typed your roommate's term paper because you are a fast typist—in return for which she will do your laundry for a month. In each of these actions, describe how your individual choices interacted with the individual choices made by others. Were other people left better off or worse off by your choices in each case?

6. When you bought the bagel and coffee, you paid a price for them. You would not have bought that breakfast if your enjoyment of it (your welfare) had not been greater than the price you paid. Similarly, the café owner would not have sold you the bagel and coffee if the price he received from you were less than the cost to him of making them. This is an example of how everybody gains from trade: both you and the café owner are better off.

When you chose to drive your car during the rush hour, you added to the congestion on the road. Your choice had a side effect for other motorists: your driving slowed everybody else down just a little bit more. Your choice made other motorists worse off.

Typing your roommate's term paper in exchange for her doing your laundry is another example of the gains that come from trade. Both of you voluntarily agreed to specialize in a task that each is comparatively better at because you expected to gain from this interaction. Your choice made both you and your roommate better off.

7. On the east side of the Hatatoochie River lives the Hatfield family, while the McCoy family lives on the west side. Each family's diet consists of fried chicken and corn-on-the-cob, and each is self-sufficient, raising their own chickens and growing their own corn. Explain the conditions under which each of the following would be true.

  a. The two families are made better off when the Hatfields specialize in raising chickens, the McCoys specialize in raising corn, and the two families trade.

  b. The two families are made better off when the McCoys specialize in raising chickens, the Hatfields specialize in raising corn, and the two families trade.

7. **a.** Gains from trade usually arise from specialization. If (compared to the McCoys) the Hatfields are better at raising chickens and (compared to the Hatfields) the McCoys are better at growing corn, then there will be gains from specialization and trade.

  b. Similar to the answer to part a, if (compared to the Hatfields) the McCoys are better at raising chickens and (compared to the McCoys) the Hatfields are better at growing corn, then there will be gains from specialization and trade.

8. Which of the following situations describes an equilibrium? Which does not? If the situation does not describe an equilibrium, what would an equilibrium look like?

  a. Many people regularly commute from the suburbs to downtown Pleasantville. Due to traffic congestion, the trip takes 30 minutes when you travel by highway, but only 15 minutes when you go by side streets.

  b. At the intersection of Main and Broadway are two gas stations. One station charges $3.00 per gallon for regular gas and the other charges $2.85 per gallon. Customers can get service immediately at the first station, but must wait in a long line at the second.

  c. Every student enrolled in Economics 101 must also attend a weekly tutorial. This year there are two sections offered: section A and section B, which meet at the same time in adjoining classrooms and are taught by equally competent instructors. Section A is overcrowded, with people sitting on the floor and often unable to see the chalkboard. Section B has many empty seats.

8. **a.** This is not an equilibrium. Assume that all that people care about is the travel time to work (not, for instance, how many turns they need to make or what the scenery is like). Some people could be better off using the side streets, which would cut down their travel time. Eventually, as the situation moves to equilibrium (that is, as more people use the side streets), travel times on the highway and along the side streets should equalize.

  b. This might be an equilibrium. Those who buy gas at the first station would be worse off by buying gas at the second if the value of their time spent waiting exceeded the savings at the pump: they would save 15 cents per gallon but would incur the opportunity cost of waiting in a long line. You should expect very busy people (a high opportunity cost of time) to buy gas at the first station. Those who buy gas at the second station might be worse off by buying gas at the first: they would not have to wait in line but would pay 15 cents more per gallon. You should expect people with a lot of free time (a low opportunity cost of time) to buy gas at the second station.

  c. This is not an equilibrium. If students from section A attended section B instead, they would be better off: they could get seats and see the chalkboard without incurring any cost (since the section meets at the same time and is taught by an equally competent instructor). Over time, you should expect students to switch from section A to section B until equilibrium is established.

9. In each of the following cases, explain whether you think the situation is efficient or not. If it is not efficient, why not? What actions would make the situation efficient?

   a. Electricity is included in the rent at your dorm. Some residents in your dorm leave lights, computers, and appliances on when they are not in their rooms.

   b. Although they cost the same amount to prepare, the cafeteria in your dorm consistently provides too many dishes that diners don't like, such as tofu casserole, and too few dishes that diners do like, such as roast turkey with dressing.

   c. The enrollment for a particular course exceeds the spaces available. Some students who need to take this course to complete their major are unable to get a space while others who are taking it as an elective do get a space.

9. a. This is not efficient. If the lights were turned off, many students could be made better off without making anyone else worse off because the college would save money on electricity that it could spend on student programs. By leaving lights and appliances on when leaving their rooms, residents do not take into account the negative side effect they impose on their college—the higher cost of electricity. If students were forced to pay their own individual electricity costs (that is, if they fully took into account the cost of their actions), then they would turn the lights and appliances off when leaving their rooms. This situation would be efficient.

   b. This is not efficient. Instead of serving dishes that many diners do not like, the cafeteria should serve more of the dishes that diners do like at the same cost. That way, some students could be made better off without others being made worse off.

   c. This is not efficient. In an efficient scheme, spaces would be allocated to those students who value them most. In this case, however, some spaces are allocated to students who value them less (those who take the course as an elective) than other students (those who need the course to graduate). Efficiency could be improved as follows: if a student who is not currently enrolled in the course values it more than a student who is enrolled, then the unenrolled student should be willing to pay the enrolled student to give up his or her space. At some price, this trade would make both students better off and the outcome would be efficient.

10. Discuss the efficiency and equity implications of each of the following policies. How would you go about balancing the concerns of equity and efficiency in these areas?

   a. The government pays the full tuition for every college student to study whatever subject he or she wishes.

   b. When people lose their jobs, the government provides unemployment benefits until they find new ones.

10. a. Although this policy is equitable, it may not be efficient, depending on the beneficial side effects of education. It does allow everyone, regardless of ability to pay, to attend college. But it may not be efficient: subsidizing the full cost of tuition for everyone lowers the opportunity cost of going to college, and this might lead some people to go to college when they could more productively follow a career that does not require a college education. And since resources (including government money) are scarce, paying tuition for these people has an opportunity cost: some other (possibly more worthwhile) government projects cannot be undertaken. One way of getting around this problem is to award scholarships based on academic ability.

b. Although this policy may be equitable (it guarantees everyone a certain amount of income), it may not be efficient. People respond to incentives. If unemployment becomes more attractive because of the unemployment benefit, some unemployed people may no longer try to find a job or may not try to find one as quickly as they would without the benefit. Ways to get around this problem are to provide unemployment benefits only for a limited time or to require recipients to prove that they are actively searching for a new job.

11. Governments often adopt certain policies in order to promote desired behavior among their citizens. For each of the following policies, determine what the incentive is and what behavior the government wishes to promote. In each case, why do you think that the government might wish to change people's behavior, rather than allow their actions to be solely determined by individual choice?

   a. A tax of $5 per pack is imposed on cigarettes.

   b. The government pays parents $100 when their child is vaccinated for measles.

   c. The government pays college students to tutor children from low-income families.

   d. The government imposes a tax on the amount of air pollution that a company discharges.

11. **a.** This policy creates an incentive to smoke less by making a pack of cigarettes more costly. This is exactly what policy makers wish to promote. Cigarettes have undesirable side effects on other people, which smokers do not (or only insufficiently) take into account. One is that other people have to breathe in second-hand smoke. Another is the cost of health care: when smokers who need treatment for lung cancer are covered by Medicare or Medicaid, the rest of society has to foot the bill. Since individuals do not take these costs (costs that arise for other people) into account in deciding whether or not (or how much) to smoke, the amount of cigarettes smoked will be inefficiently high. The tax is a way to make people take these costs into account in deciding whether or not to smoke.

   b. This policy creates an incentive to have children vaccinated: it increases the benefit to parents from vaccination of their children. Getting vaccinated means not only that a child will not contract the measles but also that he or she cannot pass the measles on to other children. That is, there is a side effect on other people (their children get sick less often) that parents do not take into account in their decision of whether or not to have their own child vaccinated. The subsidy is a way to make individuals take into account in their decisions the benefit they can create for other people.

   c. This policy creates incentives for low-income families to get college students to tutor their children, since getting a tutor is now cheaper or free. This results in better performance in school by these children and higher levels of educational attainment. This has positive side effects for the rest of society: the better children do in school, the more productive, happier, and healthier citizens they will be.

   d. This tax creates the incentive to emit fewer air pollutants. Pollution has a negative side effect on others: it decreases air quality (for instance, it contributes to the formation of ozone smog) and results in a variety of health complications (for instance, asthma). In deciding how much pollution to discharge, a company does not take these negative side effects sufficiently into account. The tax is a way to make pollution more expensive, that is, to make the company face the cost it imposes on others.

12. In each of the following situations, explain how government intervention could improve society's welfare by changing people's incentives. In what sense is the market going wrong?

    a. Pollution from auto emissions has reached unhealthy levels.

    b. Everyone in Woodville would be better off if streetlights were installed in the town. But no individual resident is willing to pay for installation of a streetlight in front of his or her house because it is impossible to recoup the cost by charging other residents for the benefit they receive from it.

12. a. In deciding how much to drive, each driver does not take into account the cost of auto emissions he or she imposes on others. That is, the market will lead to there being too much pollution. One way for governments to intervene would be to tax fuel or to tax cars that get low gas mileage. Or governments could subsidize new and cleaner fuels or technologies, such as hybrid cars. This would create incentives for people to switch to cars that use less polluting gas or to drive less.

    b. The market in this situation leads to too few (or no) streetlights in Woodville. Government could improve residents' welfare by paying for streetlight installation from the taxes paid by residents.

Economic Models: Trade-offs and Trade

1. Atlantis is a small, isolated island in the South Atlantic. The inhabitants grow potatoes and catch fresh fish. The accompanying table shows the maximum annual output combinations of potatoes and fish that can be produced. Obviously, given their limited resources and available technology, as they use more of their resources for potato production, there are fewer resources available for catching fish.

Maximum annual output options	Quantity of potatoes (pounds)	Quantity of fish (pounds)
A	1,000	0
B	800	300
C	600	500
D	400	600
E	200	650
F	0	675

a. Draw a production possibility frontier with potatoes on the horizontal axis and fish on the vertical axis illustrating these options, showing points *A–F*.

b. Can Atlantis produce 500 pounds of fish and 800 pounds of potatoes? Explain. Where would this point lie relative to the production possibility frontier?

c. What is the opportunity cost of increasing the annual output of potatoes from 600 to 800 pounds?

d. What is the opportunity cost of increasing the annual output of potatoes from 200 to 400 pounds?

e. Can you explain why the answers to parts c and d are not the same? What does this imply about the slope of the production possibility frontier?

1. **a.** The accompanying diagram shows the production possibility frontier for Atlantis.

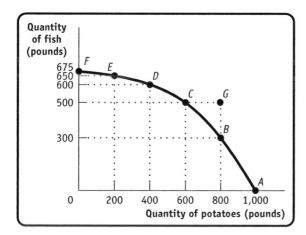

b. No, Atlantis cannot produce 500 pounds of fish and 800 pounds of potatoes. If it produces 500 pounds of fish, the most potatoes it can produce is 600 pounds. This point would lie outside the production possibility frontier, at point *G* on the diagram.

c. The opportunity cost of increasing output from 600 to 800 pounds of potatoes is 200 pounds of fish. If Atlantis increases output from 600 to 800 pounds of potatoes, it has to cut fish production from 500 pounds to 300 pounds, that is, by 200 pounds.

d. The opportunity cost of increasing output from 200 to 400 pounds of potatoes is 50 pounds of fish. If Atlantis increases output from 200 to 400 pounds of potatoes, it has to cut fish production from 650 pounds to 600 pounds, that is, by 50 pounds.

e. The answers to parts c and d imply that the more potatoes Atlantis produces, the higher the opportunity cost becomes. For instance, as you grow more and more potatoes, you have to use less and less suitable land to do so. As a result, you have to divert increasingly more resources away from fishing as you grow more pota-toes, meaning that you can produce increasingly less fish. This implies, of course, that the production possibility frontier becomes steeper the farther you move along it to the right; that is, the production possibility frontier is bowed out. (Mathematicians call this shape *concave*.)

2. In the ancient country of Roma, only two goods, spaghetti and meatballs, are pro-duced. There are two tribes in Roma, the Tivoli and the Frivoli. By themselves, the Tivoli each month can produce either 30 pounds of spaghetti and no meatballs, or 50 pounds of meatballs and no spaghetti, or any combination in between. The Frivoli, by themselves, each month can produce 40 pounds of spaghetti and no meat-balls, or 30 pounds of meatballs and no spaghetti, or any combination in between.

a. Assume that all production possibility frontiers are straight lines. Draw one dia-gram showing the monthly production possibility frontier for the Tivoli and another showing the monthly production possibility frontier for the Frivoli. Show how you calculated them.

b. Which tribe has the comparative advantage in spaghetti production? In meatball production?

In A.D. 100 the Frivoli discover a new technique for making meatballs that doubles the quantity of meatballs they can produce each month.

c. Draw the new monthly production possibility frontier for the Frivoli.

d. After the innovation, which tribe now has the absolute advantage in producing meatballs? In producing spaghetti? Which has the comparative advantage in meat-ball production? In spaghetti production?

Solution

2. a. The accompanying diagram shows the production possibility frontier for the Tivoli in panel (a) and for the Frivoli as the line labeled "Original Frivoli *PPF*" in panel (b).

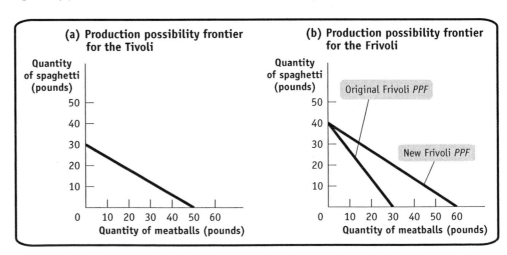

The production possibility frontier for the Tivoli was calculated as follows: The Tivoli can produce either 30 pounds of spaghetti and no meatballs, or they can produce no spaghetti but 50 pounds of meatballs. That is, the opportunity cost of 1 pound of meatballs is $\frac{3}{5}$ of a pound of spaghetti: in order to produce 1 more pound of meatballs, the Tivoli have to give up $\frac{3}{5}$ of a pound of spaghetti. This means that the slope of their production possibility frontier is $-\frac{3}{5}$. A similar argument for the Frivoli shows that their production possibility frontier has a slope of $-\frac{4}{3}$.

b. For the Tivoli, the opportunity cost of 1 pound of meatballs is $\frac{3}{5}$ of a pound of spaghetti. For the Frivoli, the opportunity cost of 1 pound of meatballs is $\frac{4}{3}$ pounds of spaghetti. That is, the Tivoli have the comparative advantage in meatball production because their opportunity cost is lower. For the Tivoli, the opportunity cost of 1 pound of spaghetti is $\frac{5}{3}$ pounds of meatballs. For the Frivoli, the opportunity cost of 1 pound of spaghetti is $\frac{3}{4}$ pound of meatballs. That is, the Frivoli have the comparative advantage in spaghetti production because their opportunity cost is lower.

c. The Frivoli's new production possibility frontier is the line labeled "New Frivoli *PPF*" in panel (b) of the diagram. Instead of producing 30 pounds of meatballs (if they produce no spaghetti), they can now produce 60 pounds.

d. Now the Frivoli have the absolute advantage in both meatball production and spaghetti production. The Frivoli's opportunity cost of meatballs has now fallen to $\frac{4}{6} = \frac{2}{3}$; that is, for each pound of meatballs that the Frivoli now produce, they have to give up producing $\frac{2}{3}$ of a pound of spaghetti. Since the Frivoli's opportunity cost of meatballs ($\frac{2}{3}$) is still higher than the Tivoli's ($\frac{3}{5}$), the Tivoli still have the comparative advantage in meatball production. The Frivoli's opportunity cost of spaghetti is $\frac{3}{2}$ pounds of meatballs and the Tivoli's is $\frac{5}{3}$ pounds of meatballs, so the Frivoli have the comparative advantage in spaghetti production.

3. Peter Pundit, an economics reporter, states that the European Union (EU) is increasing its productivity very rapidly in all industries. He claims that this productivity advance is so rapid that output from the EU in these industries will soon exceed that of the United States and, as a result, the United States will no longer benefit from trade with the EU.

a. Do you think Peter Pundit is correct or not? If not, what do you think is the source of his mistake?

b. If the EU and the United States continue to trade, what do you think will characterize the goods that the EU exports to the United States and the goods that the United States exports to the EU?

Solution

3. a. Peter Pundit is not correct. He confuses absolute and comparative advantage. Even if the EU were to have an absolute advantage over the United States in every product it produces, the United States will still have a comparative advantage in some products. And the United States should continue to produce those products: trade will make both the EU and the United States better off.

b. You should expect to see the EU export those goods in which it has the comparative advantage and the United States export those goods in which it has the comparative advantage.

4. You are in charge of allocating residents to your dormitory's baseball and basketball teams. You are down to the last four people, two of whom must be allocated to baseball and two to basketball. The accompanying table gives each person's batting average and free-throw average. Explain how you would use the concept of comparative advantage to allocate the players. Begin by establishing each player's opportunity cost of free throws in terms of batting average.

Name	Batting average	Free-throw average
Kelley	70%	60%
Jackie	50%	50%
Curt	10%	30%
Gerry	80%	70%

Why is it likely that the other basketball players will be unhappy about this arrangement but the other baseball players will be satisfied? Nonetheless, why would an economist say that this is an efficient way to allocate players for your dormitory's sports teams?

4. Let's begin by establishing the opportunity cost of free throws for each player. If you allocate Kelley to the basketball team, the team gains a player with a 60 percent free-throw average and the baseball team loses a player with a 70 percent batting average. That is, the opportunity cost of allocating Kelley to the basketball team is 7/6. Similarly, Jackie's opportunity cost of playing basketball is 1; Curt's opportunity cost of playing basketball is 1/3, and Gerry's opportunity cost of playing basketball is 8/7. Jackie and Curt have the lowest opportunity costs of playing basketball; that is, they have the comparative advantage in basketball. Therefore they should be allocated to the basketball team. Kelley and Gerry have the comparative advantage in baseball and should therefore play on the baseball team.

It is likely that the basketball team will be unhappy with this arrangement. Both Jackie and Curt have an absolute disadvantage at playing basketball, compared to the other two players. (They also have an absolute disadvantage at playing baseball, but they are comparatively less bad at basketball than at baseball.) The baseball team is likely to be happy about this allocation because both Kelley and Gerry have an absolute advantage at playing baseball. However, if you are concerned with the total number of wins for the dormitory (as an economist who would be concerned about efficiency), this allocation is the best one: it maximizes the overall chances of the dormitory winning at any sport.

5. The economy of Atlantis has developed, and the inhabitants now use money in the form of cowry shells. Draw a circular-flow diagram showing households and firms. Firms produce potatoes and fish, and households buy potatoes and fish. Households also provide the land and labor to firms. Identify where in the flows of cowry shells or physical things (goods and services, or resources) each of the following impacts would occur. Describe how this impact spreads around the circle.

a. A devastating hurricane floods many of the potato fields.

b. A very productive fishing season yields a very large number of fish caught.

c. The inhabitants of Atlantis discover the Macarena and spend several days a month at dancing festivals.

5. The accompanying diagram illustrates the circular flow for Atlantis.

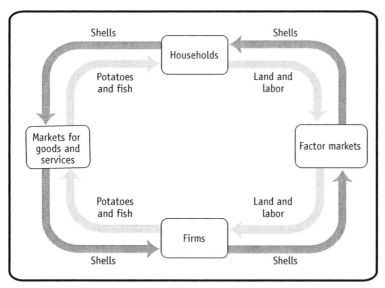

a. The flooding of the fields will destroy the potato crop. Destruction of the potato crop reduces the flow of goods from firms to households: fewer potatoes produced by firms now are sold to households. An implication, of course, is that fewer cowry shells flow from households to firms as payment for the potatoes in the market for goods and services. Since firms now earn fewer shells, they have fewer shells to pay to households in the factor market. As a result, the amount of factors flowing from households to firms is also reduced.

b. The productive fishing season leads to greater quantity of fish produced in firms to flow to households. An implication is that more money flows from households to firms through the market for goods and services. As a result, firms will want to buy more factors from households (the flow of shells from firms to households increases) and, in return, the flow of factors from households to firms increases.

c. Time spent at dancing festivals reduces the flow of labor from households to firms and therefore reduces the number of shells flowing from firms to households through the factor market. In return, households now have fewer shells to buy goods with (the flow of shells from households to firms in the goods market is reduced), implying that fewer goods flow from firms to households.

6. An economist might say that colleges and universities "produce" education, using faculty members and students as inputs. According to this line of reasoning, education is then "consumed" by households. Construct a circular-flow diagram like the one found in this chapter to represent the sector of the economy devoted to college education: colleges and universities represent firms, and households both consume education and provide faculty and students to universities. What are the relevant markets in this model? What is being bought and sold in each direction? What would happen in the model if the government decided to subsidize 50 percent of all college students' tuition?

6. The accompanying diagram shows the circular flow for the education sector.

Colleges and universities buy faculty on the academic job market and attract students from the market for students. (Many colleges and universities actively try to attract good students by offering scholarships and the like.) They sell education to households in the market for education, and households buy education in that market from one (or sometimes several) of the sellers.

If the government subsidized half of all students' tuition, households would demand more education. As a result, colleges and universities would hire more faculty, and accept more students, and more money in terms of salaries and scholarships would flow from universities and colleges to the households.

7. Your dormitory roommate plays loud music most of the time; you, however, would prefer more peace and quiet. You suggest that she buy some earphones. She responds that although she would be happy to use earphones, she has many other things that she would prefer to spend her money on right now. You discuss this situation with a friend who is an economics major. The following exchange takes place:

He: How much would it cost to buy earphones?
You: $15.

He: How much do you value having some peace and quiet for the rest of the semester?
You: $30.

He: It is efficient for you to buy the earphones and give them to your roommate. You gain more than you lose; the benefit exceeds the cost. You should do that.
You: It just isn't fair that I have to pay for the earphones when I'm not the one making the noise.

a. Which parts of this conversation contain positive statements and which parts contain normative statements?

b. Compose an argument supporting your viewpoint that your roommate should be the one to change her behavior. Similarly, compose an argument from the viewpoint of your roommate that you should be the one to buy the earphones. If your dormitory has a policy that gives residents the unlimited right to play music, whose argument is likely to win? If your dormitory has a rule that a person must stop playing music whenever a roommate complains, whose argument is likely to win?

7. a. The statement "It is efficient for you to buy the earphones" is a positive statement (it is either right or wrong); that is, it is about description. The statement "You should do that" (that is, buy the earphones) is strictly speaking a normative statement; that is, it is about prescription (although you would find all economists agree that all trades that improve efficiency should be made). The statement "It just isn't fair" is a normative statement—that is, it is about prescription—and you would likely find much disagreement about the fairness of the proposed trade.

b. One argument that your roommate should buy the earphones is that everyone has the right to peace and quiet. If your roommate therefore wants to listen to music, she should have to be responsible for making sure that others' peace and quiet is not disturbed. Your roommate might argue that since she has the right to play as much music as she wants, it is your responsibility to make sure that you are not disturbed—for instance, by buying her earphones. If the dormitory has a policy that establishes the right to unlimited music, your roommate's argument wins. If the rule is that there is a right to peace and quiet, your argument wins.

8. A representative of the American clothing industry recently made the following statement: "Workers in Asia often work in sweatshop conditions earning only pennies an hour. American workers are more productive and as a result earn higher wages. In order to preserve the dignity of the American workplace, the government should enact legislation banning imports of low-wage Asian clothing."

a. Which parts of this quote are positive statements? Which parts are normative statements?

b. Is the policy that is being advocated consistent with the preceding statements about the wages and productivities of American and Asian workers?

c. Would such a policy make some Americans better off without making any other Americans worse off? That is, would this policy be efficient from the viewpoint of all Americans?

d. Would low-wage Asian workers benefit from or be hurt by such a policy?

8. a. The positive statements are:

- workers in Asia . . . [are] earning only pennies an hour
- American workers are more productive
- American workers are more productive and as a result earn higher wages

The normative statement is:

- the government should enact legislation banning imports of low-wage Asian clothing

b. It is not. The statement about the productivity of American and Asian workers is about the absolute advantage that American workers have over Asian workers. However, Asian workers may still have a comparative advantage. And if that is the case, then banning imports would result in inefficiency.

c. If America channeled more of its productive resources into producing clothing, it would have to give up producing other goods. As a result, America would be able to consume less of all goods. And this would make some Americans clearly worse off. This policy would therefore not be efficient.

d. Low-wage Asian workers would also be hurt by this policy. The Asian country would channel its resources away from producing clothing toward producing other goods that it previously imported from America. But since it does not have the comparative advantage in those other goods, the Asian country would be able to consume less of all goods.

9. Are the following statements true or false? Explain your answers.

   a. "When people must pay higher taxes on their wage earnings, it reduces their incentive to work" is a positive statement.

   b. "We should lower taxes to encourage more work" is a positive statement.

   c. Economics cannot always be used to completely decide what society ought to do.

   d. "The system of public education in this country generates greater benefits to society than the cost of running the system" is a normative statement.

   e. All disagreements among economists are generated by the media.

9. **a.** True. This is a positive statement. It has a factual answer; that is, it is either right or wrong. There has been some debate about whether the statement is actually true or false, but in principle there is only one answer.

   b. False. This is a statement about what we should do, and this statement has no clearly right or wrong answer. Your view will depend on whether you think encouraging more work is a good or a bad idea.

   c. True. Economics is best at giving positive answers, for instance, answers about what the most efficient way is of achieving a certain aim. The question of how society ought to be organized is mostly decided in the realm of politics.

   d. False. This is a positive statement. In principle, it has an answer that is either right or wrong.

   e. False. Some disagreements among economists arise from the fact that in building a model, one economist thinks that a certain abstraction from reality is admissible but another economist may think that that abstraction is not admissible. Some disagreements arise from the fact that economists sometimes disagree about values.

10. Evaluate the following statement: "It is easier to build an economic model that accurately reflects events that have already occurred than to build an economic model to forecast future events." Do you think that this is true or not? Why? What does this imply about the difficulties of building good economic models?

10. True. With hindsight it is easier to see what the important features of the situation were that a model should have captured. For predictive purposes, a model needs to anticipate what the important features of reality are and which are the unimportant features that can therefore be ignored. This is why the British economist John Maynard Keynes referred to economics as an art as well as a science.

11. Economists who work for the government are often called on to make policy recommendations. Why do you think it is important for the public to be able to differentiate normative statements from positive statements in these recommendations?

11. Positive statements are those based on fact—or at least on our best estimate of what the facts are. These statements are also therefore those that do not depend on which political views the economist may have. Normative statements may sometimes be influenced by the economist's own values. Whether someone agrees with an economist's normative statement may depend upon whether they share values. It is therefore important that the public be able to distinguish normative from positive statements.

12. The mayor of Gotham City, worried about a potential epidemic of deadly influenza this winter, asks an economic adviser the following series of questions. Does each question require the economic adviser to make a positive assessment or a normative assessment?

    a. How much vaccine will be in stock in the city by the end of November?

    b. If we offer to pay 10 percent more per dose to the pharmaceutical companies providing the vaccines, will they provide additional doses?

    c. If there is a shortage of vaccine in the city, whom should we vaccinate first—the elderly or the very young? (Assume that a person from one group has an equal likelihood of dying from influenza as a person from the other group.)

    d. If the city charges $25 per shot, how many people will pay?

    e. If the city charges $25 per shot, it will make a profit of $10 per shot, money that can go to pay for inoculating poor people. Should the city engage in such a scheme?

12. **a.** Positive

    b. Positive

    c. Normative

    d. Positive

    e. Normative

13. Assess the following statement: "If economists just had enough data, they could solve all policy questions in a way that maximizes the social good. There would be no need for divisive political debates, such as whether the government should provide free medical care for all."

13. What is true is that if economists had enough data, they could predict precisely what the outcome would be of any proposed policy (such as free medical care). That is, economists can answer positive questions. But no amount of data can lead to a determination about what a society should do—that is a normative question. An economist can predict how much it will cost to provide free medical care and what effects different ways of raising taxes will have on people's behavior (for instance, a sales tax will reduce consumption behavior; an income tax may discourage workers from working as much as before). But whether this is a trade-off worth making is a question that can be answered only in political discourse.

Appendix: Graphs in Economics

1. Study the four accompanying diagrams. Consider the following statements and indicate which diagram matches each statement. Which variable would appear on the horizontal and which on the vertical axis? In each of these statements, is the slope positive, negative, zero, or infinity?

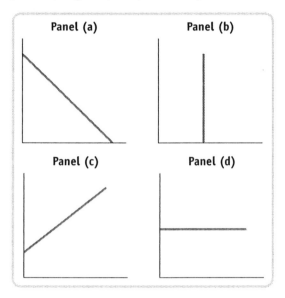

Panel (a)   Panel (b)

Panel (c)   Panel (d)

a. If the price of movies increases, fewer consumers go to see movies.

b. More experienced workers typically have higher incomes than less experienced workers.

c. Whatever the temperature outside, Americans consume the same number of hot dogs per day.

d. Consumers buy more frozen yogurt when the price of ice cream goes up.

e. Research finds no relationship between the number of diet books purchased and the number of pounds lost by the average dieter.

f. Regardless of its price, Americans buy the same quantity of salt.

Solution

1. a. Panel (a) illustrates this relationship. The higher price of movies causes consumers to see fewer movies. The relationship is negative, and the slope is therefore negative. The price of movies is the independent variable and the number of movies seen is the dependent variable. However, there is a convention in economics that, if price is a variable, it is measured on the vertical axis. So the quantity of movies is measured on the horizontal axis.

b. Panel (c) illustrates this relationship. Since it is likely that their greater experience causes firms to pay workers more, years of experience is the independent variable and would go on the horizontal axis and the resulting income, the dependent variable, on the vertical axis. The slope is positive.

c. Panel (d) illustrates this relationship. With the temperature on the horizontal axis as the independent variable, and the consumption of hot dogs on the vertical axis as the dependent variable, we see there is no change in hot dog consumption whatever the temperature. The slope is zero.

    d. Panel (c) illustrates this relationship. When the price of ice cream goes up, this would cause consumers to choose a close alternative, frozen yogurt. The price of ice cream is the independent variable and the consumption of frozen yogurt is the dependent variable. However, there is a convention in economics that, if price is a variable, it is measured on the vertical axis. The quantity that consumers buy of frozen yogurt is on the horizontal axis. The slope is positive.

    e. Panel (d) illustrates this relationship. The fact that there is no discernible relationship between the number of diet books purchased and the weight loss of the average dieter results in a horizontal curve; the slope is zero.

    f. Panel (b) illustrates this relationship. Although price is the independent variable and salt consumption the dependent variable, by convention the price appears on the vertical axis and the quantity of salt on the horizontal axis. Since salt consumption does not change whatever the price, the curve is a vertical line; the slope is infinity.

2. During the Reagan administration, economist Arthur Laffer argued in favor of lowering income tax rates in order to increase tax revenues. Like most economists, he believed that at tax rates above a certain level, tax revenue would fall because high taxes would discourage some people from working and that people would refuse to work at all if they received no income after paying taxes. This relationship between tax rates and tax revenue is graphically summarized in what is widely known as the Laffer curve. Plot the Laffer curve relationship assuming that it has the shape of a nonlinear curve. The following questions will help you construct the graph.

    a. Which is the independent variable? Which is the dependent variable? On which axis do you therefore measure the income tax rate? On which axis do you measure income tax revenue?

    b. What would tax revenue be at a 0% income tax rate?

    c. The maximum possible income tax rate is 100%. What would tax revenue be at a 100% income tax rate?

    d. Estimates now show that the maximum point on the Laffer curve is (approximately) at a tax rate of 80%. For tax rates less than 80%, how would you describe the relationship between the tax rate and tax revenue, and how is this relationship reflected in the slope? For tax rates higher than 80%, how would you describe the relationship between the tax rate and tax revenue, and how is this relationship reflected in the slope?

2. a. The income tax rate is the independent variable and so is measured on the horizontal axis. Income tax revenue is the dependent variable and so is measured on the vertical axis.

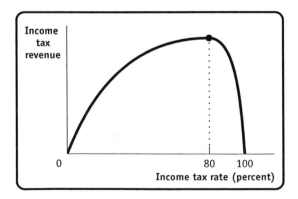

b. If the income tax rate is zero (there is no tax), tax revenue is obviously zero.

c. If the income tax rate is 100% (all your income is taxed away), you will have zero income left after tax. Since people are unwilling to work if they receive no income after tax, no income will be earned. As a result, there is no income tax revenue.

d. For tax rates less than 80%, tax rate and tax revenue are positively related and so the Laffer curve has a positive slope. For tax rates higher than 80%, the relationship between tax rate and tax revenue is negative and so the Laffer curve has a negative slope. The Laffer curve therefore looks like the diagram on page 13 with a maximum point at a tax rate of 80%.

3. In the accompanying figures, the numbers on the axes have been lost. All you know is that the units shown on the vertical axis are the same as the units on the horizontal axis.

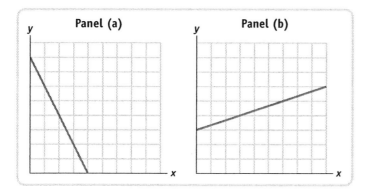

a. In panel (a), what is the slope of the line? Show that the slope is constant along the line.

b. In panel (b), what is the slope of the line? Show that the slope is constant along the line.

3. **a.** In panel (a), the slope is −2. From any point on the line, moving one unit to the right along the horizontal axis requires moving down two units along the vertical axis in order to remain on the line. The slope is the "rise" (−2) over the "run" (+1); that is, the slope is $^{-2}/_1 = -2$. The same is true starting at *any* point along the line, so the slope at every point is the same. The slope is constant.

b. In panel (b), the slope is ⅓. From any point on the line, moving three units to the right along the horizontal axis requires moving up one unit along the vertical axis in order to remain on the line. The slope is the "rise" (+1) over the "run" (+3); that is, the slope is ⅓. The same is true starting at *any* point along the line, so the slope at every point is the same. The slope is constant.

4. The accompanying table shows the relationship between workers' hours of work per week and their hourly wage rate. Apart from the fact that they receive a different hourly wage rate and work different hours, these five workers are otherwise identical.

Name	Quantity of labor (hours per week)	Wage rate (per hour)
Athena	30	$15
Boris	35	30
Curt	37	45
Diego	36	60
Emily	32	75

a. Which variable is the independent variable? Which is the dependent variable?

b. Draw a scatter diagram illustrating this relationship. Draw a (nonlinear) curve that connects the points. Put the hourly wage rate on the vertical axis.

c. As the wage rate increases from $15 to $30, how does the number of hours worked respond according to the relationship depicted here? What is the average slope of the curve between Athena's and Boris's data points?

d. As the wage rate increases from $60 to $75, how does the number of hours worked respond according to the relationship depicted here? What is the average slope of the curve between Diego's and Emily's data points?

4. a. If the wage rate is greater than your opportunity cost of time, you will choose to work. So the wage rate is the independent variable and the number of hours worked is the dependent variable.

b. The accompanying diagram illustrates the relationship between the hourly wage rate and the number of hours worked. Since the hourly wage rate is the price paid for labor, economists place wages on the vertical axis—just as in the case of other types of prices.

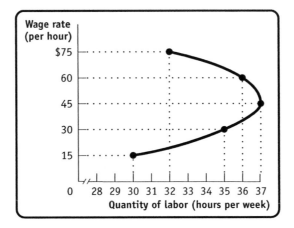

c. As the wage rate increases from $15 to $30, the number of hours worked increases by 5. The average slope of the curve between the two points is therefore $15/5 = 3$.

d. As the wage rate increases from $60 to $75, the number of hours worked decreases by 4. The average slope of the curve between the two points is therefore $15/{-4} = -3.75$.

5. Studies have found a relationship between a country's yearly rate of economic growth and the yearly rate of increase in airborne pollutants. It is believed that a higher rate of economic growth allows a country's residents to have more cars and travel more, thereby releasing more airborne pollutants.

a. Which variable is the independent variable? Which is the dependent variable?

b. Suppose that in the country of Sudland, when the yearly rate of economic growth fell from 3.0% to 1.5%, the yearly rate of increase in airborne pollutants fell from 6% to 5%. What is the average slope of a nonlinear curve between these points?

c. Now suppose that when the yearly rate of economic growth rose from 3.5% to 4.5%, the yearly rate of increase in airborne pollutants rose from 5.5% to 7.5%. What is the average slope of a nonlinear curve between these two points?

d. How would you describe the relationship between the two variables here?

5. a. According to the question, economic growth causes the increase in airborne pollutants. That is, the growth rate is the independent variable and the rate of increase in airborne pollutants is the dependent variable. So the rate of increase in airborne pollutants is measured on the vertical axis and the growth rate is measured on the horizontal axis.

b. The change in the growth rate is −1.5. The change in the rate of increase in airborne pollutants is −1. The slope is therefore $^{-1}/_{-1.5} = ^2/_3$.

c. The change in the growth rate is +1. The change in the rate of increase in airborne pollutants is +2. The slope is therefore $^2/_1 = 2$.

d. The slope is positive and, as can be seen from the answers to parts b and c, increasing.

6. An insurance company has found that the severity of property damage in a fire is positively related to the number of firefighters arriving at the scene.

a. Draw a diagram that depicts this finding with number of firefighters on the horizontal axis and amount of property damage on the vertical axis. What is the argument made by this diagram? Suppose you reverse what is measured on the two axes. What is the argument made then?

b. In order to reduce its payouts to policyholders, should the insurance company therefore ask the city to send fewer firefighters to any fire?

6. a. By drawing the diagram with number of firefighters on the horizontal axis and amount of property damage on the vertical axis, you are assuming that the number of firefighters is the independent variable and amount of property damage is the dependent variable. That graph is shown here. It makes the argument that as the number of firefighters on the scene increases, the amount of damage increases. You could also have drawn the graph with amount of property damage as the independent variable (on the horizontal axis) and the number of firefighters as the dependent variable (on the vertical axis). In this case the diagram implies that more and more firefighters come to the scene as the amount of property damage increases. (But be aware that any diagram shows only a relationship between two variables and does not imply causation).

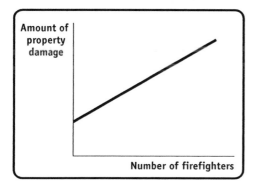

b. The statement implies that there is a causal link between the number of firefighters and the amount of property damage, and this is likely not the case. It is instead likely that there is a third, omitted, variable that is related to both the number of firefighters and the amount of property damage. This variable is the severity of the fire: more severe fires cause both greater property damage and a greater number of firefighters to be sent to the fire.

7. The accompanying table illustrates annual salaries and income tax owed by five individuals. Apart from the fact that they receive different salaries and owe different amounts of income tax, these five individuals are otherwise identical.

Name	Annual salary	Annual income tax owed
Susan	$22,000	$3,304
Bill	63,000	14,317
John	3,000	454
Mary	94,000	23,927
Peter	37,000	7,020

a. If you were to plot these points on a graph, what would be the average slope of the curve between the points for Bill's and Mary's salaries and taxes? How would you interpret this value for slope?

b. What is the average slope of the curve between the points for John's and Susan's salaries and taxes? How would you interpret that value for slope?

c. What happens to the slope as salary increases? What does this relationship imply about how the level of income taxes affects a person's incentive to earn a higher salary?

7. a. Annual salary is the independent variable and so is measured on the horizontal axis. Annual income tax owed is the dependent variable and so is measured on the vertical axis. As salary increases by $31,000 from Bill's $63,000 to Mary's $94,000, income tax owed increases by $9,610. That is, the slope of the curve is $9,610/31,000 = 0.31$. The interpretation is that in this income bracket, each additional dollar of income implies a tax of $0.31.

b. As salary increases by $19,000 from John's $3,000 to Susan's $22,000, income tax owed increases by $2,850. That is, the slope of the curve is $2,850/19,000 = 0.15$. The interpretation is that in this income bracket, each additional dollar of income implies a tax of $0.15.

c. The slope is positive and increasing. This implies that the tax scheme is "progressive": the higher the annual salary, the greater the amount of income tax owed per dollar of income. Therefore, the incentive to earn more and more income becomes weaker and weaker, since more of the additional income earned is owed as income taxes.

Supply and Demand

1. A survey indicated that chocolate ice cream is America's favorite ice-cream flavor. For each of the following, indicate the possible effects on demand and/or supply and equilibrium price and quantity of chocolate ice cream.

   a. A severe drought in the Midwest causes dairy farmers to reduce the number of milk-producing cattle in their herds by a third. These dairy farmers supply cream that is used to manufacture chocolate ice cream.

   b. A new report by the American Medical Association reveals that chocolate does, in fact, have significant health benefits.

   c. The discovery of cheaper synthetic vanilla flavoring lowers the price of vanilla ice cream.

   d. New technology for mixing and freezing ice cream lowers manufacturers' costs of producing chocolate ice cream.

Solution

1. a. By reducing their herds, dairy farmers cause the supply of cream to decrease—a leftward shift of the supply curve for cream. As a result, the market price of cream rises, which means that a unit of chocolate ice cream is more expensive to produce. This results in a leftward shift of the supply curve for chocolate ice cream as ice-cream producers reduce the quantity of chocolate ice cream supplied at any given price. This leads to a rise in the equilibrium price and a fall in the equilibrium quantity.

   b. Consumers will now demand more chocolate ice cream at any given price, representing a rightward shift of the demand curve. As a result, both equilibrium price and quantity rise.

   c. The price of a substitute (vanilla ice cream) has fallen, and consumers will tend to substitute it for chocolate ice cream. The demand for chocolate ice cream decreases, representing a leftward shift of the demand curve. Both equilibrium price and quantity fall.

   d. Because the cost of producing ice cream falls, manufacturers are willing to supply more units of chocolate ice cream at any given price. This is represented by a rightward shift of the supply curve and results in a fall in the equilibrium price and a rise in the equilibrium quantity.

2. In a supply and demand diagram, draw the shift in demand for hamburgers in your hometown due to the following events. In each case show the effect on equilibrium price and quantity.

   a. The price of tacos increases.

   b. All hamburger sellers raise the price of their french fries.

   c. Income falls in town. Assume that hamburgers are a normal good for most people.

   d. Income falls in town. Assume that hamburgers are an inferior good for most people.

   e. Hot dog stands cut the price of hot dogs.

Solution

2. **a.** A rise in the price of a substitute (tacos) causes the demand for hamburgers to increase. This represents a rightward shift of the demand curve from D_1 to D_2 and results in a rise in the equilibrium price and quantity as the equilibrium changes from E_1 to E_2.

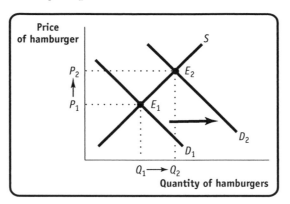

b. A rise in the price of a complement (french fries) causes the demand for hamburgers to decrease. This represents a leftward shift of the demand curve from D_1 to D_2 and results in a fall in the equilibrium price and quantity as the equilibrium changes from E_1 to E_2.

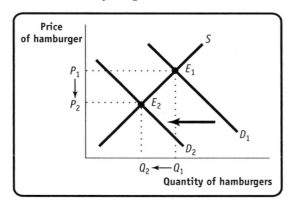

c. A fall in income causes the demand for a normal good (hamburgers) to decrease. This represents a leftward shift of the demand curve from D_1 to D_2 and results in a fall in the equilibrium price and quantity as the equilibrium changes from E_1 to E_2.

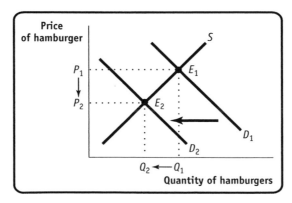

d. A fall in income causes the demand for an inferior good (hamburgers) to increase. This represents a rightward shift of the demand curve from D_1 to D_2 and results in a rise in the equilibrium price and quantity as the equilibrium changes from E_1 to E_2.

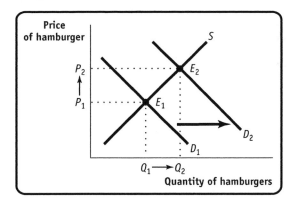

e. A fall in the price of a substitute (hot dogs) causes demand for hamburgers to decrease. This is represented by a leftward shift of the demand curve from D_1 to D_2 and results in a fall in the equilibrium price and quantity as the equilibrium changes from E_1 to E_2.

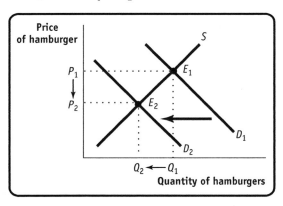

3. The market for many goods changes in predictable ways according to the time of year, in response to events such as holidays, vacation times, seasonal changes in production, and so on. Using supply and demand, explain the change in price in each of the following cases. Note that supply and demand may shift simultaneously.

a. Lobster prices usually fall during the summer peak harvest season, despite the fact that people like to eat lobster during the summer months more than during any other time of year.

b. The price of a Christmas tree is lower after Christmas than before and fewer trees are sold.

c. The price of a round-trip ticket to Paris on Air France falls by more than $200 after the end of school vacation in September. This happens despite the fact that generally worsening weather increases the cost of operating flights to Paris, and Air France therefore reduces the number of flights to Paris at any given price.

3. **a.** There is a rightward shift of the demand curve from D_1 to D_2 during the summer months, as consumers prefer to eat more lobster during the summer than during other times of the year. Other things equal, this leads to a rise in the price of lobster. Simultaneously, lobster fishermen produce more lobster during the summer peak harvest time, when it is cheaper to harvest lobster, representing a rightward shift of the supply curve of lobster from S_1 to S_2. Other things equal, this leads to a fall in the price of lobster. Given the simultaneous rightward shifts of both the demand and supply curves, the equilibrium changes from E_1 to E_2. The fall in price indicates that the rightward shift of the supply curve exceeds the rightward shift of the demand curve.

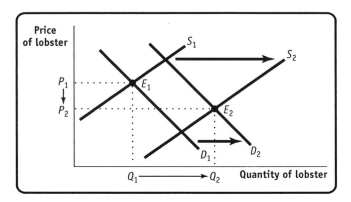

b. There is a leftward shift of the demand curve for Christmas trees after Christmas from D_1 to D_2, as fewer consumers want Christmas trees at any given price. The supply curve does not shift; the reduction in the quantity of trees supplied is a movement along the supply curve. This leads to a fall in the equilibrium price and quantity, as the equilibrium changes from E_1 to E_2.

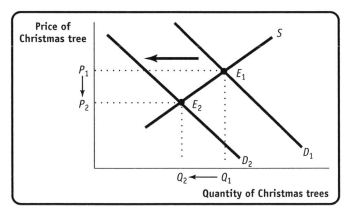

c. There is a leftward shift of the demand curve for tickets to Paris in September, after the end of school vacation, from D_1 to D_2. Other things equal, this leads to a fall in the price of tickets. At the same time, as the cost of operating flights increases, Air France decreases the number of flights, shifting the supply curve leftward from S_1 to S_2. Other things equal, this leads to a rise in price. Given the simultaneous leftward shifts of both the demand and supply curves, the equilibrium changes from E_1 to E_2. The fall in price indicates that the leftward shift of the demand curve exceeds the leftward shift of the supply curve.

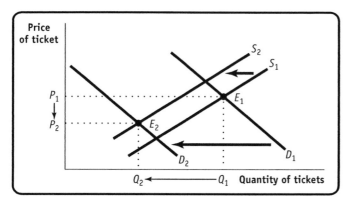

4. Show in a diagram the effect on the demand curve, the supply curve, the equilibrium price, and the equilibrium quantity of each of the following events.

a. The market for newspapers in your town.

Case 1:   The salaries of journalists go up.
Case 2:   There is a big news event in your town, which is reported in the newspapers.

b. The market for St. Louis Rams cotton T-shirts.

Case 1:   The Rams win the national championship.
Case 2:   The price of cotton increases.

c. The market for bagels.

Case 1:   People realize how fattening bagels are.
Case 2:   People have less time to make themselves a cooked breakfast.

d. The market for the Krugman and Wells economics textbook.

Case 1:   Your professor makes it required reading for all of his or her students.
Case 2:   Printing costs for textbooks are lowered by the use of synthetic paper.

4. **a. Case 1:** Journalists are an input in the production of newspapers; an increase in their salaries will cause newspaper publishers to reduce the quantity supplied at any given price. This represents a leftward shift of the supply curve from S_1 to S_2 and results in a rise in the equilibrium price and a fall in the equilibrium quantity as the equilibrium changes from E_1 to E_2.

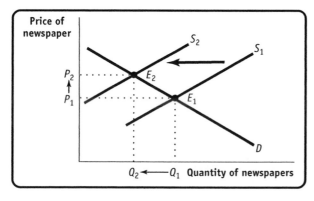

Case 2: Townspeople will wish to purchase more newspapers at any given price. This represents a rightward shift of the demand curve from D_1 to D_2 and leads to a rise in both the equilibrium price and quantity as the equilibrium changes from E_1 to E_2.

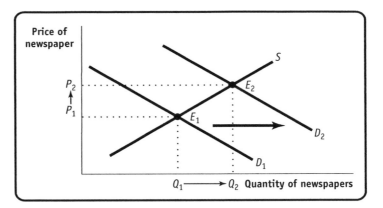

b. Case 1: Fans will demand more St. Louis Rams memorabilia at any given price. This represents a rightward shift of the demand curve from D_1 to D_2 and leads to a rise in both the equilibrium price and quantity as the equilibrium changes from E_1 to E_2.

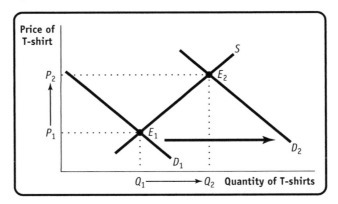

Case 2: Cotton is an input into T-shirts; an increase in its price will cause T-shirt manufacturers to reduce the quantity supplied at any given price, representing a leftward shift of the supply curve from S_1 to S_2. This leads to a rise in the equilibrium price and a fall in the equilibrium quantity as the equilibrium changes from E_1 to E_2.

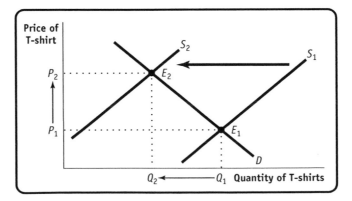

c. Case 1: Consumers will demand fewer bagels at any given price. This represents a leftward shift of the demand curve from D_1 to D_2 and leads to a fall in both the equilibrium price and quantity as the equilibrium changes from E_1 to E_2.

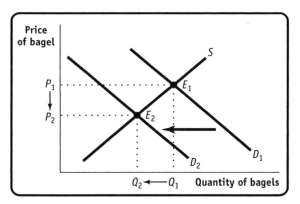

Case 2: Consumers will demand more bagels (a substitute for cooked breakfasts) at any given price. This represents a rightward shift of the demand curve from D_1 to D_2 and leads to a rise in both the equilibrium price and quantity as the equilibrium changes from E_1 to E_2.

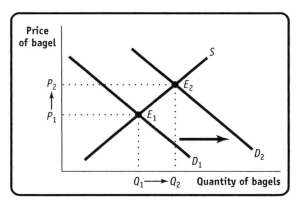

d. Case 1: A greater quantity of textbooks will be demanded at any given price, representing a rightward shift of the demand curve from D_1 to D_2. Equilibrium price and quantity will rise as the equilibrium changes from E_1 to E_2.

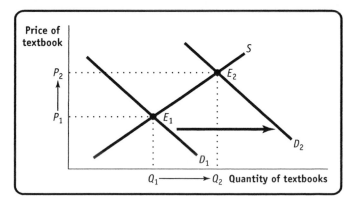

Case 2: The textbook publisher will offer more textbooks for sale at any given price, representing a rightward shift of the supply curve from S_1 to S_2. Equilibrium price will fall and equilibrium quantity will rise as the equilibrium changes from E_1 to E_2.

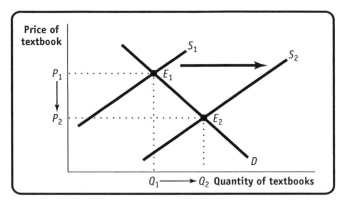

5. Suppose that the supply schedule of Maine lobsters is as follows:

Price of lobster (per pound)	Quantity of lobster supplied (pounds)
$25	800
20	700
15	600
10	500
5	400

Suppose that Maine lobsters can be sold only in the United States. The U.S. demand schedule for Maine lobsters is as follows:

Price of lobster (per pound)	Quantity of lobster demanded (pounds)
$25	200
20	400
15	600
10	800
5	1,000

a. Draw the demand curve and the supply curve for Maine lobsters. What is the equilibrium price and quantity of lobsters?

Now suppose that Maine lobsters can be sold in France. The French demand schedule for Maine lobsters is as follows:

Price of lobster (per pound)	Quantity of lobster demanded (pounds)
$25	100
20	300
15	500
10	700
5	900

b. What is the demand schedule for Maine lobsters now that French consumers can also buy them? Draw a supply and demand diagram that illustrates the new equilibrium price and quantity of lobsters. What will happen to the price at which fishermen can sell lobster? What will happen to the price paid by U.S. consumers? What will happen to the quantity consumed by U.S. consumers?

Solution

5. **a.** The equilibrium price of lobster is $15 per pound and the equilibrium quantity is 600 pounds, point *E* in the accompanying diagram.

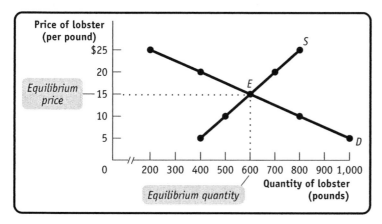

b. The new demand schedule is obtained by adding together, at any given price, the quantity demanded by American consumers and the quantity demanded by French consumers, as shown in the following table.

Price of lobster (per pound)	Quantity of lobster demanded (U.S. pounds plus French pounds)
$25	300
20	700
15	1,100
10	1,500
5	1,900

The new equilibrium price of lobster is $20 per pound and the new equilibrium quantity is 700 pounds, point *E* in the accompanying diagram. The opportunity to sell to French consumers makes Maine fishermen better off: they sell more lobster and at a higher price than before. U.S. consumers, however, are made worse off: they must pay a higher price for lobster ($20 versus $15 per pound), and as a result consume less lobster (400 versus 600 pounds).

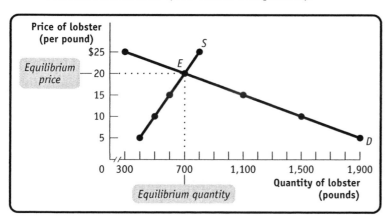

6. Find the flaws in reasoning in the following statements, paying particular attention to the distinction between shifts of and movements along the supply and demand curves. Draw a diagram to illustrate what actually happens in each situation.

   a. "A technological innovation that lowers the cost of producing a good might seem at first to result in a reduction in the price of the good to consumers. But a fall in price will increase demand for the good, and higher demand will send the price up again. It is not certain, therefore, that an innovation will really reduce price in the end."

   b. "A study shows that eating a clove of garlic a day can help prevent heart disease, causing many consumers to demand more garlic. This increase in demand results in a rise in the price of garlic. Consumers, seeing that the price of garlic has gone up, reduce their demand for garlic. This causes the demand for garlic to decrease and the price of garlic to fall. Therefore, the ultimate effect of the study on the price of garlic is uncertain."

6. **a.** This statement confuses a shift of a curve with a movement along a curve. A technological innovation lowers the cost of producing the good; as a result, producers will offer more of the good at any given price. This is represented by a rightward shift of the supply curve from S_1 to S_2. As a result, the equilibrium price falls and the equilibrium quantity rises, as shown by the change from E_1 to E_2. The statement "but a fall in price will increase demand for the good, and higher demand will send the price up again" is wrong for the following reasons. A fall in price does increase the quantity demanded and leads to an increase in the equilibrium quantity as one moves down along the demand curve. But it does not lead to an increase in demand—a rightward shift of the demand curve—and therefore does not cause the price to go up again.

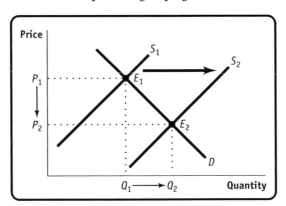

   b. This statement also confuses a shift of a curve with a movement along a curve. The health report generates an increase in demand—a rightward shift of the demand curve from D_1 to D_2. This leads to a higher equilibrium price and quantity as we move up along the supply curve, and the equilibrium changes from E_1 to E_2. The following statements are wrong: "Consumers, seeing that the price of garlic has gone up, reduce their demand for garlic. This causes the demand for garlic to decrease and the price of garlic to fall." They are wrong because they imply that the rise in the equilibrium price causes the demand for garlic to decrease—a leftward shift of the demand curve. But a rise in the equilibrium price via a movement along the supply curve does not cause the demand curve to shift leftward.

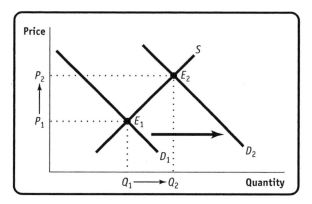

7. Some points on a demand curve for a normal good are given here:

Price	Quantity demanded
$23	70
21	90
19	110
17	130

Do you think that the increase in quantity demanded (from 90 to 110 in the table) when price decreases (from 21 to 19) is due to a rise in consumers' income? Explain clearly (and briefly) why or why not.

Solution

7. The increase in quantity demanded from 90 to 110 when the price declines from 21 to 19 is not due to a rise in consumers' income. Rather, it represents a movement along the demand curve as the price falls. In contrast, a rise in consumers' income causes the demand curve to shift rightward for a normal good; as a result, the quantity demanded will increase at any given price.

8. Aaron Hank is a star hitter for the Bay City baseball team. He is close to breaking the major league record for home runs hit during one season, and it is widely anticipated that in the next game he will break that record. As a result, tickets for the team's next game have been a hot commodity. But today it is announced that, due to a knee injury, he will not in fact play in the team's next game. Assume that season ticketholders are able to resell their tickets if they wish. Use supply and demand diagrams to explain the following.

a. Show the case in which this announcement results in a lower equilibrium price and a lower equilibrium quantity than before the announcement.

b. Show the case in which this announcement results in a lower equilibrium price and a higher equilibrium quantity than before the announcement.

c. What accounts for whether case a or case b occurs?

d. Suppose that a scalper had secretly learned before the announcement that Aaron Hank would not play in the next game. What actions do you think he would take?

8. **a.** Fewer fans want to attend the next game after the announcement is made. As a result, the demand curve will shift leftward from D_1 to D_2, as fewer tickets are demanded at any given price; other things equal, this results in a fall in both equilibrium price and quantity. In addition, the supply curve will shift rightward from S_1 to S_2, as more season ticket-holders are willing to sell tickets at any given price; other things equal, this results in a fall in equilibrium price and a rise in equilibrium quantity. In this case, the leftward shift of the demand curve exceeds the rightward shift of the supply curve; as a result, equilibrium quantity falls, shown by the change of the equilibrium from E_1 to E_2.

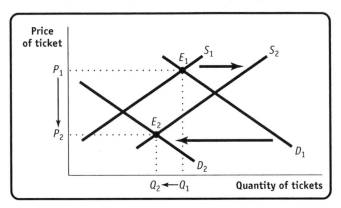

b. The supply and demand curves shift in the same manner as in part a, but in this case the rightward shift of the supply curve exceeds the leftward shift of the demand curve. Consequently, equilibrium quantity rises, shown by the change of the equilibrium from E_1 to E_2.

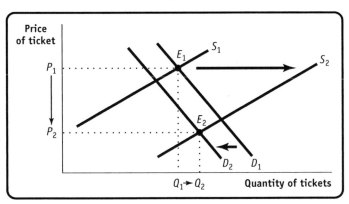

c. Case a (equilibrium quantity falls) occurs because the decrease in demand exceeds the increase in supply. Case b (equilibrium quantity rises) occurs because the increase in supply exceeds the decrease in demand.

d. A scalper who learns about the announcement secretly should take actions—such as lowering price somewhat—that ensure that he will sell all of his tickets before the announcement is made. He will do this because he knows a ticket will command a much lower price after the announcement. An expectation that the price will be lower in the future causes supply to increase today.

9. In *Rolling Stone* magazine, several fans and rock stars, including Pearl Jam, were bemoaning the high price of concert tickets. One superstar argued, "It just isn't worth $75 to see me play. No one should have to pay that much to go to a concert." Assume this star sold out arenas around the country at an average ticket price of $75.

a. How would you evaluate the arguments that ticket prices are too high?

b. Suppose that due to this star's protests, ticket prices were lowered to $50. In what sense is this price too low? Draw a diagram using supply and demand curves to support your argument.

c. Suppose Pearl Jam really wanted to bring down ticket prices. Since the band controls the supply of its services, what do you recommend they do? Explain using a supply and demand diagram.

d. Suppose the band's next CD was a total dud. Do you think they would still have to worry about ticket prices being too high? Why or why not? Draw a supply and demand diagram to support your argument.

e. Suppose the group announced their next tour was going to be their last. What effect would this likely have on the demand for and price of tickets? Illustrate with a supply and demand diagram.

Solution

9. **a.** If markets are competitive, the ticket price is simply the equilibrium price: the price at which quantity supplied is equal to quantity demanded. No one is "made" to pay $75 to go to a concert: a potential concert-goer will pay $75 if going to the concert seems worth that amount and will choose to do something else if it isn't.

b. At $50 each, the quantity of tickets demanded exceeds the quantity of tickets supplied. There is a shortage of tickets at this price as shown by the difference between the quantity demanded at this price, Q_D, and the quantity supplied at this price, Q_S.

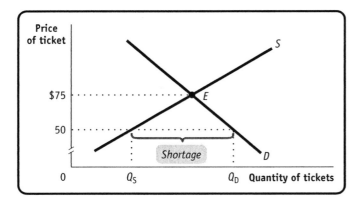

c. The band can lower the average price of a ticket by increasing supply: give more concerts. This is shown as a rightward shift of the supply curve from S_1 to S_2, resulting in a lower equilibrium price and a higher equilibrium quantity, shown by the change of the equilibrium from E_1 to E_2.

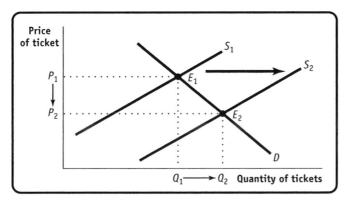

d. If the band's CD is a total dud, the demand for concert tickets is likely to decrease. This represents a leftward shift of the demand curve from D_1 to D_2, resulting in a lower equilibrium price and quantity as the equilibrium changes from E_1 to E_2. This is likely to eliminate the worry that ticket prices are "too high."

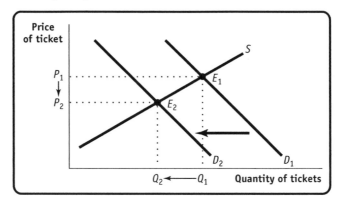

e. The announcement that this is the group's last tour causes the demand for tickets to increase. This is represented by a rightward shift of the demand curve from D_1 to D_2, resulting in an increase in both the equilibrium price and quantity as the equilibrium changes from E_1 to E_2.

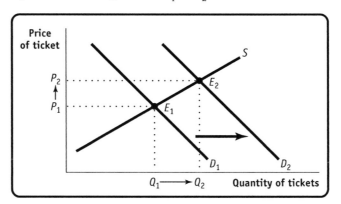

10. The accompanying table gives the annual U.S. demand and supply schedules for pickup trucks.

Price of truck	Quantity of trucks demanded (millions)	Quantity of trucks supplied (millions)
$20,000	20	14
25,000	18	15
30,000	16	16
35,000	14	17
40,000	12	18

a. Plot the demand and supply curves using these schedules. Indicate the equilibrium price and quantity on your diagram.

b. Suppose the tires used on pickup trucks are found to be defective. What would you expect to happen in the market for pickup trucks? Show this on your diagram.

c. Suppose that the U.S. Department of Transportation imposes costly regulations on manufacturers that cause them to reduce supply by one-third at any given price. Calculate and plot the new supply schedule and indicate the new equilibrium price and quantity on your diagram.

10. **a.** The supply curve is S_1 and the demand curve is D_1. The equilibrium in the market for pickup trucks is indicated by point E_1 in the diagram, with an equilibrium price of $30,000 and an equilibrium quantity of 16 million trucks bought and sold.

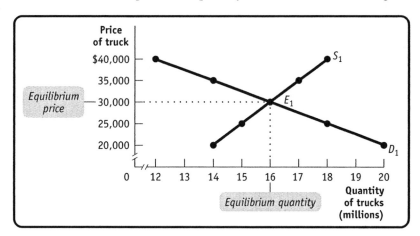

b. The announcement of a defect is likely to decrease the demand for pickup trucks. This is represented by a leftward shift of the demand curve, as shown by the shift from D_1 to D_2, and causes the equilibrium price and quantity to fall as the equilibrium changes from E_1 to E_2.

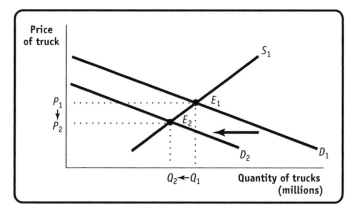

c. The new supply schedule is as follows.

Price of truck	Quantity of trucks supplied (millions)
$20,000	9.3
25,000	10.0
30,000	10.7
35,000	11.3
40,000	12.0

This one-third decrease in the quantity supplied at any given price is shown as a leftward shift of the supply curve from S_1 to S_2. It results in a new, higher equilibrium price, \$40,000 per truck, and a lower equilibrium quantity, 12 million trucks, as shown by the change of the equilibrium from E_1 to E_3.

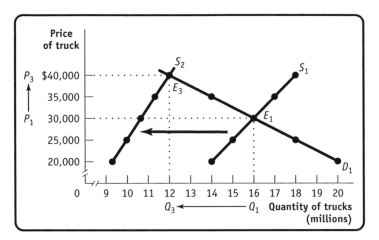

11. After several years of decline, the market for handmade acoustic guitars is making a comeback. These guitars are usually made in small workshops employing relatively few highly skilled luthiers. Assess the impact on the equilibrium price and quantity of handmade acoustic guitars as a result of each of the following events. In your answers indicate which curve(s) shift(s) and in which direction.

a. Environmentalists succeed in having the use of Brazilian rosewood banned in the United States, forcing luthiers to seek out alternative, more costly woods.

b. A foreign producer reengineers the guitar-making process and floods the market with identical guitars.

c. Music featuring handmade acoustic guitars makes a comeback as audiences tire of heavy metal and grunge music.

d. The country goes into a deep recession and the income of the average American falls sharply.

11. **a.** The cost of producing handmade acoustic guitars rises as more costly woods are used to construct them. This reduces supply, as luthiers offer fewer guitars at any given price. This is represented by a leftward shift of the supply curve and results in a rise in the equilibrium price and a fall in the equilibrium quantity.

b. This represents a rightward shift of the supply curve and results in a fall in the equilibrium price and a rise in the equilibrium quantity.

c. As more people demand music played on acoustic guitars, the demand for these guitars by musicians increases as well. (Acoustic guitars are an "input" into the production of this music.) This represents a rightward shift of the demand curve, leading to a higher equilibrium price and quantity.

d. If average American income falls sharply, then the demand for handmade acoustic guitars will decrease sharply as well because they are a normal good. This is represented by a leftward shift of the demand curve and results in a lower equilibrium price and quantity.

12. *Demand twisters:* Sketch and explain the demand relationship in each of the following statements.

   a. I would never buy a Britney Spears CD! You couldn't even give me one for nothing.

   b. I generally buy a bit more coffee as the price falls. But once the price falls to $2 per pound, I'll buy out the entire stock of the supermarket.

   c. I spend more on orange juice even as the price rises. (Does this mean that I must be violating the law of demand?)

   d. Due to a tuition rise, most students at a college find themselves with lower disposable income. Almost all of them eat more frequently at the school cafeteria and less often at restaurants, even though prices at the cafeteria have risen too. (This one requires that you draw both the demand and the supply curves for dormitory cafeteria meals.)

12. **a.** In this case the quantity demanded is 0 regardless of the price. So this person's demand curve for Britney Spears CDs is a vertical line at the quantity of 0—that is, a vertical line that lies on top of the vertical axis.

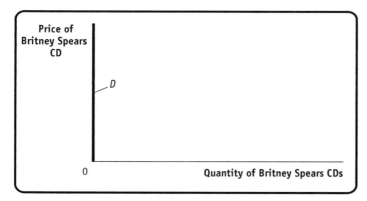

   b. The person here has the typical downward-sloping demand curve for coffee until it reaches the price of $2 per pound, at which point it becomes horizontal, showing that he or she would buy a very large quantity at that price.

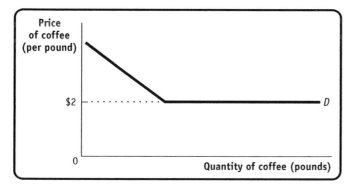

   c. This person does not necessarily violate the law of demand: the quantity of orange juice demanded may in fact fall as price goes up. The likely explanation is the following: Spending is price times the quantity demanded. Although price goes up, the total amount of money this person spends on orange juice rises because he or she does not reduce the quantity demanded enough to offset the increased cost per unit.

This person will have a steep demand curve as shown in the diagram: quantity demanded falls as price rises, but the fall in quantity demanded is proportionately less than the rise in price.

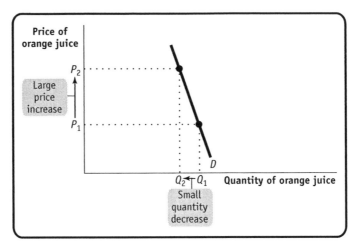

d. Since students' income has fallen, but the demand for cafeteria meals has increased, cafeteria meals must be an inferior good. The rightward shift of the demand curve, from D_1 to D_2, results in an increase in the equilibrium price and the equilibrium quantity of cafeteria meals, as the equilibrium changes from E_1 to E_2.

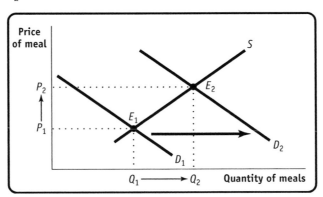

13. Will Shakespeare is a struggling playwright in sixteenth-century London. As the price he receives for writing a play increases, he is willing to write more plays. For the following situations, use a diagram to illustrate how each event affects the equilibrium price and quantity in the market for Shakespeare's plays.

a. The playwright Christopher Marlowe, Shakespeare's chief rival, is killed in a bar brawl.

b. The bubonic plague, a deadly infectious disease, breaks out in London.

c. To celebrate the defeat of the Spanish Armada, Queen Elizabeth declares several weeks of festivities, which involves commissioning new plays.

13. **a.** The death of Marlowe means that the supply of a substitute good (Marlowe's plays) has decreased, and therefore the price of Marlowe's plays will rise. As a result, the demand for Shakespeare's plays will increase, inducing a rightward shift of the demand curve in the market for Shakespeare's plays from D_1 to D_2. As a result, equilibrium price and quantity will rise as the equilibrium changes from E_1 to E_2.

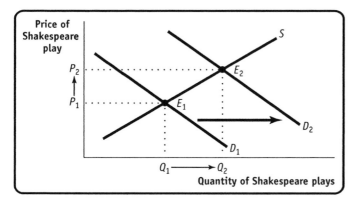

b. After the outbreak of the plague, fewer Londoners will wish to see Shakespeare's plays to avoid contracting the illness, inducing a leftward shift of the demand curve from D_1 to D_2. Equilibrium price and quantity will fall as the equilibrium changes from E_1 to E_2.

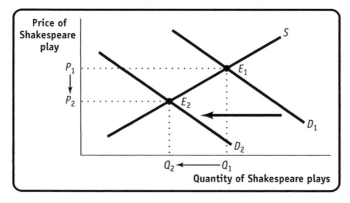

c. Queen Elizabeth's commissions result in a greater quantity of Shakespeare's plays demanded at any given price. This represents a rightward shift of the demand curve from D_1 to D_2, resulting in a higher equilibrium price and quantity as the equilibrium changes from E_1 to E_2.

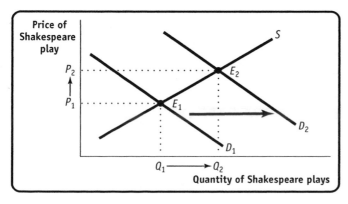

14. The small town of Middling experiences a sudden doubling of the birth rate. After three years, the birth rate returns to normal. Use a diagram to illustrate the effect of these events on the following.

   a. The market for an hour of babysitting services in Middling today

   b. The market for an hour of babysitting services 14 years into the future, after the birth rate has returned to normal, by which time children born today are old enough to work as babysitters

   c. The market for an hour of babysitting services 30 years into the future, when children born today are likely to be having children of their own

14. **a.** There are more babies today, so the demand for an hour of babysitting services has increased. This produces a rightward shift of the demand curve for babysitting services from D_1 to D_2, resulting in a rise in the equilibrium price and quantity as the equilibrium changes from E_1 to E_2.

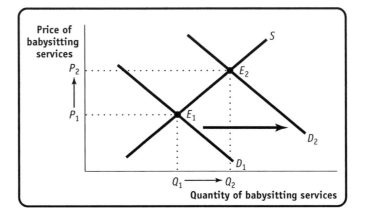

   b. The children born today will cause an increase in the supply of babysitters available 14 years from now, when there will be a rightward shift of the supply curve for babysitting services from S_1 to S_2. It will result in a lower equilibrium price and a higher equilibrium quantity as the equilibrium changes from E_1 to E_2.

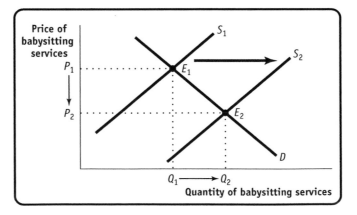

c. It is likely that there will be an increase in the birthrate 30 years from now. Therefore, there will be an increase in the demand for babysitting services, shifting the demand curve rightward from D_1 to D_2. It will result in a higher equilibrium quantity and price as the equilibrium changes from E_1 to E_2.

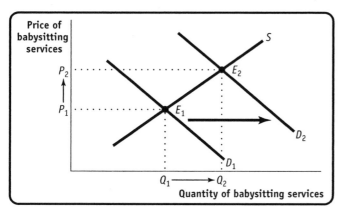

15. Use a diagram to illustrate how each of the following events affects the equilibrium price and quantity of pizza.

a. The price of mozzarella cheese rises.

b. The health hazards of hamburgers are widely publicized.

c. The price of tomato sauce falls.

d. The incomes of consumers rise and pizza is an inferior good.

e. Consumers expect the price of pizza to fall next week.

Solution

15. **a.** Mozzarella is an input in the production of pizza. Since the cost of an input has risen, pizza producers will reduce the quantity supplied at any given price, a leftward shift of the supply curve from S_1 to S_2. As a result, the equilibrium price of pizza will rise and the equilibrium quantity will fall as the equilibrium changes from E_1 to E_2.

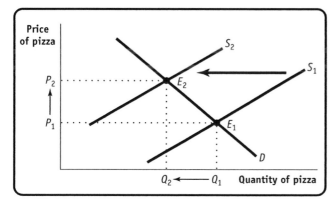

b. Consumers will substitute pizza for hamburgers, resulting in an increased demand for pizza at any given price. This generates a rightward shift of the demand curve from D_1 to D_2 and results in a rise in the equilibrium price and quantity as the equilibrium changes from E_1 to E_2.

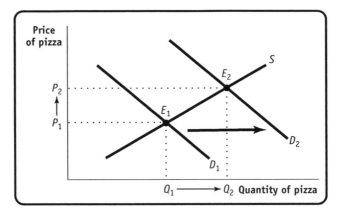

c. Tomato sauce is an input in the production of pizza. Since the cost of an input has fallen, pizza producers will increase the quantity supplied at any given price, a rightward shift of the supply curve from S_1 to S_2. As a result, the equilibrium price of pizza will fall and the equilibrium quantity will rise as the equilibrium changes from E_1 to E_2.

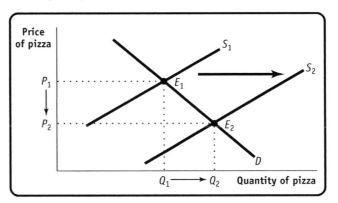

d. The demand for an inferior good decreases when the incomes of consumers rise. So a rise in consumer incomes produces a leftward shift of the demand curve from D_1 to D_2 and results in a lower equilibrium price and quantity as the equilibrium changes from E_1 to E_2.

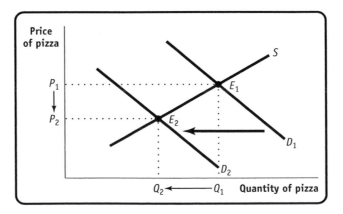

e. Consumers will delay their purchases of pizza today in anticipation of consuming more pizza next week. As a result, the demand curve shifts leftward from D_1 to D_2 and results in a lower equilibrium price and quantity as the equilibrium changes from E_1 to E_2.

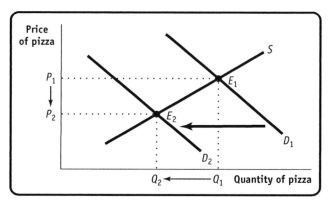

16. Although he was a prolific artist, Pablo Picasso painted only 1,000 canvases during his "Blue Period." Picasso is now dead, and all of his Blue Period works are currently on display in museums and private galleries throughout Europe and the United States.

a. Draw a supply curve for Picasso Blue Period works. Why is this supply curve different from ones you have seen?

b. Given the supply curve from part a, the price of a Picasso Blue Period work will be entirely dependent on what factor(s)? Draw a diagram showing how the equilibrium price of such a work is determined.

c. Suppose that rich art collectors decide that it is essential to acquire Picasso Blue Period art for their collections. Show the impact of this on the market for these paintings.

16. a. There are no more Picasso Blue Period works available. Hence the supply curve is a vertical line at the quantity 1,000.

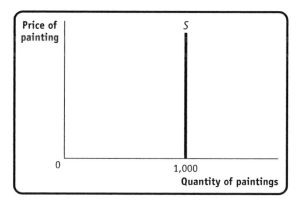

b. Since supply is fixed, the price of a Picasso Blue Period work is entirely determined by demand. Any change in demand is fully reflected in a change in price.

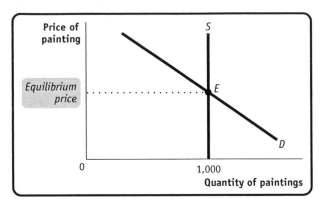

c. This results in a rightward shift of the demand curve for these works from D_1 to D_2, and the equilibrium changes from E_1 to E_2. But since no more works are available, this increase in demand simply results in an increase in the equilibrium price.

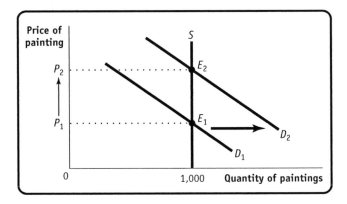

17. Draw the appropriate curve in each of the following cases. Is it like or unlike the curves you have seen so far? Explain.

a. The demand for cardiac bypass surgery, given that the government pays the full cost for any patient

b. The demand for elective cosmetic plastic surgery, given that the patient pays the full cost

c. The supply of Rembrandt paintings

d. The supply of reproductions of Rembrandt paintings

17. **a.** Since the government pays the full cost of cardiac bypass surgery, the price paid by the patient is always zero. Consequently, the demand for surgery is constant, regardless of the price actually paid by the government. The quantity demanded is constant at the quantity that would be demanded by patients if the government, not the patient, pays for surgery. That is, it is a vertical line at the quantity that patients would demand if the price of surgery to them were zero.

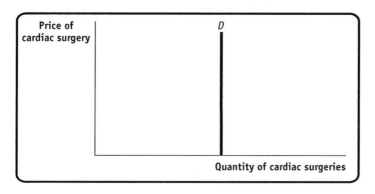

b. In this case the patient must pay the cost of the surgery; therefore, the quantity demanded is affected by price, and the demand curve has its usual downward-sloping shape.

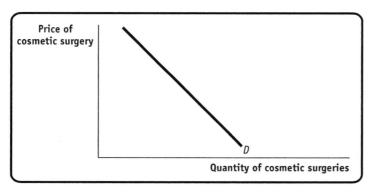

c. The supply of Rembrandt paintings is fixed because Rembrandt is dead. Therefore, unlike the typical upward-sloping supply curve, the supply curve is a vertical line, where the quantity supplied is equal to the number of Rembrandt paintings in existence.

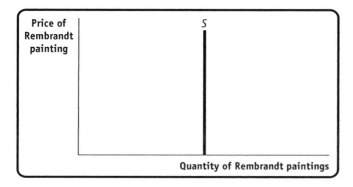

d. The supply of Rembrandt reproductions is not fixed because they can be created by existing artists. Therefore, the supply curve of these reproductions has the familiar upward-sloping shape.

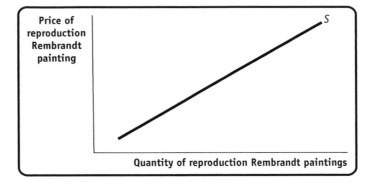

The Market Strikes Back

1. Suppose it is decided that rent control in New York City will be abolished and that market rents will now prevail. Assume that all rental units are identical and are therefore offered at the same rent. To address the plight of residents who may be unable to pay the market rent, an income supplement will be paid to all low-income households equal to the difference between the old controlled rent and the new market rent.

   a. Use a diagram to show the effect on the rental market of the elimination of rent control. What will happen to the quality and quantity of rental housing supplied?

   b. Now use a second diagram to show the additional effect of the income-supplement policy on the market. What effect does it have on the market rent and quantity of rental housing supplied in comparison to your answers to part a?

   c. Are tenants better or worse off as a result of these policies? Are landlords better or worse off?

   d. From a political standpoint, why do you think cities have been more likely to resort to rent control rather than a policy of income supplements to help low-income people pay for housing?

Solution

1. a. With a price ceiling at $P_{CEILING}$, the quantity bought and sold is $Q_{CEILING}$, indicated by point A. The ceiling at $P_{CEILING}$ is eliminated and the rent returns to the market equilibrium E_1, with an equilibrium rent of P_1. The quantity supplied increases from $Q_{CEILING}$ to the equilibrium quantity Q_1. At the same time, you should expect the quality of rental housing to improve. As you learned in this chapter, one of the inefficiencies caused by price ceilings is inefficiently low quality. As the rent returns to the equilibrium rent, landlords again have the incentive to invest in the quality of their apartments in order to attract renters.

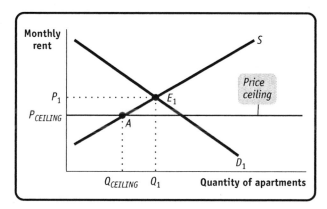

b. The income-supplement policy causes a rightward shift of the demand curve from D_1 to D_2. This results in an increase in the equilibrium rent, from P_1 to P_2, and an increase in the equilibrium quantity, from Q_1 to Q_2, as the equilibrium changes from E_1 to E_2.

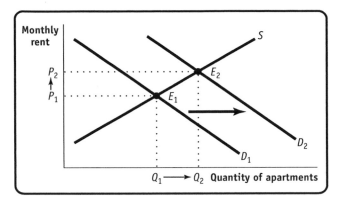

c. Landlords are clearly better off as a result of these two policies: more landlords rent out apartments, and at a higher monthly rent. It is not clear whether tenants are better or worse off. Some tenants who previously could not get apartments can now do so, but at a higher rent. In particular, those tenants who do not receive the income supplement and who used to rent cheap apartments under the price ceiling are now worse off.

d. It is likely that tenants who currently live in rent-controlled housing are better organized than tenants who cannot currently find rental housing. And more organized groups can generally exert greater influence over city policy.

2. In order to ingratiate himself with voters, the mayor of Gotham City decides to lower the price of taxi rides. Assume, for simplicity, that all taxi rides are the same distance and therefore cost the same. The accompanying table shows the demand and supply schedules for taxi rides.

Fare (per ride)	Quantity of rides (millions per year)	
	Quantity demanded	Quantity supplied
$7.00	10	12
6.50	11	11
6.00	12	10
5.50	13	9
5.00	14	8
4.50	15	7

a. Assume that there are no restrictions on the number of taxi rides that can be supplied in the city (i.e., there is no medallion system). Find the equilibrium price and quantity.

b. Suppose that the mayor sets a price ceiling at $5.50. How large is the shortage of rides? Illustrate with a diagram. Who loses and who benefits from this policy?

c. Suppose that the stock market crashes and, as a result, people in Gotham City are poorer. This reduces the quantity of taxi rides demanded by 6 million rides per year at any given price. What effect will the mayor's new policy have now? Illustrate with a diagram.

d. Suppose that the stock market rises and the demand for taxi rides returns to normal (that is, returns to the demand schedule given in the table). The mayor now decides to ingratiate himself with taxi drivers. He announces a policy in which operating licenses are given to existing taxi drivers; the number of licenses is restricted such that only 10 million rides per year can be given. Illustrate the effect of this policy on the market and indicate the resulting price and quantity transacted. What is the quota rent per ride?

Solution

2. **a.** The equilibrium in the market for taxi rides is shown by E_1 in the accompanying diagram. The equilibrium price is $6.50; at that price, the quantity demanded equals the quantity supplied—11 million taxi rides per year. The demand and supply curves $(D_1$ and $S)$ illustrate this initial situation.

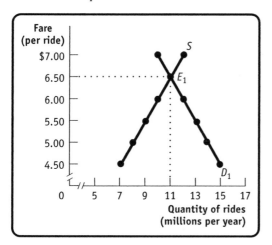

b. With a price ceiling of $5.50, the quantity supplied is 9 million taxi rides and the quantity demanded is 13 million. The shortage therefore is 13 million–9 million = 4 million. Taxi drivers clearly lose out: there are fewer taxi rides supplied than before, and at a lower price. The impact on consumers is unclear: fewer people now manage to get rides, but those who do, get them at a lower price.

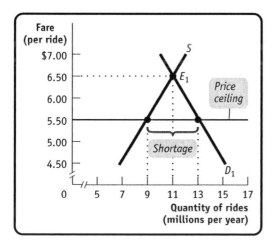

c. The new demand curve is D_2. Now the price ceiling has no effect: the equilibrium is point E_2 and the market price settles at $5, which is below the mandated price ceiling of $5.50. There will be 8 million taxi rides demanded and supplied, at a price of $5 each.

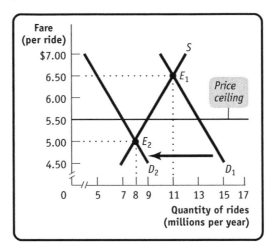

d. The accompanying diagram illustrates the effect of the quota of 10 million taxi rides. The quantity of taxi rides is now 10 million, at a price of $7. The quota rent per ride is $1.

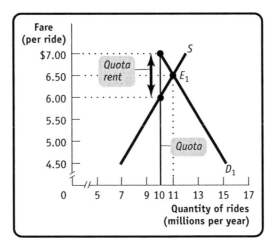

3. In the late eighteenth century, the price of bread in New York City was controlled, set at a predetermined price above the market price.

a. Draw a diagram showing the effect of the policy. Did the policy act as a price ceiling or a price floor?

b. What kinds of inefficiencies were likely to have arisen when the controlled price of bread was above the market price? Explain in detail.

One year during this period, a poor wheat harvest caused a leftward shift in the supply of bread and therefore an increase in its market price. New York bakers found that the controlled price of bread in New York was below the market price.

c. Draw a diagram showing the effect of the price control on the market for bread during this one-year period. Did the policy act as a price ceiling or a price floor?

d. What kinds of inefficiencies do you think occurred during this period? Explain in detail.

3. **a.** Panel (a) of the accompanying diagram illustrates the effect of this policy. Since the price is set *above* the market equilibrium price, this policy acts as a price floor: it raises the price artificially above the equilibrium. As a result, too much bread is produced: there is a surplus.

b. As with all price floors above the equilibrium price, there are several associated inefficiencies. Since bakers cannot compete on price, they will compete on quality: you should expect excessively high quality (bread that is more fancy than customers really want). You should also, of course, expect to see surplus production of bread that does not get bought but is thrown away instead. Furthermore, some bakers are less efficient than others (they operate at a higher cost); if the market were allowed to reach equilibrium, they would find it too costly to operate so there is an inefficient allocation among producers. Finally, there is always an opportunity for black market activity—illegal trade in bread that is priced below the set price.

c. Panel (b) illustrates the effect of the fixed price if the market equilibrium is above that price. The set price now acts like a price ceiling, preventing the price from rising to the equilibrium. There is a shortage, as occurs with every price ceiling below the equilibrium price.

d. One inefficiency is that, since there is an incentive for bakers to locate outside the city, where they can get higher prices, some consumers who cannot buy bread in the city (where there is a shortage) will travel outside the city to buy bread. And the opportunity cost of travel time is, of course, wasteful. Also, some people who manage to buy bread in the city are not those who value it most highly: there might be others who are in greater need but cannot buy bread so there is an inefficient allocation to consumers. Since the price of bread is kept artificially low, some bakers will skimp on quality. Finally, there is an opportunity for black market trade in bread that is resold at much higher prices.

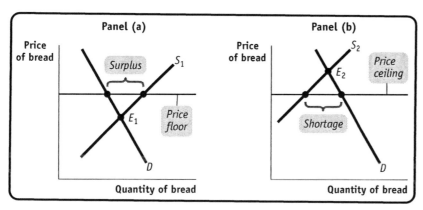

4. The accompanying table shows the demand and supply schedules for milk per year. The U.S. government decides that the incomes of dairy farmers should be maintained at a level that allows the traditional family dairy farm to survive. It therefore implements a price floor of $1 per pint by buying surplus milk until the market price is $1 per pint.

Price of milk (per pint)	Quantity of milk (millions of pints per year)	
	Quantity demanded	Quantity supplied
$1.20	550	850
1.10	600	800
1.00	650	750
0.90	700	700
0.80	750	650

a. How much surplus milk will be produced as a result of this policy?

b. What will be the cost to the government of this policy?

c. Since milk is an important source of protein and calcium, the government decides to provide the surplus milk it purchases to elementary schools at a price of only $0.60 per pint. Assume that schools will buy any amount of milk available at this low price. But parents now reduce their purchases of milk at any price by 50 million pints per year because they know their children are getting milk at school. How much will the dairy program now cost the government?

d. Give two examples of inefficiencies arising from wasted resources that are likely to result from this policy. What is the missed opportunity in each case?

4. a. With demand of D_1, and supply of S, the equilibrium would be at point E_1 in the accompanying diagram. However, with a price floor at $1, the quantity supplied is 750 million pints and the quantity demanded is 650 million pints. The policy therefore causes a surplus of milk of 100 million pints per year.

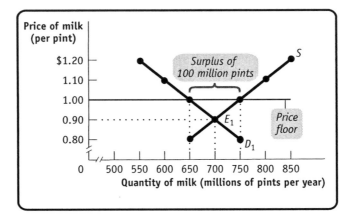

b. In order to sustain this price floor (to prevent black market sales of surplus milk below the price floor), the government would have to buy up the surplus of milk. Buying 100 million pints of milk at a price of $1 each costs the government $100 million.

c. As a result of sales of cheap milk to schools, the quantity demanded falls by 50 million pints per year at any price: the demand curve shifts leftward to the new demand curve D_2. Without the price floor, the equilibrium would now be at point E_2. However, with the price floor at $1, there is now a surplus of 150 million pints. In order to sustain the price floor of $1, the government needs to buy up 150 million pints at $1 each; that is, it needs to spend $150 million. It does, however, sell those 150 million pints to schools at $0.60 each (and from those sales makes $0.60 × 150 million = $90 million), so that the policy costs the government $150 million − $90 million = $60 million.

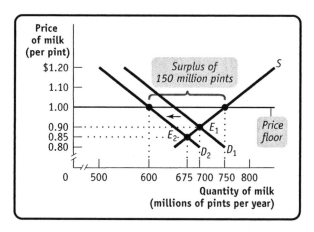

d. Some milk producers are inefficient: if the price were allowed to reach equilibrium, they would find it too costly to produce. In their absence, milk would be produced only by the most efficient producers. This is a missed opportunity. Furthermore, resources are being wasted: although no milk is poured away outright, the government spends significant amounts of money on purchases of milk. This is money that might be used more effectively for purposes other than providing cheap milk to schoolchildren, such as improving the quality of public schools. This, too, is a missed opportunity.

5. As noted in the text, European governments tend to make greater use of price controls than does the American government. For example, the French government sets minimum starting yearly wages for new hires who have completed *le bac,* certification roughly equivalent to a high school diploma. The demand schedule for new hires with *le bac* and the supply schedule for similarly credentialed new job seekers are given in the accompanying table. The price here—given in euros, the currency used in France—is the same as the yearly wage.

Wage (per year)	Quantity demanded (new job offers per year)	Quantity supplied (new job seekers per year)
€45,000	200,000	325,000
40,000	220,000	320,000
35,000	250,000	310,000
30,000	290,000	290,000
25,000	370,000	200,000

a. In the absence of government interference, what is the equilibrium wage and number of graduates hired per year? Illustrate with a diagram. Will there be anyone seeking a job at the equilibrium wage who is unable to find one—that is, will there be anyone who is involuntarily unemployed?

b. Suppose the French government sets a minimum yearly wage of €35,000. Is there any involuntary unemployment at this wage? If so, how much? Illustrate with a diagram. What if the minimum wage is set at €40,000? Also illustrate with a diagram.

c. Given your answer to part b and the information in the table, what do you think is the relationship between the level of involuntary unemployment and the level of the minimum wage? Who benefits from such a policy? Who loses? What is the missed opportunity here?

5. **a.** The equilibrium wage is €30,000, and 290,000 workers are hired. There is full employment: nobody is involuntarily unemployed. The equilibrium is at point E.

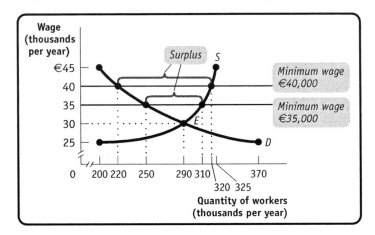

b. With a minimum wage of €35,000, there is a surplus of workers of 60,000 (the quantity supplied is 310,000 and the quantity demanded is 250,000). That is, there are 60,000 workers that are involuntarily unemployed. At a minimum wage of €40,000, there is a surplus of workers of 100,000: this is the number of involuntarily unemployed workers.

c. The higher the minimum wage, the larger the amount of involuntary unemployment. The people who benefit from this policy are those workers who succeed in getting hired: they now enjoy a higher wage. Those workers who do not get hired, however, lose: if the market were allowed to reach equilibrium, more workers would be employed. Employers also lose: fewer employers can now afford to hire workers, and they need to pay higher wages. The missed opportunity is that there are workers who want to work at a wage lower than the minimum wage and firms that would willingly hire them at a lower wage; but because the wage is not allowed to fall below the minimum wage, these hires are not made.

6. Until recently, the standard number of hours worked per week for a full-time job in France was 39 hours, just as in the United States. But in response to social unrest over high levels of involuntary unemployment, the French government instituted a 35-hour workweek—a worker could not work more than 35 hours per week even if both the worker and employer wanted it. The motivation behind this policy was that if current employees worked fewer hours, employers would be forced to hire more new workers. Assume that it is costly for employers to train new workers. French employers were greatly opposed to this policy and threatened to move their operations to neighboring countries that did not have such employment restrictions. Can you explain their attitude? Give an example of both an inefficiency and an illegal activity that are likely to arise from this policy.

6. The introduction of a quota limit, limiting the work week to 35 hours, below the current equilibrium quantity, implies that there is quota rent earned by the suppliers of labor. So it should not come as a surprise that workers who expected to keep their jobs under the new policy were in favor of the policy. The demand price (the price paid by the demanders of labor, that is, firms), compared to what the wage had been before the introduction of the policy, had risen. Furthermore, since it is costly to train new workers, firms could not completely make up through new hiring for the shortfall in the hours that their current employees were working. As a result, firms had to produce less output and earn lower revenue than before the policy. Like every quota that is below the equilibrium quantity, this quota introduced inefficiency: even if workers wanted to work more (and firms were willing to employ them for longer), such trades were no longer legally possible. You might expect a certain amount of black market activity to occur: workers working longer hours off the books.

7. For the last 70 years the U.S. government has used price supports to provide income assistance to American farmers. At times the government has used price floors, which it maintains by buying up the surplus farm products. At other times, it has used target prices, a policy by which the government gives the farmer an amount equal to the difference between the market price and the target price for each unit sold. Consider the market for corn depicted in the accompanying figure.

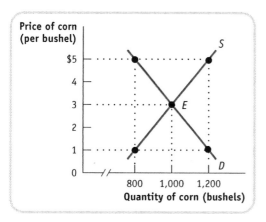

a. If the government sets a price floor of $5 per bushel, how many bushels of corn are produced? How many are purchased by consumers? By the government? How much does the program cost the government? How much revenue do corn farmers receive?

b. Suppose the government sets a target price of $5 per bushel for any quantity supplied up to 1,000 bushels. How many bushels of corn are purchased by consumers and at what price? By the government? How much does the program cost the government? How much revenue do corn farmers receive?

c. Which of these programs (in parts a and b) costs corn consumers more? Which program costs the government more? Explain.

d. What are the inefficiencies that arise in each of these cases (parts a and b)?

7. a. With a price floor of $5, the quantity of corn supplied is 1,200 bushels. The quantity demanded is only 800 bushels: there is a surplus of 400 bushels. The government therefore has to buy up the surplus of 400 bushels, at a price of $5 each: the program costs the government $400 \times \$5 = \$2,000$. Corn farmers sell 1,200 bushels (800 to consumers and 400 to the government) and therefore make $1,200 \times \$5 = \$6,000$ in revenue.

b. If the government sets a target price of $5, the market reaches equilibrium at a price of $3 and a quantity of 1,000 bushels. There is no surplus (or shortage). The government does not buy any corn under this policy. On each bushel sold the government pays farmers $2 (to make up the difference between the market price of $3 and the target price of $5), so the government pays a total of 1,000 × $2 = $2,000. Corn farmers sell 1,000 bushels and make $5 for each bushel ($3 come from consumers and $2 from the government), for a total of $5,000 of revenue.

c. The price-floor policy is more expensive for consumers: they pay $5 per bushel (compared to the $3 under the target price policy). Both policies are equally expensive for the government.

d. When there is a price floor for corn, the most striking inefficiency is the waste of resources (the corn bought by the government is presumably thrown away). This does not occur under the target price policy: under that policy all corn that is produced is also bought by consumers.

8. The waters off the North Atlantic coast were once teeming with fish. Now, due to overfishing by the commercial fishing industry, the stocks of fish are seriously depleted. In 1991, the National Marine Fishery Service of the U.S. government implemented a quota to allow fish stocks to recover. The quota limited the amount of swordfish caught per year by all U.S.-licensed fishing boats to 7 million pounds. As soon as the U.S. fishing fleet had met the quota limit, the swordfish catch was closed down for the rest of the year. The accompanying table gives the hypothetical demand and supply schedules for swordfish caught in the United States per year.

Price of swordfish (per pound)	Quantity of swordfish (millions of pounds per year)	
	Quantity demanded	Quantity supplied
$20	6	15
18	7	13
16	8	11
14	9	9
12	10	7

a. Use a diagram to show the effect of the quota on the market for swordfish in 1991.

b. How do you think fishermen will change how they fish in response to this policy?

c. Use your diagram from part a to show an excise tax that achieves the same reduction in the amount of pounds of swordfish caught as the quota. What is the amount of the tax per pound?

d. What kinds of activities do you think an excise tax will tempt people to engage in?

e. The excise tax is collected from the fishermen, who protest that they alone are bearing the burden of this policy. Why might this protest be misguided?

8. a. The quantity sold is 7 million pounds, at a price of $18 per pound. On each pound of fish caught, each fisherman earns quota rent of $6, as shown in the accompanying diagram.

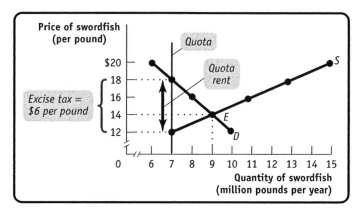

b. Because each pound of swordfish gives a fisherman $6 quota rent, each fisherman will attempt to fish as much as possible as soon as the swordfish catch opens. You should therefore see fishermen scramble to fish right at the beginning of the season, and you should see the catch being closed down very soon thereafter (which is exactly what happens).

c. If an excise tax of $6 per pound were introduced, this would similarly reduce the quantity bought and sold to 7 million pounds, as shown in accompanying diagram.

d. Any tax always creates the incentive for tax evasion—in this case, selling fish privately, or in the black market, while circumventing the imposition of the tax on those sales.

e. The fishermen are confusing who is responsible for paying the excise tax with the economic *incidence* of the tax: the burden of the tax is normally shared between consumers and producers. In this case, consumers pay $4 more per pound than they would in an equilibrium without tax (point E in the diagram), and fishermen receive $2 less per pound than they would in an equilibrium without tax. Both sides suffer from the missed opportunity to trade further amounts of fish.

9. The U.S. government would like to help the American auto industry compete against foreign automakers that sell trucks in the United States. It can do this either by imposing a quota on the number of foreign trucks imported or by imposing an excise tax on each foreign truck sold in the United States. The hypothetical demand and supply schedules for imported trucks are given in the accompanying table.

Price of imported truck	Quantity of imported trucks (thousands)	
	Quantity demanded	Quantity supplied
$32,000	100	400
31,000	200	350
30,000	300	300
29,000	400	250
28,000	500	200
27,000	600	150

a. In the absence of government interference, what is the price of an imported truck? How many are sold in the United States? Illustrate with a diagram.

b. Suppose the government adopts a quota, allowing no more than 200,000 foreign trucks to be imported. What is the effect on the market for these trucks? Illustrate using your diagram from part a and explain.

c. Now suppose that, instead of a quota, the government imposes an excise tax of $3,000 per truck. Illustrate the effect of this excise tax in your diagram from part a. How many trucks will now be purchased and at what price? What will the foreign automaker receive per truck?

d. Calculate the government revenue raised by the excise tax in part c. Then illustrate it on your diagram from that part. Do you think the government, from a revenue standpoint, prefers an excise tax or a quota?

9. a. The equilibrium price without government interference is $30,000, and 300,000 trucks are bought and sold, as shown by point E in the accompanying diagram.

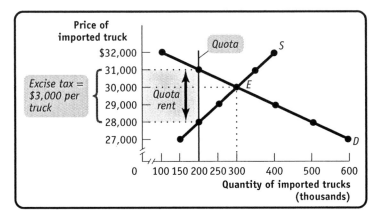

b. The effect of the quota is illustrated in the diagram: 200,000 trucks are sold at a price of $31,000, and producers receive a quota rent of $3,000 per truck.

c. The excise tax is also illustrated in the diagram: a tax of $3,000 per truck puts a wedge between the price paid by consumers, or the demand price ($31,000), and the price received by producers, or the supply price ($28,000). The quantity sold is 200,000 trucks. The foreign automaker receives $28,000 per truck (after tax).

d. Since 200,000 trucks are sold, and the government earns a tax of $3,000 on each truck, the total tax revenue is 200,000 × $3,000 = $600 million. This is the shaded area in the diagram. The government, of course, prefers the tax to a quota. Under the quota policy, the foreign automakers benefit (in the form of quota rent); under the tax policy, the government benefits (in the form of tax revenue).

10. In Maine, you must have a license to harvest lobster commercially; these licenses are issued yearly. The state of Maine is concerned about the dwindling supplies of lobsters found off its coast. The state fishery department has decided to place a yearly quota of 80,000 pounds of lobsters harvested in all Maine waters. It has also decided to give licenses this year only to those fishermen who had licenses last year. The accompanying figure shows the demand and supply curves for Maine lobsters.

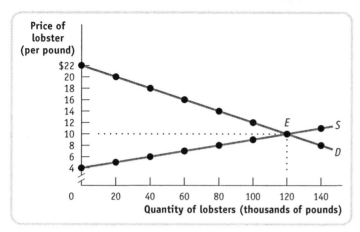

a. In the absence of government restrictions, what are the equilibrium price and quantity?

b. What is the *demand price* at which consumers wish to purchase 80,000 pounds of lobsters?

c. What is the *supply price* at which suppliers are willing to supply 80,000 pounds of lobsters?

d. What is the *quota rent* per pound of lobster when 80,000 pounds are sold?

e. Find an excise tax that achieves the same reduction in the harvest of lobsters. Show it on the figure. What is the government revenue collected from this tax?

f. Explain a transaction that benefits both buyer and seller but is prevented by the quota restriction. Explain a transaction that benefits both buyer and seller but is prevented by the excise tax.

10. a. Without government intervention, the equilibrium in the market for lobsters is at point *E*. The equilibrium price for lobsters is $10 per pound. At that price, the quantity demanded and the quantity supplied is 120,000 pounds of lobsters.

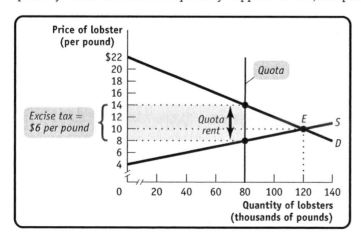

b. The demand price of 80,000 pounds of lobsters is $14.

c. The supply price of 80,000 pounds of lobsters is $8.

d. The quota rent per pound of lobster is $14 − $8 = $6.

e. An excise tax of $6 per pound would have the same effect, as the diagram illustrates. The tax reduces the quantity sold to 80,000 pounds; since the government earns a tax of $6 per pound, the government tax revenue is 80,000 × $6 = $480,000, the area of the shaded rectangle in the diagram.

f. Under the quota policy, if the 80,001st producer could sell a lobster to the 80,001st consumer, they could both be better off: the producer would be willing to sell for just a little more than $8, and the consumer would be willing to buy for just a little less than $14. The quota, however, prevents this trade. Under the tax policy, the 80,001st producer would be willing to sell to the 80,001st consumer if the tax on that 80,001st pound of lobster was reduced to a little less than $6. But since the tax is $6, selling the 80,001st pound of lobster does not cover the producer's cost, and therefore that trade is not made.

Elasticity

1. TheNile.com, the online bookseller, wants to increase its total revenue. Currently, every book it sells is priced at $10.50. One suggested strategy is to offer a discount that lowers the price of a book to $9.50, a 10% reduction in price using the midpoint method. TheNile.com knows that its customers can be divided into two distinct groups according to their likely responses to the discount. The accompanying table shows how the two groups respond to the discount.

	Group A (sales per week)	Group B (sales per week)
Volume of sales before the 10% discount	1.55 million	1.50 million
Volume of sales after the 10% discount	1.65 million	1.70 million

   a. Calculate the price elasticities of demand for Group A and Group B.

   b. Explain how the discount will affect total revenue from each group.

   c. Suppose TheNile.com knows which group each customer belongs to when he or she logs on and can choose whether or not to offer the 10% discount. If TheNile.com wants to increase its total revenue, should discounts be offered to Group A or to Group B, to neither group, or to both groups?

Solution

1. **a.** The percent change in the quantity demanded by Group A is

$$\frac{1.65 \text{ million} - 1.55 \text{ million}}{(1.55 \text{ million} + 1.65 \text{ million})/2} \times 100 = \frac{0.1 \text{ million}}{1.6 \text{ million}} \times 100 = 6.25\%$$

and since the change in price is 10%, the price elasticity of demand for Group A is

$$\frac{6.25\%}{10\%} = 0.625$$

The percent change in the quantity demanded by Group B is

$$\frac{1.7 \text{ million} - 1.5 \text{ million}}{(1.5 \text{ million} + 1.7 \text{ million})/2} \times 100 = \frac{0.2 \text{ million}}{1.6 \text{ million}} \times 100 = 12.5\%$$

and since the change in price is 10%, the price elasticity of demand for Group B is

$$\frac{12.5\%}{10\%} = 1.25$$

   b. For Group A, since the price elasticity of demand is 0.625 (demand is inelastic), total revenue will decrease as a result of the discount. For Group B, since the price elasticity of demand is 1.25 (demand is elastic), total revenue will increase as a result of the discount.

   c. If TheNile.com wants to increase total revenue, then it should definitely not offer the discount to Group A and it should definitely offer the discount to Group B.

2. Do you think the price elasticity of demand for Ford sport-utility vehicles (SUVs) will increase, decrease, or remain the same when each of the following events occurs? Explain your answer.

   a. Other car manufacturers, such as General Motors, decide to make and sell SUVs.

   b. SUVs produced in foreign countries are banned from the American market.

   c. Due to ad campaigns, Americans believe that SUVs are much safer than ordinary passenger cars.

   d. The time period over which you measure the elasticity lengthens. During that longer time, new models such as four-wheel-drive cargo vans appear.

2. **a.** The price elasticity of demand for Ford SUVs will increase because more substitutes are available.

   b. The price elasticity of demand for Ford SUVs will decrease because fewer substitutes are available.

   c. The price elasticity of demand for Ford SUVs will decrease because other cars are viewed as less of a substitute.

   d. The price elasticity of demand for Ford SUVs will increase over time because more substitutes (such as four-wheel-drive cargo vans) become available.

3. U.S. winter wheat production increased dramatically in 1999 after a bumper harvest. The supply curve shifted rightward; as a result, the price decreased and the quantity demanded increased (a movement along the demand curve). The accompanying table describes what happened to prices and the quantity demanded of wheat.

	1998	1999
Quantity demanded (bushels)	1.74 billion	1.9 billion
Average price (per bushel)	$3.70	$2.72

   a. Calculate the price elasticity of demand for winter wheat.

   b. What is the total revenue for U.S. wheat farmers in 1998 and 1999?

   c. Did the bumper harvest increase or decrease the total revenue of American wheat farmers? How could you have predicted this from your answer to part a?

3. **a.** The percent change in the quantity demanded of U.S. winter wheat is

$$\frac{1.9 \text{ billion} - 1.74 \text{ billion}}{(1.74 \text{ billion} + 1.9 \text{ billion})/2} \times 100 = \frac{0.16 \text{ billion}}{1.82 \text{ billion}} \times 100 = 8.8\%$$

and the percent change in the price of U.S. winter wheat is

$$\frac{\$3.70 - \$2.72}{(\$3.70 + \$2.72)/2} \times 100 = \frac{\$0.98}{\$3.21} \times 100 = 30.5\%$$

The price elasticity of demand is therefore

$$\frac{8.8\%}{30.5\%} = 0.29$$

   b. The total revenue in 1998 is the price per bushel in 1998 times the quantity of bushels demanded in 1998. That is, total revenue in 1998 is $3.70 × 1.74 billion = $6.438 billion. Similarly, total revenue in 1999 is $2.72 × 1.9 billion = $5.168 billion.

c. The fall in price from 1998 to 1999 reduced U.S. wheat farmers' total revenue. This could have been predicted by knowing that demand is inelastic: in part a we calculated a price elasticity of demand of 0.29. In this case, the price effect of this price fall (which tends to reduce total revenue) outweighed the quantity effect (which tends to increase total revenue).

4. The accompanying table gives part of the supply schedule for personal computers in the United States.

Price of computer	Quantity of computers supplied
$1,100	12,000
900	8,000

a. Calculate the price elasticity of supply when the price increases from $900 to $1,100.

b. Suppose firms produce 1,000 more computers at any given price due to improved technology. As price increases from $900 to $1,100, is the price elasticity of supply now greater than, less than, or the same as it was in part a?

c. Suppose a longer time period under consideration means that the quantity supplied at any given price is 20% higher than the figures given in the table. As price increases from $900 to $1,100, is the price elasticity of supply now greater than, less than, or the same as it was in part a?

Solution

4. a. The percent change in the quantity supplied is

$$\frac{12,000 - 8,000}{(8,000 + 12,000)/2} \times 100 = \frac{4,000}{10,000} \times 100 = 40\%$$

and the percent change in the price is

$$\frac{\$1,100 - \$900}{(\$900 + \$1,100)/2} \times 100 = \frac{\$200}{\$1,000} \times 100 = 20\%$$

The price elasticity of supply is therefore

$$\frac{40\%}{20\%} = 2$$

b. The elasticity estimate would be lower. A price change from $900 to $1,100 is a 20% price change, just as calculated in part a. Previously, when the quantity supplied changed from 8,000 to 12,000, that was a 40% change in the quantity supplied. Now that the quantity supplied at each price is higher by 1,000, the same price change would imply a change in the quantity supplied from 9,000 to 13,000, which is a 36% change using the midpoint method. The new price elasticity of demand is 36%/20% = 1.8, which is lower than in part a.

c. The elasticity estimate would be unchanged. The price increase from $900 to $1,100 is a 20% increase, just as calculated in part a. But now that all quantities are 20% higher, the quantity supplied increases from 9,600 to 14,400. Using the midpoint method, this is an increase of

$$\frac{14,400 - 9,600}{(9,600 + 14,400)/2} \times 100 = \frac{4,800}{12,000} \times 100 = 40\%$$

so that the price elasticity of supply is

$$\frac{40\%}{20\%} = 2$$

Therefore the price elasticity of demand is the same as in part a.

5. The accompanying table lists the cross-price elasticities of demand for several goods, where the percent price change is measured for the first good of the pair, and the percent quantity change is measured for the second good.

Good	Cross-price elasticities of demand
Air-conditioning units and kilowatts of electricity	−0.34
Coke and Pepsi	+0.63
High-fuel-consuming sport-utility vehicles (SUVs) and gasoline	−0.28
McDonald's burgers and Burger King burgers	+0.82
Butter and margarine	+1.54

a. Explain the sign of each of the cross-price elasticities. What does it imply about the relationship between the two goods in question?

b. Compare the absolute values of the cross-price elasticities and explain their magnitudes. For example, why is the cross-price elasticity of McDonald's and Burger King less than the cross-elasticity of butter and margarine?

c. Use the information in the table to calculate how a 5% increase in the price of Pepsi affects the quantity of Coke demanded.

d. Use the information in the table to calculate how a 10% decrease in the price of gasoline affects the quantity of SUVs demanded.

5. **a.** A negative cross-price elasticity of demand implies that the two goods are complements. So air-conditioning units and kilowatts of electricity are complements, as are sport-utility vehicles and gasoline. A positive cross-price elasticity of demand implies that the two goods are substitutes. So Coke and Pepsi are substitutes, as are McDonald's and Burger King burgers as well as butter and margarine.

b. The larger (and positive) the cross-price elasticity of demand is, the more closely the two goods are substitutes. Since the cross-price elasticity of butter and margarine is larger than the cross-price elasticity of McDonald's burgers and Burger King burgers, butter and margarine are closer substitutes than are McDonald's and Burger King burgers. Similarly, the greater (and negative) the cross-price elasticity of demand is, the more strongly the two goods are complements.

c. A cross-price elasticity of 0.63 implies that a 1% increase in the price of Pepsi would increase the quantity of Coke demanded by 0.63%. Therefore, a 5% increase in the price of Pepsi would increase the quantity of Coke demanded by five times as much, that is, by $5 \times 0.63\% = 3.15\%$.

d. A cross-price elasticity of −0.28 implies that a 1% fall in the price of gasoline would increase the quantity of SUVs demanded by 0.28%. Therefore, a 10% fall in the price of gasoline would increase the quantity of SUVs demanded by 10 times as much, that is, by $10 \times 0.28\% = 2.8\%$.

6. What can you conclude about the price elasticity of demand in each of the following statements?

   a. "The pizza delivery business in this town is very competitive. I'd lose half my customers if I raised the price by as little as 10%."

   b. "I owned both of the two Jerry Garcia autographed lithographs in existence. I sold one on eBay for a high price. But when I sold the second one, the price dropped a lot."

   c. "My economics professor has chosen to use the Krugman/Wells/Olney textbook for this class. I have no choice but to buy this book."

   d. "I always spend a total of exactly $10 per week on coffee."

6. a. This statement says that a 10% increase in price reduces the quantity demanded by 50%. That is, the price elasticity of demand is

$$\frac{50\%}{10\%} = 5$$

   Demand is therefore elastic.

   b. The fact that it was necessary for price to drop a lot in order to sell one more unit indicates that the demand for Jerry Garcia autographed lithographs is inelastic.

   c. There is no substitute available, so demand is inelastic. (Although, over time, as more used Krugman/Wells/Olney textbooks become available, the price elasticity of demand will increase.)

   d. Demand is unit-elastic: no matter what the price of coffee is, the total revenue to the producer (which is my total expenditure on coffee) remains the same.

7. The accompanying table shows the price and yearly quantity sold of souvenir T-shirts in the town of Crystal Lake according to the average income of the tourists visiting.

Price of T-shirt	Quantity of T-shirts demanded when average tourist income is $20,000	Quantity of T-shirts demanded when average tourist income is $30,000
$4	3,000	5,000
5	2,400	4,200
6	1,600	3,000
7	800	1,800

   a. Calculate the price elasticity of demand when the price of a T-shirt rises from $5 to $6 when the average tourist income is $20,000. Also calculate it when the average tourist income is $30,000.

   b. Calculate the income elasticity of demand when the average tourist income increases from $20,000 to $30,000 when the price of a T-shirt is $4. Also calculate it when the price is $7.

7. **a.** Suppose the average tourist income is $20,000. The percent change in the quantity demanded is

$$\frac{2,400 - 1,600}{(1,600 + 2,400)/2} \times 100 = \frac{800}{2,000} \times 100 = 40\%$$

and the percent change in the price is

$$\frac{\$6 - \$5}{(\$5 + \$6)/2} \times 100 = \frac{\$1}{\$5.50} \times 100 = 18.2\%$$

The price elasticity of demand is therefore

$$\frac{40\%}{18.2\%} = 2.2$$

Now suppose the average tourist income is $30,000. The percent change in the quantity demanded is

$$\frac{4,200 - 3,000}{(3,000 + 4,200)/2} \times 100 = \frac{1,200}{3,600} \times 100 = 33.3\%$$

and the percent change in the price is, as before,

$$\frac{\$6 - \$5}{(\$5 + \$6)/2} \times 100 = \frac{\$1}{\$5.50} \times 100 = 18.2\%$$

The price elasticity of demand is therefore

$$\frac{33.3\%}{18.2\%} = 1.8$$

b. Suppose the price of a T-shirt is $4. The percent change in the quantity demanded is

$$\frac{5,000 - 3,000}{(3,000 + 5,000)/2} \times 100 = \frac{2,000}{4,000} \times 100 = 50\%$$

and the percent change in income is

$$\frac{\$30,000 - \$20,000}{(\$20,000 + \$30,000)/2} \times 100 = \frac{\$10,000}{\$25,000} \times 100 = 40\%$$

The income elasticity of demand is therefore

$$\frac{50\%}{40\%} = 1.25$$

Now suppose the price is $7. The percent change in the quantity demanded is

$$\frac{1,800 - 800}{(800 + 1,800)/2} \times 100 = \frac{1,000}{1,300} \times 100 = 76.9\%$$

and the percent change in income is, as before,

$$\frac{\$30,000 - \$20,000}{(\$20,000 + \$30,000)/2} \times 100 = \frac{\$10,000}{\$25,000} \times 100 = 40\%$$

The income elasticity of demand is therefore

$$\frac{76.9\%}{40\%} = 1.9$$

8. A recent study determined the following elasticities for Volkswagen Beetles:

Price elasticity of demand = 2
Income elasticity of demand = 1.5

The supply of Beetles is elastic. Based on this information, are the following statements true or false? Explain your reasoning.

a. A 10% increase in the price of a Beetle will reduce the quantity demanded by 20%.

b. An increase in consumer income will increase the price and quantity sold of Beetles. Since price elasticity of demand is greater than 1, total revenue will go down.

8. **a.** True. The price elasticity of demand for Beetles is 2. That is, a 1% increase in the price would reduce the quantity demanded by 2%. Therefore, a 10% increase in the price would reduce the quantity demanded by 20%.

b. The first part of the statement is true. The income elasticity of demand for Beetles is positive (they are a normal good). That is, an increase in income will increase the demand for Beetles. The demand curve shifts rightward, and the price and quantity of Beetles supplied both increase. However, the second part of the statement is false. Since both price and quantity increase, regardless of the price elasticity of demand, total revenue will go up. So the statement is false.

9. In each of the following cases, do you think the price elasticity of supply is (i) perfectly elastic; (ii) perfectly inelastic; (iii) elastic, but not perfectly elastic; or (iv) inelastic, but not perfectly inelastic? Explain using a diagram.

a. An increase in demand this summer for luxury cruises leads to a huge jump in the sales price of a cabin on the Queen Mary.

b. The price of a kilowatt of electricity is the same during periods of high electricity demand as during periods of low electricity demand.

c. Fewer people want to fly during February than during any other month. The airlines cancel about 10% of their flights as ticket prices fall about 20% during this month.

d. Owners of vacation homes in Maine rent them out during the summer. Due to the soft economy this year, a 30% decline in the price of a vacation rental leads more than half of homeowners to occupy their vacation homes themselves during the summer.

9. **a.** Supply is perfectly inelastic: the quantity of cabins on the Queen Mary is fixed. As demand increases (a rightward shift in the demand curve), the price of a cabin on the Queen Mary increases, without an increase in the quantity supplied. See the accompanying diagram.

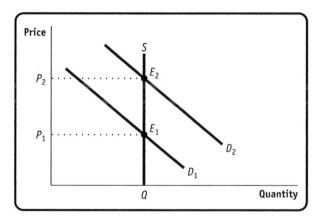

b. Supply is perfectly elastic. As demand changes (for instance, as demand increases in times of high electricity demand), price does not change but the quantity supplied does change. See the accompanying diagram.

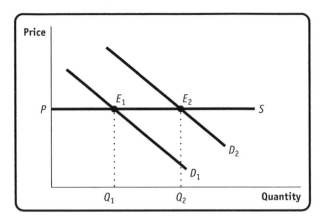

c. Supply is inelastic. As price falls by 20%, the quantity supplied falls by 10%. This implies a price elasticity of supply of

$$\frac{10\%}{20\%} = 0.5$$

which is inelastic. See the accompanying diagram.

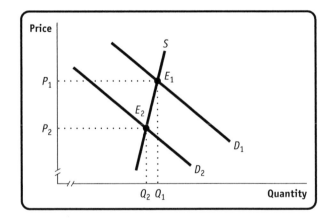

d. Supply is elastic. As price falls by 30%, the quantity supplied falls by more than 50%. This implies a price elasticity of supply greater than 50%/30%, that is, a price elasticity of supply greater than 1.7. See the accompanying diagram.

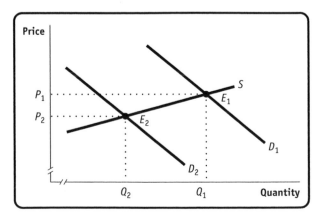

10. Use an elasticity concept to explain each of the following observations.

 a. During economic boom times, the number of new personal care businesses, such as gyms and tanning salons, is proportionately greater than the number of other new businesses, such as grocery stores.

 b. Cement is the primary building material in Mexico. After new technology makes cement cheaper to produce, the supply curve for the Mexican cement industry becomes relatively flatter.

 c. Some goods that were once considered luxuries, like a telephone, are now considered virtual necessities. As a result, the demand curve for telephone services has become steeper over time.

 d. Consumers in a less developed country like Guatemala spend proportionately more of their income on equipment for producing things at home, like sewing machines, than consumers in a more developed country like Canada.

10. **a.** During times of economic boom, incomes rise. Whether, and by how much, demand responds to changes in income is determined by the income elasticity of demand. Since the demand for personal care services increases as income increases, personal care services are a normal good. If the demand for personal care services is more responsive to changes in income than the demand for other products, the income elasticity of demand for personal care services is greater than the income elasticity of demand for other products. As a result of the proportionately greater increase in demand, you would see the quantity of personal care services supplied increase by proportionately more.

 b. New technology has made cement easier to produce. This implies that as the price of cement rises, many more firms are now willing to supply cement than before; that is, supply has become more elastic, leading to a relatively flatter supply curve.

 c. As telephones have become less and less of a luxury, the price elasticity of demand for telephones has fallen: telephones have becomes so much a necessity of daily life that it is now more difficult for consumers to substitute away from telephones. As demand for telephones has become less elastic (less responsive to changes in the price), the demand curve for telephones has become steeper.

 d. Incomes in Canada are higher than those in Guatemala. The statement therefore implies that as income rises, the demand for sewing machines increases by proportionately less than the change in income, making the income elasticity of demand inelastic. Maybe the demand for sewing machines even decreases as income rises, implying that sewing machines are an inferior good, with a negative income elasticity of demand.

11. Taiwan is a major world supplier of semiconductor chips. A recent earthquake severely damaged the production facilities of Taiwanese chip-producing companies, sharply reducing the amount of chips they could produce.

 a. Assume that the total revenue of a typical non-Taiwanese chip manufacturer rises due to these events. In terms of an elasticity, what must be true for this to happen? Illustrate the change in total revenue with a diagram, indicating the price effect and the quantity effect of the Taiwan earthquake on this company's total revenue.

 b. Now assume that the total revenue of a typical non-Taiwanese chip manufacturer falls due to these events. In terms of an elasticity, what must be true for this to happen? Illustrate the change in total revenue with a diagram, indicating the price effect and the quantity effect of the Taiwan earthquake on this company's total revenue.

11. The earthquake led to a leftward shift in the world supply curve of semiconductor chips, leading to an increase in price and a decrease in the quantity demanded.

   a. If the increase in price results in an increase in total revenue, then the price effect (which tends to increase total revenue) must outweigh the quantity effect (which tends to reduce total revenue). That is, demand must have been inelastic. In the accompanying diagram, as supply shifted leftward from S_1 to S_2, the fall in total revenue due to the quantity effect (area A) is outweighed by the gain in total revenue due to the price effect (area B).

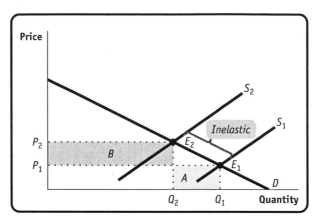

   b. If the increase in price results in a fall in total revenue, then the quantity effect (which tends to reduce total revenue) must outweigh the price effect (which tends to increase total revenue). That is, demand must have been elastic. In the accompanying diagram, as supply shifted leftward from S_1 to S_2, total revenue falls by the amount of the quantity effect (area A) but rises by the amount of the price effect (area B). The quantity effect (area A) is larger than the price effect (area B) so total revenue declines.

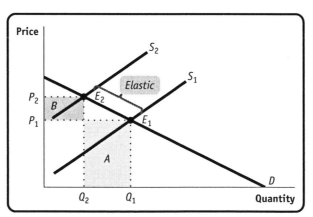

12. There is a debate about whether sterile hypodermic needles should be passed out free of charge in cities with high drug use. Proponents argue that doing so will reduce the incidence of diseases, such as HIV/AIDS, that are often spread by needle sharing among drug users. Opponents believe that doing so will encourage more drug use by reducing the risks of this behavior. As an economist asked to assess the policy, you must know the following: (i) how responsive the spread of diseases like HIV/AIDS is to the price of sterile needles; and (ii) how responsive drug use is to the price of sterile needles. Assuming that you know these two things, use the concepts of price elasticity of demand for sterile needles and the cross-price elasticity between drugs and sterile needles to answer the following questions.

   a. In what circumstances do you believe this is a beneficial policy?

   b. In what circumstances do you believe this is a bad policy?

12. a. Handing out free needles lowers the price of needles to zero. First consider the demand for needles. The higher the price elasticity of demand for sterile needles, the greater the increase in the quantity of sterile needles demanded in response to a price change. And the greater the increase in the quantity of sterile needles demanded, the lower the spread of diseases like HIV/AIDS. Now consider the demand for drugs. Drugs and sterile needles are complements: as the price of sterile needles falls, the demand between drugs increases. This implies that the cross-price elasticity of demand between drugs and sterile needles is negative. The less negative (the closer to zero) the cross-price elasticity of demand between drugs and sterile needles is, the less responsive is the demand for drugs to the price of sterile needles. So the policy would be beneficial if the price elasticity of demand for sterile needles is high (elastic) and the cross-price elasticity of demand between drugs and sterile needles is negative and low (close to zero, that is, weakly complementary).

b. Similar reasoning as in part (a) implies that the policy would be a bad idea if the price elasticity of demand for sterile needles is low (inelastic) and the cross-price elasticity of demand between drugs and sterile needles is high and negative (strongly complementary).

13. Suppose the government imposes an excise tax of $1 for every gallon of gas sold. Before the tax, the price of a gallon of gas is $2. Consider the following four after-tax scenarios. In each case, (i) use an elasticity concept to explain what must be true for this scenario to arise; (ii) determine who bears relatively more of the burden of the tax, producers or consumers; and (iii) illustrate your answer with a diagram.

a. The price of gasoline paid by consumers rises to $3 per gallon. Assume that the demand curve is downward sloping.

b. The price paid by consumers remains at $2 per gallon after the tax is imposed. Assume that the supply curve is upward sloping.

c. The price of gasoline paid by consumers rises to $2.75.

d. The price of gasoline paid by consumers rises to $2.25.

13. a. If supply is perfectly elastic, and the demand curve is downward sloping, then any tax will be fully passed on to consumers. The price paid by consumers rises to $3, and the price received by producers remains at $2. Consumers bear the full burden of the tax. See the accompanying diagram.

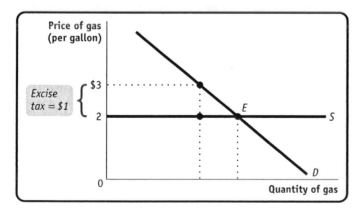

b. If demand is perfectly elastic, and the supply curve is upward sloping, then none of the tax can be passed on to consumers. The price paid by consumers remains at $2, and the price received by producers falls to $1. Producers bear the full burden of the tax. See the accompanying diagram.

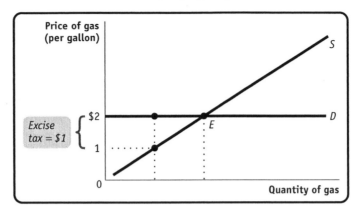

c. If demand is less elastic than supply, consumers bear a larger portion of the tax than producers. That is, the price paid by consumers rises by more than the price received by producers falls. See the accompanying diagram.

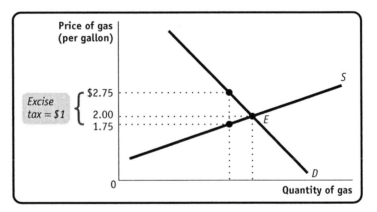

d. If demand is more elastic than supply, producers bear a larger portion of the tax than consumers. That is, the price paid by consumers rises by less than the price received by producers falls. See the accompanying diagram.

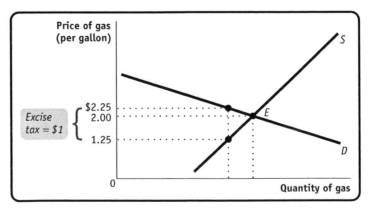

14. Describe how the following events will affect the incidence of taxation—that is, after the event, will the tax fall more heavily on consumers or producers in comparison to before the event? Use the concept of elasticity to explain your answer.

   a. Sales of gasoline are taxed. Ethanol, a substitute for gasoline, becomes widely available.

   b. Sales of electricity to California residents are taxed. Regulations are introduced that make it much more difficult for California utility companies to divert supplies of electricity from the California market to markets in neighboring states like Nevada.

   c. Sales of electricity to California residents are taxed. Regulations are introduced that make it much easier for California utility companies to divert supplies of electricity from the California market to markets in neighboring states like Nevada.

   d. The sale of municipally provided water is taxed. Legislation is introduced that forbids the use of private sources of water such as wells and the diversion of rivers.

14. a. The wide availability of ethanol, a substitute for gasoline, increases the price elasticity of demand for gasoline: demand becomes more elastic. This implies that the fraction of the tax that falls on consumers decreases and the fraction that falls on producers increases. The tax falls more heavily on producers.

   b. As it becomes harder to divert supply away from California as the price of electricity in California falls, supply of electricity in California becomes less elastic: the price elasticity of supply decreases. This implies that the fraction of the tax that falls on producers increases and the fraction that falls on consumers decreases. The tax falls more heavily on producers.

   c. As it becomes easier to divert supply away from California as the price of electricity in California falls, supply of electricity in California becomes more elastic: the price elasticity of supply increases. This implies that the fraction of the tax that falls on producers decreases and the fraction that falls on consumers increases. The tax falls more heavily on consumers.

   d. Legislation that forbids the use of substitutes for municipally provided water decreases the price elasticity of demand for municipally provided water: demand becomes less elastic. This implies that the fraction of the tax that falls on consumers increases and the fraction that falls on producers decreases. The tax falls more heavily on consumers.

15. In devising taxes, there is often a debate about (i) who bears the burden of the tax and (ii) whether the tax achieves some desirable social goal, such as discouraging undesirable behavior by making it more expensive. In the case of cigarettes, smokers tend to be highly addicted and have lower income than the average nonsmoker. Taxes on cigarettes have historically had the effect of raising the price to consumers almost one for one with the size of the tax.

   a. Why might such a tax be undesirable when considering issues of tax equity—that is, whether or not the tax burden falls more heavily on lower-income people? How do the price elasticities of supply and demand for cigarettes affect the equity of cigarette taxation?

   b. How do the price elasticities of supply and demand for cigarettes affect the effectiveness of the tax in discouraging smoking?

   c. In light of your answers to parts a and b and the historical response of price to the tax, what trade-offs must policy makers make when considering a cigarette tax?

15. The fact that smokers tend to be highly addicted means that demand for cigarettes is highly inelastic. In addition, the fact that taxes on cigarettes result in an almost one-for-one increase in the price of cigarettes means that the demand for cigarettes is almost perfectly inelastic: the demand curve is almost vertical.

   a. Since the demand for cigarettes is almost perfectly inelastic, the tax on cigarettes falls almost entirely on consumers. If you also believe that most consumers of cigarettes live in lower-than-average income households, then the tax on cigarettes is largely a tax on low-income households. That is, the tax on cigarettes distributes income away from the poor, which is not equitable.

   b. Since the demand for cigarettes is almost perfectly inelastic (almost vertical), the tax will have a negligible effect on reducing the quantity demanded. (The tax could, however, have a large effect on people who do not yet smoke—teenagers, for instance. Since these consumers are not yet addicted, their price elasticity of demand is likely to be much higher.)

   c. Policy makers must weigh the benefit of tax revenue (and, possibly, the benefit of discouraging people from taking up smoking) with the inequity of the tax falling largely on low-income households and the fact that the tax does not appreciably reduce smoking among current smokers nor the associated health care costs.

16. Worldwide, the average coffee grower has increased the amount of acreage under cultivation over the past few years. The result has been that the average coffee plantation produces significantly more coffee than it did 10 to 20 years ago. Unfortunately for the growers, however, this has also been a period in which their total revenues have plunged. In terms of an elasticity, what must be true for these events to have occurred? Illustrate these events with a diagram, indicating the quantity effect and the price effect that gave rise to these events.

16. An increase in the amount of acreage that is cultivated results in a rightward shift in the supply of coffee. This reduces the price of coffee and increases the quantity demanded. If total revenue from coffee sales have decreased, this means that the price effect (which tends to lower total revenue) must have outweighed the quantity effect (which tends to increase total revenue). This implies that demand must have been inelastic. As shown in the accompanying diagram, the price effect results in a loss of total revenue equal to the size of area A. The quantity effect (the quantity demanded increases as a result of the price fall) results in an increase in total revenue equal to the size of area B. Area A exceeds area B, so total revenue falls.

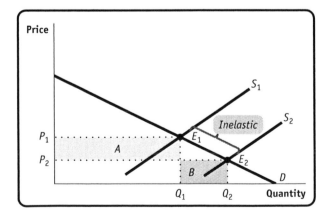

Consumer and Producer Surplus

1. Determine the amount of consumer surplus generated in each of the following situations.

    a. Paul goes to the clothing store to buy a new T-shirt, for which he is willing to pay up to $10. He picks out one he likes with a price tag of exactly $10. At the cash register, he is told that his T-shirt is on sale for half the posted price.

    b. Robin goes to the CD store hoping to find a used copy of the *Eagles Greatest Hits* for up to $10. The store has one copy selling for $10.

    c. After soccer practice, Phil is willing to pay $2 for a bottle of mineral water. The 7-Eleven sells mineral water for $2.25 per bottle.

1. a. Paul's consumer surplus is $5. This is the difference between how much he is willing to pay ($10) and how much he does pay ($5).

    b. Since Robin's willingness to pay is $10 and the price of the CD is $10, she gets no consumer surplus if she buys the CD.

    c. No trade will take place since Phil's willingness to pay is less than the price. So no consumer surplus is created.

2. Determine the amount of producer surplus generated in each of the following situations.

    a. Bob lists his old Lionel electric trains on eBay. He sets a minimum acceptable price, known as his *reserve price*, of $75. After five days of bidding, the final high bid is exactly $75.

    b. Jenny advertises her car for sale in the used-car section of the student newspaper for $2,000, but she is willing to sell the car for any price higher than $1,500. The best offer she gets is $1,200.

    c. Sanjay likes his job so much that he would be willing to do it for free. However, his annual salary is $80,000.

2. a. Bob will receive no producer surplus since the price paid for the trains is equal to his cost.

    b. No trade will take place since Jenny's cost is $1,500, which is higher than the price of $1,200 she is offered. So no producer surplus is created.

    c. Sanjay's cost is zero. The price he is paid for his time is $80,000, so his producer surplus is $80,000.

3. Hollywood writers negotiate a new agreement with movie producers that they will receive 10 percent of the revenue from every video rental of a movie they worked on. They have no such agreement for movies shown on pay-per-view television.

    a. When the new writers' agreement comes into effect, what will happen in the market for video rentals—that is, will supply or demand shift, and how? As a result, how will consumer surplus in the market for video rentals change? Illustrate with a diagram. Do you think the writers' agreement will be popular with consumers who rent videos?

b. Consumers consider video rentals and pay-per-view movies substitutable to some extent. When the new writers' agreement comes into effect, what will happen in the market for pay-per-view movies—that is, will supply or demand shift, and how? As a result, how will producer surplus in the market for pay-per-view movies change? Illustrate with a diagram. Do you think the writers' agreement will be popular with cable television companies that show pay-per-view movies?

Solution

3. a. The payment to writers will increase the cost of providing video rentals. In the accompanying diagram, the supply curve shifts leftward from S_1 to S_2, the equilibrium price of video rentals rises from P_1 to P_2 and the quantity of video rentals bought and sold falls from Q_1 to Q_2. As a result, consumer surplus will decrease by the shaded amount. The writers' agreement will not be popular with consumers.

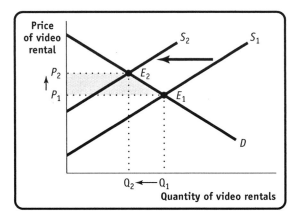

b. The higher price of video rentals will make pay-per-view movies more popular. They are substitute goods, and the demand for them will increase when the price of video rentals rises. In the accompanying diagram, demand shifts rightward from D_1 to D_2. The price rises from P_1 to P_2, and the equilibrium quantity rises from Q_1 to Q_2. Producer surplus will increase by the shaded amount. This change will be popular with the cable television companies that show pay-per-view movies.

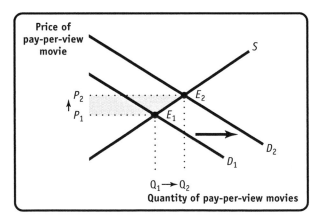

4. There are six potential consumers of computer games, each willing to buy only one game. Consumer 1 is willing to pay $40 for a computer game, consumer 2 is willing to pay $35, consumer 3 is willing to pay $30, consumer 4 is willing pay $25, consumer 5 is willing to pay $20, and consumer 6 is willing to pay $15.

   a. Suppose the market price is $29. What is the total consumer surplus?

   b. Now the market price decreases to $19. What is the total consumer surplus now?

   c. When the price fell from $29 to $19, how much did each consumer's individual consumer surplus change?

4. **a.** Consumer 1 buys a game since her willingness to pay is greater than the price. She gains $40 − $29 = $11.

   Consumer 2 buys a game since his willingness to pay is greater than the price. He gains $35 − $29 = $6.

   Consumer 3 buys a game since her willingness to pay is greater than the price. She gains $30 − $29 = $1.

   The total consumer surplus is $11 + $6 + $1 = $18.

   b. Consumer 1 buys a game since her willingness to pay is greater than the price. She gains $40 − $19 = $21.

   Consumer 2 buys a game since his willingness to pay is greater than the price. He gains $35 − $19 = $16.

   Consumer 3 buys a game since her willingness to pay is greater than the price. She gains $30 − $19 = $11.

   Consumer 4 buys a game since his willingness to pay is greater than the price. He gains $25 − $19 = $6.

   Consumer 5 buys a game since her willingness to pay is greater than the price. She gains $20 − $19 = $1.

   The total consumer surplus is $21 + $16 + $11 + $6 + $1 = $55.

   c. Total consumer surplus has increased by $55 − $18 = $37 as a result of the price decrease. For consumers 1, 2, and 3 (the consumers who would also have bought games at the higher price), individual consumer surplus increases by $10 each, the amount of the price reduction. This accounts for $30 of the increase in consumer surplus. But consumers 4 and 5 now also get consumer surplus, since the lower price leads them to buy computer games also. Consumer 4 gets $6 of consumer surplus, and consumer 5 gets $1.

5. In an effort to provide more affordable rental housing for low-income families, the city council of Collegetown decides to impose a rent ceiling well below the current market equilibrium rent.

   a. Illustrate the effect of this policy in a diagram. Indicate consumer and producer surplus before and after the introduction of the rent ceiling.

   b. Will this policy be popular with renters? With landlords?

   c. An economist explains to the city council that this policy is creating a deadweight loss. Illustrate the deadweight loss in your diagram.

5. **a.** Before the introduction of the rent ceiling, the market is in equilibrium at a price of P_E and a quantity of Q_E. Consumer surplus is the area $P_E E A$. Producer surplus is the area $P_E B E$. The rent ceiling at $P_{CEILING}$ leads to a reduction in the quantity from Q_E to $Q_{CEILING}$. Consumer surplus is the area $P_{CEILING} F C A$. Producer surplus is the area $P_{CEILING} B F$.

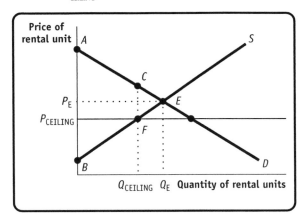

b. It is not clear whether consumers are better off with the rent ceiling: The consumers who rent housing both before and after the introduction of the price ceiling gain consumer surplus. However, some consumers who used to rent housing can no longer do so after the introduction of the price ceiling, and they lose all consumer surplus. It is clear that the policy will be unpopular with landlords: producer surplus decreases unambiguously.

c. The deadweight loss from this policy is the area CFE: it is a measure of how much consumer surplus and producer surplus is lost because of the introduction of the rent ceiling.

6. On Thursday nights, a local restaurant has a pasta special. Ari likes the restaurant's pasta, and his willingness to pay for each serving is shown in the accompanying table.

Quantity of pasta (servings)	Willingness to pay for pasta (per serving)
1	$10
2	8
3	6
4	4
5	2
6	0

a. If the price of a serving of pasta is $4, how many servings will Ari buy? How much consumer surplus does he receive?

b. The following week, Ari is back at the restaurant again, but now the price of a serving of pasta is $6. By how much does his consumer surplus decrease compared to the previous week?

c. One week later, he goes to the restaurant again. He discovers that the restaurant is offering an "all you can eat" special for $25. How much pasta will Ari eat, and how much consumer surplus does he receive now?

d. Suppose you own the restaurant and Ari is a "typical" customer. What is the highest price you can charge for the "all you can eat" special and still attract customers?

6. **a.** Ari will buy four servings of pasta. His consumer surplus is equal to $12, that is: ($10 − $4) + ($8 − $4) + ($6 − $4) + ($4 − $4) = $12.

 b. Ari will buy three servings of pasta. His consumer surplus is ($10 − $6) + ($8 − $6) + ($6 − $6) = $6, so his consumer surplus falls by $6, from $12 to $6.

 c. If there is an "all you can eat" special, the price Ari pays per serving is zero. Therefore, he will eat six servings of pasta. The total amount he is willing to pay for those six servings is $30: the sum of the amount he is willing to pay for each individual serving. Since he actually pays $25, his consumer surplus is $5.

 d. When there is an "all you can eat" special, Ari will consume six servings. His consumer surplus from consuming six servings is $30. Therefore, the most he is willing to pay for an "all you can eat" special is $30. This is the highest price you can charge for the special.

7. The accompanying diagram shows the market for cigarettes. The current equilibrium price per pack is $4, and every day 40 million packs of cigarettes are sold. In order to recover some of the health care costs associated with smoking, the government imposes a tax of $2 per pack. This will raise the equilibrium price to $5 per pack and reduce the equilibrium quantity to 30 million packs.

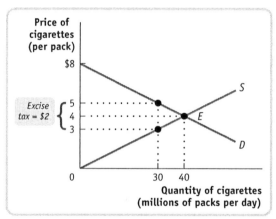

The economist working for the tobacco lobby claims that this tax will reduce consumer surplus for smokers by $40 million per day, since 40 million packs now cost $1 more per pack. The economist working for the lobby for sufferers of second-hand smoke argues that this is an enormous overestimate and that the reduction in consumer surplus will be only $30 million per day, since after the imposition of the tax only 30 million packs of cigarettes will be bought and each of these packs will now cost $1 more. They are both wrong. Why?

7. The economist working for the tobacco lobby is overestimating the change in consumer surplus. She is assuming that there will be no change in the quantity demanded and that consumers will continue to smoke 40 million packs of cigarettes per day even when the price has risen by $1 per pack. The economist working for the second-hand smoke lobby is underestimating the loss of consumer surplus. He expects that the quantity demanded will be reduced to 30 million packs per day. He is then looking at the loss of consumer surplus experienced by the consumers of those 30 million packs per day. The loss is $1 per pack, the increase in the price per pack. He is not counting the loss of consumer surplus experienced by those who are no longer smoking 10 million packs per day because consumption dropped from 40 million to 30 million packs per day.

The reduction in consumer surplus resulting from the new tax is the $30 million reduction experienced by the smokers of the 30 million packs plus the $5 million reduction in consumer surplus experienced by those smokers who are smoking 10 million fewer packs. The total reduction in consumer surplus is $35 million.

One way of calculating this answer is to look at the total consumer surplus before and after the new tax. Before the tax the consumer surplus was $\frac{1}{2} \times (\$8 - \$4) \times 40$ million = $80 million. After the tax, the consumer surplus is $\frac{1}{2} \times (\$8 - \$5) \times 30$ million = $45 million. The reduction in consumer surplus is $80 million − $45 million = $35 million. (Recall that the area of a triangle is $\frac{1}{2} \times$ the base of the triangle $\times$ the height of the triangle.)

8. Consider the original market for pizza in Collegetown, illustrated in the accompanying table. Collegetown officials decide to impose an excise tax on pizza of $4 per pizza.

Price of pizza	Quantity of pizza demanded	Quantity of pizza supplied
$10	0	6
9	1	5
8	2	4
7	3	3
6	4	2
5	5	1
4	6	0
3	7	0
2	8	0
1	9	0

a. What is the quantity of pizza bought and sold after the imposition of the tax? What is the price paid by consumers? What is the price received by producers?

b. Calculate the consumer surplus and the producer surplus after the imposition of the tax. By how much has the imposition of the tax reduced consumer surplus? By how much has it reduced producer surplus?

c. How much tax revenue does Collegetown earn from this tax?

d. Calculate the deadweight loss from this tax.

8. a. The tax drives a wedge between the price paid by consumers and the price received by producers. Consumers now pay $9, and producers receive $5. After the imposition of the tax, the quantity bought and sold will therefore be one pizza.

b. Consumer surplus is now zero (the one consumer who still buys a pizza at $9 has a willingness to pay of just $9, so that the consumer surplus is $9 − $9 = $0). Compared to the situation before the imposition of the tax where the equilibrium price was $7, consumer surplus has been reduced by $3. Similarly, the producer of the one pizza has a cost of $5, and this is the price he receives, so producer surplus is also zero: compared to the situation before, it has decreased by $3.

c. Collegetown earns a tax of $4 per pizza sold, that is, a total tax revenue of $4.

d. Total surplus has been decreased by $6. Of those $6, the town earns $4 in revenue, but $2 of surplus is lost. That is the deadweight loss from this tax.

9. Consider once more the original market for pizza in Collegetown, illustrated in the table in Problem 8. Now Collegetown officials impose a price floor on pizza of $8.

    a. What is the quantity of pizza bought and sold after the imposition of the price floor?

    b. Calculate the consumer surplus and the producer surplus after the imposition of the price floor.

9. a. After the imposition of the price floor, the price of pizza is $8. The demand schedule tells you that the quantity bought and sold is now two pizzas.

    b. At a price of $8, consumer surplus is now ($9 − $8) + ($8 − $8) = $1. Producer surplus is ($8 − $5) + ($8 − $6) = $5.

10. You are the manager of Fun World, a small amusement park. The accompanying diagram shows the demand curve of a typical customer at Fun World.

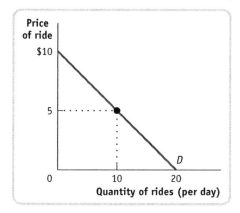

    a. Suppose that the price of each ride is $5. At that price, how much consumer surplus does an individual consumer get? (Recall that the area of a triangle is $\frac{1}{2} \times$ the base of the triangle $\times$ the height of the triangle.)

    b. Suppose that Fun World considers charging an admission fee, even though it maintains the price of each ride at $5. What is the maximum admission fee it could charge? (Assume that all potential customers have enough money to pay the fee.)

    c. Suppose that Fun World lowered the price of each ride to zero. How much consumer surplus does an individual consumer get? What is the maximum admission fee Fun World could therefore charge?

10. a. From the demand curve, you can see that with a price per ride of $5, the customer takes 10 rides. At this point her consumer surplus is $\frac{1}{2} \times$ ($10 − $5) $\times$ 10 = $25.

    b. Since a consumer obtains consumer surplus of $25 from going to Fun World when each ride costs $5, that is the most that she would be willing to pay to go to Fun World. And it is therefore the maximum admission fee that Fun World could charge. (Charging consumers both an entrance fee and a price for each unit of a good bought is called a *two-part tariff*.)

    c. If Fun World charged nothing for each ride, a typical consumer would consume 20 rides, and this would give her a consumer surplus of $\frac{1}{2} \times$ $10 $\times$ 20 = $100. This is therefore the maximum admission fee that Fun World can charge with a price per ride of zero.

11. The accompanying diagram illustrates a taxi driver's individual supply curve (assume that each taxi ride is the same distance).

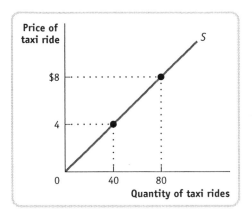

a. Suppose the city sets the price of taxi rides at $4 per ride. What is this taxi driver's producer surplus? (Recall that the area of a triangle is $\frac{1}{2} \times$ the base of the triangle $\times$ the height of the triangle.)

b. Suppose now that the city keeps the price of a taxi ride set at $4, but it decides to charge taxi drivers a "licensing fee." What is the maximum licensing fee the city could extract from this taxi driver?

c. Suppose that the city allowed the price of taxi rides to increase to $8 per ride. How much producer surplus does an individual taxi driver now get? What is the maximum licensing fee the city could charge this taxi driver?

11. a. At a price of $4, the taxi driver supplies 40 rides. His producer surplus is therefore $\frac{1}{2} \times \$4 \times 40 = \$80$.

b. Since the taxi driver's producer surplus is $80, this is the most he is willing to pay to supply 40 rides at $4. And it is therefore the most the city can charge him as a licensing fee.

c. At a price of $8, the taxi driver supplies 80 rides. His producer surplus is therefore $\frac{1}{2} \times \$8 \times 80 = \$320$. Therefore, $320 is the most the city can charge as a licensing fee when the price per ride is $8.

12. The state needs to raise money, and the governor has a choice of imposing an excise tax of the same amount on one of two previously untaxed goods: the state can tax either sales of restaurant meals or sales of gasoline. Both the demand for and the supply of restaurant meals are more elastic than the demand for and the supply of gasoline. If the governor wants to minimize the deadweight loss caused by the tax, which good should be taxed? For each good, draw a diagram that illustrates the deadweight loss from taxation.

12. The tax should be imposed on sales of gasoline. Since both demand for and supply of gasoline are less elastic, changes in the price of gasoline will result in smaller reductions in the quantity demanded and quantity supplied. As a result, fewer transactions are discouraged by the tax—in other words, less total surplus (consumer and producer surplus) is lost. Panel (a) of the accompanying diagram illustrates a tax imposed on sales of gasoline, for which both demand and supply are less elastic; panel (b) illustrates a tax imposed on sales of restaurant meals, for which both demand and supply are more elastic. As you can see, deadweight loss, the shaded triangle, is larger in panel (b) than in panel (a).

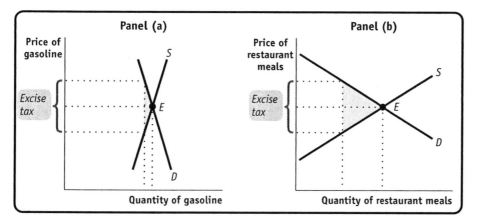

13. In each of the following cases involving taxes, explain: (i) whether the incidence of the tax falls more heavily on consumers or producers, (ii) why government revenue raised from the tax is not a good indicator of the true cost of the tax, and (iii) what missed opportunity, or inefficiency, arises.

a. The government imposes an excise tax on the sale of all college textbooks. Before the tax was imposed, 1 million textbooks were sold every year at a price of $50. After the tax is imposed, 600,000 books are sold yearly; students pay $55 per book, $30 of which publishers receive.

b. The government imposes an excise tax on the sale of all airplane tickets. Before the tax was imposed, 3 million airline tickets were sold every year at a price of $500. After the tax is imposed, 1.5 million tickets are sold yearly; travelers pay $550 per ticket, $450 of which the airlines receive.

c. The government imposes an excise tax on the sale of all toothbrushes. Before the tax, 2 million toothbrushes were sold every year at a price of $1.50. After the tax is imposed, 800,000 toothbrushes are sold every year; consumers pay $2 per toothbrush, $1.25 of which producers receive.

13. **a.** After the imposition of the tax, consumers pay $5 more per book than before; publishers receive $20 less per book than before. Producers (publishers) bear more of the tax. The tax is $55 − $30 = $25 per book, and 600,000 books are sold. Government revenue is therefore $15 million. This, however, is a poor estimate of the cost of the tax, since it does not take into account the fact that, in addition to the higher price, there are now 400,000 potential consumers who would have bought the books without the tax but no longer will buy them. The missed opportunity is that, were it not for the tax, there are 400,000 potential consumers that would buy the books and to whom publishers would sell them; but with the tax these trades are not made.

b. After the imposition of the tax, travelers pay $50 more per ticket than before; airlines receive $50 less than before. The tax is split evenly between consumers and producers. The tax is $550 − $450 = $100 per ticket, and 1.5 million tickets are sold. Government revenue is therefore $150 million. This, however, is a poor estimate of the cost of the tax, since it does not take into account the fact that, in addition to 1.5 million travelers paying higher prices, there are now 1.5 million potential consumers who would have bought tickets without the tax but no longer buy tickets. The missed opportunity is that, were it not for the tax, there are 1.5 million potential consumers who would want to travel and to whom airlines would want to sell tickets; but with the tax these trades are not made.

c. After the imposition of the tax, consumers pay $0.50 more per toothbrush than before; producers receive $0.25 less than before. The incidence of the tax falls mainly on consumers. The tax is $2.00 − $1.25 = $0.75 per toothbrush, and 800,000 toothbrushes are sold. Government revenue therefore is $600,000. This, however, is a poor estimate of the cost of the tax, since it does not take into account the fact that, in addition to 800,000 toothbrushes now being more expensive, there are 1.2 million toothbrushes that would have been sold without the tax but are no longer sold. The missed opportunity is that, were it not for the tax, there are 1.2 million toothbrushes that could be produced at a lower cost than consumers are willing to pay for them: this would be an improvement for both consumers and producers.

Behind the Supply Curve:
Inputs and Costs

1. Marty's Frozen Yogurt is a small shop that sells cups of frozen yogurt in a university town. Marty owns three frozen-yogurt machines. His other inputs are refrigerators, frozen-yogurt mix, cups, sprinkle toppings, and, of course, workers. He estimates that his daily production function when he varies the number of workers employed (and at the same time, of course, yogurt mix, cups, and so on) is as shown in the accompanying table.

Quantity of labor (workers)	Quantity of frozen yogurt (cups)
0	0
1	110
2	200
3	270
4	300
5	320
6	330

a. What are the fixed inputs and variable inputs in the production of cups of frozen yogurt?

b. Draw the total product curve. Put the quantity of labor on the horizontal axis and the quantity of frozen yogurt on the vertical axis.

c. What is the marginal product of the first worker? The second worker? The third worker? Why does marginal product decline as the number of workers increases?

Solution

1. **a.** The fixed inputs are those whose quantities do not change as the quantity of output changes: frozen-yogurt machines, refrigerators, and the shop. The variable inputs are those whose quantities do change as the quantity of output changes: frozen-yogurt mix, cups, sprinkle toppings, and workers.

b. The accompanying diagram illustrates the total product curve.

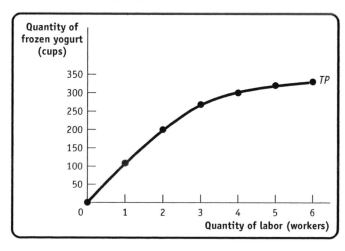

   c. The marginal product, *MPL*, of the first worker is 110 cups. The *MPL* of the second worker is 90 cups. The *MPL* of the third worker is 70 cups. The *MPL* of labor declines as more and more workers are added due to the principle of diminishing returns. Since the number of frozen-yogurt machines is fixed, as workers are added there are fewer and fewer machines for each worker to work with, making each additional worker less and less productive.

2. The production function for Marty's Frozen Yogurt is given in Problem 1. Marty pays each of his workers $80 per day. The cost of his other variable inputs is $0.50 per cup of yogurt. His fixed cost is $100 per day.

   a. What is Marty's variable cost and total cost when he produces 110 cups of yogurt? 200 cups? Calculate variable and total cost for every level of output given in Problem 1.

   b. Draw Marty's variable cost curve. On the same diagram, draw his total cost curve.

   c. What is the marginal cost per cup for the first 110 cups of yogurt? For the next 90 cups? Calculate the marginal cost for all remaining levels of output.

2. a. Marty's variable cost, *VC*, is his wage cost ($80 per worker per day) and his other input costs ($0.50 per cup). His total cost, *TC*, is the sum of the variable cost and his fixed cost of $100 per day. The answers are given in the accompanying table.

Quantity of frozen yogurt (cups)	Quantity of labor (workers)	VC	TC	MC of cup
0	0	$0	$100	
				$1.23
110	1	1 × 80 + 110 × 0.5 = 135	235	
				1.39
200	2	2 × 80 + 200 × 0.5 = 260	360	
				1.64
270	3	3 × 80 + 270 × 0.5 = 375	475	
				3.17
300	4	4 × 80 + 300 × 0.5 = 470	570	
				4.50
320	5	5 × 80 + 320 × 0.5 = 560	660	
				8.50
330	6	6 × 80 + 330 × 0.5 = 645	745	

   b. The accompanying diagram shows the variable cost and total cost curves.

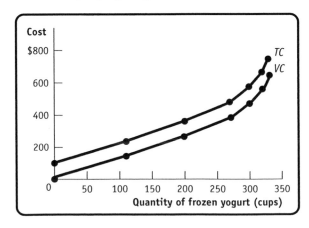

   c. Marginal cost, *MC*, per cup of frozen yogurt is shown in the table in part a; it is the change in total cost divided by the change in quantity of output.

3. The production function for Marty's Frozen Yogurt is given in Problem 1. The costs are given in Problem 2.

    a. For each of the given levels of output, calculate the average fixed cost (*AFC*), average variable cost (*AVC*), and average total cost (*ATC*) per cup of frozen yogurt.

    b. On one diagram, draw the *AFC*, *AVC*, and *ATC* curves.

    c. What principle explains why the *AFC* declines as output increases? What principle explains why the *AVC* increases as output increases? Explain your answers.

    d. How many cups of frozen yogurt are produced when average total cost is minimized?

3. **a.** The average fixed cost, average variable cost, and average total cost per cup of yogurt are given in the accompanying table. (Numbers are rounded.)

Quantity of frozen yogurt (cups)	VC	TC	AFC of cup	AVC of cup	ATC of cup
0	$0	$100	—	—	—
110	135	235	$0.91	$1.23	$2.14
200	260	360	0.50	1.30	1.80
270	375	475	0.37	1.39	1.76
300	470	570	0.33	1.57	1.90
320	560	660	0.31	1.75	2.06
330	645	745	0.30	1.95	2.26

    b. The accompanying diagram shows the *AFC*, *AVC*, and *ATC* curves.

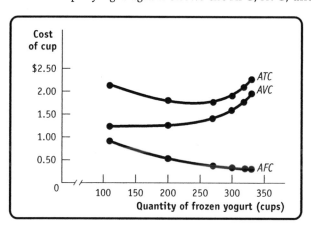

    c. *AFC* declines as output increases due to the spreading effect. The fixed cost is spread over more and more units of output as output increases. *AVC* increases as output increases due to the diminishing returns effect. Due to diminishing returns to labor, it costs more to produce each additional unit of output.

    d. Average total cost is minimized when 270 cups of yogurt are produced. At lower quantities of output, the fall attributable to the spreading effect dominates changes in average total cost. At higher quantities of output, the rise attributable to the diminishing returns effect dominates changes in average total cost.

4. The accompanying table shows a car manufacturer's total cost of producing cars.

Quantity of cars	TC
0	$500,000
1	540,000
2	560,000
3	570,000
4	590,000
5	620,000
6	660,000
7	720,000
8	800,000
9	920,000
10	1,100,000

a. What is this manufacturer's fixed cost?

b. For each level of output, calculate the variable cost (VC). For each level of output except zero output, calculate the average variable cost (AVC), average total cost (ATC), and average fixed cost (AFC). What is the minimum-cost output?

c. For each level of output, calculate this manufacturer's marginal cost (MC).

d. On one diagram, draw the manufacturer's AVC, ATC, and MC curves.

4. a. The manufacturer's fixed cost is $500,000. Even when no output is produced, the manufacturer has a cost of $500,000.

b. The accompanying table shows VC, calculated as TC − FC; AVC, calculated as VC/Q; ATC, calculated as TC/Q; and AFC, calculated as FC/Q. (Numbers are rounded.) The minimum-cost output is eight cars, the level at which ATC is minimized.

c. The table also shows MC, the additional cost per additional car produced. Notice that MC is below ATC for levels of output less than the minimum-cost output and above ATC for levels of output greater than the minimum-cost output.

Quantity of cars	TC	MC of car	VC	AVC of car	ATC of car	AFC of car
0	$500,000		$0	—	—	—
		$40,000				
1	540,000		40,000	$40,000	$540,000	$500,000
		20,000				
2	560,000		60,000	30,000	280,000	250,000
		10,000				
3	570,000		70,000	23,333	190,000	166,667
		20,000				
4	590,000		90,000	22,500	147,500	125,000
		30,000				
5	620,000		120,000	24,000	124,000	100,000
		40,000				
6	660,000		160,000	26,667	110,000	83,333
		60,000				
7	720,000		220,000	31,429	102,857	71,429
		80,000				
8	800,000		300,000	37,500	**100,000**	62,500
		120,000				
9	920,000		420,000	46,667	102,222	55,556
		180,000				
10	1,100,000		600,000	60,000	110,000	50,000

d. The *AVC*, *ATC*, and *MC* curves are shown in the accompanying diagram.

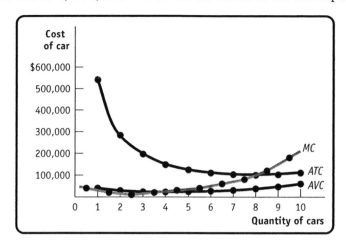

5. Amy, Bill, and Carla all mow lawns for money. Each of them operates a different lawn mower. The accompanying table shows the total cost to Amy, Bill, and Carla of mowing lawns.

Quantity of lawns mowed	Amy's total cost	Bill's total cost	Carla's total cost
0	$0	$0	$0
1	20	10	2
2	35	20	7
3	45	30	17
4	50	40	32
5	52	50	52
6	53	60	82

a. Calculate Amy's, Bill's, and Carla's marginal costs, and draw each of their marginal cost curves.

b. Who has increasing marginal cost, who has decreasing marginal cost, and who has constant marginal cost?

5. **a.** The table shows Amy's, Bill's, and Carla's marginal costs.

Quantity of lawns mowed	Amy's total cost	Amy's marginal cost of lawn mowed	Bill's total cost	Bill's marginal cost of lawn mowed	Carla's total cost	Carla's marginal cost of lawn mowed
0	$0		$0		$0	
		$20		$10		$2
1	20		10		2	
		15		10		5
2	35		20		7	
		10		10		10
3	45		30		17	
		5		10		15
4	50		40		32	
		2		10		20
5	52		50		52	
		1		10		30
6	53		60		82	

The diagram shows Amy's, Bill's, and Carla's marginal cost curves.

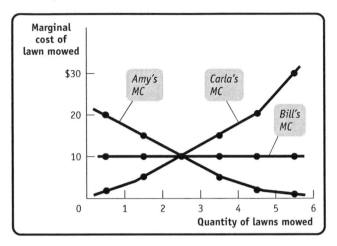

b. From the information in the table or from the diagram, you can see that Amy has decreasing marginal cost, Bill has constant marginal cost, and Carla has increasing marginal cost. (Also note that all of them have increasing *total* cost.)

6. Magnificent Blooms is a florist specializing in floral arrangements for weddings, graduations, and other events. Magnificent Blooms has a fixed cost associated with space and equipment of $100 per day. Each worker is paid $50 per day. The daily production function for Magnificent Blooms is shown in the accompanying table.

Quantity of labor (workers)	Quantity of floral arrangements
0	0
1	5
2	9
3	12
4	14
5	15

a. What is the marginal product, *MPL*, of the first, second, third, fourth, and fifth workers? What principle explains why the marginal product per worker declines as the number of workers employed increases?

b. What is the marginal cost (*MC*) of producing each of the first 5 floral arrangements? The sixth through ninth floral arrangements? The remaining levels of output? What principle explains why the marginal cost per floral arrangement increases as the number of arrangements increases?

6. a. *MPL*, shown in the accompanying table for the five workers, is the change in output resulting from the employment of one additional worker per day. *MPL* falls as the quantity of labor increases due to the principle of diminishing returns.

Quantity of labor L (workers)	Quantity of floral arrangements Q	Marginal product of labor MPL = $\Delta Q/\Delta L$ (floral arrangements per worker)	Variable cost VC = number of workers x wage rate	Total cost TC = FC + VC	Marginal cost of floral arrangement MC = $\Delta TC/\Delta Q$
0	0		$0	$100	
		5			$10.00 (= 50/5)
1	5		50	150	
		4			12.50 (= 50/4)
2	9		100	200	
		3			16.67 (= 50/3)
3	12		150	250	
		2			25.00 (= 50/2)
4	14		200	300	
		1			50.00 (= 50/1)
5	15		250	350	

b. The marginal cost, *MC*, of floral arrangements is the change in total cost divided by the change in output. So, to compute *MC*, we first need to compute total cost, *TC = FC + VC*, as shown in the table. *MC* per floral arrangement is also shown in the table. *MC* increases as output increases due again to the principle of diminishing returns.

7. You have the information shown in the accompanying table about a firm's costs. Complete the missing data.

Quantity	TC	MC	ATC	AVC
0	$20			
		$20		
1	?		?	?
		10		
2	?		?	?
		16		
3	?		?	?
		20		
4	?		?	?
		24		
5	?		?	?

7. The accompanying table contains the complete cost data. The total cost of producing one unit of output is the total cost of producing zero units of output plus the marginal cost of increasing output from zero to one, and so forth. The average total cost is just the total cost divided by output. Since the total cost of producing zero output is $20, the variable cost is $TC - \$20$. The average variable cost is then just the variable cost divided by output.

Quantity	TC	MC of unit	ATC of unit	AVC of unit
0	$20.00		—	—
		$20.00		
1	40.00		$40.00	$20.00
		10.00		
2	50.00		25.00	15.00
		16.00		
3	66.00		22.00	15.33
		20.00		
4	86.00		21.50	16.50
		24.00		
5	110.00		22.00	18.00

8. Evaluate each of the following statements: If a statement is true, explain why; if it is false, identify the mistake and try to correct it.

a. A decreasing marginal product tells us that marginal cost must be rising.

b. An increase in fixed cost increases the minimum-cost output.

c. An increase in fixed cost increases marginal cost.

d. When marginal cost is above average total cost, average total cost must be falling.

8. a. True. If each additional unit of the input adds less to output than the previous unit (decreasing marginal product), then in order to produce additional output, the firm needs to use increasingly more of the input; that is, the marginal cost of production increases.

b. True. As the fixed cost rises, the average fixed cost also rises; that is, the spreading effect is now larger. It is the spreading effect that causes average total cost to decline. Since this effect is now larger, it dominates the diminishing returns effect over a greater quantity of outputs; that is, average total cost decreases over a greater quantity of outputs.

c. False. An increase in fixed cost does not change marginal cost. Marginal cost is the additional cost of producing an additional unit of output. Fixed cost does not change as output is increased, and so the additional cost of producing an additional unit of output is independent of the fixed cost.

d. False. When marginal cost is above average total cost, average total cost must be rising. If the additional cost of producing one more unit of output is greater than what it costs to produce each unit of output on average, then producing that one more unit of output must increase the average total cost.

9. Mark and Jeff operate a small company that produces souvenir footballs. Their fixed cost is $2,000 per month. They can hire workers for $1,000 per worker per month. Their monthly production function for footballs is as given in the accompanying table.

Quantity of labor (workers)	Quantity of footballs
0	0
1	300
2	800
3	1,200
4	1,400
5	1,500

a. For each quantity of labor, calculate average variable cost (*AVC*), average fixed cost (*AFC*), average total cost (*ATC*), and marginal cost (*MC*).

b. On one diagram, draw in the *AVC*, *ATC*, and *MC* curves.

c. At what level of output is Mark and Jeff's average total cost minimized?

9. **a.** The *AVC*, *AFC*, *ATC*, *TC*, and *MC* are given in the accompanying table.

Quantity of labor (workers)	Quantity of footballs	AVC of football	AFC of football	ATC of football	TC of football	MC of football
0	0	—	—	—	$2,000.00	
						$3.33
1	300	$3.33	$6.67	$10.00	3,000.00	
						2.00
2	800	2.50	2.50	5.00	4,000.00	
						2.50
3	1,200	2.50	1.67	4.17	5,000.00	
						5.00
4	1,400	2.86	1.43	4.29	6,000.00	
						10.00
5	1,500	3.33	1.33	4.67	7,000.00	

b. See the accompanying diagram.

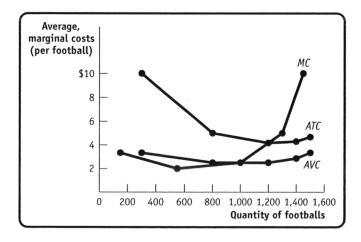

c. According to the table, Mark and Jeff's average total cost is minimized at 1,200 footballs per month, where the *ATC* is $4.17.

10. You produce widgets. Currently you produce 4 widgets at a total cost of $40.

  a. What is your average total cost?

  b. Suppose you could produce one more (the fifth) widget at a marginal cost of $5. If you do produce that fifth widget, what will your average total cost be? Has your average total cost increased or decreased? Why?

  c. Suppose instead that you could produce one more (the fifth) widget at a marginal cost of $20. If you do produce that fifth widget, what will your average total cost be? Has your average total cost increased or decreased? Why?

10. **a.** Your average total cost is $40/4 = $10 per widget.

  b. If you produce one more widget, you are producing five widgets at a total cost of $40 + $5 = $45. Your average total cost is therefore $45/5 = $9. Your average total cost has decreased because the marginal cost of the additional widget is below the average total cost before you produced the additional widget.

  c. If you produce one more widget, you are producing five widgets at a total cost of $40 + $20 = $60. Your average total cost is therefore $60/5 = $12. Your average total cost has increased because the marginal cost of the additional widget is above the average total cost before you produced the additional widget.

11. In your economics class, each homework problem set is graded on the basis of a maximum score of 100. You have completed 9 out of 10 of the problem sets for the term, and your current average grade is 88. What range of grades for your 10th problem set will raise your overall average? What range will lower your overall average? Explain.

11. Any grade for your 10th problem set greater than 88 will raise your overall average; any grade lower than 88 will lower it. This is the same principle at work as that for average total cost and marginal cost. If the marginal cost curve (the 10th grade) is above the average total cost curve (the average over the first 9 grades), then the average total cost is rising (that is, the average over the 10 sets is greater than the average over the 9 sets). And if the marginal cost curve (the 10th grade) is below the average total cost curve (the average over the first 9 grades), then the average total cost is falling (that is, the average over the 10 sets is lower than the average over the 9 sets). To see this arithmetically, note that your current average, 88, is found by

$$\frac{\text{Sum of grades for first 9 sets}}{9} = 88 = \text{Average over first 9 sets}$$

Hence,

$$\text{Sum of grades for first 9 sets} = 88 \times 9 = 792$$

So your overall grade—the grade over all 10 problem sets—is

$$\frac{792}{10} + \frac{\text{Grade for 10th set}}{10} = \text{Overall average}$$

If your 10th grade is 90, then your overall grade is

$$\frac{792}{10} + \frac{90}{10} = 79.2 + 9.0 = 88.2$$

which is greater than 88. And if your 10th grade is 86, then your overall grade is

$$\frac{792}{10} + \frac{86}{10} = 79.2 + 8.6 = 87.8$$

which is less than 88.

12. Don owns a small concrete-mixing company. His fixed cost is the cost of the concrete-batching machinery and his mixer trucks. His variable cost is the cost of the sand, gravel, and other inputs for producing concrete; the gas and maintenance for the machinery and trucks; and his workers. He is trying to decide how many mixer trucks to purchase. He has estimated the costs shown in the accompanying table based on estimates of the number of orders his company will receive per week.

Quantity of trucks	FC	VC 20 orders	VC 40 orders	VC 60 orders
2	$6,000	$2,000	$5,000	$12,000
3	7,000	1,800	3,800	10,800
4	8,000	1,200	3,600	8,400

a. For each level of fixed cost, calculate Don's total cost for producing 20, 40, and 60 orders per week.

b. If Don is producing 20 orders per week, how many trucks should he purchase and what will his average total cost be? Answer the same questions for 40 and 60 orders per week.

12. a. The answers are given in the accompanying table.

Quantity of trucks	TC 20 orders	TC 40 orders	TC 60 orders
2	$8,000	$11,000	$18,000
3	8,800	10,800	17,800
4	9,200	11,600	16,400

b. Don should choose the number of trucks that minimizes average total cost for each level of output. Given this, Don should buy two trucks if he is producing 20 orders per week. His average total cost per order will be $400. He should buy three trucks if he is producing 40 orders per week. His average total cost per order will then be $270. He should buy four trucks if he is producing 60 orders per week. His average total cost per order will then be $273.

13. Consider Don's concrete-mixing business described in Problem 12. Suppose Don purchased 3 trucks, expecting to produce 40 orders per week.

a. Suppose that, in the short run, business declines to 20 orders per week. What is Don's average total cost per order in the short run? What will his average total cost per order in the short run be if his business booms to 60 orders per week?

b. What is Don's long-run average total cost for 20 orders per week? Explain why his short-run average total cost of producing 20 orders per week when the number of trucks is fixed at 3 is greater than his long-run average total cost of producing 20 orders per week.

c. Sketch Don's long-run average total cost curve. Sketch his short-run average total cost curve if he owns 3 trucks.

13. **a.** In the short run, producing 20 orders per week with three trucks, Don's average total cost per order will be ($7,000 + $1,800)/20 = $440. If he instead produces 60 orders per week with three trucks, his average total cost per order will be $297.

b. The long-run average total cost of producing 20 orders per week is $400 because Don would choose the number of trucks (2 trucks) that minimizes the total cost of producing 20 orders. His short-run average total cost is greater than the long-run minimum because, using 3 trucks, the level of the fixed input is greater than he needs to optimally produce 20 orders per week.

c. See the accompanying diagram.

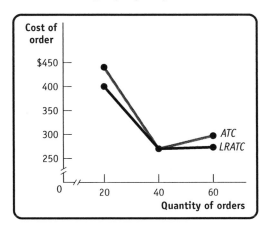

14. True or False? Explain your reasoning.

a. The short-run average total cost can never be less than the long-run average total cost.

b. The short-run average variable cost can never be less than the long-run average total cost.

c. In the long run, choosing a higher level of fixed cost shifts the long-run average total cost curve upward.

14. **a.** True. The long-run average total cost is the average total cost you get by choosing the most favorable level of fixed cost in the long run; that is, it is the lowest average total cost that is possible when you can adjust how much of the fixed input you use. In other words, the long-run average total cost of producing a certain level of output is the lowest average total cost with which that level of output can be produced.

b. False. The long-run average total cost is the lowest average total cost possible. But average variable cost will always be less than average total cost (it is lower than the average total cost by just the amount of the average fixed cost). So short-run average variable cost can be lower than long-run average total cost.

c. False. In the long run, choosing a higher level of fixed cost allows you to move along and to the right on the long-run average total cost curve. In the long run, if you want to produce a larger quantity of output, you would optimally increase the level of fixed cost (this will decrease the average variable cost). You will do this in such a way as to spend the lowest possible average total cost; that is, you will be on the long-run average total cost curve but farther to the right (at a larger quantity of output).

15. Wolfsburg Wagon (WW) is a small automaker. The accompanying table shows WW's long-run average total cost.

Quantity of cars	LRATC of car
1	$30,000
2	20,000
3	15,000
4	12,000
5	12,000
6	12,000
7	14,000
8	18,000

a. For which levels of output does WW experience economies of scale?

b. For which levels of output does WW experience diseconomies of scale?

c. For which levels of output does WW experience constant returns to scale?

15. a. WW's long-run average total cost is decreasing over the range of output between one and four cars. So over that range, WW experiences economies of scale.

b. WW's long-run average total cost is increasing over the range of output between six and eight cars. So over that range, WW experiences diseconomies of scale.

c. WW's long-run average total cost is constant over the range of output between four and six cars. So over that range, WW experiences constant returns to scale.

Perfect Competition and the Supply Curve

1. For each of the following, is the business a price-taking producer? Explain your answers.

   a. A cappuccino café in a university town where there are dozens of very similar cappuccino cafés

   b. The makers of Pepsi-Cola

   c. One of many sellers of zucchini at a local farmers' market

1. a. The cappuccino café is probably a price-taking producer, especially if there are a large number of cafés in town, since each will have a small market share and produces a standardized product.

   b. There is only one manufacturer of Pepsi-Cola, and it works hard to differentiate its product from others in the minds of consumers. It is not a price-taking producer.

   c. Zucchini sellers at the farmers' market are price-taking producers; there are many of them, none of whom can affect the market price for zucchini, and zucchini are a standardized product.

2. For each of the following, is the industry perfectly competitive? Referring to market share, standardization of the product, and/or free entry and exit, explain your answers.

   a. Aspirin

   b. Shania Twain concerts

   c. SUVs

2. a. Yes, aspirin is produced in a perfectly competitive industry. Many manufacturers produce aspirin, the product is standardized, and new manufacturers can easily enter and existing manufacturers can easily exit the industry.

   b. No, Shania Twain concerts are not produced in a perfectly competitive industry. There is not free entry into the industry—there is only one Shania Twain.

   c. No, SUVs are not produced in a perfectly competitive industry. There are only a few manufacturers of SUVs, each holding a large market share and SUVs are not a standardized product in the minds of consumers.

3. Hiro owns and operates a small business that provides economic consulting services. During the year he spends $55,000 on travel to clients and other expenses, and the computer that he owns depreciates by $2,000. If he didn't use the computer, he could sell it and earn yearly interest of $100 on the money created through this sale. Hiro's total revenue for the year is $100,000. Instead of working as a consultant for the year, he could teach economics at a small local college and make a salary of $50,000.

   a. What is Hiro's accounting profit?

   b. What is Hiro's economic profit?

   c. Should Hiro continue working as a consultant, or should he teach economics instead?

3. a. Hiro's accounting profit is:

$100,000 (total revenue)
− $55,000 (travel and other expenses)
− $2,000 (depreciation)

$43,000 (accounting profit)

b. Hiro's economic profit is:

$100,000 (total revenue)
− $55,000 (travel and other expenses)
− $2,000 (depreciation)
− $100 (interest forgone)
− $50,000 (salary as economics professor)

− $7,100 (economic profit)

c. Since Hiro's economic profit is negative, he would be better off if he didn't operate the consulting business and taught economics instead.

4. You own and operate a bike store. Each year, you receive revenue of $200,000 from your bike sales, and it costs you $100,000 to obtain the bikes. In addition, you pay $20,000 for electricity, taxes, and other expenses per year. Instead of running the bike store, you could become an accountant and receive a yearly salary of $40,000. A large clothing retail chain wants to expand and offers to rent the store from you for $50,000 per year. How do you explain to your friends that despite making a profit, it is too costly for you to continue running your store?

4. a. Your yearly accounting profit is:

$200,000 (total revenue)
− $100,000 (cost of bikes)
− $20,000 (electricity, taxes, and other expenses)

$80,000 (accounting profit)

But not renting the store to the retail chain is an opportunity cost, and not being able to make $40,000 as an accountant is also an opportunity cost, so your yearly economic profit is:

$200,000 (total revenue)
− $100,000 (cost of bikes)
− $20,000 (electricity, taxes, and other expenses)
− $40,000 (opportunity cost of your time)
− $50,000 (opportunity cost of not renting the store)

− $10,000 (economic profit)

So although you make an accounting profit each year, you would be better off renting the store to the large chain and becoming an accountant yourself, since your opportunity cost of continuing to run your own store is too high.

5. Kate's Katering provides catered meals, and the catered meals industry is perfectly competitive. Kate's machinery costs $100 per day and is the only fixed input. Her variable cost is comprised of the wages paid to the cooks and the food ingredients. The variable cost associated with each level of output is given in the accompanying table.

Quantity of meals	VC
0	$0
10	200
20	300
30	480
40	700
50	1,000

a. Calculate the total cost, the average variable cost, the average total cost, and the marginal cost for each quantity of output.

b. What is the break-even price? What is the shut-down price?

c. Suppose that the price at which Kate can sell catered meals is $21 per meal. In the short run, will Kate earn a profit? In the short run, should she produce or shut down?

d. Suppose that the price at which Kate can sell catered meals is $17 per meal. In the short run, will Kate earn a profit? In the short run, should she produce or shut down?

e. Suppose that the price at which Kate can sell catered meals is $13 per meal. In the short run, will Kate earn a profit? In the short run, should she produce or shut down?

5. **a.** From Kate's variable cost (VC), the accompanying table calculates Kate's total cost (TC), average variable cost (AVC), average total cost (ATC), and marginal cost (MC).

Quantity of meals	VC	TC	MC of meal	AVC of meal	ATC of meal
0	$0.00	$100.00		—	—
			$20.00		
10	200.00	300.00		$20.00	$30.00
			10.00		
20	300.00	400.00		15.00	20.00
			18.00		
30	480.00	580.00		16.00	19.33
			22.00		
40	700.00	800.00		17.50	20.00
			30.00		
50	1,000.00	1,100.00		20.00	22.00

b. Kate's break-even price, the minimum average total cost, is $19.33, at an output quantity of 30 meals. Kate's shut-down price, the minimum average variable cost, is $15.

c. When the price is $21, Kate will make a profit: the price is above her break-even price. And since the price is above her shut-down price, Kate should produce in the short run, not shut down.

d. When the price is $17, Kate will incur a loss: the price is below her break-even price. But since the price is above her shut-down price, Kate should produce in the short run, not shut down.

e. When the price is $13, Kate will incur a loss: the price is below her break-even price. And since the price is also below her shut-down price, Kate should shut down in the short run.

6. You are the manager of a gym, and you have to decide how many customers to admit each hour. Assume that each customer stays exactly one hour. Customers are costly to admit because they inflict wear and tear on the exercise equipment. Moreover, each additional customer generates more wear and tear than the customer before. As a result, the gym faces increasing marginal cost. The accompanying table shows the marginal costs associated with each number of customers per hour.

Quantity of customers per hour	Marginal cost of customer
0	$14.00
1	14.50
2	15.00
3	15.50
4	16.00
5	16.50
6	17.00
7	

a. Suppose that each customer pays $15.25 for a one-hour workout. Use the principle of marginal analysis to find the optimal number of customers that you should admit per hour.

b. You increase the price of a one-hour workout to $16.25. What is the optimal number of customers per hour that you should admit now?

6. a. The marginal benefit of each customer is $15.25: each additional customer you admit increases the total benefit to the gym by $15.25. You should therefore admit three customers per hour. Here is how you could think about that decision. Suppose currently you admit no customers. Admitting the first customer gives the gym a marginal benefit of $15.25 and a marginal cost of $14.00. Since the marginal benefit of that first customer exceeds the marginal cost, you want to admit the first customer. For the second customer, the marginal benefit ($15.25) also exceeds the marginal cost ($14.50), so you do want to admit the second customer, too. The same is true for the third customer: the marginal benefit ($15.25) exceeds the marginal cost ($15.00), so you also want to admit the third customer. For the fourth customer, however, the marginal cost ($15.50) exceeds the marginal benefit ($15.25), so you do not want to admit a fourth customer.

b. By reasoning similar to that in part a, you now want to admit five customers: for the fifth customer, the marginal benefit ($16.25) exceeds the marginal cost ($16.00). For the sixth customer, however, the marginal cost ($16.50) exceeds the marginal benefit, so you do not want to admit a sixth customer.

7. Bob produces DVD movies for sale, which requires only a building and a machine that copies the original movie onto a DVD. Bob rents a building for $30,000 per month and rents a machine for $20,000 a month. Those are his fixed costs. His variable cost is given in the accompanying table.

Quantity of DVDs	VC
0	$0
1,000	5,000
2,000	8,000
3,000	9,000
4,000	14,000
5,000	20,000
6,000	33,000
7,000	49,000
8,000	72,000
9,000	99,000
10,000	150,000

a. Calculate Bob's average variable cost, average total cost, and marginal cost for each quantity of output.

b. There is free entry into the industry: anyone who enters will face the same costs as Bob. Suppose that currently the price of a DVD is $23. What will Bob's profit be? Is this a long-run equilibrium? If not, what will the price of DVD movies be in the long run?

Solution

7. a. See the accompanying table.

Quantity of DVDs	VC	MC of DVD	AVC of DVD	ATC of DVD
0	$0.00		—	—
		$5.00		
1,000	5,000.00		$5.00	$55.00
		3.00		
2,000	8,000.00		4.00	29.00
		1.00		
3,000	9,000.00		3.00	19.67
		5.00		
4,000	14,000.00		3.50	16.00
		6.00		
5,000	20,000.00		4.00	14.00
		13.00		
6,000	33,000.00		5.50	13.83
		16.00		
7,000	49,000.00		7.00	14.14
		23.00		
8,000	72,000.00		9.00	15.25
		27.00		
9,000	99,000.00		11.00	16.56
		51.00		
10,000	150,000.00		15.00	20.00

b. When the price is $23, Bob will sell 8,000 DVDs per month and make a profit of $62,000. If there is free entry into the industry, this profit will attract new firms. As firms enter, the price of DVDs will eventually fall until it is equal to the minimum average total cost. Here, the average total cost reaches its minimum of $13.83 at 6,000 DVDs per month. So the long-run price of DVDs will be $13.83.

8. Consider Bob's DVD company described in Problem 7. Assume that DVD production is a perfectly competitive industry. In each case, explain your answers.

a. What is Bob's break-even price? What is his shut-down price?

b. Suppose the price of a DVD is $2. What should Bob do in the short run?

c. Suppose the price of a DVD is $7. What is the profit-maximizing quantity of DVDs that Bob should produce? What will his total profit be? Will he produce or shut down in the short run? Will he stay in the industry or exit in the long run?

d. Suppose instead that the price of DVDs is $20. Now what is the profit-maximizing quantity of DVDs that Bob should produce? What will his total profit be now? Will he produce or shut down in the short run? Will he stay in the industry or exit in the long run?

8. a. Bob's break-even price is $13.83 because this is the minimum average total cost. His shut-down price is $3, the minimum average variable cost, because below that price his revenue does not even cover his variable costs.

b. If the price of DVDs is $2, the price is below Bob's shut-down price of $3. So Bob should shut down in the short run.

c. If DVDs sell for $7, Bob should produce 5,000 DVDs because for any greater quantity his marginal cost exceeds his marginal revenue (the market price). His total profit will be $−35,000, a loss of $35,000. In the short run, he will produce because his short-run loss if he were to shut down would be greater; it would equal his fixed costs of $50,000. In the long run, he will exit the industry because his profit is negative.

d. If DVDs sell instead for $20, Bob should produce 7,000 DVDs because at this quantity his marginal cost equals his marginal revenue (the market price). His total profit will be $41,000. In the short run, he will produce because he is covering his variable cost. In the long run, he will stay in the industry because his profit is not negative.

9. Consider again Bob's DVD company described in Problem 7.

a. Draw Bob's marginal cost curve.

b. Over what range of prices will Bob produce no DVDs in the short run?

c. Draw Bob's individual supply curve.

9. a. Bob's marginal cost curve is shown in the accompanying diagram.

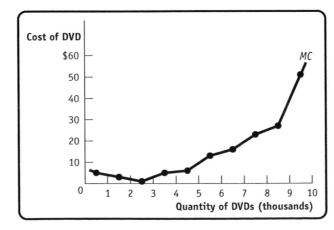

b. Bob will produce no DVDs if the price falls below $3 because $3 is the lowest point on the average variable cost curve—his shut-down price.

c. The individual supply curve is shown in the accompanying diagram. It is his *MC* curve above the minimum average variable cost.

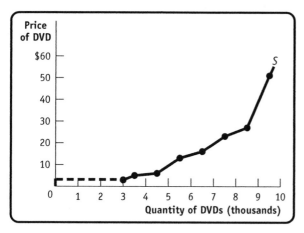

10. a. A profit-maximizing business incurs an economic loss of $10,000 per year. Its fixed cost is $15,000 per year. Should it produce or shut down in the short run? Should it stay in the industry or exit in the long run?

b. Suppose instead this business has a fixed cost of $6,000 per year. Should it produce or shut down in the short run? Should it stay in the industry or exit in the long run?

Solution

10. a. In the short run, the business should produce. If it shuts down, the short-run annual loss will be $15,000, its fixed cost; but if it produces, the loss will be only $10,000. In the long run, the business should exit the industry because it is incurring a loss.

b. In the short run, the business should shut down. If it shuts down, the short-run loss will be $6,000, its fixed cost; if it continues to produce, the loss will be $10,000. In the long run, the firm should exit the industry because it is incurring a loss.

11. Four students have each started companies selling late-night snack deliveries to dorms and student apartment complexes. Each student has estimated her or his individual supply schedule as given in the accompanying table.

Delivery charge	Quantity supplied by:			
	Aleesha	Brent	Christine	Dominic
$1	1	5	3	7
2	3	8	6	12
3	5	11	9	17
4	7	15	12	21
5	9	21	15	23

a. Draw the four individual supply curves.

b. Determine the short-run industry supply schedule. Draw the short-run industry supply curve.

11. a. The four individual supply curves are shown in the accompanying diagram. Aleesha's supply curve is labeled S_A, Brent's is labeled S_B, Christine's is labeled S_C, and Dominic's is labeled S_D.

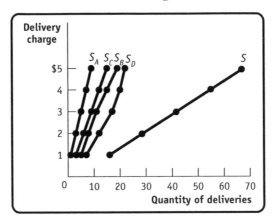

b. The short-run industry supply schedule is shown in the accompanying table, and the short-run industry supply curve is labeled S in the diagram above.

Delivery charge	Quantity supplied by industry
$1	16
2	29
3	42
4	55
5	68

12. The first sushi restaurant opens in town. Initially people are very cautious about eating tiny portions of raw fish, as this is a town where large portions of grilled meat have always been popular. Soon, however, an influential health report warns consumers against grilled meat and suggests that they increase their consumption of fish, especially raw fish. The sushi restaurant becomes very popular and its profit increases.

a. What will happen to the short-run profit of the sushi restaurant? What will happen to the number of sushi restaurants in town in the long run? Will the first sushi restaurant be able to sustain its short-run profit over the long run? Explain your answers.

b. Local steakhouses suffer from the popularity of sushi and start incurring losses. What will happen to the number of steakhouses in town in the long run? Explain your answer.

12. a. The short-run profit of the sushi restaurant will rise, enticing others to open sushi restaurants. The number of sushi restaurants in town will increase. Over time, as the supply of sushi restaurants increases, the equilibrium price of sushi will decrease, lowering the short-run profit of the original sushi restaurant.

b. The number of steakhouses in town will decrease in the long run, as owners incur losses and exit from the industry.

13. A perfectly competitive firm has the following short-run total cost:

Quantity	TC
0	$5
1	10
2	13
3	18
4	25
5	34
6	45

Market demand for the firm's product is given by the following market demand schedule:

Price	Quantity demanded
$12	300
10	500
8	800
6	1,200
4	1,800

a. Calculate this firm's marginal cost and, for all output levels except zero, the firm's average variable cost and average total cost.

b. There are 100 firms in this industry that all have identical costs to those of this firm. Draw the short-run industry supply curve. In the same diagram, draw the market demand curve.

c. What is the market price, and how much profit will each firm make?

13. a. This firm's fixed cost is $5, since even when the firm produces no output, it incurs a total cost of $5. The marginal cost ($MC$), average variable cost (AVC), and average total cost (ATC) are given in the accompanying table.

Quantity	TC	MC	AVC	ATC
0	$5.00		—	—
		$5.00		
1	10.00		$5.00	$10.00
		3.00		
2	13.00		4.00	6.50
		5.00		
3	18.00		4.33	6.00
		7.00		
4	25.00		5.00	6.25
		9.00		
5	34.00		5.80	6.80
		11.00		
6	45.00		6.67	7.50

b. This firm's minimum average variable cost is $4, at 2 units of output. So the firm will produce only if the price is greater than $4, making its individual supply curve the same as its marginal cost curve above the shut-down price of $4. The same is true for all other firms in the industry. That is, if the price is $4, the quantity supplied by all 100 firms is 200. The quantity supplied by all 100 firms at a price of $6 is 300, and so on. The accompanying diagram illustrates this principle.

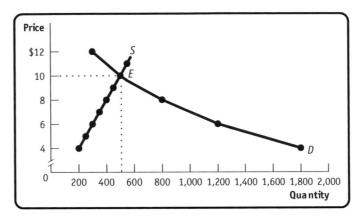

c. The quantity supplied equals the quantity demanded at a price of $10—the (short-run) market price. So the quantity bought and sold in this market is therefore 500 units. Each firm will therefore maximize profit by producing 5 units of output—the greatest quantity at which price equals or exceeds marginal cost. At 5 units of output, each firm's revenue is $10 × 5 = $50. Its total cost is $34. It therefore makes a profit of $16.

14. A new vaccine against a deadly disease has just been discovered. Presently, 55 people die from the disease each year. The new vaccine will save lives, but it is not completely safe. Some recipients of the shots will die from adverse reactions. The projected effects of the inoculation are given in the accompanying table:

Percent of population inoculated	Total deaths due to disease	Total deaths due to inoculation	Marginal benefit of inoculation	Marginal cost of inoculation	"Profit" of inoculation
0	55	0	—	—	—
10	45	0	—	—	—
20	36	1	—	—	—
30	28	3	—	—	—
40	21	6	—	—	—
50	15	10	—	—	—
60	10	15	—	—	—
70	6	20	—	—	—
80	3	25	—	—	—
90	1	30	—	—	—
100	0	35	—	—	—

a. What are the interpretations of "marginal benefit" and "marginal cost" here? Calculate marginal benefit and marginal cost per each 10 percent increase in the rate of inoculation. Write your answers in the table.

b. What proportion of the population should optimally be inoculated?

c. What is the interpretation of "profit" here? Calculate the profit for all levels of inoculation.

14. a. The "marginal benefit" is the additional lives saved due to inoculation. The "marginal cost" is the additional deaths due to inoculation. The values are given in the accompanying table.

Percent of population inoculated	Total deaths due to disease	Total deaths due to inoculation	Marginal benefit of inoculation	Marginal cost of inoculation	"Profit" of inoculation
0	55	0			0
			10	0	
10	45	0			10 − 0 = 10
			9	1	
20	36	1			19 − 1 = 18
			8	2	
30	28	3			27 − 3 = 24
			7	3	
40	21	6			34 − 6 = 28
			6	4	
50	15	10			40 − 10 = 30
			5	5	
60	10	15			45 − 15 = 30
			4	5	
70	6	20			49 − 20 = 29
			3	5	
80	3	25			52 − 25 = 27
			2	5	
90	1	30			54 − 30 = 24
			1	5	
100	0	35			55 − 35 = 20

b. People should be inoculated until the marginal cost equals the marginal benefit from the inoculations. This occurs when $MB = MC = 5$, at which point 50 or 60% of the population should be inoculated (both result in the greatest number of lives saved).

c. "Profit" is the total lives saved minus the total lives lost. The profit at each level of inoculation in the population is shown in the table. The maximum number of lives saved is 30, which occurs at inoculation levels of both 50 and 60%.

15. Evaluate each of the following statements. If a statement is true, explain why; if it is false, identify the mistake and try to correct it.

a. A profit-maximizing firm should select the output level at which the difference between the market price and marginal cost is greatest.

b. An increase in fixed cost lowers the profit-maximizing quantity of output produced in the short run.

15. a. False. Profit is maximized by producing a quantity at which marginal cost is equal to the market price.

b. False. Changes in fixed cost do not affect marginal cost and so do not change the profit-maximizing quantity of output produced. Changes in fixed cost do, however, change the amount of profit earned and the firm's break-even price: the higher the fixed cost, the higher the firm's break-even price and the lower its profit.

Factor Markets and the Distribution of Income

1. In 2001, national income in the United States was $8,122.0 billion. In the same year, 135 million workers were employed, at an average wage of $43,518 per worker per year.

   a. How much compensation of employees was paid in the United States in 2001?

   b. Analyze the factor distribution of income. What percentage of national income was received in terms of compensation of employees in 2001?

   c. Suppose that a huge wave of corporate downsizing leads many terminated employees to open their own businesses. What is the effect on the factor distribution of income?

   d. Suppose the supply of labor rises due to an increase in the retirement age. What happens to the percentage of national income received in terms of compensation of employees?

1. a. Since 135 million workers were employed at an average yearly wage of $43,518, the total amount of compensation of employees was 135 million × $43,518 = $5,874.9 billion.

   b. Of a total of $8,122.0 billion, the amount received by workers was $5,874.9 billion. In percentage terms, this is ($5,874.9 billion/$8,122.0 billion) × 100% = 72%.

   c. The effect of this change is to diminish the share of income going to compensate employees and increase the share going to proprietors' income.

   d. As the supply of labor increases, the equilibrium wage rate falls, but the equilibrium number of workers employed rises. So it is not clear whether more or less of national income is paid to workers in terms of compensation.

2. Marty's Frozen Yogurt has the production function per day shown in the accompanying table. The equilibrium wage rate for a worker is $80 per day. Each cup of frozen yogurt sells for $2.

Quantity of labor (workers)	Quantity of frozen yogurt (cups)
0	0
1	110
2	200
3	270
4	300
5	320
6	330

   a. Calculate the marginal product of labor for each worker and the value of the marginal product per worker.

   b. How many workers should Marty employ?

2. **a.** The accompanying table shows the marginal product of labor (*MPL*) and the value of the marginal product (*VMPL*) of each worker. Remember that $VMPL = P \times MPL$. Here that means that $VMPL = \$2 \times MPL$.

Quantity of labor (workers)	Quantity of frozen yogurt (cups)	MPL (cups per worker)	VMPL (per worker)
0	0		
		110	$220
1	110		
		90	180
2	200		
		70	140
3	270		
		30	60
4	300		
		20	40
5	320		
		10	20
6	330		

b. Marty should employ 3 workers. The value of the marginal product of the third worker ($140) is above the wage rate of $80: Marty should hire the third worker. But the fourth worker's value of the marginal product is only $60. This is less than Marty would have to pay this worker, so Marty should not hire a fourth worker.

3. Patty's Pizza Parlor has the production function per hour shown in the accompanying table. The hourly wage rate for each worker is $10. Each pizza sells for $2.

Quantity of labor (workers)	Quantity of pizza
0	0
1	9
2	15
3	19
4	22
5	24

a. Calculate the marginal product of labor for each worker and the value of the marginal product per worker.

b. Draw the value of the marginal product curve. Use your diagram to determine how many workers Patty should employ.

c. Now the price of pizza increases to $4. Calculate the value of the marginal product per worker, and draw the new value of the marginal product curve into your diagram. Use your diagram to determine how many workers Patty should employ now.

3. **a.** The accompanying table shows the marginal product of labor (*MPL*) and the value of the marginal product of labor (*VMPL$_1$*).

Number of workers	Quantity of pizza	MPL (pizzas per worker)	VMPL$_1$ (per worker) (price of pizza = $2)	VMPL$_2$ (per worker) (price of pizza = $4)
0	0			
		9	$18	$36
1	9			
		6	12	24
2	15			
		4	8	16
3	19			
		3	6	12
4	22			
		2	4	8
5	24			

b. The accompanying diagram shows the value of the marginal product curve (*VMPL$_1$*). The value of the marginal product of labor equals the wage rate at 2 workers. So Patty should employ 2 workers.

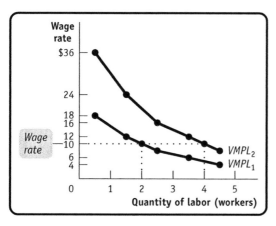

c. The table shows the new value of the marginal product (*VMPL$_2$*). The value of the marginal product curve is labeled *VMPL$_2$* in the diagram. The new value of the marginal product of labor equals the wage rate at 4 workers. So Patty should employ 4 workers.

4. The production function for Patty's Pizza Parlor is given in the table in Problem 3. The price of pizza is $2, but the hourly wage rate rises from $10 to $15. Use a diagram to determine how Patty's demand for workers responds as a result of this wage rate increase.

4. The accompanying diagram shows the value of the marginal product curve and the wage rates of $10 and $15. As the wage rate increases from $10 to $15, Patty's demand for workers decreases from 2 workers to 1 worker. So, as the wage rate increases, Patty should hire fewer workers.

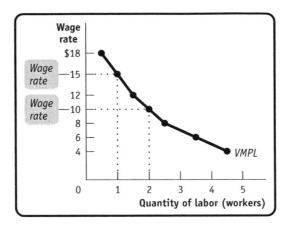

5. Patty's Pizza Parlor initially had the production function given in the table in Problem 3. A worker's hourly wage rate was $10, and pizza sold for $2. Now Patty buys a new high-tech pizza oven that allows her workers to become twice as productive as before. That is, the first worker now produces 18 pizzas per hour instead of 9, and so on.

  a. Calculate the new marginal product of labor and the new value of the marginal product of labor.

  b. Use a diagram to determine how Patty's hiring decision responds to this increase in the productivity of her workforce.

5. a. The accompanying table shows the new production function for Patty's Pizza Parlor, the new marginal product of labor (MPL_3), and the new value of the marginal product of labor ($VMPL_3$).

Quantity of labor (workers)	Quantity of pizza	MPL_3 (pizzas per worker)	$VMPL_3$ (per worker)
0	0		
		18	$36
1	18		
		12	24
2	30		
		8	16
3	38		
		6	12
4	44		
		4	8
5	48		

  b. The accompanying diagram shows the original value of the marginal product curve from Problem 3 ($VMPL_1$) and the new value of the marginal product curve ($VMPL_3$). The value of the marginal product of labor now equals the wage rate at 4 workers. So Patty should employ 4 workers. As the value of the marginal product of labor increases—in this case as a result of a technological innovation (the new pizza oven)—Patty should hire more workers.

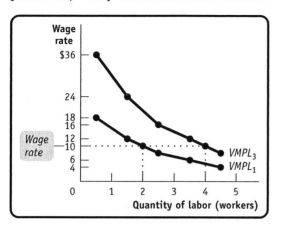

6. Jameel runs a driver education school. The more driving instructors he hires, the more driving lessons he can sell. But because he owns a limited number of training automobiles, each additional driving instructor adds less to Jameel's output of driving lessons. The accompanying table shows Jameel's production function per day. Each driving lesson can be sold at $35 per hour.

Quantity of labor (driving instructors)	Quantity of driving lessons (hours)
0	0
1	8
2	15
3	21
4	26
5	30
6	33

Determine Jameel's labor demand schedule (his demand schedule for driving instructors) for each of the following daily wage rates for driving instructors: $160, $180, $200, $220, $240, and $260.

6. The accompanying table calculates the marginal product of labor (*MPL*) and the value of the marginal product of labor (*VMPL*).

Quantity of labor (driving instructors)	Quantity of driving lessons (hours)	MPL (hours per driving instructor)	VMPL (per driving instructor)
0	0		
		8	$280
1	8		
		7	245
2	15		
		6	210
3	21		
		5	175
4	26		
		4	140
5	30		
		3	105
6	33		

If the daily wage rate of driving instructors is $160, Jameel should hire 4 instructors: the fourth instructor has a value of the marginal product of $175, which is greater than the wage rate; but the fifth instructor would have a value of the marginal product of only $140, which is less than the wage rate. By similar reasoning for the other wage rates, Jameel's demand schedule for labor is as shown in the accompanying table.

Daily wage rate	Quantity of labor demanded (driving instructors)
$160	4
180	3
200	3
220	2
240	2
260	1

7. Dale and Dana work at a self-service gas station and convenience store. Dale opens up everyday and Dana arrives later to help stock the store. They are both paid the current market wage of $9.50 per hour. But Dale feels he should be paid much more because the revenue generated from the gas pumps he turns on every morning is much higher than the revenue generated by the items that Dana stocks. Assess this argument.

7. Dale's argument is incorrect because the owner of the business will hire workers until the hourly value of the marginal product of the last person hired equals $9.50. This implies that all other workers hired will have an hourly value of the marginal product higher than $9.50 but will be paid a wage of $9.50. Or to put it a slightly different way, any worker who opens the station, regardless of whether it is Dale or Dana, will have a higher value of the marginal product than the second person to report for work.

8. In the Shire, farmers can rent land for $100 per acre per year. All the acres are identical. Merry Brandybuck rents 30 acres on which he grows carrots. Pippin Took rents 20 acres on which he grows corn. They sell their produce in a perfectly competitive market. Merry boasts that his value of the marginal product of land is twice as large as Pippin's. Pippin replies that, if this is true and if Merry wants to maximize his profit, Merry is renting too much land. Is Pippin right? Explain your answer.

8. Without more information, we can't determine if Pippin is wrong or right. As you know, a profit-maximizing farmer should use the quantity of land at which the value of the marginal product of land equals the rental rate of land. The law of diminishing returns implies that the value of the marginal product of land declines as a farmer uses more land. So if Merry's value of the marginal product of land is greater than the rental rate of land, he should use *more* land, not less, and Pippin is wrong. If, however, Merry's value of the marginal product of land is less than the rental rate of land, then he should use less land and Pippin is right. (In fact, in that case, Pippin's value of the marginal product of land is certainly also less than the rental rate of land—remember Pippin's value of the marginal product is half that of Merry's—so Pippin is doing even worse than Merry, and Pippin should also use less land.)

9. For each of the following situations in which similar workers are paid different wages, give the most likely explanation for these wage differences.

   a. Test pilots for new jet aircraft earn higher wages than airline pilots.

   b. College graduates usually have higher earnings in their first year on the job than workers without college degrees have in their first year on the job.

   c. Full professors command higher salaries than assistant professors for teaching the same class.

   d. Unionized workers are generally better paid than non-unionized workers.

9. **a.** This is most likely because being a test pilot for a new aircraft design is more dangerous than flying a commercial airliner. So the most likely explanation is that of compensating differentials.

   b. This is probably due to differences in human capital. More education gives a worker greater amounts of human capital. So more education usually translates into greater earnings.

   c. This is also probably due to differences in human capital. Because full professors have been teaching longer than assistant professors, their greater on-the-job experience has given them greater human capital. And greater human capital translates into higher salaries.

   d. Unions exercise considerable bargaining power in negotiating wages for their members. This results in higher wages and therefore wage differences that are not explained by marginal productivity theory.

10. Research consistently finds that despite nondiscrimination policies, African-American workers on average receive lower wages than white workers do. What are the possible reasons for this? Are these reasons consistent with marginal productivity theory?

10. One possible reason is that this is the result of discrimination in the workplace. And, as you know, discrimination is not consistent with marginal productivity theory. But another possible reason for this income disparity is that it may be a result of *past* discrimination, which is consistent with marginal productivity theory. In the past, because of overt discrimination, the educational opportunities for African-American children were severely limited. These children are today's workers, and if their educational attainment is lower, they embody less human capital and are therefore paid a lower wage. So the current income disparity may imply past discrimination but is consistent with marginal productivity theory. But even if this is true, keep in mind that marginal productivity theory does not give *moral* justification to the current distribution of income.

11. Greta is an enthusiastic amateur gardener and spends a lot of her free time working in her yard. She also has a demanding and well-paid job as a freelance advertising consultant. The advertising business is going through a difficult time and the hourly consulting fee Greta can charge falls. Greta decides to spend more time gardening and less time consulting. Explain her decision in terms of income and substitution effects.

11. As Greta's hourly consulting fee falls, the opportunity cost of leisure—time spent working in her yard—also falls. So the substitution effect will push Greta toward spending more time gardening and less time consulting. However, the income effect of a fall in the consulting fee makes Greta poorer and—since leisure is a normal good—less inclined to consume leisure. That is, the income effect will push Greta toward working more. If, overall, Greta decides to work less, the substitution effect must have dominated the income effect.

12. Wendy works at a fast-food restaurant. When her wage rate was $5 per hour, she worked 30 hours per week. When her wage rate rose to $6 per hour, she decided to work 40 hours. But when her wage rate rose further to $7, she decided to work only 35 hours.

　a. Draw Wendy's individual labor supply curve.

　b. Is Wendy's behavior irrational, or can you find a rational explanation? Explain your answer.

12. a. Wendy's individual labor supply curve has the "backward-bending" shape shown in the accompanying diagram.

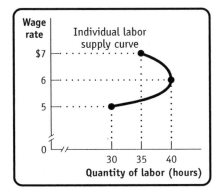

　b. Wendy's behavior has a perfectly rational explanation. As the wage rate increases, the opportunity cost of leisure increases. So the substitution effect says to consume less leisure and work more. At the same time, an increase in the wage rate makes Wendy richer in a real sense. And since leisure is a normal good, the income effect says to consume more leisure and work less. Income and substitution effects work in opposite directions. As Wendy's wage rate rises from $5 to $6, the substitution effect dominates the income effect. As her wage rate rises further to $7, the income effect dominates the substitution effect.

13. You are the governor's economic policy adviser. The governor wants to put in place policies that encourage employed people to work more hours at their jobs and that encourage unemployed people to find and take jobs. Assess each of the following policies in terms of reaching that goal. Explain your reasoning in terms of income and substitution effects, and indicate when the impact of the policy may be ambiguous.

　a. The state income tax rate is lowered, which has the effect of increasing workers' after-tax wage rate.

　b. The state income tax rate is increased, which has the effect of decreasing workers' after-tax wage rate.

　c. The state property tax rate is increased, which reduces workers' after-tax income.

13. **a.** The effect of this policy on the incentive to work is ambiguous. A lower income tax rate has the effect of raising workers' wages in a real sense. The substitution effect will induce people to work more, but the income effect will induce them to work less. So this is an effective policy only if the substitution effect is stronger than the income effect.

b. The effect of this policy on incentive to work is also ambiguous. A higher income tax rate has the effect of reducing workers' wages in a real sense. The substitution effect will induce people to work less, but the income effect will induce them to work more. So this is an effective policy only if the income effect is stronger than the substitution effect.

c. This policy will unambiguously encourage people to work more. The increase in the property tax rate makes people feel poorer, and as a result, they will consume less of all normal goods. Since leisure is a normal good, people will consume less leisure and work more. This policy influences how much labor is supplied only through the income effect. There is no substitution effect on the quantity of labor supplied in this case since the opportunity cost of leisure has not changed.

Efficiency, Inefficiency, and Equity

1. Lakshmi and Sam have a cake that they want to divide in an efficient way, and the cake is the only good in their little economy. Both Lakshmi and Sam like cake and would always prefer to have more of it. Using the standard of efficiency in consumption, determine whether the following ways of dividing the cake are efficient.

   a. Lakshmi and Sam each get half of the cake.

   b. Lakshmi and Sam each get one-third of the cake and one-third is thrown away.

   c. Lakshmi gets the whole cake and Sam gets nothing.

1. a. If Lakshmi has half a cake and Sam has half a cake, giving any more cake to Sam would mean taking it away from Lakshmi. That is, the only way of making Sam better off is to make Lakshmi worse off. Similarly, taking some away from Sam and giving it to Lakshmi would miake Lakshmi better off but Sam worse off. So there is no way of making one consumer better off without making the other worse off. The allocation is efficient.

   b. The allocation is not efficient. If Lakshmi has one-third of the cake and Sam has one-third, and one-third is thrown away, there is a way of making at least one person better off without making anyone else worse off: instead of throwing cake away, we could give it to Lakshmi. That would make her better off without making Sam worse off. Since cake is the only good, any division of the cake is efficient, as long as nothing is thrown away.

   c. If Lakshmi has the whole cake, the only way to make Sam better off is to give him some cake and take some away from Lakshmi. But that makes Lakshmi worse off, so there is no way of making one consumer better off without making the other worse off. The allocation is efficient (if not necessarily equitable).

2. In the town of Rockport, only two goods are produced: left shoes and right shoes. And this economy produces on the production possibility frontier. That is, there is no way of producing more left shoes without producing fewer right shoes, and vice versa. What else would you need to know, if anything, to determine whether the economy of Rockport as a whole is efficient? That is, does it satisfy efficiency in production, efficiency in consumption, and efficiency in output levels? Explain your answer.

2. We know that the economy of Rockport is efficient in production: there is no way of reallocating factors to produce more of one good without producing less of the other. But the efficiency of an economy as a whole requires not only efficiency in production but also efficiency in consumption and efficiency in output levels. And we do not know whether the economy of Rockport is also efficient in consumption and in output levels. For instance, although left and right shoes are produced efficiently, there might not be efficiency in consumption: some consumers might get only left shoes and others only right shoes. And there might not be efficiency in output levels: the economy might be producing 100 left shoes and 20 right shoes, even though it would certainly be more efficient to produce equal numbers of left and right shoes.

3. The economy of Dunk, IN, produces only two goods, bagels and doughnuts, using labor as the only factor of production. There are 8 workers in Dunk and all are paid the same wage. The accompanying table shows the amount of output that can be produced with a certain number of workers.

Quantity of labor in doughnut production (workers)	Quantity of doughnuts	Quantity of labor in bagel production (workers)	Quantity of bagels
0	0	0	0
1	34	1	50
2	40	2	86
3	46	3	92
4	49	4	98
5	52	5	104
6	53	6	106

a. Suppose that the price of a doughnut is $0.50 and the price of a bagel is also $0.50. There are 2 workers producing doughnuts and 3 workers producing bagels. The other 3 workers are unemployed. Given what you know about the relationship between the value of the marginal products and efficiency, determine whether this economy is efficient in the production of doughnuts versus the production of bagels—that is, is the economy efficient in output levels? Also determine whether the economy is efficient in production—that is, is it producing on the production possibility frontier?

b. Suppose that the price of doughnuts is $0.20, and the price of bagels is $0.10. There are 4 workers producing doughnuts and 4 workers producing bagels, and nobody is unemployed. Is this economy efficient in production? Is it efficient in output levels?

c. Initially, the price of doughnuts is $0.20, the price of bagels is $0.10, and there are 4 workers producing doughnuts and 4 workers producing bagels, just as in part b. Now consumers' tastes change: due to health concerns, consumers are now willing to pay $0.75 per bagel but only $0.10 per doughnut. These new prices act as signals of consumers' preferences. In response to this change, will the allocation of workers to bagel or doughnut production change?

3. a. Since the wage rate is the same in both industries, efficiency in output levels implies that the value of the marginal product of labor has to be equal across all goods. That is, the value of the marginal product of labor in doughnuts ($VMPL_D$) has to be equal to the value of the marginal product of labor in bagels ($VMPL_B$). Since currently 2 workers produce doughnuts, the marginal product of labor in doughnuts (MPL_D) is 6. And with 3 workers producing bagels, the marginal product of labor in bagels (MPL_B) is 6. So with 2 workers producing doughnuts, the $VMPL_D = \$0.50 \times 6 = \$3.00$. And with 3 workers producing bagels, $VMPL_B = \$0.50 \times 6 = \$3.00$. That is, the value of the marginal product of labor is equal across all goods. So the economy is efficient in output levels. But the economy is not efficient in production: there are 3 workers who are not producing. By having these workers also produce (either bagels or doughnuts), the economy could produce more of one good without producing less of the other good.

b. The economy is efficient in production: if 1 worker were reallocated from producing bagels to producing doughnuts, the economy would produce more doughnuts but also fewer bagels, and vice versa. That is, there is no way to produce more of one good without producing less of another good. And the economy is also efficient in output levels. Since currently 4 workers are employed producing doughnuts, the MPL_D is 3. And the MPL_B is 6. Therefore, $VMPL_D = \$0.20 \times 3 = \$0.60$. And $VMPL_B = \$0.10 \times 6 = \$0.60$. That is, the value of the marginal product of labor is equal across all goods.

c. Consumers' willingness to pay for bagels has risen, and their willingness to pay for doughnuts has fallen. If the 4 workers remained in doughnut production, $VMPL_D$ would now be $\$0.10 \times 3 = \$0.30$. And if 4 workers remained in bagel production, $VMPL_B$ would now be $\$0.75 \times 6 = \$4.50$. Since $VMPL_B > VMPL_D$, firms would reallocate workers away from doughnut production and toward bagel production.

4. Land in the Shire can be used for growing carrots or potatoes, and the only variable input into production is labor (land is fixed). All workers are paid the same wage. There are two farmers: Sam grows carrots, and the marginal product of labor on his farm is 30 pounds of carrots per month. Merry grows potatoes, and the marginal product of labor on his farm is 44 pounds of potatoes per month. Each experiences diminishing returns to labor. The price of carrots is $3 per pound, and the price of potatoes is $2 per pound.

   a. Calculate the value of the marginal product of labor in carrots and in potatoes to assess whether the economy of the Shire is efficient in output levels. Is the economy in general equilibrium?

   b. Do the prices of carrots and potatoes signal that farmers should produce more or less of their crops? In which direction will employment levels adjust in response to the market prices for the two crops? Describe how the economy reaches general equilibrium.

4. **a.** This economy is not in general equilibrium. In an economy in general equilibrium, the value of the marginal product of labor would have to be the same across all goods. The value of the marginal product of labor in carrots ($VMPL_C$) is $\$3 \times 30 = \$90$. The value of the marginal product of labor in potatoes ($VMPL_P$) is $\$2 \times 44 = \$88$. Since they are not the same, the economy is not efficient in output levels and so cannot be in general equilibrium.

   b. Since Sam's $VMPL_C$ is higher than Merry's $VMPL_P$, Sam will want to employ more workers and will therefore produce more carrots, and Merry will employ fewer workers and will therefore produce fewer potatoes. So since more workers are employed in carrot production, the marginal product of labor in carrots falls. As a result, $VMPL_C$ falls. As fewer workers are employed in potato production, the marginal product of labor in potatoes rises. As a result, $VMPL_P$ rises. This process continues until the value of the marginal product of labor is the same in potatoes and in carrots. At that point, the economy is in general equilibrium and so will also be efficient in output levels.

5. The economy of Leisureville, CO, produces only two goods: skis and bikes. Labor is the only variable input into production, there are diminishing returns to labor, and all workers are paid the same wage. All markets are competitive, and initially the economy is in general equilibrium. Now, due to a change in tastes, consumers' preferences change away from skis and toward bikes.

   a. What will happen to consumers' willingness to pay for bikes and for skis? What will therefore happen to the market prices for bikes and skis?

b. As the prices adjust, what will happen to the value of the marginal product of labor in bikes and in skis? What will happen to bike producers' and ski producers' willingness to pay for workers?

c. As adjustments are made in employment, what happens to the output of bikes and of skis? How does the marginal product of labor in bikes and in skis respond? What therefore happens to the value of the marginal product of labor in bikes and in skis?

d. At what point does this process stop?

Solution

5. a. As consumers' preferences change toward bikes, the willingness to pay for bikes rises (the demand curve for bikes shifts to the right) and the willingness to pay for skis falls (the demand curve for skis shifts to the left). So the price of bikes rises and the price of skis falls.

b. As the price of bikes rises, the value of the marginal product of labor in bikes rises. And as the price of skis falls, the value of the marginal product of labor in skis falls. As a result, bike producers' willingness to pay for workers rises, and they will hire more workers. Ski producers' willingness to pay for workers falls, and they will hire fewer workers.

c. As adjustments in employment are made, bike producers produce more bikes and ski producers produce fewer skis. As a result, the marginal product of labor in bikes falls and the marginal product of labor in skis rises. The value of the marginal product of labor in bikes therefore falls and the value of the marginal product of labor in skis rises.

d. This process will continue until the value of the marginal product of labor in bikes and in skis is the same. At that point, the economy is in general equilibrium again.

6. Consider the utility possibility frontier in the accompanying diagram.

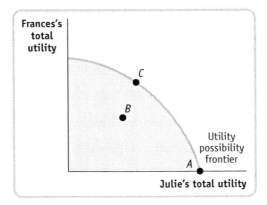

a. Is point *A* efficient? Would you describe point *A* as fair? Why or why not?

b. Is point *B* efficient?

c. Is point *C* better than point *B*? Why or why not?

d. Is point *A* better than point *B*? Why or why not?

6. **a.** Point *A* is efficient: it lies on the utility possibility frontier. That is, there is no way of making Frances better off without making Julie worse off. But most people would agree that it may not be fair: at *A*, Julie has all the utility and Frances has none.

b. Point *B* is not efficient. There is a way of making at least one person better off without making the other worse off. For instance, moving from *B* to *C* would make both Julie and Frances better off.

c. Moving from *B* to *C* makes Julie better off without making Frances worse off—in fact, it also makes Frances better off. So *C* is clearly better than point *B*.

d. Although *A* is efficient and *B* is not, moving from *B* to *A* is not clearly better. Although Julie is made better off, Frances is made worse off. So moving from *B* to *A* is not straightforwardly better: for Frances, that move is worse.

7. The table shows how much total utility Jeremy and John Stuart experience from various amounts of income. (Utility is measured in units of utils.)

Jeremy's income	Jeremy's total utility (utils)	John Stuart's income	John Stuart's total utility (utils)
$0	0	$0	0
1	12	1	12
2	22	2	22
3	30	3	30
4	36	4	36
5	40	5	40
6	42	6	42

a. There are $6 that we can distribute between Jeremy and John Stuart. Suppose that Jeremy and John Stuart live in a utilitarian society that tries to distribute income in such a way as to create the greatest sum of the total utility of each member. How can we distribute $6 between Jeremy and John Stuart so that the sum of their total utilities is the greatest?

b. Now Jeremy falls ill, and his illness requires expensive treatment. As a result, the utility he gets from each dollar of income is now only half of what the table above shows. If our aim is to distribute income in such a way as to create the greatest sum of the total utility of both Jeremy and John Stuart, how should we distribute the $6 now? Does this seem fair to you?

7. a. If we give $3 to Jeremy, his total utility is 30 utils. If we give the remaining $3 to John Stuart, his total utility is 30 utils. The sum of their total utilities is therefore 30 + 30 = 60 utils. There is no other way of distributing $6 between them that creates a greater sum of their total utilities.

b. The table of Jeremy's and John Stuart's total utility now looks like this:

Jeremy's income	Jeremy's total utility (utils)	John Stuart's income	John Stuart's total utility (utils)
$0	0	$0	0
1	6	1	12
2	11	2	22
3	15	3	30
4	18	4	36
5	20	5	40
6	21	6	42

If we give $2 to Jeremy, his total utility is 11 utils. If we give the remaining $4 to John Stuart, his total utility is 36 utils. The sum of their total utility is therefore 11 + 36 = 47 utils. There is no other way of distributing $6 between them that creates a greater sum of their total utilities. But that doesn't seem fair—we are now giving Jeremy less money than before! As we explained in For Inquiring Minds on p. 240, this is one of the reasons that utilitarianism has pretty much vanished from economic thought.

8. What type of externality (positive or negative) is described in each of the following examples? Is the marginal social benefit of the activity greater than or equal to the marginal benefit to the individual? Is the marginal social cost of the activity greater than or equal to the marginal cost to the individual? Consequently, without intervention, will there be too little or too much (relative to what would be socially optimal) of this activity?

a. Mrs. Chau plants lots of colorful flowers in her front yard.

b. Anna Crombie and Fritz, a popular clothing store, opens in a mall, attracting more shoppers who also visit other stores.

c. The fraternity next to your dorm plays loud music, keeping you from studying.

d. Maija, who lives next to an apple orchard, decides to keep bees to produce honey.

e. Justine buys a large SUV that consumes a lot of gasoline.

8. a. This is a positive externality: since other people enjoy looking at Mrs. Chau's flowers, the marginal social benefit of looking at the flowers is greater than the marginal benefit to Mrs. Chau of looking at them. As a result, fewer flowers will be planted than is socially optimal.

b. This is a positive externality: since additional shoppers lead to additional business for other stores in the mall, the store's decision to locate there confers external benefits on other stores. The marginal social benefit is greater than the marginal benefit to Anna Crombie and Fritz alone. Since Anna Crombie and Fritz do not take the external benefit into account in their decision making, they will open fewer stores in malls than is socially optimal.

c. This is a negative externality: since you cannot study, an external cost is imposed on you. That is, the marginal social cost is greater than the marginal cost incurred by the fraternity. Since the fraternity does not take this external cost into account, there will be more music played (or the music will be louder) than is socially optimal.

d. This is a positive externality: since bees pollinate her neighbor's apple trees and therefore confer an external benefit on the owner of the apple orchard, the marginal social benefit is greater than the marginal benefit to Maija. Since Maija does not take the external benefit into account, she will keep fewer bees than is socially optimal.

e. This is a negative externality: the burning of gasoline produces toxic gases that impose an external cost on others. The marginal social cost is greater than the marginal cost incurred by Justine. As a result, more people will purchase SUVs than is socially optimal.

9. The accompanying table shows the total social benefit from steel production and the total cost to steel producers of producing steel. Producing a ton of steel imposes a marginal external cost of $60 per ton.

Quantity of steel (tons)	Total social benefit	Total cost to producers
1	$115	$10
2	210	30
3	285	60
4	340	100
5	375	150

a. Calculate the marginal social benefit per ton of steel and the marginal cost per ton of steel to steel producers. Then calculate the marginal social cost per ton of steel.

b. What is the market equilibrium quantity of steel production?

c. What is the socially optimal quantity of steel production?

d. If you wanted to impose a Pigouvian tax to remedy the problem created by the negative externality, how high would the Pigouvian tax have to be per ton of steel?

9. a. The accompanying table calculates the marginal social benefits and costs from steel production and the marginal cost to steel producers.

Quantity (tons of steel)	Total social benefit	Marginal social benefit per ton	Total cost to steel producers per ton	Marginal cost to steel producers per ton	Marginal social cost per ton
1	$115		$10		
		$95		$20	$80
2	210		30		
		75		30	90
3	285		60		
		55		40	100
4	340		100		
		35		50	110
5	375		150		

b. The market equilibrium quantity of steel production is 4 tons. The marginal social benefit of going from the third ton to the fourth ton is $55, which is more than $40, the marginal cost to steel producers of going from the third ton to the fourth ton. But in going from the fourth to the fifth ton, the marginal social benefit, $35, is less than the marginal cost to steel producers, $50.

c. The socially optimal level of steel production is 2 tons. The marginal social benefit of going from the first to the second ton is $95, more than the marginal social cost of going from the first to the second ton. But the marginal social benefit of going from 2 tons to 3 tons is $75, less than the marginal social cost, which is $90.

d. A Pigouvian tax would have to bring the marginal cost to steel producers in line with the marginal social cost. That is, a Pigouvian tax of $60 per ton of steel produced would increase the marginal cost to steel producers, so that their marginal cost would equal the marginal social cost. As a result, the steel producers would produce the socially optimal quantity of steel.

10. Education is an example of a positive externality: acquiring more education benefits the individual student and having a more highly educated work force is good for the economy as a whole. The accompanying table illustrates the marginal benefit to Sian per year of education and the marginal cost per year of education. Each year of education has a marginal external benefit to society equal to $8,000. Assume that the marginal social cost is the same as the marginal cost paid by an individual student.

Quantity of education (years)	Sian's marginal benefit per year	Sian's marginal cost per year
9		
	$20,000	$15,000
10		
	19,000	16,000
11		
	18,000	17,000
12		
	17,000	18,000
13		
	16,000	19,000
14		
	15,000	20,000
15		
	14,000	21,000
16		
	13,000	22,000
17		

a. Find Sian's market equilibrium number of years of education.

b. Calculate the marginal social benefit schedule. What is the socially optimal number of years of education?

c. You are in charge of education funding. Would you use a Pigouvian tax or a Pigouvian subsidy to induce Sian to choose the socially optimal amount of education? How high would you set this tax or subsidy per year of education?

10. **a.** Sian's market equilibrium number of years of education is 12 years: at a smaller number of years, Sian's marginal benefit exceeds her marginal cost; at a greater number of years, her marginal cost exceeds her marginal benefit.

b. The marginal social benefit includes not only Sian's benefit but also the external benefit to society. The accompanying table calculates the marginal social benefit. From the table you can see that the socially optimal number of years of education would be 16 years.

Years of education	Sian's marginal benefit per year	Marginal social benefit per year	Sian's marginal cost per year
9			
	$20,000	$28,000	$15,000
10			
	19,000	27,000	16,000
11			
	18,000	26,000	17,000
12			
	17,000	25,000	18,000
13			
	16,000	24,000	19,000
14			
	15,000	23,000	20,000
15			
	14,000	22,000	21,000
16			
	13,000	21,000	22,000
17			

c. You would choose to use a Pigouvian subsidy to increase Sian's marginal benefit so that it equals the marginal social benefit. That is, you should introduce a Pigouvian subsidy of $8,000 per year of education.

11. Getting a flu shot reduces not only your chance of getting the flu but also the chance that you will pass it on to someone else.

a. Draw a diagram showing the supply and demand curves of inoculating different proportions of the population. Assume that the marginal cost of each flu shot is constant and is equal to the marginal social cost, and that the demand curve is downward sloping.

b. Will the marginal social benefit curve be higher, lower, or the same as the demand curve? Why? Draw the marginal social benefit curve into your diagram.

c. In your diagram, show the market equilibrium quantity and the socially optimal quantity of flu shots. Is the market equilibrium quantity of flu shots socially efficient? Why or why not?

d. Many university health centers offer free flu shots to students and employees. Does this solution necessarily achieve efficiency? Explain, using your diagram.

11. a. Supply (S) and demand (D) of inoculating different proportions of the population are shown in the accompanying diagram.

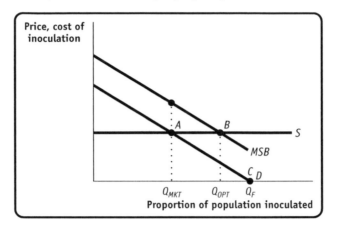

b. The marginal social benefit will be higher than the marginal benefit of the person inoculated because there is an external benefit: others who come into contact with this person now cannot get the flu from him or her. The curve labeled *MSB* illustrates this.

c. The market equilibrium quantity of flu shots is quantity Q_{MKT} at point *A*, where supply and demand are equal. The socially optimal quantity of flu shots is quantity Q_{OPT} at point *B*, where supply and marginal social benefit are equal. The market-determined quantity is not efficient: at that quantity, the marginal social benefit is greater than the marginal cost (represented by the supply curve). That is, immunizing one more person would bring greater benefit to society, including the immunized person and those in contact with her, than it would cost to provide the immunization.

d. If a health center provides flu shots for free, the marginal cost to patients falls to zero. This results in equilibrium at point *C*. As you can see, this quantity is greater than that at point *A*, the (inefficient) market equilibrium outcome. But it is not necessarily the same quantity as the socially optimal outcome. A Pigouvian subsidy leads to the efficient outcome only if it is equal to the difference between private and marginal social benefit. Providing flu shots for free means giving students a subsidy equal to the (constant) marginal cost. Hence the optimal quantity would be achieved only if the cost of providing flue shots were exactly equal to the difference between social and private marginal benefits of immunization.

12. Ronald owns a cattle farm at the source of a long river. His cattle's waste flows into the river, and down many miles to where Carla lives. Carla gets her drinking water from the river. By allowing his cattle's waste to flow into the river, Ronald imposes a negative externality on Carla. In each of the two following cases, do you think that through negotiation, Ronald and Carla can find an efficient solution? What might this solution look like?

a. There are no telephones, and for Carla to talk to Ronald, she has to travel for two days on a rocky road.

b. Carla and Ronald both have e-mail access, making it costless for them to communicate.

12. **a.** The Coase theorem states that an economy can always reach an efficient solution, as long as transaction costs are sufficiently low. Here, transaction costs are not low: Carla has to spend several days traveling to negotiate with Ronald. Since the transaction cost is large, it is likely that no efficient solution will be reached.

b. Now transaction costs are zero: it is costless for Carla and Ronald to negotiate with each other. There are two possible solutions: either Carla pays Ronald to reduce pollution of her drinking water or Ronald pays Carla to accept some waste in her water. Either way, negotiation will result in a socially efficient outcome, in which Carla and Ronald internalize the externality.

13. In many planned communities, various aspects of community living are subject to regulation by a homeowners' association. These rules can regulate house architecture; require snow removal from sidewalks; exclude outdoor equipment, such as backyard swimming pools; and so on. There has been some conflict, as some homeowners feel that some of the regulations are overly intrusive. You have been called in to mediate. Using economics, how would you decide what types of regulations are warranted and what types are not?

13. Using efficiency as the goal, a regulation is warranted if it provides a public good. The enjoyment of pleasing and harmonious architecture and snow removal from sidewalks are examples of public goods: they are nonexcludable and nonrival in consumption. But it is questionable whether or not aspects such as backyard swimming pools should be regulated: their presence in someone's yard does not benefit or hurt neighbors (so they are rival in consumption) and they are solely for the benefit of the homeowner who owns them (they are excludable). Hence they are private goods and should not be subject to regulation by the homeowners' association. The regulation of private goods in the community is unwarranted.

14. A residential community has 100 residents who are concerned about security. The accompanying table gives the total cost of hiring a 24-hour security service as well as each individual resident's total benefit.

Quantity of security guards	Total cost	Total individual benefit to each resident
0	$0	$0
1	150	10
2	300	16
3	450	18
4	600	19

a. Explain why the security service is a public good for the residents of the community.

b. Calculate the marginal cost, the individual marginal benefit for each resident, and the marginal social benefit.

c. If an individual resident were to decide about hiring and paying for security guards on his or her own, how many guards would that resident hire?

d. If the residents act together, how many security guards will they hire?

14. **a.** Security services are nonexcludable: as soon as security is provided to the community, every resident benefits from it. Security services are nonrival: if one resident enjoys protection, this does not diminish any other resident's ability to enjoy the service.

b. The accompanying table calculates the marginal cost, the individual marginal benefit, and the marginal social benefit. The marginal social benefit is just the individual marginal benefit times 100, since there are 100 residents.

Quantity of security guards	Total cost	Marginal cost	Total individual benefit to each resident	Individual marginal benefit	Marginal social benefit
0	$0		$0		
		$150		$10	$1,000
1	150		10		
		150		6	600
2	300		16		
		150		2	200
3	450		18		
		150		1	100
4	600		19		

c. An individual resident would compare the marginal cost of hiring an additional security guard against his or her individual marginal benefit. Since the marginal cost of hiring even the first security guard exceeds the individual marginal benefit to the resident, the resident would decide to hire no security guards on his or her own.

d. If the residents act together, they will compare the marginal cost of hiring an additional security guard against the marginal social benefit. They will therefore decide to hire 3 security guards. For the third security guard, the marginal social benefit of $200 exceeds the marginal cost of $150. But for the fourth security guard, the marginal cost of $150 would exceed the marginal social benefit of $100.

15. The accompanying table shows Tanisha's and Ari's individual marginal benefit of different amounts of street cleanings per month. Suppose that the marginal cost of street cleanings is constant at $9 each.

Quantity of street cleanings per month	Tanisha's individual marginal benefit	Ari's individual marginal benefit
0		
	$10	$8
1		
	6	4
2		
	2	1
3		

a. If Tanisha had to pay for street cleaning on her own, how many street cleanings would there be?

b. Calculate the marginal social benefit of street cleaning. What is the optimal number of street cleanings?

c. Consider the optimal number of street cleanings. The last street cleaning of that number costs $9. Is Tanisha willing to pay for that last cleaning on her own? Is Ari willing to pay for that last cleaning on his own?

15. **a.** If Tanisha had to pay for street cleaning on her own, she would pay for the street to be cleaned once: her individual marginal benefit of the first cleaning, $10, exceeds the marginal cost of $9.

b. The accompanying table shows the marginal social benefit of street cleaning. The optimal number of street cleanings is 2: the marginal social benefit of the second cleaning is $10, which exceeds the marginal cost of $9.

Quantity of street cleanings per month	Tanisha's individual marginal benefit	Ari's individual marginal benefit	Marginal social benefit
0			
	$10	$8	$18
1			
	6	4	10
2			
	2	1	3
3			

c. Tanisha on her own would be willing to pay only $6 (her individual marginal benefit) for the second cleaning. Ari on his own would be willing to pay only $4 (his individual marginal benefit) for the second cleaning. So neither would be individually willing to pay for the second cleaning.

16. Anyone with a radio receiver can listen to public radio, which is funded largely by donations.

a. Is public radio excludable or nonexcludable? Is it rival in consumption or nonrival? What type of good is it?

b. Should the government support public radio? Explain your reasoning.

16. **a.** Public radio is nonexcludable: anyone with a radio receiver can pick up the radio waves. It is nonrival: if I listen to public radio, that does not diminish your opportunity to listen to it also. So public radio is a public good.

b. As with all public goods, private markets lead to an inefficient quantity of the good being supplied. The individual marginal benefit from a certain amount of public radio programming is less than the marginal social benefit from that amount of public radio programming. As a result, individuals are not willing to pay for the efficient level of public radio programming, and as a result the privately provided quantity of programming would be inefficiently low. There is a case for government support of public radio.

Monopoly

1. Each of the following firms possesses market power. Explain its source.

   a. Merck, the producer of the patented cholesterol-lowering drug Zetia

   b. Verizon, a provider of local telephone service

   c. Chiquita, a supplier of bananas and owner of most banana plantations

1. a. Merck has a patent for Zetia. This is an example of a government-created barrier to entry, which gives Merck market power.

   b. There are economies of scale in the provision of local telephone service. There is a large fixed cost associated with building a network of copper cables to each household; the more telephone calls Verizon produces, the lower its average total cost becomes. This gives Verizon a cost advantage over other companies. This cost advantage gives Verizon market power.

   c. Chiquita controls most banana plantations. Control over a scarce resource gives Chiquita market power.

2. Skyscraper City has a subway system, for which a one-way fare is $1.50. There is pressure on the mayor to reduce the fare by one-third, to $1.00. The mayor is dismayed, thinking that this will mean Skyscraper City is losing one-third of its revenue from sales of subway tickets. The mayor's economic adviser reminds her that she is focusing only on the price effect and ignoring the quantity effect. Explain why the mayor's estimate of a one-third loss of revenue is likely to be an overestimate. Illustrate with a diagram.

2. A reduction in fares from $1.50 to $1.00 will reduce the revenue on each ticket that is currently sold by one-third; this is the price effect. But a reduction in price will lead to more tickets being sold at the lower price of $1.00, which creates additional revenue; this is the quantity effect. The accompanying diagram illustrates this.

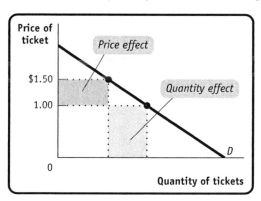

The price effect is the loss of revenue on all the currently sold tickets. The quantity effect is the increase in revenue from increased sales as a result of the lower price.

3. Consider an industry with the demand curve and marginal cost (MC) curve shown in the accompanying diagram. There is no fixed cost. If the industry is a single-price monopoly, the monopolist's marginal revenue curve would be MR. Answer the following questions by naming the appropriate points or areas.

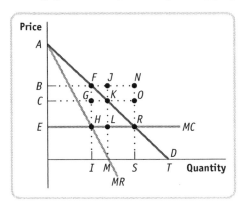

a. If the industry is perfectly competitive, what will be the total quantity produced? At what price?

b. Which area reflects consumer surplus under perfect competition?

c. If the industry is a single-price monopoly, what quantity will the monopolist produce? Which price will it charge?

d. Which area reflects the single-price monopolist's profit?

e. Which area reflects consumer surplus under single-price monopoly?

f. Which area reflects the deadweight loss to society from single-price monopoly?

g. If the monopolist can price-discriminate perfectly, what quantity will the perfectly price-discriminating monopolist produce?

3. a. In a perfectly competitive industry, each firm maximizes profit by producing the quantity at which price equals marginal cost. That is, all firms together produce a quantity S where the marginal cost curve crosses the demand curve. Price will be equal to marginal cost, E.

b. Consumer surplus is the area under the demand curve and above price. In part a, we saw that the perfectly competitive price is E. Consumer surplus in perfect competition is therefore the triangle ARE.

c. A single-price monopolist produces the quantity at which marginal cost equals marginal revenue, that is, quantity I. Accordingly, the monopolist charges price B, the highest price it can charge if it wants to sell quantity I.

d. The single-price monopolist's profit per unit is the difference between price and the average total cost. Since there is no fixed cost and the marginal cost is constant (each unit costs the same to produce), the marginal cost is the same as the average total cost. That is, profit per unit is the distance BE. Since the monopolist sells I units, its profit is BE times I, or the rectangle BEHF.

e. Consumer surplus is the area under the demand curve and above price. In part d, we saw that the monopoly price is B. Consumer surplus in monopoly is therefore the triangle AFB.

f. Deadweight loss is the surplus that would have been available (either to consumers or producers) under perfect competition but that is lost when there is a single-price monopolist. It is the triangle FRH.

g. If a monopolist can price-discriminate perfectly, it will sell the first unit at price *A*, the second unit at a slightly lower price, and so forth. That is, it will extract from each consumer just that consumer's willingness to pay, as indicated by the demand curve. It will sell *S* units, because for the last unit, it can just make a consumer pay a price of *E* (equal to its marginal cost), and that just covers its marginal cost of producing that last unit. For any further units, it could not make any consumer pay more than its marginal cost, and it therefore stops selling units at quantity *S*.

4. Bob, Bill, Ben, and Brad Baxter have just made a documentary movie about their basketball team. They are thinking about making the movie available for download on the Internet, and they can act as a single-price monopolist if they choose to. Each time the movie is downloaded, their Internet service provider charges them a fee of $4. The Baxter brothers are arguing about which price to charge customers per download. The accompanying table shows the demand schedule for their film.

Price of download	Quantity of downloads demanded
$10	0
8	1
6	3
4	6
2	10
0	15

a. Calculate the total revenue and the marginal revenue per download.

b. Bob is proud of the film and wants as many people as possible to download it. Which price would he choose? How many downloads would be sold?

c. Bill wants as much total revenue as possible. Which price would he choose? How many downloads would be sold?

d. Ben wants to maximize profit. Which price would he choose? How many downloads would be sold?

e. Brad wants to charge the efficient price. Which price would he choose? How many downloads would be sold?

4. a. The accompanying table calculates total revenue (*TR*) and marginal revenue (*MR*). Recall that marginal revenue is the additional revenue *per unit of output*, that is, $\Delta TR/\Delta Q$.

Price of download	Quantity of downloads demanded	TR	MR
$10	0	$0	
			$8
8	1	8	
			5
6	3	18	
			2
4	6	24	
			−1
2	10	20	
			−4
0	15	0	

b. Bob would charge $0. At that price, there would be 15 downloads, the largest quantity they can sell.

c. Bill would charge $4. At that price, total revenue is greatest ($24). At that price, there would be 6 downloads.

d. Ben would charge $6. At that price, there would be 3 downloads. For any more downloads, marginal revenue would be below marginal cost, and further downloads would therefore lose the Baxters money.

e. Brad would charge $4. A price equal to marginal cost is efficient. At that price, there would be 6 downloads.

5. Jimmy has a room that overlooks, from some distance, a major league baseball stadium. He decides to rent a telescope for $50.00 a week and charge his friends and classmates to use it to peep at the game for 30 seconds. He can act as a single-price monopolist for renting out "peeps." For each person who takes a 30-second peep, it costs Jimmy $0.20 to clean the eyepiece. The accompanying table shows the information Jimmy has gathered about the demand for the service.

Price of peep	Quantity of peeps demanded
$1.20	0
1.00	100
0.90	150
0.80	200
0.70	250
0.60	300
0.50	350
0.40	400
0.30	450
0.20	500
0.10	550

a. For each price in the table, calculate the total revenue from selling peeps and the marginal revenue per peep.

b. At what quantity will Jimmy's profit be maximized? What price will he charge? What will his total profit be?

c. Jimmy's landlady complains about all the visitors coming into the building and tells Jimmy to stop selling peeps. Jimmy discovers, however, that if he gives the landlady $0.20 for every peep he sells, she will stop complaining. What effect does the $0.20-per-peep bribe have on Jimmy's marginal cost per peep? What is the new profit-maximizing quantity of peeps? What effect does the $0.20-per-peep bribe have on Jimmy's total profit?

Solution

5. a. Total revenue (*TR*) and marginal revenue (*MR*) are given in the accompanying table.

Price of peep	Quantity of peeps demanded	TR	MR
$1.20	0	$0	
			$1.00
1.00	100	100	
			0.70
0.90	150	135	
			0.50
0.80	200	160	
			0.30
0.70	250	175	
			0.10
0.60	300	180	
			−0.10
0.50	350	175	
			−0.30
0.40	400	160	
			−0.50
0.30	450	135	
			−0.70
0.20	500	100	
			−0.90
0.10	550	55	

b. Jimmy's profit will be maximized when he sells 250 peeps, since for the first 250 peeps his marginal revenue exceeds his marginal cost of $0.20. He will charge $0.70 per peep. His total profit is 250 × $0.70 − 250 × $0.20 − $50.00 = $75.00.

c. When Jimmy pays the landlady $0.20 per peep, his marginal cost increases to $0.40 per peep, so the profit-maximizing quantity decreases to 200 and the profit-maximizing price increases to $0.80. His total profit will now be 200 × $0.80 − 200 × $0.40 − $50.00 = $30.00.

6. Suppose that De Beers is a single-price monopolist in the market for diamonds. De Beers has five potential customers: Raquel, Jackie, Joan, Mia, and Sophia. Each of these customers will buy at most one diamond—and only if the price is just equal to, or lower than, her willingness to pay. Raquel's willingness to pay is $400; Jackie's, $300; Joan's, $200; Mia's, $100; and Sophia's, $0. De Beers's marginal cost per diamond is $100. This leads to the demand schedule for diamonds shown in the accompanying table.

Price of diamond	Quantity of diamonds demanded
$500	0
400	1
300	2
200	3
100	4
0	5

a. Calculate De Beers's total revenue and its marginal revenue. From your calculation, draw the demand curve and the marginal revenue curve.

b. Explain why De Beers faces a downward-sloping demand curve.

c. Explain why the marginal revenue from an additional diamond sale is less than the price of the diamond.

d. Suppose De Beers currently charges $200 for its diamonds. If it lowered the price to $100, how large is the price effect? How large is the quantity effect?

e. Draw the marginal cost curve into your diagram and determine which quantity maximizes De Beers's profit and which price De Beers will charge.

6. a. Total revenue (TR) and marginal revenue (MR) are given in the accompanying table.

Price of diamond	Quantity of diamonds demanded	TR	MR
$500	0	$0	
			$400
400	1	400	
			200
300	2	600	
			0
200	3	600	
			−200
100	4	400	
			−400
0	5	0	

The accompanying diagram illustrates De Beers's demand curve and marginal revenue (MR) curve.

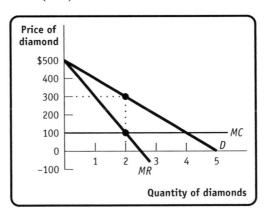

b. De Beers is the only producer of diamonds, so its demand curve is the market demand curve. And the market demand curve slopes downward: the lower the price, the more customers will buy diamonds.

c. If De Beers lowers the price sufficiently to sell one more diamond, it earns extra revenue equal to the price of that one extra diamond. This is the quantity effect of lowering the price. But there is also a price effect: lowering the price means that De Beers also has to lower the price on all other diamonds, and that lowers its revenue. So the marginal revenue of selling an additional diamond is less than the price at which the additional diamond can be sold.

d. If the price is $200, then De Beers sells to Raquel, Jackie, and Joan. If it lowers the price to $100, it will additionally sell a diamond to Mia. The price effect is that De Beers loses $100 (the amount by which it lowered the price) each from selling to Raquel, Jackie, and Joan. So the price effect lowers De Beers's revenue by 3 × $100 = $300. The quantity effect is that De Beers sells one more diamond (to Mia), at $100. So the quantity effect is to raise De Beers's revenue by $100.

e. The marginal cost (MC) curve is constant at $100, as shown in the diagram. Marginal revenue equals marginal cost at a quantity of 2 diamonds. So De Beers will sell 2 diamonds at a price of $300 each.

7. Use the demand schedule for diamonds given in Problem 6. The marginal cost of producing diamonds is constant at $100. There is no fixed cost.

   a. If De Beers charges the monopoly price, how large is the individual consumer surplus that each buyer experiences? Calculate total consumer surplus by summing the individual consumer surpluses. How large is producer surplus?

   Suppose that upstart Russian and Asian producers enter the market and the market becomes perfectly competitive.

   b. What is the perfectly competitive price? What quantity will be sold in this perfectly competitive market?

   c. At the competitive price and quantity, how large is the consumer surplus that each buyer experiences? How large is total consumer surplus? How large is producer surplus?

   d. Compare your answer to part c to your answer to part a. How large is the deadweight loss associated with monopoly in this case?

7. **a.** The monopoly price is $300. At that price Raquel and Jackie buy diamonds. Raquel's consumer surplus is $400 − $300 = $100; Jackie's is $300 − $300 = $0. So total consumer surplus is $100 + $0 = $100. Producer surplus is $300 − $100 = $200 for each diamond sold; 2 × $200 = $400.

   b. In a perfectly competitive market, P = MC. That is, the perfectly competitive price is $100, and at that price 4 diamonds will be sold—to Raquel, Jackie, Joan, and Mia.

   c. At the competitive price, Raquel's consumer surplus is $400 − $100 = $300; Jackie's, $300 − $100 = $200; Joan's, $200 − $100 = $100; and Mia's, $100 − $100 = $0. So total consumer surplus is $300 + $200 + $100 + $0 = $600. Since the price is equal to marginal cost, there is no producer surplus.

   d. Under perfect competition, the sum of consumer and producer surplus is $600 + $0 = $600. Under monopoly, the sum of consumer and producer surplus is $100 + $400 = $500. So the loss of surplus to society from monopoly—the deadweight loss—is $600 − $500 = $100.

8. Use the demand schedule for diamonds given in Problem 6. De Beers is a monopolist, but it can now price-discriminate perfectly among all five of its potential customers. De Beers's marginal cost is constant at $100. There is no fixed cost.

   a. If De Beers can price-discriminate perfectly, to which customers will it sell diamonds and at what prices?

   b. How large is each individual consumer surplus? How large is total consumer surplus? Calculate producer surplus by summing the producer surplus generated by each sale.

8. a. If De Beers can price-discriminate perfectly, it will charge each customer that customer's willingness to pay. That is, it will charge Raquel $400, Jackie $300, Joan $200, and Mia $100. De Beers does not want to sell to Sophia since she will only buy at a price of $0, and that would be below De Beers's marginal cost.

b. Since each consumer is charged exactly her willingness to pay, there is no consumer surplus. De Beers's producer surplus is $400 − $100 = $300 from selling to Raquel; $300 − $100 = $200 from selling to Jackie; $200 − $100 = $100 from selling to Joan; $100 − $100 = $0 from selling to Mia. So producer surplus is $300 + $200 + $100 + $0 = $600.

9. Download Records decides to release an album by the group Mary and the Little Lamb. It produces the album with no fixed cost, but the total cost of downloading an album to a CD and paying Mary her royalty is $6 per album. Download Records can act as a single-price monopolist. Its marketing division finds that the demand schedule for the album is as shown in the accompanying table.

Price of album	Quantity of albums demanded
$22	0
20	1,000
18	2,000
16	3,000
14	4,000
12	5,000
10	6,000
8	7,000

a. Calculate the total revenue and the marginal revenue per album.

b. The marginal cost of producing each album is constant at $6. To maximize profit, what level of output should Download Records choose, and which price should it therefore charge?

c. Mary renegotiates her contract and now needs to be paid a royalty of $14 per album. So the marginal cost rises to be constant at $14. To maximize profit, what level of output should Download Records now choose, and which price should it charge for each album?

9. a. Total revenue (*TR*) and marginal revenue per album (*MR*) is shown in the accompanying table.

Price of album	Quantity of albums demanded	TR	MR
$22	0	$0	
			$20
20	1,000	20,000	
			16
18	2,000	36,000	
			12
16	3,000	48,000	
			8
14	4,000	56,000	
			4
12	5,000	60,000	
			0
10	6,000	60,000	
			−4
8	7,000	56,000	

b. If the marginal cost of each album is $6, Download Records will maximize profit by producing 4,000 albums, since for each album up to 4,000, marginal revenue is greater than marginal cost. For any further albums, marginal cost would exceed marginal revenue. Producing 4,000 albums, Download Records will charge $14 for each album.

c. If the marginal cost of each album is $14, Download Records will maximize profit by producing 2,000 albums, and it will charge $18 per album.

10. The accompanying diagram illustrates your local electricity company's natural monopoly. The diagram shows the demand curve for kilowatt-hours (kWh) of electricity, the company's marginal revenue (*MR*) curve, the marginal cost (*MC*) curve, and its average total cost (*ATC*) curve. The government wants to regulate the monopolist by imposing a price ceiling.

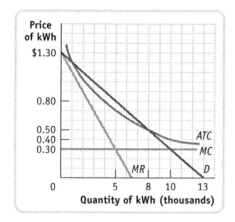

a. If the government does not regulate this monopolist, which price will it charge? Illustrate the inefficiency this creates by shading the deadweight loss from monopoly.

b. If the government imposes a price ceiling equal to the marginal cost, $0.30, will the monopolist make profits or lose money? Shade the area of profit (or losses) for the monopolist. If the government does impose this price ceiling, do you think the firm will continue to produce in the long run?

c. If the government imposes a price ceiling of $0.50, will the monopolist make a profit or lose money?

10. a. The monopolist would choose a price of $0.80. Deadweight loss is shaded and labeled in the accompanying figure.

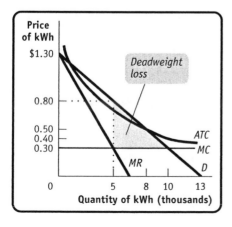

b. If the government imposes a price ceiling of $0.30, the quantity demanded is 10,000. The monopolist will incur a loss equal to the shaded rectangle in the accompanying figure. Since the firm is incurring a loss, in the long run it will exit the market.

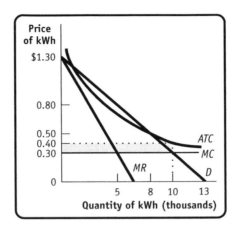

c. If the government imposes a price ceiling of $0.50, the quantity demanded is 8,000. The price equals the monopolist's average total cost, and the firm will therefore make zero profit.

11. The movie theater in Collegetown serves two kinds of customers: students and professors. There are 900 students and 100 professors in Collegetown. Each student's willingness to pay for a movie ticket is $5. Each professor's willingness to pay for a movie ticket is $10. Each will buy at most one ticket. The movie theater's marginal cost per ticket is constant at $3, and there is no fixed cost.

a. Suppose the movie theater cannot price-discriminate and needs to charge both students and professors the same price per ticket. If the movie theater charges $5, who will buy tickets and what will the movie theater's profit be? How large is consumer surplus?

b. If the movie theater charges $10, who will buy movie tickets and what will the movie theater's profit be? How large is consumer surplus?

c. Now suppose that, if it chooses to, the movie theater can price-discriminate between students and professors by requiring students to show their student ID. If the movie theater charges students $5 and professors $10, how much profit will the movie theater make? How large is consumer surplus?

11. **a.** If the movie theater charges $5 per ticket, both students and professors will buy tickets. The movie theater will sell to 1,000 customers (students and professors), at a price of $5 each. Since the movie theater's cost per ticket is $3, its profit is $2 per ticket for a total profit of 1,000 × $2 = $2,000. Students will experience no consumer surplus, but each of the 100 professors will experience consumer surplus of $10 − $5 = $5 for a total consumer surplus of 100 × $5 = $500.

b. If the movie theater charges $10 per ticket, only professors will buy tickets. The movie theater will sell to 100 customers (professors) at a price of $10 each. Since the movie theater's cost per ticket is $3, its profit is $7 per ticket for a total profit of 100 × $7 = $700. Students experience no consumer surplus since they do not buy any tickets. Each of the 100 professors experiences no consumer surplus since the price is equal to their willingness to pay. So consumer surplus is $0.

c. If the movie theater charges students a price of $5, it sells 900 tickets at a profit of $5 – $3 = $2 each for a profit from selling to students of 900 × $2 = $1,800. Charging professors $10, it sells 100 tickets at a profit of $10 – $3 = $7 each for a profit from selling to professors of 100 × $7 = $700. So the theater's total profit is $1,800 + $700 = $2,500. Since each customer is charged exactly his or her willingness to pay, there is no consumer surplus.

12. A monopolist knows that if it expands the quantity of output it produces from 8 to 9 units, that will lower the price of its output from $2 to $1. Calculate the quantity effect and the price effect. Use these results to calculate the monopolist's marginal revenue of producing the 9th unit. The marginal cost of producing the 9th unit is positive. Is is a good idea for the monopolist to produce the 9th unit?

12. The quantity effect is $1 (the increase in total revenue from selling the 9th unit at $1). The price effect is 8 × (–$1) = –$8 (the decrease in total revenue from having to lower the price of 8 units by $1 each). The marginal revenue of producing the 9th unit therefore is $1 – $8 = –$7. Since marginal revenue is negative, producing the 9th unit is definitely not a good idea: it lowers revenue (since marginal revenue is negative), and it increases the total cost (since marginal cost is positive). So it will definitely lower profit. Instead, the monopolist should produce less output.

Oligopoly, Monopolistic Competition, and Product Differentiation

1. To preserve the North Atlantic fish stocks, it is initially decided that only two fishing fleets, one from the United States and one from the European Union (EU) can fish in these waters. But soon the fisheries agreement breaks down, so that the fleets behave noncooperatively. Assume that the U.S. and the EU each can send out either one or two fleets. Also assume that the more fleets in the area, the more fish they catch in total but the lower the catch of each fleet. The accompanying matrix shows the profit (in dollars) per week earned by the two sides.

a. What is the noncooperative Nash equilibrium? Will each side choose to send out one or two fleets?

b. Suppose that the fish stocks are being depleted. Each region considers the future and comes to a "tit-for-tat" agreement whereby each side will send only one fleet out as long as the other does the same. If either of them breaks the agreement and sends out a second fleet, the other will also send out two and will continue to do so until its competitor sends out only one fleet. If both play this "tit for tat" strategy, how much profit will each make every week?

Solution

1. **a.** If the European Union has only one fleet, the United States will have a higher profit if it sends out two fleets ($12,000 rather than $10,000). If the EU sends out two fleets, the United States will have a higher profit if it also sends out two fleets ($7,500 rather than $4,000). The same reasoning will persuade the EU that its best strategy is also to send out two fleets whether the United States sends out one or two. Both parties will send out two fleets, each earning only $7,500 each instead of the $10,000 they would each have earned if they had each limited themselves to one fleet.

b. If both play a "tit for tat" strategy, they each will begin by sending out one fleet. The week after that, each does what the other one did the week before—that is, each again sends out one fleet, and so on. As a result, each week the United States and the EU will each have a profit of $10,000 every week.

2. Untied and Air 'R' Us are the only two airlines operating flights between Collegeville and Bigtown. That is, they operate in a duopoly. Each airline can charge either a high price or a low price for a ticket. The accompanying matrix shows their payoffs, in profits per seat (in dollars), for any choice that the two airlines can make.

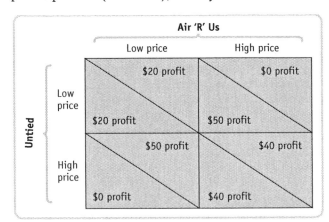

a. Suppose the two airlines play a one-shot game—that is, they interact only once and never again. What will be the Nash (noncooperative) equilibrium in this one-shot game?

b. Now suppose the two airlines play this game twice. And suppose each airline can play one of two strategies: it can play either "always charge the low price" or "tit for tat"—that is, it starts off charging the high price in the first period, and then in the second period it does whatever the other airline did in the previous period. Write down the payoffs to Untied from the following four possibilities:

  i. Untied plays "always charge the low price" when Air 'R' Us also plays "always charge the low price."

  ii. Untied plays "always charge the low price" when Air 'R' Us plays "tit for tat."

  iii. Untied plays "tit for tat" when Air 'R' Us plays "always charge the low price."

  iv. Untied plays "tit for tat" when Air 'R' Us also plays "tit for tat."

2. a. This is a prisoners' dilemma situation. Whatever Air 'R' Us does, it is best for Untied to charge the low price; whatever Untied does, it is best for Air 'R' Us to charge the low price. So the Nash (noncooperative) equilibrium is for both airlines to charge the low price.

b. These are Untied's payoffs:

  i. Both airlines charge the low price in both periods, so Untied's payoffs are $20 in the first period and $20 in the second period, for a total of $20 + $20 = $40.

  ii. In the first period, Untied charges the low price and Air 'R' Us charges the high price for a payoff to Untied of $50. In the second period, Untied and Air 'R' Us both charge the low price for a payoff to Untied of $20. Untied's payoffs are therefore $50 + $20 = $70.

  iii. In the first period, Untied charges the high price and Air 'R' Us charges the low price for a payoff to Untied of $0. In the second period, both airlines charge the low price for a payoff to Untied of $20. Untied's total payoff is therefore $0 + $20 = $20.

  iv. Both airlines charge the high price in both periods, so Untied's payoffs are $40 in both periods, for a total of $40 + $40 = $80.

3. Philip Morris and R.J. Reynolds spend huge sums of money each year to advertise their tobacco products in an attempt to steal customers from each other. Suppose each year Philip Morris and R.J. Reynolds have to decide whether or not they want to spend money on advertising. If neither firm advertises, each will earn a profit of $2 million. If they both advertise, each will earn a profit of $1.5 million. If one firm advertises and the other does not, the firm that advertises will earn a profit of $2.8 million and the other firm will earn $1 million.

    a. Use a payoff matrix to depict this problem.

    b. Suppose Philip Morris and R.J. Reynolds can write an enforceable contract about what they will do. What is the cooperative solution to this game?

    c. What is the Nash equilibrium without an enforceable contract? Explain why this is the likely outcome.

3. a. See the accompanying payoff matrix.

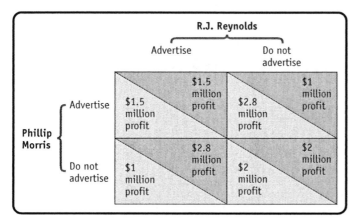

    b. Each firm should not advertise, since this would maximize joint profits. Each firm then earns a profit of $2 million.

    c. Each firm will consider what its best action is depending on the action of the other firm. If R.J. Reynolds advertises, Philip Morris should as well, since it will earn $1.5 million instead of $1 million. If R.J. Reynolds does not advertise, Philip Morris should advertise, since $2.8 million is better than $2 million. So no matter what R.J. Reynolds does, the best action for Philip Morris is to advertise. The same logic applies to R.J. Reynolds. As a result, each firm will advertise, yielding profit of $1.5 million for each firm. This is a prisoners' dilemma situation.

4. Over the last 30 years the Organization of Petroleum Exporting Countries (OPEC) has had varied success in forming and maintaining its cartel agreements. Explain how the following factors may contribute to the difficulty of forming and/or maintaining its price and output agreements.

    a. New oil fields are discovered and increased drilling is undertaken in the Gulf of Mexico and the North Sea by nonmembers of OPEC.

    b. Crude oil is a product that is differentiated by sulfur content: it costs less to refine low-sulfur crude oil into gasoline. Different OPEC countries possess oil reserves of different sulfur content.

    c. Cars powered by hydrogen are developed.

4. a. With the discovery of new oil by nonmembers of OPEC, there is increased competition. This will lead to a fall in market price and make the cartel agreement harder to maintain.

b. The OPEC countries sell a differentiated and complex product. This complicates the decision about what prices to set for what types of oil and makes enforcement of a cartel agreement more difficult. Much of the conflict within OPEC rests on the price differential that is set between "high"- and "low"-quality oils.

c. The development of a hydrogen-powered car would make it more difficult to maintain or form an agreement. Remember that a cartel essentially acts like a monopoly. A cartel's (or a monopoly's) market power is eroded if there is entry of new firms or the development of substitute products.

5. Suppose you are an economist working for the Antitrust Division of the Department of Justice. In each of the following cases you are given the task of determining whether the behavior warrants an antitrust investigation for possible illegal acts, or is just an example of undesirable, but not illegal, tacit collusion. Explain your reasoning.

a. Two companies dominate the industry for industrial lasers. Several people sit on the boards of directors of both companies.

b. Three banks dominate the market for banking in a given state. Their profits have been going up recently as they add new fees for customer transactions. Advertising among the banks is fierce, and new branches are springing up in many locations.

c. The two oil companies that produce most of the petroleum for the western half of the United States have decided to forgo building their own pipelines and to share a common pipeline, the only means of transporting petroleum products to that market.

d. The two major companies that dominate the market for herbal supplements have each created a subsidiary that sells the same product as the parent company in large quantities but with a generic name.

e. The two largest credit card companies, Passport and OmniCard, have required all banks and retailers who accept their cards to agree to limit their use of rival credit cards.

5. a. This warrants an antitrust investigation because it is likely that having the same set of people sit on the two boards will facilitate cartel-like behavior.

b. This does not warrant an antitrust investigation. The intensity of advertising and competition by location indicates that the banks are engaged in nonprice competition.

c. This warrants an antitrust investigation. By using the same pipeline, each company can monitor how much output the other is producing. This facilitates cartel-like behavior.

d. This does not warrant an antitrust investigation. These two companies are actively competing, albeit by using their subsidiaries.

e. This warrants an antitrust investigation. These two companies are acting together to shut out a rival.

6. Use the three conditions for monopolistic competition discussed in the chapter to decide which of the following firms are likely to be operating as monopolistic competitors. If they are not monopolistically competitive firms, are they monopolists, oligopolists, or perfectly competitive firms?

   a. A local band that plays for weddings, parties, and so on

   b. Minute Maid, a producer of individual-serving juice boxes

   c. Your local dry cleaner

   d. A farmer who produces soybeans

6. The three conditions for monopolistic competition are (1) a large number of producers, (2) differentiated products, and (3) free entry and exit.

   a. There are many bands that play at weddings, parties, and so on. There are no significant barriers to entry or exit. And products are differentiated by quality (for instance, some bands have better musicians or better electronic equipment) or by style (for instance, different bands play different types of music). All three conditions for monopolistic competition are fulfilled.

   b. The industry for individual-serving juice boxes is dominated by a few very large firms (for example, Minute Maid, Welch's, and Kool Aid), and there are significant barriers to entry, in part because of the large costs (for example, advertising) involved in gaining any market share of the national market. Products are, however, differentiated—if perhaps only in the minds of consumers. Because of the small number of competitors, the industry is closer to oligopoly.

   c. There is a large number of dry cleaners, and each produces a product differentiated by location: customers are likely to prefer to use the dry cleaner closest to their home or workplace. Finally, there are no significant barriers to entry. This is a monopolistically competitive market.

   d. There is a large number of soybean farmers, and there is free entry and exit in this industry. However, soybeans are not differentiated from each other—they are a standardized product. No individual soybean farmer has market power. This industry is therefore a perfectly competitive industry.

7. You are thinking of setting up a coffee shop. The market structure for coffee shops is monopolistic competition. There are three Starbucks shops and two other coffee shops very much like Starbucks in your town already. In order for you to have some degree of market power, you may want to differentiate your coffee shop. Thinking about the three different ways in which products can be differentiated, explain how you would decide whether you should copy Starbucks or whether you should sell coffee in a completely different way.

7. There are three ways in which you can differentiate your product: by style or type; by location; and by quality.

   If you decide to copy Starbucks both in style (for example, you copy the décor of the shop and the service) and in quality (for example, you serve coffee made from the same coffee beans, brewed in exactly the same way), you will still most likely differentiate your product by location: your coffee shop will be closer for some people than any of the other shops, and that gives you some degree of market power.

   But you could further differentiate your product by style (for example, you could serve coffee in porcelain cups brought to the table by waiters) or by quality (for example, you could serve only organic shade-grown coffee). All these will help you create a differentiated product that gives you more market power—that is, the power to raise prices. You would, of course, need to determine whether it allows you to raise prices sufficiently to cover the cost of paying for waiters and higher-quality coffee.

8. The restaurant business in town is a monopolistically competitive industry in long-run equilibrium. One restaurant owner asks for your advice. She tells you that, each night, not all tables in her restaurant are full. She also tells you that if she lowered the prices on her menu, she would attract more customers and that doing so would lower her average total cost. Should she lower her prices? Draw a diagram showing the demand curve, marginal revenue curve, marginal cost curve, and average total cost curve for this restaurant to explain your advice. Show in your diagram what would happen to the restaurant owner's profit if she were to lower the price so that she sells the minimum-cost output.

8. She should not lower her price. Since the industry is in long-run equilibrium, each restaurant makes zero profit. That is, the restaurant's demand, marginal revenue, marginal cost, and average total cost curves are as shown in the accompanying diagram.

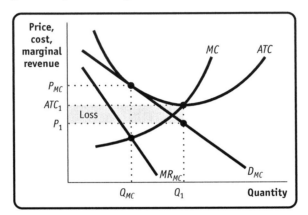

The restaurant owner produces output (the number of tables served), Q_{MC}, at a price of P_{MC}. The price is equal to average total cost, and she therefore makes zero profit. If she were to lower the price to P_1, she would attract more customers and sell the minimum-cost output Q_1. That is, there is excess capacity: each restaurant in town could produce more output at a lower average total cost. But lowering the price to P_1 would cause the restaurant owner to incur a loss equal to the shaded rectangle in the diagram, since price is now below average total cost, ATC_1. In fact, there is no price other than P_{MC} at which the restaurant owner does not make a loss. She should therefore not change the prices on her menu.

9. The local hairdresser industry has the structure of monopolistic competition. Your hairdresser boasts that he is making a profit and that if he continues to do so, he will be able to retire in five years. Use a diagram to illustrate your hairdresser's current situation. Do you expect this to last? In a separate diagram, draw what you expect to happen in the long run. Explain your reasoning.

9. Your hairdresser currently makes a profit. His demand, marginal revenue, marginal cost, and average total cost curves are shown in the diagram below.

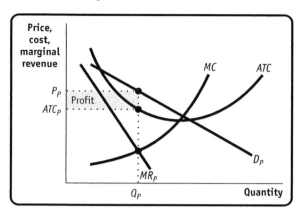

Since this hairdresser (and all other hairdressers) makes a profit equal to the shaded rectangle by producing quantity Q_P at a price P_P, there will be entry into this industry. As more hairdressers open shops in town, demand for the typical existing hairdresser will fall—the demand curve and marginal revenue curve shift leftward. This will continue to the point at which no hairdresser makes positive profit. This eliminates the incentive for further entry into the industry and long-run equilibrium is reached. The situation is illustrated in the diagram below.

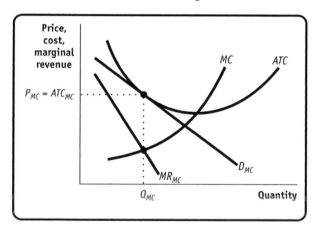

The best the typical hairdresser can do is to produce quantity Q_{MC} at a price of P_{MC}. Since price equals average total cost at this quantity, each hairdresser will make exactly zero profit.

10. Magnificent Blooms is a florist in a monopolistically competitive industry. It is a successful operation, producing the quantity that minimizes its average total cost and making a profit. The owner also boasts that at its current level of output, its marginal cost is above marginal revenue. Illustrate the current situation of Magnificent Blooms in a diagram. Answer the following questions by illustrating with a diagram.

a. In the short run, could Magnificent Blooms increase its profit?

b. In the long run, could Magnificent Blooms increase its profit?

10. The current situation of Magnificent Blooms is illustrated in the accompanying diagram. It produces quantity Q_1 at the minimum point of its average total cost curve, and it charges price P_1, thus making profit equal to the shaded rectangular area.

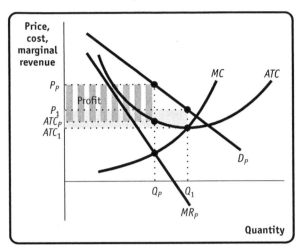

a. Yes, Magnificent Blooms could increase its profit in the short run by producing less. It would maximize its profit by producing quantity Q_P, the quantity at which marginal revenue equals marginal cost, and selling it at a price P_P and making a profit equal to the striped area.

b. No. In the long run, Magnificent Blooms will make zero profit. The fact that it is making profits in the short run induces other firms to enter the industry. This shifts its demand curve and marginal revenue curve leftward to the point where it makes zero profit, as shown in the accompanying diagram.

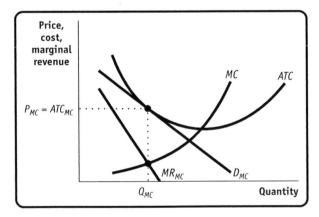

11. "In both the short run and in the long run, the typical firm in monopolistic competition and a monopolist each make a profit." Do you agree with this statement? Explain your reasoning.

11. In the short run, a monopolist makes positive profit. Whether a firm in monopolistic competition makes a profit depends on how many firms there are in the industry. If there are "too few" firms in the industry (relative to the long-run equilibrium number of firms), then a typical firm in monopolistic competition will make a profit. But if there are "too many" firms in the industry (relative to the long-run equilibrium number of firms), then a typical firm in monopolistic competition will incur a loss.

In the long run, a monopolist also makes positive profit. But in the long-run equilibrium in a monopolistically competitive industry, all firms make zero profit. This is because in the long run, in a monopolistically competitive industry, enough firms have entered or left the market to shift a typical firm's demand curve so that it is tangent to the firm's average total cost curve at the firm's profit-maximizing quantity. The typical firm makes zero profit.

12. For each of the following situations, decide whether advertising is directly informative about the product or simply an indirect signal of its quality. Explain your reasoning.

   a. Golf champion Tiger Woods drives a Buick in a TV commercial and claims that he prefers it to any other car.

   b. A newspaper ad states "For sale: 1989 Honda Civic, 160,000 miles, new transmission."

   c. McDonald's spends millions of dollars on an advertising campaign that proclaims: "I'm lovin' it."

   d. Subway advertises one of its sandwiches claiming that it contains 6 grams of fat and fewer than 300 calories.

12. **a.** This commercial is not directly informative about the product since every car manufacturer can claim that its car is better than any other; this is not a statement that can be easily verified by the purchaser before purchase. However, Tiger Woods commands a very high fee for advertising. What the commercial therefore signals is something like "we can afford to pay Tiger Woods's fee since we are a company with a superior product."

   b. This ad is directly informative about the product. It states specific information (that, on inspection of the car, you could easily verify before purchase). Since it can be so easily verified, this information is likely to be true.

   c. This type of advertising provides indirect signal of the quality of McDonald's food. By spending millions on advertising, McDonald's signals that it is confident that once it attracts a buyer to its product, that buyer will buy its products again (creating more profit for McDonald's in the future).

   d. This type of advertising is directly informative about the product because it contains specific information that could easily be verified. If this claim were false, it would very quickly be discredited. So the claim is likely to be true and informs you directly about the product.

13. In each of the following cases, explain how the advertisement functions as a signal to a potential buyer. Explain what information the buyer lacks that is being supplied by the advertisement and how the information supplied by the advertisement is likely to affect the buyer's willingness to buy the good.

   a. "Looking for work. Excellent references from previous employers available."

   b. "Electronic equipment for sale. All merchandise carries a one-year, no-questions-asked warranty."

   c. "Car for sale by original owner. All repair and maintenance records available."

13. a. The seller here is the job-seeker, who is selling his or her labor to a potential employer. The potential employer lacks information on how good an employee the job-seeker is—how dependable, diligent, and so on. By being willing to provide excellent references from previous employers, the job-seeker signals that he or she is a good employee. As a result, the potential employer is more willing to hire that person.

b. The potential buyer lacks information on how good the merchandise is. By being willing to provide a one-year, no-questions-asked warranty, the seller signals to the potential buyer that the merchandise is of high quality. As a result, the potential buyer is more willing to buy the good.

c. The potential buyer lacks information on how good the used car is. By being willing to provide the repair and maintenance records, the seller signals to the potential buyer that this is a good-quality used car. As a result, the potential buyer is more willing to buy it.

14. McDonald's spends millions of dollars each year on legal protection of its brand name, thereby preventing any unauthorized use of it. Explain what information this conveys to you as a consumer about the quality of McDonald's products.

14. The fast-food industry is a monopolistically competitive one, and companies attempt to differentiate their product from that of other firms. McDonald's invests money in maintaining its brand name that differentiates it from other companies. The amount of money spent on creating and maintaining a brand name does not convey any *specific* information about McDonald's products. But it does convey, indirectly, that McDonald's is in this market for the long haul, that it has a reputation to protect, and that it will interact repeatedly with its customers. In this sense, the amount of money spent on maintaining a brand name signals to you as a consumer that McDonald's will provide products of consistent quality.

International Trade

1. For each of the following trade relationships, explain the likely source of the comparative advantage of each of the exporting countries.

   a. The United States exports software to Venezuela, and Venezuela exports oil to the United States.

   b. The United States exports airplanes to China, and China exports clothing to the United States.

   c. The United States exports wheat to Colombia, and Colombia exports coffee to the United States.

1. a. The United States has the comparative advantage in software production because of a factor endowment: a relatively large supply of human capital. Venezuela has the comparative advantage in oil production because of a factor endowment: large oil reserves.

   b. The United States has the comparative advantage in airplane production because of an advantage in human capital: it has the human capital needed to produce airplanes. China has the comparative advantage in clothing production because of a factor endowment: it has a relatively large supply of unskilled labor.

   c. The United States has the comparative advantage in wheat production because of an advantage in climate: it has a climate suitable for growing wheat. Colombia has the comparative advantage in coffee production because of an advantage in climate: it has a climate suitable for growing coffee.

2. Shoes are labor-intensive and satellites are capital-intensive to produce. The United States has abundant capital. China has abundant labor. According to the Heckscher–Ohlin model, which good will China export? Which good will the United States export? In the United States, what will happen to the price of labor (the wage) and to the price of capital?

2. The Heckscher–Ohlin model predicts that a country will have a comparative advantage in the good whose production is intensive in the factor the country has abundantly available: the United States has the comparative advantage in satellite production, and China has the comparative advantage in shoe production. So the United States will export satellites, and China will export shoes. In the United States, demand for capital increases, raising the price of capital, but the demand for labor decreases, lowering the wage.

3. Before the North American Free Trade Agreement (NAFTA) gradually eliminated import tariffs on goods, the autarky price of tomatoes in Mexico was below the world price and in the United States was above the world price. Similarly, the autarky price of poultry in Mexico was above the world price and in the United States was below the world price. Draw diagrams with domestic supply and demand curves for each country and each of the two goods. As a result of NAFTA, the United States now imports tomatoes from Mexico and the United States now exports poultry to Mexico. How would you expect the following groups to be affected?

   a. Mexican and U.S. consumers of tomatoes. Illustrate the effect on consumer surplus in your diagram.

   b. Mexican and U.S. producers of tomatoes. Illustrate the effect on producer surplus in your diagram.

   c. Mexican and U.S. tomato workers.

   d. Mexican and U.S. consumers of poultry. Illustrate the effect on consumer surplus in your diagram.

   e. Mexican and U.S. producers of poultry. Illustrate the effect on producer surplus in your diagram.

   f. Mexican and U.S. poultry workers.

3. The four accompanying diagrams illustrate the U.S. and Mexican domestic demand and supply curves.

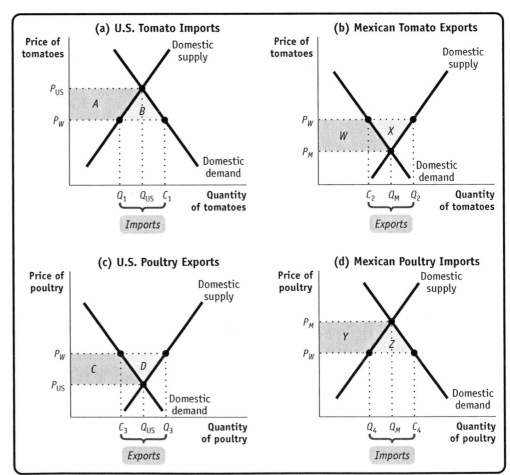

a. As shown in panel (b), consumer surplus of Mexican tomato consumers decreases by the size of area W as the price rises from P_M to P_W. As shown in panel (a), consumer surplus of U.S. tomato consumers increases by the size of the area $A + B$ as the price falls from P_{US} to P_W.

b. As shown in panel (a), production of tomatoes decreases in the United States from Q_{US} to Q_1; producer surplus decreases by the area A. As shown in panel (b), in Mexico, production of tomatoes increases from Q_M to Q_2, so producer surplus increases by the area $W + X$.

c. As production of tomatoes decreases in the United States, the demand for U.S. tomato workers falls and so the wages of U.S. tomato workers fall. In Mexico, as the production of tomatoes increases, the wages of Mexican tomato workers rise.

d. As shown in panel (d), consumer surplus increases in Mexico by the size of the area $Y + Z$ as the price falls from P_M to P_W. As shown in panel (c), consumer surplus decreases in the United States by the size of area C as the price rises from P_{US} to P_W.

e. As shown in panel (d), production of poultry decreases in Mexico, from Q_M to Q_4; therefore producer surplus in Mexico decreases by area Y. As shown in panel (c), U.S. production of poultry increases from Q_{US} to Q_3; therefore producer surplus in the United States increases by the area $C + D$.

f. As production of poultry increases in the United States, the demand for poultry workers rises and therefore the wages of poultry workers rise. In Mexico, as the production of poultry decreases, the wages of poultry workers fall.

4. The accompanying table indicates the U.S. domestic demand schedule and domestic supply schedule for commercial jet airplanes. Suppose that the world price of a commercial jet airplane is $100 million.

Price of jet (millions)	Quantity of jets demanded	Quantity of jets supplied
$120	100	1,000
110	150	900
100	200	800
90	250	700
80	300	600
70	350	500
60	400	400
50	450	300
40	500	200

a. In autarky, how many commercial jet airplanes does the United States produce, and at what price are they bought and sold?

b. With trade, what will the price for commercial jet airplanes be? Will the United States import or export airplanes? How many?

Solution

4. a. In autarky, the equilibrium price will be $60 million, and 400 airplanes will be bought and sold at that price.

b. When there is trade, the price rises to the world price of $100 million. At that price, the domestic quantity supplied is 800, and the domestic quantity demanded is 200. So 600 airplanes are exported.

5. The accompanying table shows the U.S. domestic demand schedule and domestic supply schedule for oranges. Suppose that the world price of oranges is $0.30 per orange.

Price of orange	Quantity of oranges demanded (thousands)	Quantity of oranges supplied (thousands)
$1.00	2	11
0.90	4	10
0.80	6	9
0.70	8	8
0.60	10	7
0.50	12	6
0.40	14	5
0.30	16	4
0.20	18	3

a. Draw the U.S. domestic supply curve and domestic demand curve.

b. With free trade, how many oranges will the United States import or export?

Suppose that the U.S. government imposes a tariff on oranges of $0.20 per orange.

c. How many oranges will the United States import or export after introduction of the tariff?

d. In your diagram, shade the gain or loss to the economy as a whole from the introduction of this tariff.

5. a. The U.S. domestic supply and demand curves are illustrated in the accompanying diagram.

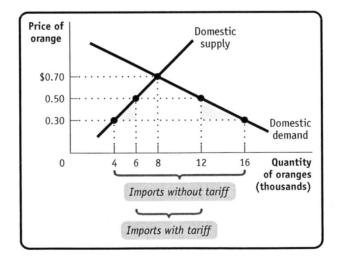

b. With free trade, the price will be the world price, $0.30, the domestic quantity demanded will be 16,000 oranges, and the domestic quantity supplied will be 4,000 oranges. The United States therefore imports 12,000 oranges.

c. With the tariff, the domestic price rises to $0.50. At that price, the domestic quantity demanded exceeds the domestic quantity supplied by 6,000. The United States imports 6,000 oranges.

d. The shaded areas indicate the deadweight loss to the economy as a whole due to the tariff.

6. The U.S. domestic demand schedule and domestic supply schedule for oranges was given in Problem 8. Suppose that the world price of oranges is $0.30. The United States introduces an import quota of 3,000 oranges. Draw the domestic demand and supply curves and answer the following questions.

a. What will the domestic price of oranges be after introduction of the quota?

b. What is the value of the quota rents that importers of oranges receive?

6. The domestic demand and domestic supply curves are shown in the accompanying diagram.

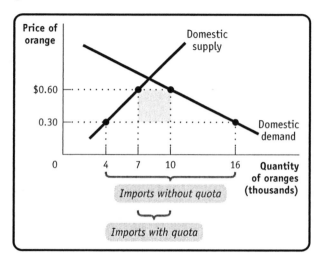

a. After imposition of the quota, instead of importing 16,000 − 4,000 = 12,000 oranges, the United States imports only 3,000 oranges. The price rises to $0.60.

b. The importers of oranges receive quota rent of $0.30 × 3,000 = $900.

7. The accompanying diagram illustrates the U.S. domestic demand curve and domestic supply curve for beef.

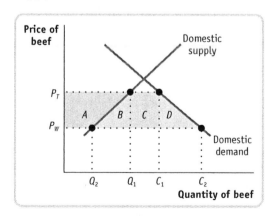

The world price of beef is P_W. The United States currently imposes an import tariff on beef, so the price of beef is P_T. Congress decides to eliminate the tariff. In terms of the areas marked in the diagram, answer the following questions.

a. What is the gain/loss in consumer surplus?

b. What is the gain/loss in producer surplus?

c. What is the gain/loss to the government?

d. What is the gain/loss to the economy as a whole?

7. a. As the price falls from P_T to P_W, consumer surplus increases by the area $A + B + C + D$.

b. As the price falls, producer surplus decreases by the area A.

c. As the tariff is eliminated, the government loses revenue of area C, which is the amount of imports under the tariff $(C_1 - Q_1)$ times the tariff.

d. The gain to the economy as a whole is the gain to consumers minus the loss to producers minus the loss to the government: $A + B + C + D - A - C = B + D$.

8. As the United States has opened up to trade, it has lost many of its low-skill manufacturing jobs, but it has gained jobs in high-skill industries, such as the software industry. Explain whether the United States as a whole has been made better off by trade.

8. As the United States has opened up to trade, it has specialized in producing goods that use high-skill labor (such as software design) in which it has a comparative advantage, and it has allowed other countries to specialize in producing low-skill manufactured goods in which they have the comparative advantage. As a result, the country has lost low-skill manufacturing jobs (and the wage to low-skill workers has fallen), and it has gained jobs in high-skill industries (and the wage to high-skill workers has risen). That is, demand for labor in exporting industries has risen, and demand for labor in the import-competing industries has fallen, as the Heckscher-Ohlin model predicts. But as a result of trade, the United States can now consume more of all goods than before. That is, overall the economy is better off: so the gains to highly skilled workers outweigh the losses to low-skill workers.

9. The United States is highly protective of its agricultural industry, imposing import tariffs, and sometimes quotas, on imports of agricultural goods. The chapter has presented three arguments for trade protection. For each argument, discuss whether it is a valid justification for trade protection of U.S. agricultural products.

9. The three arguments for trade protection are the national security, job creation, and infant industry arguments. Agriculture is not an infant industry, so this argument does not apply. Some argument can be made that agricultural products are necessary for national security: if we depended completely on imports for our agricultural goods, we would be vulnerable if our trading partners cut off our imports. And protecting agriculture does not create jobs. It does protect farming jobs; but it is likely that if agriculture lost its protection from imports, those workers could find other jobs in industries that expand due to lower food costs (such as the restaurant industry). The rationale for protecting agricultural markets from imports must lie elsewhere—in the political power of the farm lobby.

10. In World Trade Organization (WTO) negotiations, if a country agrees to reduce trade barriers (tariffs or quotas), it usually refers to this as a *concession* to other countries. Do you think that this terminology is appropriate?

10. The word *concession* implies that when a country lowers its trade barriers, it is giving up something to other countries. As discussed in this chapter, free trade is beneficial to all countries, including the country that lowers its trade barriers. In fact, even if no other country reduces its trade barriers, the country that does lower its trade barriers still benefits from trade. By allowing more international trade, each country's economy simply gains overall.

11. Producers in import-competing industries often make the following argument: "Other countries have an advantage in production of certain goods purely because workers abroad are paid lower wages. In fact, American workers are much more productive than foreign workers. So import-competing industries need to be protected." Is this a valid argument? Explain your answer.

11. Even if American workers are better at everything than are foreign workers (that is, even if America has the absolute advantage in everything), this does not mean that the United States should restrict trade. What matters for trade is who has the comparative advantage. In fact, other countries will have a comparative advantage in some good or service, and specialization and trade will mean welfare improvements for both countries. Claiming that other countries have an advantage only because labor is so cheap relies on the pauper labor fallacy.

Macroeconomics: The Big Picture

1. Which of the following questions are relevant for the study of macroeconomics and which for microeconomics?

    a. How will Ms. Martin's tips change when a large manufacturing plant near the restaurant where she works closes?

    b. What will happen to spending by consumers when the economy enters a downturn?

    c. How will the price of oranges change when a late frost damages Florida's orange groves?

    d. How will wages at a manufacturing plant change when its workforce is unionized?

    e. What is the relationship between a nation's unemployment rate and its inflation rate?

1. a. This is a microeconomic question because it addresses the effects of a single firm's actions (the closure of a manufacturing plant) on a single individual (the waitress).

    b. This is a macroeconomic question because it considers how overall spending by consumers is affected by the state of the macroeconomy.

    c. This is a microeconomic question because it looks at how a single market (oranges) will be affected by a late frost.

    d. This is a microeconomic question because it addresses how wages in a particular plant will change when the firm's workforce is unionized.

    e. This is a macroeconomic question because it addresses the relationship between two aggregate measures of economic activity, inflation and unemployment.

2. When one person saves, that person's wealth is increased, meaning that he or she can consume more in the future. But when everyone saves, everyone's income falls, meaning that everyone must consume less today. Explain this seeming contradiction.

2. This question concerns the Paradox of Thrift; what is true for an individual—that saving makes you better off—is not always true for the economy as a whole. When an individual saves, she adds to her wealth, providing for higher consumption in the future. However, if everyone saves, firms will not sell as much and will lay off workers. Individuals find that their incomes fall as a result. Hence they must consume less today.

3. What was the Great Depression? How did it affect the role of government in the economy and the macroeconomic toolkit?

3. Great Depression refers to the high rates of unemployment that the United States and other nations experienced during the 1930s. In the United States, unemployment rates reached a high of almost 25%. Economists focused on understanding how such a prolonged period of unemployment could have happened and how it could be alleviated. John Maynard Keynes's *The General Theory of Employment, Interest, and Money,* as well as interpretations and critiques of his work, are seen as the beginning of macroeconomics as we know it today. It is from this that the modern macroeconomic toolkit of fiscal policy (control of government spending and taxation) and monetary policy (control of interest rates and money supply in circulation) was developed.

4. There are 100,000 inhabitants in Macronesia. Among those 100,000 inhabitants, 25,000 are too old to work and 15,000 inhabitants are too young to work. Among the remaining 60,000 inhabitants, 10,000 are not working and have given up looking for work, 45,000 are currently employed, and the remaining 5,000 are looking for work but do not currently have a job.

   a. What is the number of people in the labor force in Macronesia?

   b. What is the unemployment rate in Macronesia?

   c. How many people in Macronesia are discouraged workers?

4. a. The labor force is the sum of employed and unemployed people. There are 45,000 employed people and 5,000 unemployed people. The size of the labor force therefore is 45,000 + 5,000 = 50,000 people.

   b. The unemployment rate is the ratio of people unemployed to the total number of people in the labor force. Here it is (5,000/50,000) × 100 = 10%.

   c. There are 10,000 people in Macronesia who are discouraged workers, since they are capable of working but not actively looking for a job.

5. College tuition has risen significantly in the last few decades. From the 1971–1972 academic year to the 2001–2002 academic year, total tuition, room, and board paid by full-time undergraduate students went from $1,357 to $8,022 at public institutions and from $2,917 to $21,413 at private institutions. This is an average annual tuition increase of 6.1% at public institutions and 6.9% at private institutions. Over the same time, average personal income after taxes rose from $3,860 to $26,156 per year, which is an average annual rate of growth of personal income of 6.6%. Have these tuition increases made it more difficult for the average student to afford college tuition?

5. To determine whether it is more or less difficult for a typical person to afford college, we would need to know how much tuition had increased relative to average income in the United States. Average personal income after taxes rose from $3,860 to $26,156 from 1971 to 2001, or an average annual increase of 6.6%. So it was easier for the average person to afford a public institution, where tuition increased 6.1% annually, but more difficult to afford a private institution, where tuition rose 6.9% annually.

Tracking the Macroeconomy

chapter 15

1. Below is a simplified circular-flow diagram for the economy of Micronia.

   a. What is the value of GDP in Micronia?

   b. What is the value of net exports?

   c. What is the value of disposable income?

   d. Does the total flow of money out of households—the sum of taxes paid, consumer spending, and private savings—equal the total flow of money into households?

   e. How does the government of Micronia finance its purchases of goods and services?

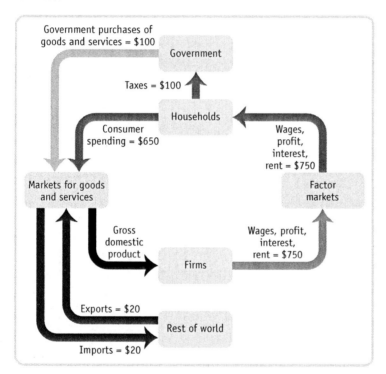

1. a. We can measure GDP in Micronia as the sum of all spending on domestically produced final goods and services. Spending consists of consumer spending, government purchases of goods and services, and exports less imports, or $750 ($650 + $100 + $20 − $20).

   b. Net exports are exports less imports. In Micronia, net exports equal zero ($20 − $20).

   c. Disposable income is income received by households less taxes plus government transfers. In Micronia, disposable income equals $650 ($750 − $100).

   d. Yes, consumer spending plus taxes equals $750—the same as the wages, profit, interest, and rent received by households.

   e. The government finances its purchases of goods and services with tax revenue.

2. A more complex circular-flow diagram for the economy of Macronia is shown below.

   a. What is the value of GDP in Macronia?

   b. What is the value of net exports?

   c. What is the value of disposable income?

   d. Does the total flow of money out of households—the sum of taxes paid, consumer spending, and private savings—equal the total flow of money into households?

   e. How does the government finance its spending?

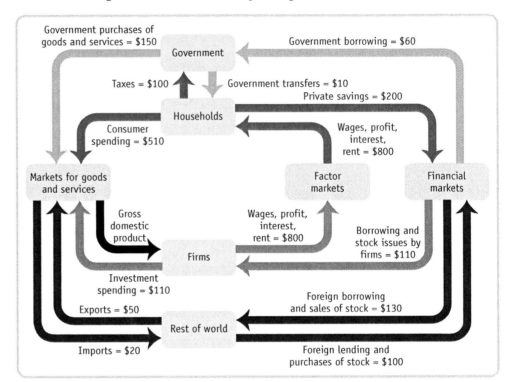

2. **a.** We can measure GDP in Macronia as the sum of all spending on domestically produced final goods and services. Spending consists of consumer spending, investment spending, government purchases of goods and services, and exports less imports, or $800 ($510 + $110 + $150 + $50 − $20).

   b. Net exports are exports less imports. In Macronia, net exports equal $30 ($50 − $20).

   c. Disposable income is income received by households less taxes plus government transfers. In Macronia, disposable income equals $710 ($800 − $100 + $10).

   d. Yes, consumer spending plus taxes plus private savings equals $810—the same as the wages, profit, interest, rent, and government transfers received by households.

   e. In Macronia, the government needs to finance $160 in spending ($150 on purchases of goods and services and $10 in government transfers). The government finances $100 of its spending with tax revenue and the other $60 through borrowing in financial markets.

3. The small economy of Pizzania produces three goods (bread, cheese, and pizza), each produced by a separate company. The bread and cheese companies produce all the inputs they need to make bread and cheese, respectively; the pizza company uses the bread and cheese from the other companies to make its pizzas. All three companies employ labor to help produce their goods, and the difference between the value of goods sold and the sum of labor and input costs is the firm's profit. This table summarizes the activities of the three companies when all the bread and cheese produced are sold to the pizza company as inputs in the production of pizzas.

	Bread company	Cheese company	Pizza company
Cost of inputs	$0	$0	$50 Bread
			35 Cheese
Wages	15	20	75
Value of output	50	35	200

a. Calculate GDP as the value added in production.

b. Calculate GDP as spending on final goods and services.

c. Calculate GDP as factor income.

3. a. To calculate GDP as the value added in production, we need to sum all value added (value of output less input costs) for each company. Value added in the bread company is $50; in the cheese company, $35; and in the pizza company, $115 ($200 − $50 − $35). The total value added in production is $200.

b. To calculate GDP as spending on final goods and services, we only need to estimate the value of pizzas because all bread and cheese produced are intermediate goods used in the production of pizzas. Spending on final goods and services is $200.

c. To calculate GDP as factor income, we need to sum factor income (wages and profits) for each firm. For the bread company, factor income is $50: labor earns $15 and profit is $35. For the cheese company, factor income is $35: labor earns $20 and profit is $15. For the pizza company, factor income is $115; labor earns $75 and profit is $40 ($200 − $75 − $50 − $35). Factor income is $200 ($50 + $35 + $115).

4. In the economy of Pizzania (from Problem 3), bread and cheese produced are sold both to the pizza company for inputs in the production of pizzas and to consumers as final goods. The accompanying table summarizes the activities of the three companies.

	Bread company	Cheese company	Pizza company
Cost of inputs	$0	$0	$50 Bread
			35 Cheese
Wages	25	30	75
Value of output	100	60	200

a. Calculate GDP as the value added in production.

b. Calculate GDP as spending on final goods and services.

c. Calculate GDP as factor income.

4. **a.** To calculate GDP as the value added in production, we need to sum all value added (value of output less input costs) for each company. Value added in the bread company is $100; in the cheese company, $60; and in the pizza company, $115 ($200 − $50 − $35). The total value added in production is $275.

b. To calculate GDP as spending on final goods and services, we need to sum the value of bread, cheese, and pizzas sold as final goods. GDP equals $275 because the bread company sells $50 worth as final goods, the cheese company sells $25 worth as final goods, and all $200 worth of pizzas are final goods.

c. To calculate GDP as factor income, we need to sum factor income (labor and profits) for each firm. For the bread company, factor income is $100: labor earns $25 and profit is $75. For the cheese company, factor income is $60: labor earns $30 and profit is $30. For the pizza company, factor income is $115: labor earns $75 and profit is $40 ($200 − $75 − $50 − $35). As factor income, GDP equals $275 ($100 + $60 + $115).

5. Which of the following transactions will be included in GDP for the United States?

a. Coca-Cola builds a new bottling plant in the United States.

b. Delta sells one of its existing airplanes to Korean Air.

c. Ms. Moneybags buys an existing share of Disney stock.

d. A California winery produces a bottle of Chardonnay and sells it to a customer in Montreal, Canada.

e. An American buys a bottle of French perfume.

f. A book publisher produces too many copies of a new book; the books don't sell this year, so the publisher adds the surplus books to inventories.

5. **a.** When Coca-Cola builds a new bottling plant, it is investment spending and included in GDP.

b. If Delta sells one of its airplanes to Korean Air, this transaction is not included in GDP because it does not represent production during the current time period. The airplane would have been included in GDP when it was produced; now it is just a sale of a used item.

c. When an individual buys an existing share of stock, the transaction is not included in GDP because there is no production.

d. If a California winery sells a bottle of Chardonnay to a customer in Montreal, it is a U.S. export and is entered as such in U.S. GDP.

e. When an American buys a bottle of French perfume, it is a consumption expenditure as measured by GDP. But since it does not represent production in the United States, it is also deducted from GDP as an import. The net effect of the transaction does not change GDP in the United States.

f. If a book publisher produces too many copies of a new book and the books don't sell in the year they are produced, the publisher adds the surplus books to inventories. These books are considered investment spending and added to GDP. It is as if the publisher bought the books itself.

6. The economy of Britannica produces three goods: computers, DVDs, and pizza. The accompanying table shows the prices and output of the three goods for the years 2002, 2003, and 2004.

Year	Computers Price	Computers Quantity	DVDs Price	DVDs Quantity	Pizza Price	Pizza Quantity
2002	$900	10	$10	100	$15	2
2003	1,000	10.5	12	105	16	2
2004	1,050	12	14	110	17	3

a. What is the percent change in production of each of the goods from 2002 to 2003 and from 2003 to 2004?

b. What is the percent change in prices of each of the goods from 2002 to 2003 and from 2003 to 2004?

c. Calculate nominal GDP in Britannica for each of the three years. What is the percent change in nominal GDP from 2002 to 2003 and from 2003 to 2004?

d. Calculate real GDP in Britannica using 2002 prices for each of the three years. What is the percent change in real GDP from 2002 to 2003 and from 2003 to 2004?

6. a. From 2002 to 2003, the percent change in the production of computers is 5.0% (equal to $(10.5 - 10)/10 \times 100$); of DVDs, 5.0% (equal to $(105 - 100)/100 \times 100$); and of pizza, 0% (equal to $(2 - 2)/2 \times 100$). From 2003 to 2004, the percent change in the production of computers is 14.3% (equal to $(12 - 10.5)/10.5 \times 100$); of DVDs, 4.8% (equal to $(110 - 105)/105 \times 100$); and of pizza, 50.0% (equal to $(3 - 2)/2 \times 100$).

b. From 2002 to 2003, the percent change in the price of computers is 11.1% (equal to $(\$1,000 - \$900)/\$900 \times 100$); of DVDs, 20.0% (equal to $(\$12 - \$10)/\$10 \times 100$); and of pizza, 6.7% (equal to $(\$16 - \$15)/\$15 \times 100$). From 2003 to 2004, the percent change in the price of computers is 5.0% (equal to $(\$1,050 - \$1,000)/\$1,000 \times 100$); of DVDs, 16.7% (equal to $(\$14 - \$12)/\$12 \times 100$); and of pizza, 6.25% (equal to $(\$17 - \$16)/\$16 \times 100$).

c. Nominal GDP for each year is calculated by summing up the value of the three goods produced in that year:

Year	Nominal GDP	Nominal GDP rate of change
2002	$10,030	
2003	11,792	17.6%
2004	14,191	20.3%

d. Real GDP in 2002 prices is calculated by summing up the value of the three goods produced each year using 2002 prices:

Year	Real GDP (2002 dollars)	Real GDP rate of change
2002	$10,030	
2003	10,530	5.0%
2004	11,945	13.4%

7. The accompanying table shows data on nominal GDP (in billions of dollars), real GDP (in billions of dollars) using 2000 as the base year, and population (in thousands) of the U.S. in 1960, 1970, 1980, 1990, 2000, and 2004, years in which the U.S. price level consistently rose.

Year	Nominal GDP (billions of dollars)	Real GDP (billions of 2000 dollars)	Population (thousands)
1960	$526.4	$2,501.8	180,671
1970	1,038.5	3,771.9	205,052
1980	2,789.5	5,161.7	227,726
1990	5,803.1	7,112.5	250,132
2000	9,817.0	9,817.0	282,388
2004	11,734.0	10,841.9	293,907

a. Why is real GDP greater than nominal GDP for all years before 2000 and lower for 2004? Does nominal GDP have to equal real GDP in 2000?

b. Calculate the percent change in real GDP from 1960 to 1970, 1970 to 1980, 1980 to 1990, and 1990 to 2000. Which period had the highest growth rate?

c. Calculate real GDP per capita for each of the years in the table.

d. Calculate the percent change in real GDP per capita from 1960 to 1970, 1970 to 1980, 1980 to 1990, and 1990 to 2000. Which period had the highest growth rate?

e. How do the percent change in real GDP and the percent change in real GDP per capita compare? Which is larger? Do we expect them to have this relationship?

7. a. Real GDP is greater than nominal GDP for all years before 2000 because from 1960 to 2000 prices rose. So to calculate real GDP for the years 1960, 1970, 1980, and 1990, we would multiply output in those years by the higher prices that existed in 2000. To calculate nominal GDP, we would multiply output by the lower prices that existed in those particular years. Since prices rose from 2000 to 2004, valuing the output in 2004 using 2000 prices (real GDP) will result in a lower number than valuing the output in 2004 using 2004 prices. Real GDP equals nominal GDP in 2000 because the year 2000 is the base year and we use the same set of prices to value both real and nominal GDP in that year.

b. The accompanying table shows the percent change in real GDP from 1960 to 1970, 1970 to 1980, 1980 to 1990, and 1990 to 2000. The percent change in real GDP was the highest during the 1960s.

Year	Real GDP (billions of 2000 dollars)	Real GDP rate of change
1960	$2,501.8	
1970	3,771.9	50.8%
1980	5,161.7	36.8%
1990	7,112.5	37.8%
2000	9,817.0	38.0%

c. We can calculate real GDP per capita by dividing real GDP by population. The accompanying table shows real GDP per capita for each of the years in the table. Remember that real GDP is measured in billions and population is measured in thousands. Real GDP per capita in 1960 was $13,847.27 ($2,501,800,000,000/180,671,000).

Year	Real GDP (billions of 2000 dollars)	Population (thousands)	Real GDP per capita
1960	$2,501.8	180,671	$13,847.27
1970	3,771.9	205,052	18,394.85
1980	5,161.7	227,726	22,666.27
1990	7,112.5	250,132	28,434.99
2000	9,817.0	282,388	34,764.23
2004	10,841.9	293,907	36,888.88

d. The accompanying table shows the percent change in real GDP per capita from 1960 to 1970, 1970 to 1980, 1980 to 1990, and 1990 to 2000. The percent change in real GDP per capita was the highest during the 1960s.

Year	Real GDP (billions of 2000 dollars)	Population (thousands)	Real GDP per capita	Real GDP per capita rate of change
1960	$2,501.8	180,671	$13,847.27	
1970	3,771.9	205,052	18,394.85	32.8%
1980	5,161.7	227,726	22,666.27	23.2%
1990	7,112.5	250,132	28,434.99	25.5%
2000	9,817.0	282,388	34,764.23	22.3%

e. The percent change in real GDP is always larger than the percent change in GDP per capita; as long as the population is growing, the two will always have this relationship.

8. This table shows the Human Development Index (HDI) and real GDP per capita in U.S. dollars for six nations in 2002.

	HDI	Real GDP per capita
Brazil	0.775	$7,770
Canada	0.943	29,480
Japan	0.938	26,940
Mexico	0.802	8,970
Saudi Arabia	0.768	12,650
United States	0.939	35,750

Rank the nations according to HDI and according to real GDP per capita. Why do the two vary?

8. The accompanying table shows the Human Development Index (HDI) and real GDP per capita in dollars for six nations in 2002, along with their HDI and real GDP per capita rank. The two differ in that a nation's rank in real GDP per capita relates how much production is available per person in that country compared with other nations and the rank in HDI relates how a nation stands relative to various determinants of human welfare (such as infant mortality, life expectancy, and literacy).

	HDI	Real GDP per capita	Rank HDI	Rank real GDP per capita
Brazil	0.775	$7,770	5	6
Canada	0.943	29,480	1	2
Japan	0.938	26,940	3	3
Mexico	0.802	8,970	4	5
Saudi Arabia	0.768	12,650	6	4
United States	0.939	35,750	2	1

9. In general, how do changes in the unemployment rate vary with changes in real GDP? After several quarters of a severe recession, explain why we might observe a decrease in the official unemployment rate. Could we see an increase in the official unemployment rate after several quarters of a strong expansion?

9. In general, the change in the unemployment rate varies inversely with the rate of growth in real GDP: when the economy is growing, we expect the unemployment rate to be falling rapidly. However, after several quarters of a severe recession, unemployed workers may become discouraged and stop looking for work. Since the definition of unemployed persons requires that they be looking for work, unemployment falls as workers become discouraged and stop looking. We could see an increase in the official unemployment rate after several quarters of a strong expansion as existing workers, encouraged by an increase in wages to attract new workers, leave existing jobs to search for new ones and discouraged workers begin to search for a job again.

10. Each month, usually on the first Friday of the month, the Bureau of Labor Statistics releases the Employment Situation Summary for the previous month. Go to www.bls.gov and find the latest report. (On the Bureau of Labor Statistics home page, click on "National unemployment rate" and then choose "Employment Situation Summary.") How does the unemployment rate compare to the rate one year earlier? What percentage of unemployed workers are long-term unemployed workers?

10. Answers will vary with the latest data. For September 2005, the unemployment rate was 5.1%, unchanged from September 2004 when it was also 5.1%. The number of long-term unemployed workers represented 19.4% of the unemployed in September 2005.

11. Eastland College is concerned about the rising price of textbooks that students must purchase. To better identify the increase in the price of textbooks, the dean asks you, the Economics Department's star student, to create an index of textbook prices. The average student purchases three English, two math, and four economics textbooks. The prices of these books are given in the accompanying table.

	2002	2003	2004
English textbook	$50	$55	$57
Math textbook	70	72	74
Economics textbook	80	90	100

a. Create the price index for these books for all years with a base year of 2002.

b. What is the percent change in the price of an English textbook from 2002 to 2004?

c. What is the percent change in the price of a math textbook from 2002 to 2004?

d. What is the percent change in the price of an economics textbook from 2002 to 2004?

e. What is the percent change in the market index from 2002 to 2004?

11. a. To create an index of textbook prices, you must first calculate the cost of the market basket (three English, two math, and four economics textbooks) in each of the three years; then normalize it by dividing the cost of the market basket in a given year by the cost of the market basket in the base period; and then multiply by 100 to get an index value (base period of 2002 = 100).

$$\text{Cost of textbooks in 2002} = 3 \times \$50 + 2 \times \$70 + 4 \times \$80 = \$610$$
$$\text{Cost of textbooks in 2003} = 3 \times \$55 + 2 \times \$72 + 4 \times \$90 = \$669$$
$$\text{Cost of textbooks in 2004} = 3 \times \$57 + 2 \times \$74 + 4 \times \$100 = \$719$$

$$\text{Index value for 2002} = \$610/\$610 \times 100 = 100$$
$$\text{Index value for 2003} = \$669/\$610 \times 100 = 109.7$$
$$\text{Index value for 2004} = \$719/\$610 \times 100 = 117.9$$

b. The percent change in the price of an English textbook from 2002 to 2004 is 14.0% (equal to ($57 − $50)/$50 × 100).

c. The percent change in the price of a math textbook from 2002 to 2004 is 5.7% (equal to ($74 − $70)/$70 × 100).

d. The percent change in the price of an economics textbook from 2002 to 2004 is 25% (equal to ($100 − $80)/$80 × 100).

e. The percent change in the market index for textbooks from 2002 to 2004 is 17.9% (equal to (117.9 − 100)/100 × 100).

12. The consumer price index, or CPI, measures the cost of living for the average consumer by multiplying the price for each category of expenditure (housing, food, and so on) times a measure of the importance of that expenditure in the average consumer's market basket and summing over all categories. However, using data from the consumer price index, we can see that changes in the cost of living for different types of consumers can vary a great deal. Let's compare the cost of living for a hypothetical retired person and a hypothetical college student. Let's assume that the market basket of a retired person is allocated in the following way: 10% on housing, 15% on food,

5% on transportation, 60% on medical care, 0% on education, and 10% on recreation. The college student's market basket is allocated as follows: 5% on housing, 15% on food, 20% on transportation, 0% on medical care, 40% on education, and 20% on recreation. The accompanying table shows the December 2004 CPI for each of the relevant categories.

	CPI, December 2004
Housing	190.7
Food	188.9
Transportation	164.8
Medical care	314.9
Education	112.6
Recreation	108.5

Calculate the overall CPI for the retired person and for the college student by multiplying the CPI for each of the categories by the relative importance of that category to the individual and then summing each of the categories. The CPI for all items in December 2004 was 190.3. How do your calculations for a CPI for the retired person and the college student compare to the overall CPI?

12. To calculate the CPI for the retired person and for the college student, we need to weight the CPI for each component with the importance of that component in his or her market basket. The CPI for the retired person is 255.45 and for the college student is 138.58. Since the CPI for the average consumer was 190.3, the CPI overstates the increase in the cost of living for the college student and understates it for the retired person.

For the retired person:

	Weight	CPI—December 2004	CPI for retired person
Housing	0.10	190.7	19.07
Food	0.15	188.9	28.34
Transportation	0.05	164.8	8.24
Medical Care	0.60	314.9	188.94
Education	0.00	112.6	0.00
Recreation	0.10	108.5	10.85
			255.44

For the college student:

	Weight	CPI—December 2004	CPI for college student
Housing	0.05	190.7	9.54
Food	0.15	188.9	28.34
Transportation	0.20	164.8	32.96
Medical Care	0.00	314.9	0.00
Education	0.40	112.6	45.04
Recreation	0.20	108.5	21.70
			137.58

13. Each month the Bureau of Labor Statistics releases the Consumer Price Index Summary for the previous month. Go to www.bls.gov and find the latest report. (On the Bureau of Labor Statistics home page, click on "CPI" under "Latest Numbers" and then choose "Consumer Price Index Summary.") What was the CPI for the previous month? How did it change from the previous month? How does the CPI compare to the same month one year ago?

13. Answers will vary with the latest data. For September 2005, the CPI was 198.8; it rose 1.2% from August 2005. The CPI was 4.7% higher than in September 2004.

14. The accompanying table contains two price indexes for the years 2002, 2003, and 2004: the GDP deflator and the CPI. For each price index, calculate the inflation rate from 2002 to 2003 and from 2003 to 2004.

Year	GDP deflator	CPI
2002	104.1	179.9
2003	106.0	184.0
2004	108.3	188.9

14. The accompanying table calculates the inflation rates based on the GDP deflator and on the CPI.

Year	GDP deflator	Inflation rate (based on GDP deflator)	CPI	Inflation rate (based on CPI)
2002	104.1		179.9	
2003	106.0	1.8%	184.0	2.3%
2004	108.3	2.2%	188.9	2.7%

Aggregate Supply and Aggregate Demand

1. Your study partner is confused by the upward-sloping short-run aggregate supply curve and the vertical long-run aggregate supply curve. How would you explain this?

1. The short-run aggregate supply curve slopes upward because nominal wages are sticky in the short run. Nominal wages are fixed by either formal contracts or informal agreements in the short run. So, as the aggregate price level falls and nominal wages remain the same, production costs will not fall by the same proportion as the aggregate price level. This will reduce profit per unit of output, leading producers to reduce output in the short run. Similarly, as the aggregate price level rises, production costs will not rise by the same proportion because nominal wages will remain fixed in the short run. Profit per unit of output will increase, leading producers to increase output in the short run. So there is a positive relationship between the aggregate price level and the quantity of aggregate output producers are willing to supply in the short run because nominal wages are fixed. However, in the long run, nominal wages can and will be renegotiated. Nominal wages will change along with the aggregate price level. As the aggregate price level rises, production costs will rise by the same proportion. When the aggregate price level and production costs rise by the same percentage, every unit of output that had been profitable to produce before the price rise is still profitable, and every unit of output that had been unprofitable to produce before the price rise is still unprofitable. So aggregate output does not change. In the long run, when nominal wages are perfectly flexible, an increase or decrease in the aggregate price level will not change the quantity of aggregate output produced. So the long-run aggregate supply curve is vertical.

2. Suppose that in Wageland all workers sign annual wage contracts each year on January 1. No matter what happens to prices of final goods and services during the year, all workers earn the wage specified in their annual contract. This year, prices of final goods and services fall unexpectedly after the contracts are signed. Answer the following questions using a diagram and assume that the economy starts at potential output.

   a. In the short run, how will the quantity of aggregate output supplied respond to the fall in prices?

   b. What will happen when firms and workers renegotiate their wages?

2. **a.** In the short run, the prices of final goods and services in Wageland fall unexpectedly but nominal wages don't change; they are fixed in the short run by the annual contract. So firms earn a lower profit per unit and reduce output. In the accompanying diagram, Wageland moves along $SRAS_1$ from point A on January 1 to point B after the fall in prices.

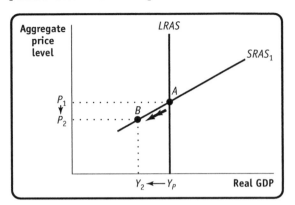

b. When firms and workers renegotiate their wages, nominal wages will decrease, shifting the short-run aggregate supply curve rightward from $SRAS_1$ to a curve such as $SRAS_2$.

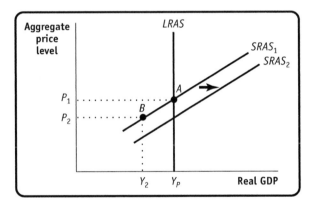

3. In each of the following cases, in the short run, determine whether the events cause a shift of a curve or a movement along a curve. Determine which curve is involved and the direction of the change.

a. As a result of an increase in the value of the dollar in relation to other currencies, American producers now pay less in dollar terms for foreign steel, a major commodity used in production.

b. An increase in the quantity of money by the Federal Reserve increases the quantity of money that people wish to lend, lowering interest rates.

c. Greater union activity leads to higher nominal wages.

d. A fall in the aggregate price level increases the purchasing power of households' money holdings. As a result, they borrow less and lend more.

3. **a.** As the value of the dollar in terms of other currencies increases and American producers pay less in dollar terms for foreign steel, producers' profit per unit increases and they are willing to supply a greater quantity of aggregate output at any given aggregate price level. The short-run aggregate supply curve will shift to the right.

b. As the Federal Reserve increases the quantity of money, households and firms have more money, which they are willing to lend out, and interest rates fall. The lower interest rates will increase investment spending and consumer spending, leading to a greater quantity of aggregate output demanded at any given aggregate price level. The aggregate demand curve will shift to the right.

c. If unions are able to negotiate higher nominal wages for a large portion of the workforce, this will increase production costs and reduce profit per unit at any given aggregate price level. The short-run aggregate supply curve will shift to the left.

d. As the aggregate price level falls and the purchasing power of households' and firms' money holdings increases, the public tries to reduce its money holdings by borrowing less and lending more. So interest rates fall, leading to a rise in both investment spending and consumer spending. This is the interest rate effect of a change in the aggregate price level, represented as a movement down along the aggregate demand curve.

4. A fall in the value of the dollar against other currencies makes U.S. final goods and services cheaper to foreigners even though the U.S. aggregate price level stays the same. As a result, foreigners demand more American aggregate output. Your study partner says that this represents a movement down the aggregate demand curve because foreigners are demanding more in response to a lower price. You, however, insist that this represents a rightward shift of the aggregate demand curve. Who is right? Explain.

4. You are right. When a fall in the value of the dollar against other currencies makes U.S. final goods and services cheaper to foreigners, this represents a shift of the aggregate demand curve. Although foreigners may be demanding more U.S. goods because the price of those goods in their own currency is lower, there is no change in the U.S. aggregate price level. From the U.S. perspective, there is an increase in aggregate output demanded at any given aggregate price level.

5. Suppose that local, state and federal governments were obliged to cut government purchases whenever consumer spending falls. Then suppose that consumer spending falls due to a fall in the stock market. Draw a diagram and explain the full effect of the fall in the stock market on the aggregate demand curve and on the economy. How is this similar to the experience of stagflation in the 1970s?

5. If a fall in the stock market reduces consumer spending, the aggregate demand curve will shift to the left from AD_1 to AD_2 in the accompanying diagram. At any given aggregate price level, consumer spending is lower and the amount of aggregate output demanded falls. However, if governments must cut government purchases whenever consumer spending falls, this will lead to a further leftward shift of the aggregate demand curve from AD_2 to AD_3. At any given aggregate price level, government purchases are lower and the amount of aggregate output demanded falls again. This is similar to the "knock on" effect during the stagflation of the 1970s in that one adverse change led to another. The increase in the price of oil during the 1970s reduced short-run aggregate supply (the short-run aggregate supply curve shifted leftward) and raised aggregate prices. At this time many wage contracts included cost-of-living allowances that automatically raised the nominal wage when consumer prices increased. As nominal wages rose, there was a second leftward shift of the short-run aggregate supply curve.

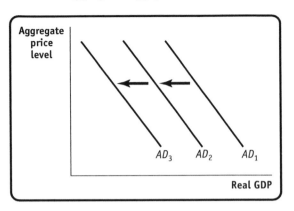

6. Due to an increase in consumer wealth, there is a $40 billion autonomous increase in consumer spending in the economies of Westlandia and Eastlandia. Assuming that the aggregate price level is constant, the interest rate is fixed in both countries, and there are no taxes and no foreign trade, complete the accompanying tables to show the various rounds of increased spending that will occur in both economies if the marginal propensity to consume is 0.5 in Westlandia and 0.75 in Eastlandia. What do your results indicate about the relationship between the size of the marginal propensity to consume and the multiplier?

Westlandia

Rounds	Incremental change in GDP		Total change in GDP
1	$\Delta C = \$40$ billion		?
2	$MPC \times \Delta C =$	?	?
3	$MPC \times MPC \times \Delta C =$	?	?
4	$MPC \times MPC \times MPC \times \Delta C =$	?	?
. . .		. . .	. . .
Total change in GDP	$(1/(1 - MPC)) \times \Delta C =$		?

Eastlandia

Rounds	Incremental change in GDP		Total change in GDP
1	$\Delta C = \$40$ billion		?
2	$MPC \times \Delta C =$	?	?
3	$MPC \times MPC \times \Delta C =$	?	?
4	$MPC \times MPC \times MPC \times \Delta C =$	?	?
. . .	. . .	. . .	
Total change in GDP	$(1/(1 - MPC)) \times \Delta C =$		?

6.

Westlandia

Rounds	Incremental change in GDP	Total change in GDP
1	$\Delta C = \$40$ billion	$40 billion
2	$MPC \times \Delta C = \$20$ billion	$60 billion
3	$MPC \times MPC \times \Delta C = \$10$ billion	$70 billion
4	$MPC \times MPC \times MPC \times \Delta C = \$5$ billion	$75 billion
. . .	. . .	. . .

Total change in GDP $(1/(1 - MPC)) \times \Delta C - 1/(1 - 0.5) \times \$40$ billion   **$80 billion**

Eastlandia

Rounds	Incremental change in GDP	Total change in GDP
1	$\Delta C = \$40$ billion	$40 billion
2	$MPC \times \Delta C = \$30$ billion	$70 billion
3	$MPC \times MPC \times \Delta C = \$22.5$ billion	$92.5 billion
4	$MPC \times MPC \times MPC \times \Delta C = \$16.88$ billion	$109.38 billion
. . .	. . .	. . .

Total change in GDP $(1/(1 - MPC)) \times \Delta C = 1/(1 - 0.75) \times \$40$ billion   **$160 billion**

The accompanying tables clearly show that the larger the marginal propensity to consume, the larger the size of the multiplier. In Westlandia, with the marginal propensity to consume of 0.5, the multiplier equals 2. In Eastlandia, with the marginal propensity to consume of 0.75, the multiplier equals 4.

7. Assuming that the aggregate price level is constant, the interest rate is fixed, and there are no taxes and no foreign trade, how much will the aggregate demand curve shift and in what direction if the following events occur?

a. An autonomous increase in consumer spending of $25 billion; the marginal propensity to consume is 2/3.

b. Firms reduce investment spending by $40 billion; the marginal propensity to consume is 0.8.

c. The government increases its purchases of military equipment by $60 billion; the marginal propensity to consume is 0.6.

7. a. An autonomous increase in consumer spending of $25 billion, with a marginal propensity to consume of 2/3, will shift the aggregate demand curve to the right by $75 billion.

Total change in real GDP $= (1/(1 - MPC)) \times \Delta C$

Total change in real GDP $= (1/(1 - 2/3)) \times \$25$ billion

Total change in real GDP $= 3 \times \$25$ billion

Total change in real GDP $= \$75$ billion

b. If firms reduce investment spending by $40 billion and the marginal propensity to consume is 0.8, the aggregate demand curve will shift to the left by $200 billion.

Total change in GDP = $(1/(1 - MPC)) \times \Delta I$

Total change in GDP = $(1/(1 - 0.8)) \times (-\$40 \text{ billion})$

Total change in GDP = $5 \times (-\$40 \text{ billion})$

Total change in GDP = $-\$200$ billion

c. If government purchases of goods and services rise by $60 billion and the marginal propensity to consume is 0.6, the aggregate demand curve will shift to the right by $150 billion.

Total change in GDP = $(1/(1 - MPC)) \times \Delta G$

Total change in GDP = $(1/(1 - 0.6)) \times \$60 \text{ billion}$

Total change in GDP = $2.5 \times \$60 \text{ billion}$

Total change in GDP = $\$150$ billion

8. The economy is at point A in the accompanying diagram. Suppose that the aggregate price level rises from P_1 to P_2. How will aggregate supply adjust in the short run and in the long run to the increase in the aggregate price level?

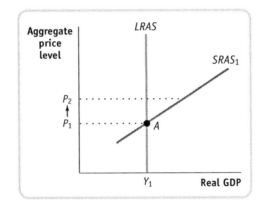

8. In the short run, as the aggregate price level rises from P_1 to P_2, nominal wages will not change. So profit per unit will rise, leading to an increase in production from Y_1 to Y_2. The economy will move from point A to point B in the accompanying diagram. In the long run, however, nominal wages will be renegotiated upward in reaction to low unemployment at Y_2. As nominal wages increase, the short-run aggregate supply curve will shift leftward from $SRAS_1$ to a position such as $SRAS_2$. The exact position of $SRAS_2$ depends on factors such as the aggregate demand curve.

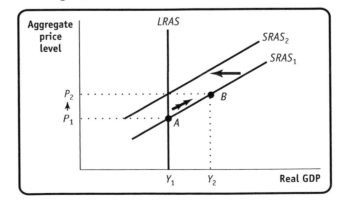

9. Suppose that all households hold all their wealth in assets that automatically rise in value when the aggregate price level rises (an example of this is what is called an "inflation-indexed bond"—a bond whose interest rate, among other things, changes one-for-one with the inflation rate). What happens to the wealth effect of a change in the aggregate price level as a result of this allocation of assets? What happens to the slope of the aggregate demand curve? Will it still slope downward? Explain.

9. If all households hold all their wealth in assets that automatically rise in value when the aggregate price level rises, this will eliminate the wealth effect of a change in the aggregate price level. The purchasing power of consumers' wealth will not vary with a change in the aggregate price level, so there will be no change in consumer spending due to the change in the aggregate price level. The aggregate demand curve will still slope downward because of the interest rate effect of a change in the aggregate price level. As the aggregate price level rises, the purchasing power of households' money holdings will decrease and they will be eager to borrow more and lend less, increasing interest rates. The increase in interest rates will discourage investment spending and consumer spending. The aggregate demand curve will be steeper because the wealth effect of a change in the aggregate price level has been eliminated. As prices rise, the amount of aggregate output demanded will fall by a smaller amount, an amount corresponding to the interest rate effect of a change in the aggregate price level.

10. Suppose that the economy is currently at potential output. Also suppose that you are an economic policy maker and that a college economics student asks you to rank, if possible, your most preferred to least preferred type of shock: positive demand shock, negative demand shock, positive supply shock, negative supply shock. How would you rank them and why?

10. The most preferred shock would be a positive supply shock. The economy would have higher aggregate output without the danger of inflation. The government would not need to respond with a change in policy. The least preferred shock would be a negative supply shock. The economy would experience stagflation. There would be lower aggregate output and inflation. There is no good policy remedy for a negative supply shock: policies to counteract the slump in aggregate output would worsen inflation, and policies to counteract inflation would further depress aggregate output. It is unclear how economic policy makers would rank positive and negative demand shocks. A positive demand shock brings a higher level of aggregate output but at a higher aggregate price level. A negative demand shock brings a lower level of aggregate output but at a lower aggregate price level. With either a positive or negative demand shock, policy makers could try to use either monetary or fiscal policy to lessen the effects of the shock.

11. Explain whether the following government policies affect the aggregate demand curve or the short-run aggregate supply curve and how.

a. The government reduces the minimum nominal wage.

b. The government increases Temporary Assistance to Needy Families (TANF) payments, government transfers to families with dependent children.

c. To reduce the budget deficit, the government announces that households will pay much higher taxes beginning next year.

d. The government reduces military spending.

11. a. If the government reduces the minimum nominal wage, it is similar to a fall in nominal wages. Aggregate supply will increase, and the short-run aggregate supply curve will shift to the right.

b. If the government increases TANF, consumer spending will increase because disposable income increases (disposable income equals income plus government transfers, such as TANF payments, less taxes). Aggregate demand will increase, and the aggregate demand curve will shift to the right.

c. If the government announces a large increase in taxes on households for next year, consumer spending will fall this year. Since households base their spending in part on their expectations about the future, the anticipated increase in taxes will lower their spending this year. There will be a decrease in aggregate demand and the aggregate demand curve will shift to the left.

d. If the government reduces military spending, this will decrease aggregate demand. The amount of aggregate output demanded at any given aggregate price level will fall and the aggregate demand curve will shift to the left.

12. In Wageland, all workers sign an annual wage contract each year on January 1. In late January, a new computer operating system is introduced that increases labor productivity dramatically. Explain how Wageland will move from one short-run macroeconomic equilibrium to another. Illustrate with a diagram.

12. As labor productivity increases, producers will experience a reduction in production costs and profit per unit of output will increase. Producers will respond by increasing the quantity of aggregate output supplied at any given aggregate price level. The short-run aggregate supply curve will shift to the right. Beginning at short-run equilibrium, E_1 in the accompanying diagram, the short-run aggregate supply curve will shift from $SRAS_1$ to $SRAS_2$. The aggregate price level will fall, and real GDP will increase in the short run.

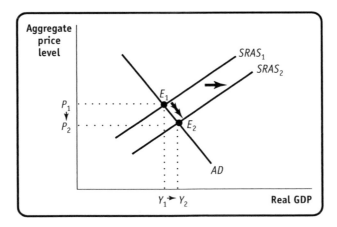

13. Using aggregate demand, short-run aggregate supply, and long-run aggregate supply curves, explain the process by which each of the following economic events will move the economy from one long-run macroeconomic equilibrium to another. Illustrate with diagrams. In each case, what are the short-run and long-run effects on the aggregate price level and aggregate output?

a. There is a decrease in households' wealth due to a decline in the stock market.

b. The government lowers taxes, leaving households with more disposable income, with no corresponding reduction in government purchases.

13. a. A decrease in households' wealth will reduce consumer spending. Beginning at long-run macroeconomic equilibrium, E_1 in the accompanying diagram, the aggregate demand curve will shift from AD_1 to AD_2. In the short run, nominal wages are sticky, and the economy will be in short-run macroeconomic equilibrium at point E_2. The aggregate price level will be lower than at E_1, and aggregate output will be lower than potential output. The economy faces a recessionary gap. As wage contracts are renegotiated, nominal wages will fall and the short-run aggregate supply curve will shift gradually to the right over time until it reaches $SRAS_2$ and intersects AD_2 at point E_3. At E_3, the economy is back at its potential output but at a much lower aggregate price level.

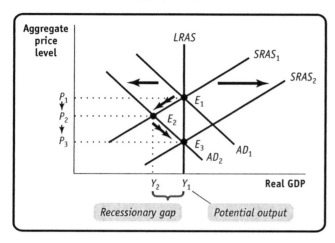

b. An increase in disposable income will increase consumer spending; at any given aggregate price level, the aggregate demand curve will shift to the right. Beginning at long-run macroeconomic equilibrium E_1 in the accompanying diagram, the aggregate demand curve will shift from AD_1 to AD_2. In the short run, nominal wages are sticky, and the economy will be in short-run macroeconomic equilibrium at point E_2. The aggregate price level is higher than at E_1, and aggregate output will be higher than potential output. The economy faces an inflationary gap. As wage contracts are renegotiated, nominal wages will rise and the short-run aggregate supply curve will shift gradually to the left over time until it reaches $SRAS_2$ and intersects AD_2 at point E_3. At E_3, the economy is back at its potential output but at a much higher aggregate price level.

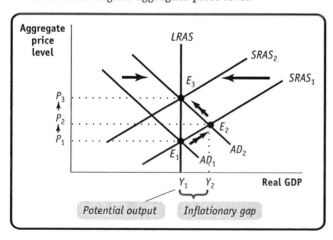

14. Using aggregate demand, short-run aggregate supply, and long-run aggregate supply curves, explain the process by which each of the following government policies will move the economy from one long-run macroeconomic equilibrium to another. Illustrate with diagrams. In each case, what are the short-run and long-run effects on the aggregate price level and aggregate output?

a. There is an increase in taxes on households.

b. There is an increase in the quantity of money.

c. There is an increase in government spending.

14. a. An increase in taxes will decrease consumer spending by households. Beginning at E_1 in the accompanying diagram, the aggregate demand curve will shift left from AD_1 to AD_2. In the short run, nominal wages are sticky, and the economy will be in short-run macroeconomic equilibrium at point E_2. The aggregate price level is lower than at E_1, and aggregate output is lower than potential output. The economy faces a recessionary gap. As wage contracts are renegotiated, nominal wages will fall and the short-run aggregate supply curve will shift gradually to the right over time until it reaches $SRAS_2$ and intersects AD_2 at point E_3. At E_3, the economy is back at its potential output but at a much lower aggregate price level.

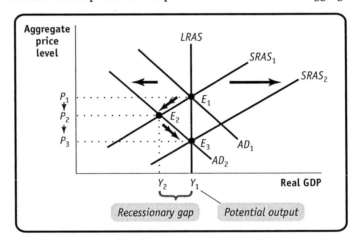

b. An increase in the quantity of money will encourage people to lend, lowering interest rates and increasing investment and consumer spending; at any given aggregate price level, the quantity of aggregate output demanded will be higher. Beginning at long-run macroeconomic equilibrium E_1 in the accompanying diagram, the aggregate demand curve will shift from AD_1 to AD_2. In the short run, nominal wages are sticky, and the economy will be in short-run macroeconomic equilibrium at point E_2. The aggregate price level is higher than at E_1, and aggregate output is higher than potential output. The economy faces an inflationary gap. As wage contracts are renegotiated, nominal wages will rise and the short-run aggregate supply curve will shift gradually to the left over time until it reaches $SRAS_2$ and intersects AD_2 at point E_3. At E_3, the economy is back at its potential output but at a much higher aggregate price level.

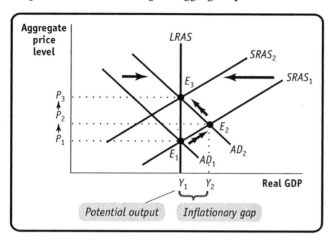

c. An increase in government spending will increase aggregate demand; at any given aggregate price level, the quantity of aggregate output demanded will be higher. Beginning at long-run macroeconomic equilibrium, E_1 in the accompanying diagram, the aggregate demand curve will shift from AD_1 to AD_2. In the short run, nominal wages are sticky, and the economy will be in short-run macroeconomic equilibrium at point E_2. The aggregate price level is higher than at E_1, and aggregate output is higher than potential output. The economy faces an inflationary gap. As wage contracts are renegotiated, nominal wages will rise and the short-run aggregate supply curve will shift gradually to the left over time until it reaches $SRAS_2$ and intersects AD_2 at point E_3. At E_3, the economy is back at its potential output but at a much higher aggregate price level.

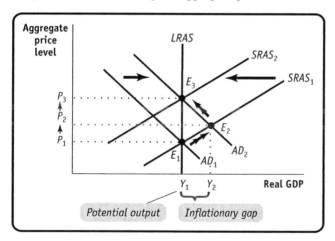

15. The economy is in short-run macroeconomic equilibrium at point E_1 in the accompanying diagram.

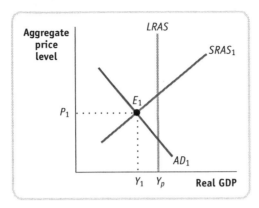

a. Is the economy facing an inflationary or a recessionary gap?

b. What policies can the government implement that might bring the economy back to long-run macroeconomic equilibrium? Illustrate with a diagram.

c. If the government did not intervene to close this gap, would the economy return to long-run macroeconomic equilibrium? Explain and illustrate with a diagram.

d. What are the advantages and disadvantages of the government's implementing policies to close the gap?

15. a. The economy is facing a recessionary gap because Y_1 is less than the potential output of the economy, Y_P.

b. The government could use either fiscal policy (increases in government spending or reductions in taxes) or monetary policy (increases in the quantity of money in circulation to reduce the interest rate) to move the aggregate demand curve from AD_1 to AD_2 in the accompanying diagram. This will move the economy back to potential output, and the aggregate price level will rise from P_1 to P_2.

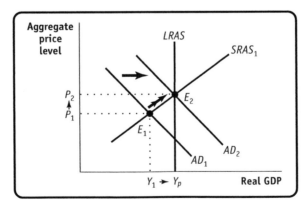

c. If the government did not intervene to close the recessionary gap, the economy would eventually self-correct and move back to potential output on its own. Due to unemployment, nominal wages will fall in the long run. The short-run aggregate supply curve will shift to the right, and eventually it will shift from $SRAS_1$ to $SRAS_2$ in the accompanying diagram. The economy will be back at potential output but at a lower aggregate price level.

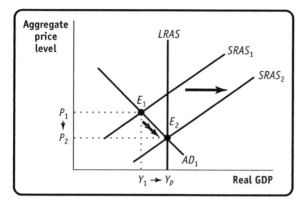

d. If the government implements fiscal or monetary policies to move the economy back to long-run macroeconomic equilibrium, the recessionary gap may be eliminated faster than if the economy were left to adjust on its own. However, because policy makers aren't perfectly informed and policy effects can be unpredictable, policies to close the recessionary gap can lead to greater macronomic instability. Furthermore, if the government uses fiscal or monetary policies, the price level will be higher than it will be if the economy is left to return to long-run macroeconomic equilibrium by itself. In addition, a policy that increases the budget deficit may lead to lower long-run growth through crowding-out.

16. In the accompanying diagram, the economy is in long-run macroeconomic equilibrium at point E_1 when an oil shock shifts the short-run aggregate supply curve to $SRAS_2$.

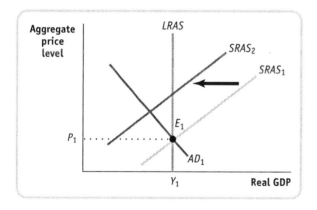

a. How do the aggregate price level and aggregate output change in the short run as a result of the oil shock? What is this phenomenon known as?

b. What fiscal or monetary policies can the government use to address the effects of the supply shock? Use a diagram that shows the effect of policies chosen to address the change in real GDP. Use another diagram to show the effect of policies chosen to address the change in the aggregate price level.

c. Why do supply shocks present a dilemma for government policy makers?

16. **a.** As a result of the increase in the price of oil and the shift to the left of the short-run aggregate supply curve, real GDP decreases to Y_2 (and with it unemployment rises) and the aggregate price level increases to P_2 as shown in the accompanying diagram. This combined problem of inflation and unemployment is known as stagflation.

b. The government can use fiscal and monetary policies to either increase real GDP or lower the aggregate price level, but not both. If the government increases government spending, decreases taxes, or increases the quantity of money in circulation, it can raise real GDP but it will also raise the aggregate price level. This is illustrated in the accompanying diagram by the rightward shift of AD_1 to AD_2.

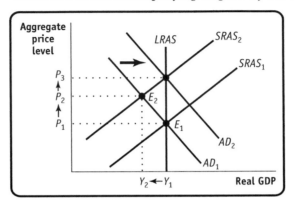

If the government decreases government spending, increases taxes, or decreases the quantity of money in circulation, it can lower the aggregate price level but it will also lower real GDP, worsening the recessionary gap. This is illustrated in the accompanying diagram by the leftward shift of AD_1 to AD_3.

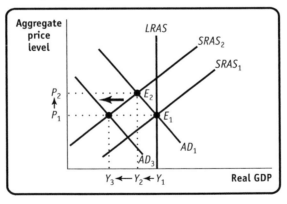

c. The government cannot use fiscal and monetary policies to correct for the lower real GDP and higher aggregate price level simultaneously. It can only use policies to alleviate one problem but at the expense of making the other worse.

17. The late 1990s in the United States were characterized by substantial economic growth with low inflation; that is, real GDP increased with little, if any, increase in the aggregate price level. Explain this experience using aggregate demand and aggregate supply curves. Illustrate with a diagram.

17. Increases in both long-run and short-run aggregate supply, along with increases in aggregate demand, can explain how real GDP grew with little if any increase in the aggregate price level. The accompanying diagram shows how the economy could move from one long-run macroeconomic equilibrium, point E_1, to another, point E_2, with an increase in real GDP and no increase in the aggregate price level. This may explain the U.S. experience during the late 1990s. During this time, increases in productivity due to increasing use of information technology may have shifted the long-run and short-run aggregate supply curves; simultaneously, increases in stock values may have led to increases in consumer spending and a shift to the right of the aggregate demand curve.

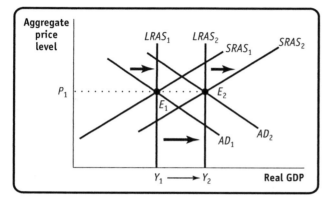

Fiscal Policy

1. The accompanying diagram shows the current macroeconomic situation for the economy of Albernia. You have been hired as an economic consultant to help the economy move to potential output, Y_P.

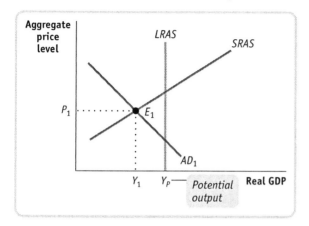

a. Is Albernia facing a recessionary or inflationary gap?

b. Which type of fiscal policy—expansionary or contractionary—would move the economy of Albernia to potential output, Y_E? What are some examples of such policies?

c. Illustrate the macroeconomic situation in Albernia with a diagram after the successful fiscal policy has been implemented.

Solution

1. **a.** Albernia is facing a recessionary gap; Y_1 is less than Y_P.

b. Albernia could use expansionary fiscal policies to move the economy to potential output. Such policies include increasing government purchases of goods and services, increasing government transfers, and reducing taxes.

c.

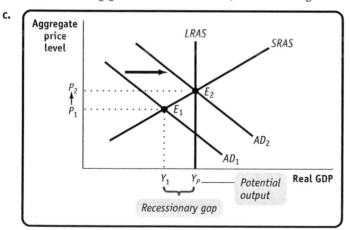

2. The accompanying diagram shows the current macroeconomic situation for the economy of Brittania; real GDP is Y_1 and the aggregate price level is P_1. You have been hired as an economic consultant to help the economy move to potential output, Y_P.

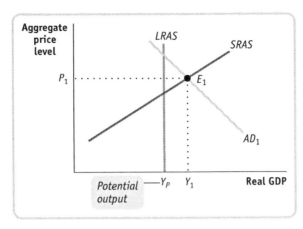

a. Is Brittania facing a recessionary or inflationary gap?

b. Which type of fiscal policy—expansionary or contractionary—would move the economy of Brittania to potential output, Y_P? What are some examples of such policies?

c. Illustrate the macroeconomic situation in Brittania with a diagram after the successful fiscal policy has been implemented.

2. a. Brittania is facing an inflationary gap; Y_1 is greater than Y_P.

b. Brittania could use contractionary fiscal policies to move the economy to potential output. Such policies include reducing government purchases of goods and services, lowering government transfers, and raising taxes.

c.

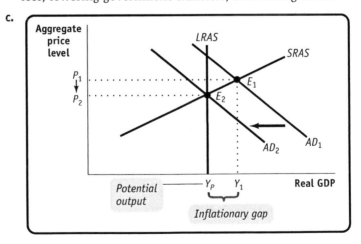

3. An economy is in long-run macroeconomic equilibrium when each of the following aggregate demand shocks occurs. What kind of gap—inflationary or recessionary—will the economy face after the shock, and what type of fiscal policies would help move the economy back to potential output?

a. A stock market boom increases the value of stocks held by households.

b. Firms come to believe that a recession in the near future is likely.

c. Anticipating the possibility of war, the government increases its purchases of military equipment.

d. Interest rates increase.

3. **a.** As the stock market booms and the value of stocks held by households increases, there will be an increase in consumer spending; this will shift the aggregate demand curve to the right. The economy will face an inflationary gap. Policy makers could use contractionary fiscal policies to move the economy back to potential output.

b. If firms become concerned about a recession in the near future, they will decrease investment spending and aggregate demand will shift to the left. The economy will face a recessionary gap. Policy makers could use expansionary fiscal policies to move the economy back to potential output.

c. If the government increases its purchases of military equipment, the aggregate demand curve will shift to the right. The economy will face an inflationary gap. Policy makers could use contractionary fiscal policies to move the economy back to potential output. The government would need to reduce its purchases of nondefense goods and services, raise taxes or reduce transfers.

d. As interest rates rise, investment spending will decrease and the aggregate demand curve will shift to the left. The economy will face a recessionary gap. Policy makers could use expansionary fiscal policies to move the economy back to potential output.

4. Show why a $10 billion decrease in government purchases will have a larger effect on real GDP than a $10 billion reduction in government transfers by completing the table at the top of page 451 for an economy with a marginal propensity to consume (MPC) of 0.6. The first and second rows of the table are filled in for you: in the first row, the $10 billion decrease in government purchases decreases real GDP and disposable income, YD, by $10 billion, leading to a decrease in consumer spending of $6 billion (MPC × change in disposable income) in row 2. However, the $10 billion reduction in transfers has no effect on real GDP in round 1 but does lower YD by $10 billion, resulting in a decrease in consumer spending of $6 billion in round 2.

	Decrease in G = −$10 billion			Decrease in TR = −$10 billion		
	Billions of dollars			Billions of dollars		
Rounds	Change in G	Change in real GDP	Change in YD	Change in TR	Change in real GDP	Change in YD
1	$\Delta G = -\$10.00$	−$10.00	−$10.00	$\Delta TR = -\$10.00$	$0.00	−$10.00
2	$\Delta C = 6.00$	−6.00	−6.00	$\Delta C = -6.00$	−6.00	−6.00
3	$\Delta C = ?$	?	?	$\Delta C = ?$	?	?
4	$\Delta C = ?$	?	?	$\Delta C = ?$	?	?
5	$\Delta C = ?$	?	?	$\Delta C = ?$	?	?
6	$\Delta C = ?$	?	?	$\Delta C = ?$	?	?
7	$\Delta C = ?$	?	?	$\Delta C = ?$	?	?
8	$\Delta C = ?$	?	?	$\Delta C = ?$	?	?
9	$\Delta C = ?$	?	?	$\Delta C = ?$	?	?
10	$\Delta C = ?$	?	?	$\Delta C = ?$	?	?

a. When government purchases decrease by $10 billion, what is the sum of the changes in real GDP after the 10 rounds?

b. When the government reduces transfers by $10 billion, what is the sum of the changes in real GDP after the 10 rounds?

c. Using the formula for the multiplier for changes in government purchases and for changes in transfers, calculate the total change in real GDP due to the $10 billion decrease in government purchases and the $10 billion reduction in transfers. What explains the difference?

Solution

4. Here is the completed table:

	Decrease in G = −$10 billion billions of dollars			Decrease in TR = −$10 billion billions of dollars		
Rounds	Change in G	Change in real GDP	Change in YD	Change in TR	Change in real GDP	Change in YD
1	$\Delta G = -\$10.00$	−$10.00	−$10.00	$\Delta TR = -\$10.00$	$0.00	−$10.00
2	$\Delta C = -6.00$	−6.00	−6.00	$\Delta C = -6.00$	−6.00	−6.00
3	$\Delta C = -3.60$	−3.60	−3.60	$\Delta C = -3.60$	−3.60	−3.60
4	$\Delta C = -2.16$	−2.16	−2.16	$\Delta C = -2.16$	−2.16	−2.16
5	$\Delta C = -1.30$	−1.30	−1.30	$\Delta C = -1.30$	−1.30	−1.30
6	$\Delta C = -0.78$	−0.78	−0.78	$\Delta C = -0.78$	−0.78	−0.78
7	$\Delta C = -0.47$	−0.47	−0.47	$\Delta C = -0.47$	−0.47	−0.47
8	$\Delta C = -0.28$	−0.28	−0.28	$\Delta C = -0.28$	−0.28	−0.28
9	$\Delta C = -0.17$	−0.17	−0.17	$\Delta C = -0.17$	−0.17	−0.17
10	$\Delta C = -0.10$	−0.10	−0.10	$\Delta C = -0.10$	−0.10	−0.10
. . . .						
Sum for 10 rounds		−$24.86			−$14.86	

a. When government purchases decrease by $10 billion, the change in real GDP is −$24.86 billion after 10 rounds.

b. When transfers fall by $10 billion, the change in real GDP is −$14.86 billion after 10 rounds.

c. When the government decreases purchases by $10 billion, the total change in real GDP is −$25 billion $[(1/(1-0.6)) \times (-\$10 \text{ billion})]$. When transfers fall by $10 billion, the total change in real GDP is −$15 billion $[(-0.6/(1-0.6)) \times \$10 \text{ billion}]$. The difference is that the $10 billion fall in transfers does not directly affect real GDP. All rounds except the first are the same in the table for a decrease in government purchases and reduction in transfers; however, in the first round, real GDP falls by the same amount that government purchases declined but real GDP is initially unaffected when transfers fall by that amount.

5. In each of the following cases, either a recessionary or inflationary gap exists. Assume that the aggregate supply curve is horizontal so that the change in real GDP arising from a shift of the aggregate demand curve equals the size of the shift of the curve. Calculate both the change in government purchases of goods and services and the change in government transfers necessary to close the gap.

a. Real GDP equals $100 billion, potential output equals $160 billion, and the marginal propensity to consume is 0.75.

b. Real GDP equals $250 billion, potential output equals $200 billion, and the marginal propensity to consume is 0.5.

c. Real GDP equals $180 billion, potential output equals $100 billion, and the marginal propensity to consume is 0.8.

5. a. The economy is facing a recessionary gap; real GDP is less than potential output. Since the multiplier for a change in government purchases of goods and services is $1/(1 - 0.75) = 4$, an increase in government purchases of $15 billion will increase real GDP by $60 billion and close the recessionary gap. Each dollar of a transfer increase will increase real GDP by $MPC/(1 - MPC)$, or $0.75/(1 - 0.75) = 3. Since real GDP needs to increase by $60 billion, the government should increase transfers by $20 billion to close the recessionary gap.

b. The economy is facing an inflationary gap; real GDP is higher than potential output. Since the multiplier for a change in government purchases of goods and services is $1/(1 - 0.5) = 2, a decrease in government purchases of $25 billion will reduce real GDP by $50 billion and close the inflationary gap. Each dollar of a transfer reduction will decrease real GDP by $MPC/(1 - MPC)$, or $0.5/(1 - 0.5) = 1. Since real GDP needs to decrease by $50 billion, the government should increase transfers by $50 billion to close the inflationary gap.

c. The economy is facing an inflationary gap; real GDP is higher than potential output. Since the multiplier for a change in government purchases of goods and services is $1/(1 - 0.8) = 5$, a decrease in government purchases of $16 billion will reduce real GDP by $80 billion and close the inflationary gap. Each dollar of a transfer reduction will reduce real GDP by $MPC/(1 - MPC)$, or $0.8/(1 - 0.8) = 4. Since real GDP needs to decrease by $80 billion, the government should reduce transfer payments by $20 billion to close the inflationary gap.

6. Most macroeconomists believe it is a good thing that taxes act as automatic stabilizers and lower the size of the multiplier. However, a smaller multiplier means that the change in government purchases of goods and services, government transfers, or taxes necessary to close an inflationary or recessionary gap is larger. How can you explain this apparent inconsistency?

6. Automatic stabilizers, such as taxes, help to dampen the business cycle. As the economy expands, taxes increase; this increase acts as a contractionary fiscal policy. In this way any autonomous change in aggregate spending will have a smaller effect on real GDP than it would in the absence of taxes and result in a smaller inflationary or recessionary gap. Consequently, the need for discretionary fiscal policy is reduced. However, if a demand shock does occur and the government decides to use discretionary fiscal policy to help eliminate it, the smaller multiplier means that the change in government purchases of goods and services, government transfers, or taxes necessary to close the gap is larger.

7. The accompanying table shows how consumers' marginal propensities to consume in a particular economy are related to their level of income:

Income range	Marginal propensity to consume
$0–$20,000	0.9
$20,001–$40,000	0.8
$40,001–$60,000	0.7
$60,001–$80,000	0.6
Above $80,000	0.5

a. What is the "bang for the buck" in terms of the increase in real GDP for an additional $1 of income for consumers in each income range?

b. If the government needed to close a recessionary or inflationary gap, what types of fiscal policies would you recommend to close the gap with the smallest change in either government purchases of goods and services or taxes?

7. a. The accompanying table shows the "bang for the buck" for an additional $1 of income for a consumer in each income range. It is calculated as $1/(1 - MPC)$.

Income range	Marginal propensity to consume	"Bang for the buck"
$0–$20,000	0.9	10
$20,001–$40,000	0.8	5
$40,001–$60,000	0.7	3.33
$60,001–$80,000	0.6	2.5
Above $80,000	0.5	2

b. Since the "bang for the buck" is highest for the lowest income group, fiscal policies aimed at that income group would require the smallest change in government purchases of goods and services or the smallest change in taxes or transfers to close a recessionary or inflationary gap.

8. The government's budget surplus in Macroland has risen consistently over the past five years. Two government policy makers disagree as to why this has happened. One argues that a rising budget surplus indicates a growing economy; the other argues that it shows that the government is using contractionary fiscal policy. Can you determine which policy maker is correct? If not, why not?

8. It's impossible to determine which policy maker is correct given the information available. The government's budget surplus will rise either if real GDP is growing or if Macroland is using contractionary fiscal policy. When the economy grows, tax revenue rises and government transfers fall, leading to an increase in the government's budget surplus. However, if the government uses contractionary fiscal policy, then the government purchases fewer goods and services, increases taxes, or reduces government transfers. Any of those three changes will result in a temporary increase in the government's budget surplus, although the reduction in real GDP will eventually cause tax revenue to fall and government transfers to rise, which will reduce the budget surplus.

9. Figure 17-9 shows the actual budget deficit and the cyclically adjusted budget deficit as a percentage of real GDP in the United States since 1970. Assuming that potential output was unchanged, use this figure to determine in which years since 1992 the government used discretionary expansionary fiscal policy and in which years it used contractionary fiscal policy.

9. Since the cyclically adjusted budget balance is an estimate of what the budget balance would be if real GDP were exactly equal to potential output, the effect of changes in income on the budget are eliminated. And since we have assumed that there are no changes in potential output, any change in the cyclically adjusted budget balance represents changes in fiscal policies. When the cyclically adjusted budget deficit falls, the government must be engaging in contractionary fiscal policies: either government purchases and transfer payments are decreasing or taxes are increasing. When the cyclically adjusted budget deficit rises, the government must be engaging in expansionary fiscal policies: either government purchases and transfer payments are increasing or taxes are decreasing. From Figure 17-9, we see that from 1992 to 2001, the cyclically adjusted budget deficit was falling; this indicates that the government was pursuing contractionary fiscal policies during that period. From 2001 to 2004, the cyclically adjusted budget deficit was rising; this indicates that the government was pursuing expansionary fiscal policies during that period.

10. You are an economic adviser to a candidate for national office. She asks you for a summary of the economic consequences of a balanced-budget rule for the federal government and for your recommendation on whether she should support such a rule. How do you respond?

10. You might respond that balanced-budget rules are usually proposed because the government is running a budget deficit and many people think of deficits as bad. When the government runs a budget deficit, it adds to the public debt. If the government persists in running budget deficits, interest payments become an increasing part of government spending and the budget deficit itself. As a result, the debt–GDP ratio may rise. However, budget deficits themselves are not the problem; the problem arises when budget deficits become persistent. In the United States, there has been a strong relationship between the federal government's budget balance and the business cycle: when the economy expands, the budget moves toward surplus, and when the economy experiences a recession, the budget moves into deficit. The major disadvantage of a balanced-budget rule is that it would undermine the role of taxes and government transfers as automatic stabilizers and force the government to respond to an inflationary gap with expansionary fiscal policies and to a recessionary gap with contractionary fiscal policies. You might recommend, as most economists do, that rather than a balanced-budget rule, the government only balance its budget on average; it should run budget deficits during recessions and budget surpluses during expansions.

11. In 2005, the policy makers of the economy of Eastlandia projected the debt–GDP ratio and the deficit–GDP ratio for the economy for the next 10 years under different scenarios for growth in the government's deficit. Real GDP is currently $1,000 billion per year and is expected to grow by 3% per year, the public debt is $300 billion at the beginning of the year, and the deficit is $30 billion in 2005.

Year	Real GDP (billions of dollars)	Debt (billions of dollars)	Budget deficit (billions of dollars)	Debt (percent of real GDP)	Budget deficit (percent of real GDP)
2005	$1,000	$300	$30	?	?
2006	1,030	?	?	?	?
2007	1,061	?	?	?	?
2008	1,093	?	?	?	?
2009	1,126	?	?	?	?
2010	1,159	?	?	?	?
2011	1,194	?	?	?	?
2012	1,230	?	?	?	?
2013	1,267	?	?	?	?
2014	1,305	?	?	?	?
2015	1,344	?	?	?	?

a. Complete the accompanying table to show the debt–GDP ratio and the deficit–GDP ratio for the economy if the government's budget deficit remains constant at $30 billion over the next 10 years. (Remember that the government's debt will grow by the previous year's deficit.)

b. Redo the table to show the debt–GDP ratio and the deficit–GDP ratio for the economy if the government's budget deficit grows by 3% per year over the next 10 years.

c. Redo the table again to show the debt–GDP ratio and the deficit–GDP ratio for the economy if the government's budget deficit grows by 20% per year over the next 10 years.

d. What happens to the debt–GDP ratio and the deficit–GDP ratio for the economy over time under the three different scenarios?

11. **a.** Here is the completed table:

Year	Real GDP (billions of dollars)	Debt (billions of dollars)	Budget deficit (billions of dollars)	Debt (percent of real GDP)	Budget deficit (percent of real GDP)
2005	$1,000	$300	$30	30.0%	3.0%
2006	1,030	330	30	32.0	2.9
2007	1,061	360	30	33.9	2.8
2008	1,093	390	30	35.7	2.7
2009	1,126	420	30	37.3	2.7
2010	1,159	450	30	38.8	2.6
2011	1,194	480	30	40.2	2.5
2012	1,230	510	30	41.5	2.4
2013	1,267	540	30	42.6	2.4
2014	1,305	570	30	43.7	2.3
2015	1,344	600	30	44.6	2.2

b. Here is the table redone:

Year	Real GDP (billions of dollars)	Debt (billions of dollars)	Budget deficit (billions of dollars)	Debt (percent of real GDP)	Budget deficit (percent of real GDP)
2005	$1,000	$300	$30	30.0%	3.0%
2006	1,030	330	31	32.0	3.0
2007	1,061	361	32	34.0	3.0
2008	1,093	393	33	35.9	3.0
2009	1,126	426	34	37.8	3.0
2010	1,159	459	35	39.6	3.0
2011	1,194	494	36	41.4	3.0
2012	1,230	530	37	43.1	3.0
2013	1,267	567	38	44.7	3.0
2014	1,305	605	39	46.3	3.0
2015	1,344	644	40	47.9	3.0

c. And here is the table again:

Year	Real GDP (billions of dollars)	Debt (billions of dollars)	Budget deficit (billions of dollars)	Debt (percent of real GDP)	Budget deficit (percent of real GDP)
2005	$1,000	$300	$30	30.0%	3.0%
2006	1,030	330	36	32.0	3.5
2007	1,061	366	43	34.5	4.1
2008	1,093	409	52	37.4	4.7
2009	1,126	461	62	40.9	5.5
2010	1,159	523	75	45.1	6.4
2011	1,194	598	90	50.1	7.5
2012	1,230	687	107	55.9	8.7
2013	1,267	795	129	62.7	10.2
2014	1,305	924	155	70.8	11.9
2015	1,344	1,079	186	80.3	13.8

d. When the deficit remains constant at $30 billion, the deficit–GDP ratio declines but the debt–GDP ratio continues to increase because debt is rising faster than GDP. When the deficit grows by 3% per year, the same rate at which real GDP grows, the deficit–GDP ratio remains constant at 3% and the debt–GDP ratio continues to increase. When the deficit grows by 20% per year, the deficit–GDP ratio rises from 3.0% to 13.8% in 10 years and the debt–GDP ratio more than doubles from 30% to more than 80%.

12. Your study partner argues that the distinction between the government's budget deficit and debt is similar to the distinction between consumer savings and wealth. He also argues that if you have large budget deficits, you must have a large debt. In what ways is your study partner correct and in what ways is he incorrect?

12. Your study partner is correct that the distinction between the government's budget deficit and debt is similar to the distinction between consumer savings and wealth. Savings and deficits refer to actions that take place over time. When the government spends more than it receives in tax revenue in a particular time period, it is running a budget deficit. When consumers spend less than their disposable income in a particular time period, they are saving. However, both debt and wealth are measured at one point in time. When the government runs a budget deficit, the deficit is almost always financed by borrowing, which adds to its debt. Similarly, consumers accumulate wealth by saving. Your study partner is wrong in that the government can run a large budget deficit and have a small debt if it hasn't run large deficits in the past.

13. In which of the following cases does the size of the government's debt and the size of the budget deficit indicate potential problems for the economy?

a. The government's debt is relatively low, but the government is running a large budget deficit as it builds a high-speed rail system to connect the major cities of the nation.

b. The government's debt is relatively high due to a recently ended deficit-financed war, but the government is now running only a small budget deficit.

c. The government's debt is relatively low, but the government is running a budget deficit to finance the interest payments on the debt.

13. **a.** If the government has relatively little debt but is running a large budget deficit as it builds a high-speed rail system, this should not indicate potential problems for the economy. Like funding a war effort, it is difficult, if not impossible, to finance major improvements in a nation's infrastructure without borrowing. As long as the budget deficit ends with the building project, this should not create long-term problems.

b. If the government's debt is relatively high but the government has reduced its budget deficit, this should not indicate potential problems for the economy. However, the government needs to be careful that the deficits do not become persistent.

c. Even if the government's debt is relatively low, if it is running a budget deficit to finance the interest payments on that debt, this portends potential problems for the future. Without any changes, the government's debt will grow over time and with it the size of the government's budget deficit because of increasing interest payments.

14. How did or would the following affect the current public debt and implicit liabilities of the U.S. government?

a. In 2003, Congress passed and President Bush signed the Medicare Modernization Act, which provides seniors and individuals with disabilities with a prescription drug benefit. Some of the benefits under this law took effect immediately, but others will not begin until sometime in the future.

b. The age at which retired persons can receive full Social Security benefits is raised to age 70 for future retirees.

c. For future retirees, Social Security benefits are limited to those with low incomes.

d. Because the cost of health care is increasing faster than the overall inflation rate, annual increases in Social Security benefits are increased by the annual increase in health care costs rather than the overall inflation rate.

14. **a.** Because of its immediate impact on government spending, the Medicare Modernization Act increased the current public debt; implicit liabilities also rose because the act commits the government to a higher level of spending in the future.

b. If the age at which future retirees can receive full Social Security benefits is raised to age 70, implicit liabilities fall because government transfers will be lower in the future. There is no effect on the current public debt.

c. If Social Security benefits for future retirees are limited to those with low incomes, implicit liabilities fall because government transfers will be lower in the future. There is no effect on the current public debt because the change occurs in the future.

d. If annual increases in Social Security benefits are increased by the annual increase in health care costs rather than the overall inflation rate, implicit liabilities will rise. The current public debt will rise as soon as the rule is implemented.

Money, the Federal Reserve System, and Monetary Policy

1. For each of the following transactions, what is the effect (increase or decrease) on M1? on M2?

   a. You sell a few shares of stock and put the proceeds into your savings account.

   b. You sell a few shares of stock and put the proceeds into your checking account.

   c. You transfer money from your savings account to your checking account.

   d. You discover $0.25 under the floor mat in your car and deposit it in your checking account.

   e. You discover $0.25 under the floor mat in your car and deposit it in your savings account.

1. a. Shares of stock are not a component of either M1 or M2, so holding fewer shares does not decrease either M1 or M2. However, depositing the money into your savings account increases M2, since the savings account is part of M2 (but not part of M1). M1 does not change.

   b. Shares of stock are not a component of either M1 or M2, and so holding fewer shares does not decrease either M1 or M2. However, depositing the money into your checking account increases M1, since checking accounts are part of M1. It also increases M2, since M1 is part of M2.

   c. Moving money from savings to checking has no effect on M2, since both savings accounts and checking accounts are included in M2. However, since savings accounts are not part of M1, moving money from savings to checking does increase M1.

   d. Depositing cash into a checking account does not change M1 or M2. You are simply transferring money from one component of M1 (currency in circulation) to another component of M1 (checkable deposits).

   e. Depositing $0.25 into your savings account has no effect on M2, since both savings accounts and currency in circulation are in M2. However, since savings accounts are not part of M1, depositing the $0.25 into your savings account reduces M1.

2. There are three types of money: commodity money, commodity-backed money, and fiat money. Which type of money is used in each of the following situations?

   a. Mother-of-pearl seashells were used to pay for goods in ancient China.

   b. Salt was used in many European countries as a medium of exchange.

   c. For a brief time, Germany used paper money (the "Rye Mark") that could be redeemed for a certain amount of grain rye.

   d. The town of Ithaca, New York, prints its own currency, the Ithaca HOURS, which can be used to purchase local goods and services.

2. a. Mother-of-pearl is commodity money since the shells have other uses (for instance, for shirt buttons).

   b. Salt is commodity money since it has other uses.

c. The "Rye Mark" is commodity-backed money since its ultimate value is guaranteed by a promise that it can be converted into valuable goods (grain rye).

d. Ithaca HOURS are fiat money because their value derives entirely from their status as a means of payment in Ithaca.

3. The table below shows the components of M1 and M2 in billions of dollars for the month of December in the years 1995 to 2004 as published in the *2005 Economic Report of the President*. Complete the table by calculating M1, M2, currency in circulation as a percentage of M1, and currency in circulation as a percentage of M2. What trends or patterns about M1, M2, currency in circulation as a percentage of M1, and currency in circulation as a percentage of M2 do you see? What might account for these trends?

Year	Currency in circulation	Traveler's checks	Checkable deposits	Money market funds	Time deposits smaller than $100,000	Savings deposits	M1	M2	Currency in circulation as a percentage of M1	Currency in circulation as a percentage of M2
1995	$372.1	$9.1	$745.9	$448.8	$931.4	$1,134.0	?	?	?	?
1996	394.1	8.8	676.5	517.4	946.8	1,273.1	?	?	?	?
1997	424.6	8.5	639.5	592.2	967.9	1,399.1	?	?	?	?
1998	459.9	8.5	627.7	732.7	951.5	1,603.6	?	?	?	?
1999	517.7	8.6	597.7	832.5	954.0	1,738.2	?	?	?	?
2000	531.6	8.3	548.1	924.2	1,044.2	1,876.2	?	?	?	?
2001	582.0	8.0	589.3	987.2	972.8	2,308.9	?	?	?	?
2002	627.4	7.8	582.0	915.5	892.1	2,769.5	?	?	?	?
2003	663.9	7.7	621.8	801.1	809.4	3,158.5	?	?	?	?
2004	699.3	7.6	656.2	714.7	814.0	3,505.9	?	?	?	?

3. Here is the completed table:

Year	Currency in circulation	Traveler's checks	Checkable bank deposits	Money market funds	Time deposits smaller than $100,000	Savings deposits	M1	M2	Currency in circulation as a percentage of M1	Currency in circulation as a percentage of M2
1995	$372.1	$9.1	$745.9	$448.8	$931.4	$1,134.0	$1,127.1	$3,641.3	33.0%	10.2%
1996	394.1	8.8	676.5	517.4	946.8	1,273.1	1,079.4	3,816.7	36.5%	10.3%
1997	424.6	8.5	639.5	592.2	967.9	1,399.1	1,072.6	4,031.8	39.6%	10.5%
1998	459.9	8.5	627.7	732.7	951.5	1,603.6	1,096.1	4,383.9	42.0%	10.5%
1999	517.7	8.6	597.7	832.5	954.0	1,738.2	1,124.0	4,648.7	46.1%	11.1%
2000	531.6	8.3	548.1	924.2	1,044.2	1,876.2	1,088.0	4,932.6	48.9%	10.8%
2001	582.0	8.0	589.3	987.2	972.8	2,308.9	1,179.3	5,448.2	49.4%	10.7%
2002	627.4	7.8	582.0	915.5	892.1	2,769.5	1,217.2	5,794.3	51.5%	10.8%
2003	663.9	7.7	621.8	801.1	809.4	3,158.5	1,293.4	6,062.4	51.3%	11.0%
2004	699.3	7.6	656.2	714.7	814.0	3,505.9	1,363.1	6,397.7	51.3%	10.9%

M1 consists of currency in circulation, traveler's checks, and checkable deposits. M2 consists of M1 plus money funds, time deposits, and savings deposits. From 1995 to 2004, there is no obvious trend in M1. M1 grew by $236 billion (or 21% from 1995 to 2004) but was essentially stable from 1995 to 2001; all of this growth occurred between 2002 and 2004. There is, however, a clear upward trend throughout the period for M2, which grew by $2,756.4 billion (or 76% from 1995 to 2004). Currency as a percentage of M1 grew from 33 percent to over 51 percent from 1995 to 2004, but currency as a percentage of M2 remained relatively constant, varying from a low of 10.2% in 1995 to a high of 11.1% in 1999. The increase in currency as a percentage of M1 could reflect increased use of credit cards, causing a reduction in the importance of traveler's checks and checkable deposits. Yet, since currency as a percentage of M2 did not change, it could also reflect a shift from checkable deposits to money funds, time deposits, and saving deposits.

4. Indicate whether each of the following is part of M1, M2, or neither:

    a. $95 on your campus meal card

    b. $0.55 in the change cup of your car

    c. $1,663 in your savings account

    d. $459 in your checking account

    e. 100 shares of stock worth $4,000

    f. A $1,000 line of credit on your Sears credit card

4. **a.** $95 on your campus meal card is similar to a gift certificate. Because it can only be used for one purpose, it is not part of either M1, M2.

    b. $0.55 in the change cup of your car is part of currency in circulation; it is part of both M1 and M2.

    c. $1,663 in your savings account isn't directly usable as a medium of exchange, so it is not part of M1; but because it can readily be converted into cash or checkable deposits, it is part of M2.

    d. A $459 balance in your checking account is part of M1 and M2; it represents a checkable deposit.

    e. 100 shares of stock are not part of either M1 or M2. Although an asset, stock is not a highly liquid asset.

    f. A $1,000 line of credit on your Sears credit card account is not part of either M1 or M2 because it does not represent an asset.

5. The government of Eastlandia uses measures of monetary aggregates similar to those used by the United States, and the central bank of Eastlandia imposes a required reserve ratio of 10%. Given the following information, answer the questions below.

Bank deposits at the central bank = $200 million
Currency held by public = $150 million
Currency in bank vaults = $100 million
Checkable bank deposits = $500 million
Traveler's checks = $10 million

    a. What is M1?

    b. Are the commercial banks holding excess reserves?

    c. Can the commercial banks increase checkable bank deposits?

5. **a.** M1 equals the sum of currency held by the public ($150 million), checkable deposits ($500 million), and traveler's checks ($10 million) or $660.

   b. Required reserves are $50 million (10% of $500 million). Because total reserves are $300 million, the commercial banks are holding $250 million ($300 million − $50 million) in excess reserves.

   c. Since the commercial banks are holding excess reserves, they can increase deposits.

6. Using Figure 18-3, find the Federal Reserve district in which you live. Go to http://www.federalreserve.gov/bios/pres.htm and identify the president of that Federal Reserve Bank. Go to http://www.federalreserve.gov/fomc/and determine if the president of the Fed is currently a voting member of the Federal Open Market Committee (FOMC).

6. Answers will vary depending on where you live and when you look up your answer. If you live in Reedley, California, in July 2005, you were in the San Francisco district of the Federal Reserve system. Janet Yellen was the president of the Federal Reserve Bank of San Francisco and an alternate (nonvoting) member of the FOMC at that time.

7. Go to the FOMC page of the Federal Reserve Board's website (http://www.federalreserve.gov/FOMC/) to find the statement issued after the most recent FOMC meeting. (Go to the bottom of the web page and click on the most recent statement listed in the calendar.)

   a. What is the target federal funds rate?

   b. Is the target federal funds rate different from the target federal funds rate from the previous FOMC statement? If yes, by how much does it differ?

   c. Does the statement comment on macroeconomic conditions in the United States? How does it describe the U.S. economy?

7. Answers will vary depending on when you look up the information. As of July 2005, the latest statement was issued June 30, after the June 29–30 FOMC meeting.

   a. On June 30, 2005, the Fed announced that it had raised its target for the federal funds rate to 3¼%.

   b. Yes, the target federal funds rate is 25 basis points higher (the target had been 3% before the June 29–30 FOMC meeting).

   c. It states that even with this increase in the federal funds rate, the committee believes that "monetary policy remains accommodative." Coupled with the growth in productivity, monetary policy is "providing ongoing support to economic activity." It also comments that "although energy prices have risen further, the expansion remains firm and labor market conditions continue to improve gradually."

8. An economy is facing the recessionary gap shown in the accompanying diagram. To eliminate the gap, should the central bank use expansionary or contractionary monetary policy? How will the interest rate, investment spending, consumer spending, real GDP, and the aggregate price level change as the monetary policy closes the recessionary gap?

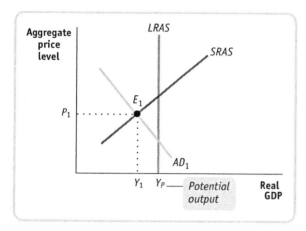

8. The central bank can use expansionary monetary policy to eliminate the recessionary gap. The central bank could engage in an open-market purchase of U.S. Treasury bills. This would increase the money supply, lowering the rate of interest and encouraging an increase in investment spending. The increase in investment spending will kick off the multiplier process, leading consumers to increase their spending. The final situation is illustrated in the accompanying diagram by the movement of the AD curve from its initial position, AD_1, to its new location, AD_2. Real GDP and the aggregate price level will rise.

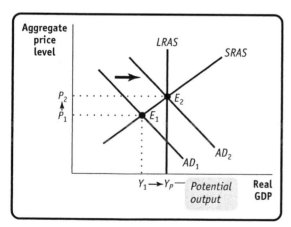

9. An economy is facing the inflationary gap shown in the accompanying diagram. To eliminate the gap, should the central bank use expansionary or contractionary monetary policy? How will the interest rate, investment spending, consumer spending, real GDP, and aggregate price level change as the monetary policy closes the inflationary gap?

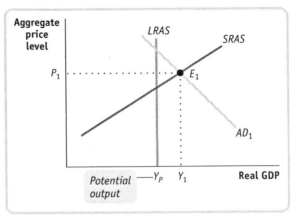

9. The central bank can use contractionary monetary policy to eliminate the inflationary gap. The central bank could engage in an open-market sale of U.S Treasury bills. This would decrease the supply of money, raising the interest rate and causing investment spending to fall. The decrease in investment spending will lead consumers to decrease their spending. The final situation is illustrated in the accompanying diagram by the movement of the AD curve from its initial position, AD_1, to its new location, AD_2. Real GDP and the aggregate price level will fall.

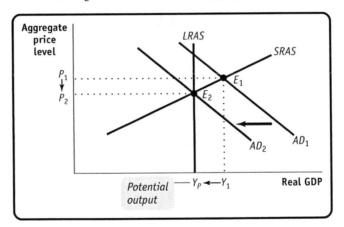

10. During the Great Depression, businesspeople in the United States were very pessimistic about the future of economic growth and reluctant to increase investment spending even when interest rates fell. How did this limit the potential for monetary policy to help alleviate the Depression?

10. Monetary policy is effective when changes in the money supply change the interest rate and, in turn, the change in the interest rate changes investment spending. If businesspeople are very pessimistic about the future of economic growth and reluctant to increase investment spending when interest rates decrease, monetary policy will not be very effective in shifting the aggregate demand curve to the right. Since this was the situation during the Great Depression, monetary policy had little to offer policy makers trying to promote economic growth.